CONTEMPORARY BLACK HISTORY

Manning Marable, Founding Series Editor

*Peniel Joseph (Tufts University) and
Yohuru Williams (Fairfield University),
Series Editors*

This series features cutting-edge scholarship in Contemporary Black History, under-lining the importance of the study of history as a form of public advocacy and political activism. It focuses on postwar African-American history, from 1945 to the early 1990s, but it also includes international black history, bringing in high-quality interdisciplinary scholarship from around the globe. It is the series editors' firm belief that outstanding critical research can also be accessible and well written. To this end, books in the series incorporate different methodologies that lend themselves to narrative richness, such as oral history and ethnography, and combine disciplines such as African American Studies, Political Science, Sociology, Ethnic and Women's Studies, Cultural Studies, Anthropology, and Criminal Justice.

Published by Palgrave Macmillan:

Biko Lives! The Contested Legacies of Steve Biko
   Edited by Andile Mngxitama, Amanda Alexander, and Nigel C. Gibson

Anticommunism and the African American Freedom Movement: "Another Side of the Story"
   Edited by Robbie Lieberman and Clarence Lang

Africana Cultures and Policy Studies: Scholarship and the Transformation of Public Policy
   Edited by Zachery Williams

Black Feminist Politics from Kennedy to Obama
   By Duchess Harris

Mau Mau in Harlem? The U.S. and the Liberation of Kenya
   By Gerald Horne

Black Power in Bermuda: The Struggle for Decolonization
   By Quito Swan

Neighborhood Rebels: Black Power at the Local Level
   Edited by Peniel E. Joseph

Living Fanon: Global Perspectives
   Edited by Nigel C. Gibson

From Black Power to Prison Power: The Making of Jones v. North Carolina Prisoners' Labor Union
   By Donald F. Tibbs

The Black Campus Movement: Black Students and the Racial Reconstitution of Higher Education, 1965–1972
   By Ibram H. Rogers

Soul Thieves: White America's Appropriation of African American Culture
   By Baruti N. Kopano and Tamara Lizette Brown (forthcoming)

Black Power Principals
   By Matthew Whitaker (forthcoming)

The Congress of African People: History, Memory, and an Ideological Journey
   By Michael Simanga (forthcoming)

The Black Campus Movement

Black Students and the Racial Reconstitution of Higher Education, 1965–1972

Ibram H. Rogers

THE BLACK CAMPUS MOVEMENT
Copyright © Ibram H. Rogers, 2012.

First published in 2012 by
PALGRAVE MACMILLAN®
in the United States—a division of St. Martin's Press LLC,
175 Fifth Avenue, New York, NY 10010.

Where this book is distributed in the UK, Europe and the rest of the world,
this is by Palgrave Macmillan, a division of Macmillan Publishers Limited,
registered in England, company number 785998, of Houndmills,
Basingstoke, Hampshire RG21 6XS.

Palgrave Macmillan is the global academic imprint of the above companies
and has companies and representatives throughout the world.

Palgrave® and Macmillan® are registered trademarks in the United States,
the United Kingdom, Europe and other countries.

ISBN: 978–0–230–11781–5 (pbk)
ISBN: 978–0–230–11780–8 (hc)

Library of Congress Cataloging-in-Publication Data

Rogers, Ibram H.
    The Black campus movement : Black students and the racial reconstitution
of higher education, 1965–1972 / Ibram H. Rogers.
        p. cm.—(Contemporary Black history)
    ISBN 978–0–230–11780–8 (hardback)—
    ISBN 978–0–230–11781–5 ()
    1. African American student movements. 2. African American college
students—Political activity—History—20th century. 3. African Americans—
Education (Higher)—History. 4. Education, Higher—United States—History.
I. Title.

LC2781.R65 2012
378.1'9820973—dc23   2012000441

A catalogue record of the book is available from the British Library.

Design by Newgen Imaging Systems (P) Ltd., Chennai, India.

First edition: March 2012

D 10 9 8 7 6 5 4 3 2

Printed in the United States of America.

In memory of the youth who died during the Black Campus Movement.

Benjamin Brown, 22, community activist, Jackson State, May 12, 1967

Leonard D. Brown Jr., 20, Southern University, November 16, 1972

Rick "Tiger" Dowdell, 19, University of Kansas, July 16, 1970

Phillip Gibbs, 21, Jackson State, May 14, 1970

James Earl Green, 17, high school student, Jackson State, May 14, 1970

Willie E. Grimes, 20, North Carolina A&T, May 22, 1969

Samuel Hammond Jr., 18, South Carolina State, February 8, 1968

Larry D. Kimmons, 15, high school student, Pepperdine, March 12, 1969

Delano Middleton, 17, high school student, South Carolina State, February 8, 1968

Harry Nicholas "Nick" Rice, 18, University of Kansas, July 20, 1970

Denver A. Smith, 20, Southern University, November 16, 1972

Henry E. Smith, 19, South Carolina State, February 8, 1968

Samuel "Sammy" Younge Jr., 21, Tuskegee, January 3, 1966

Contents

List of Illustrations   ix

Acknowledgments   xi

Abbreviations Used in the Text   xiii

Introduction   1

1   An "Island Within": Black Students and Black Higher Education
    Prior to 1965   9

2   "God Speed the Breed": New Negro in the Long Black
    Student Movement   29

3   "Strike While the Iron Is Hot": Civil Rights in the Long
    Black Student Movement   49

4   "March That Won't Turn Around": Formation and Development of
    the Black Campus Movement   67

5   "Shuddering in a Paroxysm of Black Power": A Narrative
    Overview of the Black Campus Movement   89

6   "A Fly in Buttermilk": Black Campus Movement Organizations,
    Demands, Protests, and Support   107

7   "Black Jim Crow Studies": Opposition and Repression   127

8   "Black Students Refuse to Pass the Buck": The Racial
    Reconstitution of Higher Education   145

Epilogue: Backlash and Forward Lashes of the Black Campus Movement   161

Abbreviations Used in the Notes   171

Notes   181

Index   221

Illustrations

Photo 1   Alexander Twilight   10
Photo 2   Lucy Stanton   31
Photo 3   Zora Neale Hurston   35
Photo 4   Greensboro Four   63
Photo 5   Gwen Patton as a teenager   75
Photo 6   Front cover of *The Harambee*   84
Photo 7   Howard Fuller   99
Photo 8   Jackson State dormitory, after shooting   102
Photo 9   Armed students leaving Straight Hall   128

Acknowledgments

This book is five years in the making, and during that time numerous people and institutions have contributed to its development; they are so numerous that it is rather impossible to acknowledge everyone. So first, I would like to offer a general thanks to all that aided me in producing this manuscript. I would like to give special thanks to the major funding sources (and the archivists and officials I worked with there): UCLA (Charlotte Brown), Washington University (Sonya Rooney), Michigan Tech University (Julie Blair), Kentucky History Society (Darrell Meadows), Lyndon Baines Johnson Library and Museum (Allen Fisher), Wake Forest University (Megan Mulder), Historical Society of Southern California, SUNY College at Oneonta, and Temple University. Research fellowships were crucial as well, so thank you Deborah Gray White and Donna Murch for allowing me to contribute to the Rutgers Center for Historical Analysis, Vera Davis at the Black Metropolis Research Consortium, and Carolyn Brown for treating me so kindly during my J. Franklin Jameson Fellowship in American History at the Library of Congress, supported by the American Historical Association. Your support and guidance during this process were immeasurable. I must also sincerely thank the hundreds of archivists and librarians I have worked with over these last few years. Your kindness, generosity, and knowledge have eased this trying task of writing a national story. I was told before I started my research that college archivists are usually a pleasure to work with. I now see why they have that much-deserved reputation.

To my parents, Carol and Larry Rogers—both of whom were involved in the Black Campus Movement (BCM) and are now Reverends moving people to Christ—and my big brother, Akil Rogers, I am forever grateful for your Godly love, support, compassion, and positive energy. My Aunts Jeanette, Doris, and Laurena, and my Uncles Leonard, Jimmy, and J.C.: thank you for your constant love and encouragement. My loving and funny cousins, who are full of life and too numerous to name (so I will not in fear of leaving someone out), thank you for being my role models and for always challenging me and keeping me grounded. To all of my family members and countless friends, my Q3 roommates, my friends in Manassas, Virginia, and Philadelphia, thank you for always being there for me and regularly giving me a reason to believe in myself and the goodness of our world. I would like to acknowledge Sadiqa Edmonds for patiently listening as the ideas for this book came to life. Thank you for your partnership, companionship, understanding, and love throughout this process. I would like to thank

B. T. Edmonds, a BCM participant, immensely for your thoughtful, stimulating insight, and Nyota Tucker for those thought-provoking conversations on education. I would like to thank Weckea Lilly, H. Zahra Caldwell, Jasmin Young, and Robert Chase for reading portions of the manuscript.

My colleagues at SUNY College at Oneonta—Caridad Souza, Kathleen O'Mara, Michelle and Matthew Hendley, Bill Ashbaugh, Jeffrey Fortin, Thomas Beal, Bill Simons, Miguel Leon, Chris Keegan, Rob Compton, R. Neville Choonoo, Betty Wambui, Gina Keel, Gretchen Sorin, Don Hill, B. Cecilia Zapata, Penina Kamina, Nancy Kleniewski, Susan Bernardin, Yuriy Malikov, Mette Harder, April Harper, Veronica Diver, Mary Bonderoff, Bernadette Tiapo (to name a few of the many people who have opened their minds and hearts to my academic and personal companionship)—thank you. I would like to express my gratitude to Ama Mazama for being my scholarly role model and adviser. Molefi Asante, I am grateful for having been able to learn from you and receive your critical wisdom and inspiring knowledge. At Temple University, I would also like to thank Muhammah Ahmad (Maxwell Stanford Jr.), Sonja Peterson-Lewis, Anthony Monteiro, and Kathy Walker for assisting my intellectual development. I must express my thanks to Yohuru Williams for encouraging me and providing essential assistance during this scholarly endeavor. To Peniel Joseph and the late Manning Marable, thank you for allowing me to claim a small part of this tremendous scholarly series and for forging a path for this research.

I would like to thank the former members of the SF State Black Student(s) Union (BSU) during the BCM, who I have had the pleasure of meeting and informally conversely with about the movement, including Bernard Stringer, Vern Smith, Benny Stewart, Jimmy Garrett, and Jerry Varnado. To the dozens of other BCM participants with whom I have discussed the movement during my travels and research—thank you for making this book a reality. To the countless more living and passed black campus activists who thought outside of the box and fought inside higher educational boxes that had confined black students for decades—thank you for carving out a space for me to now be able to tell your national story.

Abbreviations Used in the Text

The following abbreviations and acronyms are used in the book. Widely known shortened names of colleges or universities will be used (examples: NYU, Howard, Michigan State, Harvard, Duke, Jackson State, and Spelman), which are not listed below. To reduce confusion, present-day names of institutions will also be used. Sometimes abbreviations of states (NY, IN, CA) will follow the names of colleges and universities to locate them for the reader.

A&M	Agricultural and Mechanical
A&T	Agricultural and Technical
AAO	Afro-American Organization
AAS	Afro-American Society
AABL	Afro-Americans for Black Liberation
ABC	Association of Black Collegians
ACE	American Council on Education
ACLU	American Civil Liberties Union
ACS	American Colonization Society
AFNS	American Federation of Negro Students
AMA	American Missionary Association
AMEC	African Methodist Episcopal Church
ASU	American Student Union
BCC	Black Cultural Center
BCM	Black Campus Movement
BPM	Black Power Movement
BSA	Black Student(s) Alliance
BSO	Black Student(s) Organization
BSU	Black Student(s) Union
BUS	Black United Students
COINTELPRO	Counter-Intelligence Program, Federal Bureau of Investigation
-C or C-	College or College of
College-U	College University (example for all, like Temple University: Temple-U)
CORE	Congress of Racial Equality
CRM	Civil Rights Movement

CSU	California State University
DU	Delta Upsilon International Fraternity
EOP	Educational Opportunity Program
FBI	Federal Bureau of Investigation
FOR	Fellowship of Reconciliation
HBCUs	Historically Black Colleges and Universities
HEW	Department of Health, Education, and Welfare
HUAC	House Un-American Activities Committee
HWCUs	Historically White Colleges and Universities
-I	Institute
KKK	Ku Klux Klan
LAC	Liberal Arts College
LBSM	Long Black Student Movement
MFDP	Mississippi Freedom Democratic Party
MXLU	Malcolm X Liberation University
NAACP	National Association for the Advancement of Colored People
NABS	National Association of Black Students
NACW	National Association of College Women
NBA	National Basketball Association
NC	North Carolina
NCC	Negro-Caucasian Club
NNC	National Negro Congress
NNCM	New Negro Campus Movement
NOI	Nation of Islam
NSA	Negro Students Association
NYPD	New York Police Department
RAM	Revolutionary Action Movement
SAAS	Students Afro-American Society
SC	South Carolina
SCLC	Southern Christian Leadership Conference
SDS	Students for a Democratic Society
SF State	San Francisco State University
SGA	Student Government Association
SNYC	Southern Negro Youth Congress
SOBU	Students Organized for Black Unity
SUNY	State University of New York
TIAL	Tuskegee Institute Advancement League
-U or U-	University or University of
UC	University of California
UNCF	United Negro College Fund
UW	University of Wisconsin
YAF	Young Americans for Freedom

Introduction

Fists balled and raised, black berets, head wraps, swaying Afros, sunglasses, black leather jackets, army fatigue coats, dashikis, African garb, with Curtis Mayfield singing "We're a Winner" in the background, shouting from fuming lips and posters in the foreground: "black power, racism, relevancy, black pride, revolution, equality, non-negotiable demands, student control, Black Studies, Black University"—higher education was under siege. The academic status quo had been destabilized. On February 13, 1969, black student activism and its challenge soared to a record level. Nine hundred National Guardsmen strolled onto the UW Madison campus with fixed bayonets that Thursday. Some rode on jeeps decked with machine guns. Helicopters surveyed the thousands of protesters. If the presence of city police had stirred campus activism a few days earlier when black students kicked off their strike, then the National Guard whipped students into a frenzy. After picketing and obstructing traffic during the day, about ten thousand students, with African American torch bearers leading the way, walked in the cold from the university to the capitol in the largest student march of the Black Campus Movement (BCM). Their bodies may have been freezing that night, but their mouths were on fire: "On strike, shut it down!" "Support the black demands!"[1]

Meanwhile that day, the nationally renowned SF State strike—a protest that popularized the mantra "On strike, shut it down!"—entered its third month. At UC Berkeley, police brutality caused the two-week-old boycott of classes to escalate. Black Student(s) Alliance (BSA) members at Roosevelt-U in Chicago continued their week of disrupting classes to teach Black Studies. The night before, BSA members rejected a deal offered by Dean of Students Lawrence Silverman that included amnesty and written responses to their demands for a Black Studies department under their control. In a statement, the BSA yelled, "We will continue our program, BY ANY MEANS NECESSARY!!!" Black students at U-Illinois delivered a list of demands to administrators on February 13, calling for the establishment of a Black Cultural Center and a Black Studies department, and the hiring of fifty black residence hall counselors and five hundred black professors. At Duke, forty-eight black collegians entered the administration building in the early morning, walked to the central records section, and told the clerical workers they had to leave. They then nailed the doors shut, threatened to burn university records if the police were called, and renamed the space "Malcolm X Liberation School." They issued thirteen demands, including the creation of a Black Studies department controlled by students, money for a Black Student Union building, a black dorm, and an end to "racist policies."[2]

At City College of New York, also on February 13, with a cold wind blowing, President Buell Gallagher stood on a snow-covered lawn in front of the administration building and delivered a speech that swirled coldly around affirming the five demands issued a week earlier. Livid, since they wanted a firm commitment that day, 300 black and Puerto Rican students swarmed into the administration building and ejected its workers. They plastered their demands on walls and ceilings and one student waved a sign that read, "Free Huey: Che Guevara, Malcolm X University." While City College students occupied the building for three and half hours, in the Deep South, more than 90 percent of students at Mississippi Valley State avoided classroom buildings. Stokely Carmichael had launched the black power slogan into America's social atmosphere in 1966, in Greenwood, ten miles from Mississippi Valley State. Wilhelm Joseph Jr., from Trinidad, like Carmichael, had been radically moved by the slogan. He successfully ran for student body president on a ticket that boasted, "We are going to move this place! This is a black college." Under his leadership, students pressed for the ability to don African garb and Afros, to study people of African descent in their courses, and to terminate campus paternalism, student powerlessness, and the poor quality of faculty and facilities. In total, they presented twenty-six demands leading to the boycott. State police and campus security officers swooped in and transported 196 strikers to Jackson, imprisoned a dozen others, and put out a warrant on four leaders (including Joseph). Close to 200 protesters were expelled.[3]

February 13, 1969, looms as the most unruly day of the BCM. If there was a day, or *the* day, that black campus activists forced the racial reconstitution of higher education, it was February 13, 1969. Black students disrupted higher education in almost every area of the nation—the Midwest in Illinois and Wisconsin; the Northeast in New York; the Upper South in North Carolina; the Deep South in Mississippi; the West Coast in the Bay Area. It was a day that emitted the anger, determination, and agency of a generation that stood on the cutting edge of educational progression. It was like no other day in the history of black higher education—a history of turmoil and progress, accommodation and advancement, isolation and community. Like the BCM it highlighted, this day had been in the making for more than one hundred years and changed the course of higher education for decades to come.

* * *

February 13, 1969, stands at the apex of the BCM, the subject of this book. During this movement, which emerged in 1965 and declined in 1972, hundreds of thousands of black campus activists (and sympathizers), aided on some campuses by white, Latino/a, Chicano/a, Native American, and Asian students, requested, demanded, and protested for a relevant learning experience. Notions of relevancy differed with activist ideologies that ranged from moderate to radical nationalists. In most cases, students considered a relevant education one that interrogated progressive African American and Third World literature and gave students the intellectual tools to fix a broken society. Students crusaded at upwards of one thousand colleges and universities, in every state except Alaska. When they principally utilized *campus activism* against higher education during this eight-year social movement, they were *black campus activists* to distinguish from the many black students who chose not to participate and from students engaged off campus in the myriad of black power groups in the late 1960s and early 1970s.[4]

To disentangle this social movement from other threads of activism during the Black Power Movement (BPM), from the campus movements waged by other racial groups at the time, and from black student off-campus activism during the contemporary civil rights period (1954–1965), this struggle among black student nationalists at historically white and black institutions to reconstitute higher education from 1965 to 1972 has been termed the *Black Campus Movement*. Even though they both tend to be conceptually located in what is widely known as the Black Student Movement, this late 1960s black power campus struggle represented a profound ideological, tactical, and spatial shift from early 1960s off-campus civil rights student confrontations. They were not merely different phases of the Black Student Movement. Along with the generally unknown New Negro Campus Movement of the 1920s, they were unique social movements, or, more precisely, separate but interlocking tussles in the *Long* Black Student Movement (LBSM) from 1919 to 1972.[5]

Akin to the concomitant Black Arts Movement, Black Theology Movement, and Black Feminist Movement, to name a few of the black power social movements scholars have distinguished, this period of black student activism should be understood as a social movement in its own right. In addition, even though black students battled the same structure in the same space with similarities in their ideas and tactics, and were sometimes allies, their struggle must be conceptualized as independent from white student activism. A few scholars have already followed the *New York Times*, which published a story on May 12, 1969, with the headline "The Campus Revolutions: One is Black, One White." In sum, the BCM was at the same time a part of and apart from three larger social movements: the transhistorical LBSM, beginning after World War I; the transracial student movement of the Long Sixties; and the transobjective contemporary BPM of the late 1960s and early 1970s.[6]

At historically white and black colleges and universities, black campus activists formed the nation's first chain of politically and culturally progressive black student unions with varying names and gained control of many student government associations. They utilized these Black Student(s) Unions (BSUs) and Student Government Associations (SGAs) as pressure groups to pursue a range of campus alterations, including an end to paternalism and racism, and the addition of more black students, faculty, administrators, and Black Studies courses, programs, and departments. They fought at almost every historically black college and university for a black-dominated, oriented, and radical "Black University" to replace what they theorized as the white-controlled, Eurocentric, bourgeoisie, accommodationist "Negro University." Their ultimate aim was to revolutionize higher education.

Black campus activists did not succeed in revolutionizing higher education. However, they did succeed in shoving to the center a series of historically marginalized academic ideas, questions, frames, methods, perspectives, subjects, and pursuits. They were able to succeed in pushing into higher education a profusion of racial reforms—in the form of people, programs, and literature. Most decisively, but least chronicled, black campus activists succeeded in exchanging the academy's century-old racist ideals. The 1954 *Brown v. Board of Education of Topeka* decision, which deemed unconstitutional separate but equal public policy, did not do this. Neither did the Civil Rights Act of 1964, which outlawed discrimination. The BCM forced the rewriting of the racial constitution of higher education, the central contention of this text.

*   *   *

Although undermined since 1919 by the LBSM, and more recently by the *Brown* decision and the Civil Rights Act, in 1965 there were at least four entrenched elements that had long undergirded the racial constitution of higher education: the *moralized contraption, standardization of exclusion, normalized mask of whiteness,* and *ladder altruism.* The moralized contraption was a system of rules, in place at practically all HBCUs, that regulated student freedom and agency. Students were told when to eat, sleep, study, and socialize. Chapel, convocation, and class attendance were mandatory, and women were slapped with additional restrictions. These rules, injected by white benefactors, paternalists, and black accommodationists, were meant to Christianize and civilize, and ultimately to induce submission to the white supremacist, capitalist, patriarchal American order. The ideas that justified these rules were deeply colonialist, racist, and sexist, and the moralized contraption resembled the off-campus segregationist directives that continuously endeavored, for a century after the Civil War, to keep African Americans a step away from slavery. In place of the contraption, Black campus activists demanded moral freedom.

Moreover, the open exclusion of African Americans from faculties, student bodies, administrations, coaching staffs—from every facet of the communities at historically white colleges and universities—was standardized. Standardized (or standardization) as opposed to standard, since the exclusion was not by happenstance. Inequality is never a coincidence. African Americans were purposefully excluded by academics. The prohibition or marginalization of Africana scholarship from curricula was standardized by academics at both historically white colleges and universities (HWCUs) and HBCUs. African Americans were also customarily excluded from many (usually private) HBCU professorial bodies and presidencies into the 1920s, and from boards of trustees into the 1960s. There were instances in which black concepts and people found their way into these terrains, but these were the exceptions to the rule, to the standard. The desegregation movement created many of these exceptions, for instance, as did the slight postwar flow of African Americans into HWCUs. Black students demanded more than exceptions. They desired the standardization of inclusion.

Exclusion was not merely standardized in 1965. Those who kept African Americans at bay projected the exclusionary environment as the norm. Notions of objectivity, removed scientific inquiry, unbiased scholarly assessments, empiricism, standardized tests, universalism, evolutionism, and Eurocentric thinking are a few of the many constructs that academics, politicians, and benefactors used to mask the preponderance of whiteness—white ideas, people, and scholarship—as normal. Thus, white racists and capitalists and black accommodationists actively created and maintained this white normality by masking it, by removing the adjectives, by denigrating and downgrading everything non-European, everything outside of the Eurocentric or capitalist homily. European history and literature were not presented as such. Academics labeled it *the* history and literature. By conceiving of European (and Euro-American) scholarship as superior to all others, they racialized it, they gave it whiteness—an officious social construct of racial superiority. Academics had still veiled the academy with the normalized mask of whiteness in 1965, with few holes, compelling students to demand its removal and denormalization.

During the century preceding the BCM, when academics were not normalizing and masking whiteness, they were instituting and encouraging ladder altruism. They taught the many altruistic African American college students to believe that their personal advancement up the American ladder of success advanced African America as a whole through the societal doors that graduates opened and through their function as role models. Meanwhile, academics, politicians, and capital allowed colleges and universities to serve as ladders, removing African Americans politically, economically, and culturally from the black masses.[7] In contrast to ladder altruism, black campus activists demonstrated for the demolishing of the personal and institutional ladders, and demanded an ideological and tactical reconnection through grassroots altruism. In sum, black campus activists during the BCM challenged the rules and regulations (moralized contraption), black marginalization from practically all facets of higher education (standardization of exclusion), the irrelevant curriculum, which they termed White Studies (normalized mask of whiteness), and the fact that academia encouraged and facilitated their removal from the masses (ladder altruism).

* * *

Literature on the BCM has been largely subsumed in the historiographies of the Student, Black Student, and Black Power movements, with white student activism, early 1960s civil rights remonstrating, and off-campus engagements, respectively, receiving most of the attention. The black campus struggle has been largely relegated and scattered in these three areas of inquiry. When the BCM has been studied, the treatments have almost always been campus specific, as historians have detailed the struggle at U-Illinois, UPENN, Columbia, Rutgers, Cornell, NYU, and SF State—to name the most expansive and prominent campus studies. The SC State (1968) and Jackson State (1970) "massacres" of black students have also been examined. *The Black Campus Movement* provides the first comprehensive national examination of black campus activism at black and white four-year colleges and universities in the late 1960s and early 1970s. It situates each campus struggle in the national movement and delivers a national purview for future campus studies.[8]

The Black Campus Movement not only centers the combating of the racial constitution of higher education at the locus of this history. It bonds the activism at HWCUs and HBCUs. It continues the recent scholarly revelation of the array of radicalism at HBCUs in the late 1960s and early 1970s, the multitude of women and moderate black power activists, black power organizing with whites, and black student activism prior to 1960, all the while presenting the range and attainments of black power, negotiating local with national activism, connecting and disconnecting black power to civil rights, elaborating on the most recent golden stretch of black educational nationalism, providing the movement context for the rise of what is now called Africana Studies, and showing the vicious backlash to the BCM. It places 1969 (as opposed to 1968) at the peak of black student activism, at both HWCUs and HBCUs, and the national clamor for relevancy, including Africana Studies. It pulls the origin of the movement back from 1967 or 1968 to 1965, while demonstrating that the Orangeburg Massacre (February 8, 1968) and the assassination of the Martin Luther King (April 4, 1968) did not spark the struggle, as some scholars have claimed. Those societal tragedies only accelerated it. This book proves that the movement did not start at HWCUs nor did the most "militant" protests disrupt those institutions. It complicates the more celebrated story of campus activism at HWCUs and expounds on this emergent literature by elucidating the largely unknown struggle at rural liberal arts colleges, remote institutions in the Great Plains, Northwest, and New England, and recently desegregated southern HWCUs. The study enters the discourse at the time of an evolving battle among the increasingly powerful race-neutrality advocates, who are advancing on race-specificity and diversity, and reinscribing the pre-1965 racial constitution of higher education in the name of integration, color blindness, and racial progress. At the same time, the vines of diversity continue to ensnare the halls of the academy and grow further away from their roots of resistance—systematically unearthed and revealed for the first time in this book.[9]

Neither the cultural nor political-economic features of the movement—their cause and effect—were shortchanged during this historical analysis. The words, deeds, and perspectives of black campus activists rested at the center of this investigation. Therefore, the documents they produced and their voices, presented in publications during the movement, provided the bulk of the evidence. Oral history interviews of activists conducted after the struggle, secondary campus-specific studies, and documents produced by the marginal actors of the movement—administrators, professors, and black leaders, for instance—enhanced this delineation. Campus-specific ideas, outlooks, reactions, requests, demands, protests, and implementations were fused into a national depiction of the BCM.

The initial chapter provides an introduction to the history of black higher education in the United States before the BCM. It addresses the harsh experiences of black students and offers the top-down configuration of the racial constitution of higher education by white paternalists and capitalists, black egalitarian elites, accommodating separatists, and revolting nationalists. The next two chapters discuss the activist response to racism and segregation on and off campus through a survey of the LBSM from 1919 to 1962. More than thirty years of mass black student activism set the stage for the BCM. In particular, the successes, failures, repression, and ideological and tactical lessons emanating from the Civil Rights Movement (CRM) (and early black power) in the first half of the 1960s provided the immediate social conditions that spawned the BCM. Chapter 4 presents this making of the movement from 1963 to 1965, and ascertains the factors that refined and circulated black student ideology during the BCM. Since they on occasion reference the BCM and the 1960s, these four chapters are not "traditional" histories, but rather provide the historical context for the BCM.

With the immediate prehistory of the movement and the ideas, societal calamities, and forms of consciousness raising that energized the BCM laid out, Chapter 5 provides a narrative historical overview of the BCM. Chapter 6 delves deeper into the movement by examining the disposition of black student organizing—their demands, protests, and support—while the following chapter discloses the forms of opposition and repression students faced. The final chapter lays out the new ideals (and reforms) their struggle brought to life, or rather forced to the center. An epilogue providing a post-history of black student activism and an analysis of the revitalization of the racial constitution through egalitarian exclusion concludes *The Black Campus Movement*.

1

An "Island Within": Black Students and Black Higher Education Prior to 1965

People of African descent had educated themselves for thousands of years in scholastic centers across Africa. They learned and analyzed the social, physical, and spiritual world during antiquity in renowned universities in Egypt that taught legendary Greek philosophers, and later in the bustling West African cities of Timbuktu and Jenne. When hundreds of thousands of Africans were snatched from their communities and enslaved in the United States, they were shut out of colleges and universities for two centuries, as were most Americans. Outside of the formal academy, African people maintained their storied tradition of higher learning in informal manners and in clandestine schools. Eighteenth-century poet Phillis Wheatley and the multi-talented Benjamin Banneker both received a home-schooled higher education. Princeton president John Witherspoon secretly tutored John Chavis, who went on to study at Washington and Lee in the late 1790s. (His great-great-grandson Ben Chavis later managed the BCM at UNC Charlotte). Bound out to a religious family as a teenager, Maria Stewart peered through the family library and took advantage of religious teaching to become an intrepid nineteenth-century public speaker for women's rights and abolition. Jemmy, Gabriel Prosser, and Nat Turner are a few of the innumerable enslaved and free Africans who employed their higher learning in the planning and execution of slave revolts, which invariably led to slaveholder revolts against black learning.[1]

Alexander Twilight, who graduated from Vermont's Middlebury in 1823, became the first known person of African descent to earn an American bachelor's degree. Likely the son of mixed-race parents, he probably passed for white. He parlayed his education into positions in the pulpit and the Vermont General Assembly in 1836, becoming the earliest known state legislator with African heritage. Edward A. Jones (Amherst, a Massachusetts Liberal Arts College [LAC]) and John Russwurm (Bowdoin, a Maine LAC) became the second and third graduates in 1826. As Russwurm established the nation's first black newspaper, the *Freedom's Journal*, Jones attended Trinity-C (CT), securing African America's initial M.A. degree in 1830.[2]

Photo 1   *Alexander Twilight* (Supplied by staff, Special Collections, Middlebury College, Middlebury, Vermont)

Promoters of free black removal from the United States to Africa (or what they termed colonization) welcomed the emigration of Jones, who helped found Sierra Leone's first Western colonial college, and Russwurm, who became a school superintendent in Liberia. Quite a few of the early black graduates and educators were *accommodating separatists*. They bowed to the relatively conservative dictates of the day that posed black emigration to Africa as the solution to the slave-holding society's racial quandary: what to do with free blacks. These early accommodating separatists were imbued by their paternal Pan-Africanism, a belief that African Americans should impart their "superior" civilization to "backward" Africans. Their educational benefactors were often the American Colonization Society (ACS). Slaveholders desiring the ejection of free blacks, Christians distressed with Africa's "pagans," and those who believed emigration must follow black emancipation—the "colonizationists," as Carter G. Woodson termed them—were an antebellum force.[3]

These more tolerant white colonizationists can be classified as the original *paternal conservatives*, among the minority of whites who believed at the time that African Americans should be educated. Aside from imparting civilizing knowledge, they believed they were gifted with the charge to advance an "inferior" race through a conservative method—education for colonization. Colonizationists tried to inaugurate schools in the 1820s in Newark and Hartford, but their schemes were sometimes foiled by African Americans guided by another major ideology—*egalitarian elitism*. These black thinkers believed both races were capable of receiving the same education for the same purpose—training a talented few to lead and provide a model for the many. Joining the egalitarian elites in opposition to the colonizationists and accommodating separatists were some white abolitionists, or *paternal liberals*, who believed they were innately endowed with a civil or Christian mission to lift African Americans from their degradation by means of a liberal method—education for domestic civil equality. This relatively unknown ideological dispute—between egalitarian elites (in the company of white abolitionists) who supported a "classical" college and accommodating separatists (with paternal conservatives) who aided colonization education—was the first great debate over the function of black higher education.

Assembling in Philadelphia in 1830 and 1831, the First Annual Convention of the People of Color went on record as opposing the ACS's colonization rationale for the higher education of "African youth." The delegates proposed the establishment of a black college in New Haven, so African Americans could receive "classical knowledge which...causes man to soar up to those high intellectual enjoyments...and drowns in oblivion's cup their moral degradation." But New Haven residents voted against it. Unyielding, the convention delegates, with the support of the New England Anti-Slavery Society, struck a deal with Noyes Academy in Canaan, New Hampshire, to craft an interracial, manual labor pseudo-high school. As quickly as the daylight of upper learning beamed for New England blacks, nightfall came. In 1835, 300 white Canaan residents, with a hundred oxen, dragged the schoolhouse a mile down the road into a nearby swamp, where they set it on fire. "No sable son of Africa remains to darken our horizon," a speaker avowed after the institutional lynching.[4]

In spite of the trembling resistance, the HBCU idea gained traction, particularly since new pages were needed for the list of talented African Americans turned away from HWCUs. No more than fifteen were admitted before 1840. Even though they warmed to the black college idea, African Americans and abolitionists chilled the growth of HBCUs for colonization, compelling colonizationists to focus collegiate funding on aspiring black emigrants. African Americans' own stirring to create a black college for Americanization was likewise halted until Richard Humphreys, a Philadelphia Quaker, bequeathed $10,000 to educate people of African descent. In 1837, his money gave birth to Cheyney-U in Philadelphia.[5]

Twelve years later, in 1849, Charles Avery founded Pennsylvania's Allegheny-I. In 1851, Myrtilla Miner, a New York abolitionist, founded the U-District of Columbia amid a groundswell of antagonism in the slaveholding terrain. The Presbytery of New Castle in Pennsylvania garnered funds to build Lincoln-U in 1854. Two years later, Cincinnati Methodists founded Wilberforce-U, which served the mulatto children of slaveholders until the Civil War clogged the channel. Enmeshed in debt, school officials appealed to the African Methodist Episcopal Church (AMEC). With Bishop Daniel A. Payne leading the way as the nation's earliest African American college president, in 1863 Wilberforce became the first college controlled by African Americans.[6]

Like many HWCUs at the time, these initial HBCUs primarily provided preparatory programs—special high schools and sometimes junior colleges—for students aiming to teach, preach, embark on a mission, or attend a university.

Lincoln-U (PA) became the first bachelor's-degree-granting HBCU in 1865.[7] As racial change propelled open the doors of HBCUs, racist tradition kept the revolving doors of HWCUs closing in African American faces. In 1845, Dartmouth president Nathan Lord refused to "have a flood of blacks" at his college because he doubted "the fitness of Africans," a rare *doubt* in the age of outright dismissals "proven" by scientific racists. "They will need cultivation as a people, for centuries, before many of them will hold their way with long civilized and Christian Saxons, if, indeed, that is ever to be expected, which I doubt." Nonetheless, unlike many, President Lord kept his college open to "help a struggling people," revealing his paternal liberalism.[8]

In 1847, David John Peck, the first African American admitted to medical practice, graduated from Chicago's Rush Medical. The school was named after one of the early scientific racists, Benjamin Rush, who claimed African phenotypic features verified leprosy in a 1799 academic talk. New York Central-C allowed black students to enroll upon its opening in 1849 in upstate New York. Charles L. Reason, an abolitionist, suffragist, and son of Haitian immigrants, joined its faculty as a professor of belles lettres (Greek, Latin, French) and an adjunct professor of mathematics. As two other black scholars accompanied the nation's first known black professor at an HWCU in 1850, Lucy Stanton, the daughter of Cleveland abolitionists, became the first black woman graduate when she completed the "ladies course" of study (inferior academically to the "gentlemen's course") at Oberlin-C in Ohio.[9]

Meanwhile, that fall, Martin Delany entered Harvard's medical school along with Daniel Laing and Isaac Snowden. When the three black students entered the lecture hall for their first class, the noisy room of 113 white students drooped into a loud silence and staring separation. Harvard's white male students "endured" the three black pariahs. But when the faculty voted to admit a white woman in December 1850, within days the white males met and passed a resolution barring both women and African Americans. Concerning the latter, the resolution stated, "We cannot consent to be identified as fellow students with blacks." The faculty upheld the standardization of exclusion. Snowden and Laing finished at Dartmouth with the help of the ACS, embarking for Liberia in 1854. But Delaney, intending to practice in the States, was crushed when Boston abolitionists did not press for his readmission. The ordeal led Delaney to later write of his "sad, sad disappointment" in liberal abolitionists, hastening his ideological travel to Pan-Africanism, black emigration, and a *revolting black nationalism*. Even as he advised emigration, unlike accommodating separatists and paternal conservatives, Delaney demanded education for cultural and political self-determination and social self-respect at home, the final form of the tripartite black ideological womb that birthed black higher education.[10]

* * *

As fugitive slaves emancipated themselves and in turn dictated the course of the war in 1862, Mary Jane Patterson, the daughter of fugitives from Raleigh, became the nation's first known African American woman to receive a B.A. degree.

Fanny M. Jackson and Frances J. Norris were next in line at Oberlin-C, finishing in 1865, the year before Sarah Jane Woodson accepted a professorship—the first black woman to do so—in English and Latin at Wilberforce-U.[11] In total, twenty-seven African Americans, capable of fitting into a classroom, had received bachelor's degrees prior to the passage of the Emancipation Proclamation. When the Civil War came to a close, aside from family reunification and land, the newly freed searched for knowledge. Northern white missionaries, with an overflowing crusading cup of New England–flavored education, descended on the South to douse the "downtrodden." They found legions of African American revolting nationalists and egalitarian elites creating their own schools to garner what had been kept from them—literacy, self-determination, self-respect, equality, power, and civil rights. "They have a natural praiseworthy pride in keeping their educational institutions in their own hands," reported William Channing Grant, a white American Missionary Association (AMA) teacher from New England. "What they desire is assistance without control." Together they launched a cause for organized education between 1861 and 1871, which W. E. B. Du Bois described as "one of the marvelous occurrences of the modern world; almost without parallel in the history of civilization."[12]

They started building schools as early as 1861 in territories occupied by Union forces, which was the origin, in 1862, of Western-U in Kansas and LeMoyne-Owen in Memphis. The movement reached its pitch as the battle cries ceased. From 1865 to 1867, a staggering seventeen HBCUs were established (at the least). Five states founded institutions, along with the AMA, Presbyterians, Methodists, Baptists, Episcopalians, United Church of Christ, and AMEC. Rev. Richard C. Coulter, a former slave from Augusta, Georgia, aided in the birth of Morehouse in 1867, the same year Congress chartered Howard in Washington, DC. Presumably as many as two hundred private HBCUs opened in the 1870s and 1880s, but most closed not long after due to financial, racial, and clientele constraints.[13]

The antebellum debate over education for colonization or Americanization was eclipsed by a relative Reconstruction consensus forged by paternal liberals and egalitarian elites (and revolting nationalists) on black higher education utilizing classical academic curricula to school intellect, self-reliance, moral regeneration, Christian orthodoxy, and the tools for American citizenship. HBCUs were to raise an army of teachers and preachers (and to a lesser extent professionals, politicians, and entrepreneurs) to guide the race out of their hundreds of years of political captivity, forced illiteracy, and supposed moral degradation.

The accommodating separatists and paternal conservatives had to sit on the sidelines of history. However, they bided their time and planned. The most prominent postbellum paternal conservative, General S. C. Armstrong, founded Hampton in Southern Virginia in 1868. Compared to whites who had three centuries of "experience in organizing the forces about him," African Americans "had three centuries of experience in general demoralization and behind that, paganism," he once wrote. At Hampton, Armstrong created a model of education for paternal conservatives and accommodating separatists that would take hold of black higher education with the support of Southern segregationists and Northern capital when they deconstructed the gains of Reconstruction. He endeavored to mold teachers who would go out and fashion a submissive, stationary, easily exploitable black laboring class through the language of morals, Christianity, virtue, thrift, and freedom. "The Hampton-Tuskegee curriculum was not centered on trade or agricultural training; it was centered on the training of teachers," according to James D. Anderson. Of the 723 Hampton graduates in its first twenty classes, 84 percent became teachers. The habitually exaggerated manual-industrial component to the Hampton curriculum was to "work the perspective teachers long and hard so that they would embody, accept, and preach an ethic of hard toil or the 'dignity of labor,'" Anderson explains. Armstrong's new solution to the old race problem (what to do with free blacks) resembled the old paternal conservative model of education for colonization. Instead of training teachers for the maintenance of colonialism and white supremacy in Africa, Armstrong trained teachers for the maintenance of exploitative colonial labor relations and white supremacy in the American South. Still, Armstrong had a lot of convincing on his hands, as many Americans believed, as Virginian Bebbet Puryear did, that higher education for control was impossible. Education "instills in his mind that he is competent to share in the higher walks of life, prompts him to despise those menial pursuits to which his race has been doomed, and invites him to enter into competition with the white man," which he is destined to lose due to his inferiority, Puryear stated in 1877.[14]

*   *   *

At the dawn of black higher education in the mid-nineteenth century, white presidents, administrators, and professors were the norm at HWCUs and HBCUs, with credentialed African Americans either excluded, unavailable, or unrecognized. At every HBCU, students were imprisoned with bars of regulations by means of the widespread institutionalization of the moralized contraption. HBCUs emerged as moralizing plantations. This contraption was politically roused to teach subordination. It was philosophically roused by religious affiliations, the presence of women (who purportedly needed an additional set of patriarchal rules), the overtly mainstream racist ideas of the nineteenth century (such as the hypersexuality, immaturity, intellectual inferiority, and laziness of African Americans), the concomitant zealous desire among some egalitarian elites and paternal liberals to nurture or prove racial equality and black civilization to white Americans, and the fact that initially many colleges were only colleges in name, having mostly boarding students of elementary, junior, and high school age.

Replicating the white New England schools and colleges, egalitarian elites and paternal liberals wrote into the founding HBCU curriculums the normalized mask of whiteness. Just as these lily-white New England institutions did not label themselves Euro-American or white institutions, they did not brand their literature and scholarship European. It was "classical" education, teaching "high culture." Latin and Greek were placed on a pedagogical pedestal at HBCUs. To gain admission to the 1868–1869 freshman class at Howard, students needed to read "two books of Caesar, six orations of *Cicero*, the *Bucolics*, the *Georgics*, six books of Virgil's *Aeneid*, Sallust's *Cataline*, two books of Xenophon's *Anabasis*, and the first two books of Homer's *Illiad*," according to the graduate school dean, Dwight Oliver Wendell Holmes.

Amid the European topics, courses and content specializing in Africa were practically nonexistent. But few objected. Some African Americans believed the racist propaganda that Africa was figuratively the "dark continent," shaded from the sun of progress, civilization, and history. Many believed that people of African descent were innately inferior or that slavery/colonialism made them inferior. Academics accentuated cultural assimilation along with black civic grooming for lifelong swimming in the white American mainstream. Initially, the standardization of exclusion of Africana content seemed to not unnerve most black students. If anything, many were motivated to demonstrate that they could learn anything whites could learn. Others were like Richard Wright, who shortly after graduating from Atlanta-U in 1876 used the classics, through words from Humboldt and Herodutus, to assert that "these differences of race, so called, are a mere matter of color and not of brain."[15]

With more than 90 percent of African Americans in the South, HBCUs were practically the only option for most aspiring postbellum collegians, unless they wanted to trek up North to the meager amount of desegregated HWCUs. Discouragement, custom, and then laws preserved the standardization of exclusion of African Americans from HWCUs in the South. One of the few exceptions was Maryville, a LAC in Tennessee, which boasted thirteen African Americans among its 137 students in 1876. Berea, a Kentucky LAC that admitted its first black student in 1866, stood as the foremost exception. Thereafter, twenty-seven white students vacated the school "in a disgraceful manner." Undaunted and committed to principle, school officials kept the gates open, and African Americans inundated the school during the next few decades—96 during the 1866–1867 school year (with 91 whites), and 129 to 144 in 1877–1878. Berea alone prevailed as the only truly integrated college in the nineteenth century.[16]

Eager former slaves of varying ages poured into HBCUs during the Reconstruction Era. In the fall of 1872, a 16-year-old coal miner from West Virginia, with a small satchel containing all his possessions, made the five-hundred-mile trek to Southern Virginia, begging and working for travel money along the way. Up from slavery, with fifty cents in his dirty pocket and starving for food and admission to the school of his dreams, Booker T. Washington secured a position as a janitor and enrolled at Hampton. An astute 10-year-old "Annie" Julia Haywood (Cooper) entered Saint Augustine's in 1868. Over the next nearly fourteen years in Raleigh, she distinguished herself academically, honing her pioneering voice from the South. She followed the footsteps of Mary Jane Patterson, a fellow native of Raleigh, and enrolled at Oberlin-C in Ohio in 1881. During that historic year, the AMEC founded Morris Brown (GA), Southern-U (LA) was established, Washington created Tuskegee, and Spelman opened its doors (the only institution for black women offering college courses). Cooper pursued the classical academic track typically restricted to men at Oberlin-C, as did Ida Gibbs (Hunt) and Mary Church (Terrell), who graduated with her in 1884. Oberlin alumni made up an estimated 75 of the 194 black graduates from northern colleges between 1865 and 1895.[17]

The year after this dynamic, soon-to-be activist trio finished, a brilliant and confident 17-year-old from Massachusetts walked onto Fisk's grounds in the fall of 1885, "thrilled to be for the first time among so many people of my own color." However, in W. E. B Du Bois's three years in Nashville, there persisted "an abyss between my education and the truth of the world." Exemplifying the abyss, Du Bois selected for his commencement speech in 1888 German Chancellor Otto von Bismarck, who had just hosted a conference of European colonizers of Africa in Berlin. Like most HBCU faculty, Fisk professors did not discuss the imperial rivalry to exploit foreign materials, markets, and labor. "I was blithely European and imperialist in outlook; democratic as democracy was conceived in America," Du Bois later lamented.

On the other hand, he displayed his two-ness, his conscious blackness, by seeking out his racial peers at nearby institutions when he enrolled at Harvard in the fall of 1888. Thus the indignities he encountered on campus—being mistaken as a waiter or rejections from student organizations—were alleviated by his small support system and maturing sense of self. He had his black "island within," he said. He did not try to venture into the sea of whiteness. He knew he "was in Harvard but not of it."[18]

*   *   *

As the federal government withdrew from the South in the 1870s and the movement to disenfranchise southern African Americans and separate public space gained momentum at the turn of the century, segregationist-Democrats paved the South for the color line. Refusing to exclude white students, Atlanta-U had its state appropriation cut off by Georgia lawmen in 1888. In 1890, the U-Maryland law school ejected its "two intelligent young negroes." Tennessee legislators compelled Maryville-C to segregate in 1901. The Kentucky state legislature passed the Day Law in 1904 barring interracial schools, extinguishing America's brightest beacon of educational integration, the year after Carter G. Woodson, the father of black history, earned his Berea-C degree. The college did not begin readmitting African Americans until the 1950s..[19]

Meanwhile, segregationist-Democrats substantially reduced the funding of public HBCUs and eradicated anyone and anything at these schools that undermined southern white supremacy and capital accumulation. For instance, in 1878 Mississippi Democrats reduced Alcorn State's annual appropriation, ended state scholarships, reduced classical offerings, and gave the HBCU a new focus: "scientific and practical knowledge of agriculture, horticulture, and the mechanical arts." Accommodating separatists bent to their will. Writing a benefactor in 1894, Alabama A&M principal W. H. Councill coolly asserted, "The south has done more for the negro than any other section of the globe." Egalitarian elites and revolting nationalists stood their ground. Thomas DeSaille Tucker, a graduate of Oberlin and the founding president of Florida A&M in 1887, emphasized liberal arts in his teacher training program until state officials forced his resignation in 1901.[20]

Segregationist-Democrats were supported by northern bankers, merchants, railroad tycoons, and other corporate principals with deep pockets, including

John F. Slater and John D. Rockefeller Sr. The power of southern politicians, northern corporate philanthropists, paternal conservatives, and black accommodating separatists fractured the Reconstruction consensus of black higher education for advancement. Then the second dispute on the function of black higher education unfolded. Should black higher education teach African Americans to accommodate to disenfranchised, separate, second-class citizenship as semi-skilled agricultural, mechanical, and manual laborers controlled by white capital? Or should black higher education provide (white) liberal arts training in order to equalize the races and give African Americans the intellectual means to fight for civil rights, and for radicals—power? Accommodation or equality/power—that was higher education's demarcating line, crisscrossing the deepening color line. Tuskegee president Booker T. Washington emerged as the chief proponent of the accommodating separatists (even as he secretly supported civil rights causes). "The wisest among my race understand that the agitation of questions of social equality is the extremest folly," Washington stated at the 1895 Atlanta Exposition. W. E. B. Du Bois led the charge for the latter position, crystalizing the egalitarian elite's philosophy when he declared the need for a college trained "Talented Tenth," because "the Negro race, like all races, is going to be saved by its exception men."[21]

This Washington/Du Bois debate has been overplayed in the history of black higher education. Downplayed has been the pervasive sway of white capitalists and paternalists—those whom William H. Watkins termed the "white architects of black education." They used their power and capital to build an educational system with the normalized mask of whiteness, moralized contraption, and ladder altruism, an educational system that taught African Americans their rightful place, an educational system that buttressed the exploitation of black labor, an educational system for control. By 1900, capitalists and Christian missionaries marched in unity, like European colonialists around the globe, financing HBCUs in the name of civilization, progress, and moral growth, when their real aim had been to establish civilized racial order, progressive white supremacy, and capitalist growth. By the outbreak of the First World War, the vast majority of black students attended HBCUs affiliated by missionary societies and churches supported primarily by corporate philanthropies like the Slater Fund, Rosenwald Fund, Jeannes Foundation, Peabody Education Fund, and Carnegie Corporation. Grants were packed in accommodationism *and* concepts of evolution. "Race relations would gradually change, presumably for the better, if Blacks were willing to remain within the boundaries of 'acceptable' behavior," read the evolutionary offer, explained Watkins. Only ladder altruism uncomfortably resided within these boundaries.[22]

*   *   *

At the turn of the century, HBCUs increasingly laid out the red carpet for trustees, state and federal politicians, and philanthropists to court their political and economic favor in grand spectacles that bordered on minstrelsy. The artistic, moral, aesthetic, and manual talents of the students and the college were displayed with more pomp than intellectual acumen. Usually, African American students were ordered by HBCU presidents to sing spirituals, which to the benefactors harkened them back to the good ole days of slavery. Some singers of spirituals resented the ritual but went along out of adoration for the president or the benefactors' money or fear of punishment. In the 1920s some, calling it demeaning, refused to sing, including Howard students and Shaw-U's Ella Baker, the celebrated civil rights organizer. But the slavery shows went on and the money poured in to pacify the Talented Tenth, as many HBCUs resembled plantations with black and white slave drivers for presidents, powerless faculty as slaves, students as the cotton, and corporate capital as the slaveholders. In April 1906, Booker T. Washington welcomed a host of powerful figures, from Secretary of War William H. Taft to steel mogul Andrew Carnegie to Harvard president Charles William Eliot, to celebrate Tuskegee's four-day "silver jubilee," which intermixed speeches with spirituals sung by a student choir and flowing donations.[23]

At the same time though, during the early years of the twentieth century, HBCUs not following the Hampton-Tuskegee model, namely Atlanta-U, Fisk, Howard, and Talladega-C (AL), started to become havens for the development of African American scholarship, which blossomed after World War I. To Allen Ballard, these black scholars "provided the basic intellectual antidote to the venom of racism pouring forth from both Northern and Southern holders of white professorial chairs."[24] Despite the venom, with the reformation and deterioration of HBCUs and the South, more black students started looking north for college. At some institutions, white students prevented their admission, while at others absolute exclusion in admissions was maintained, as at George Washington. Not surprisingly then, less than seven hundred African Americans had graduated from HWCUs by 1910. In 1912, U-Michigan had the third largest enrollment (thirty-nine) behind Oberlin-C and U-Kansas. Brown-U trained five black men from 1877 to 1912 who became college presidents, including John Hope of Morehouse. Amelia Mahorney graduated from Butler-U in 1887, presumably the first black woman to earn a degree from an Indiana college. George Washington Carver earned bachelor's (1894) and master's (1896) degrees from Iowa State and became the school's first black professor, before Washington lured the scientist to Tuskegee.[25]

Like Carver in the 1890s, black students were locked out of dormitories at Iowa State well into the twentieth century. The problem grew to such a proportion that, in 1919, a recently relocated African American couple provided a rooming house for students. An untold number of families opened homes to students excluded from dorms at HWCUs, and some were vocal *supporters* of the standardization of exclusion that provided them with customers. Black students at Iowa State, like others around the nation, would not be permitted to live in dorms until after World War II. Nor would they all be permitted to attend school in peace, as black students were victims of the surge of violence that terrorized Americans during the era of lynching and urban race battles. In 1914, for example, white gang bangers brutally struck Augustus Granger, a dental student at UPENN, with stones until he fought back with a knife, stabbing an assailant. There was a report of HBCU students also carrying weapons for protection during this period.[26]

In athletics, during the early twentieth century, some teams refused to play those with African Americans and sometimes hotels and other businesses declined interracial squads, a situation that continued into the 1960s. William and Mary and Georgia Tech chose not to play Rutgers, which in the late 1910s had on its football roster All-American Paul Robeson, the future world-renowned singer, actor, and revolting nationalist. West Virginia also insisted it could not play with Robeson on the field, but ultimately Robeson did line up. At six feet, two inches, and 190 pounds, he stood four inches taller and weighed twenty pounds more than most football players at the time. On the first play of the game, the West Virginia player facing him on the other side of the line of scrimmage leaned forward. "Don't you so much as touch me, you black dog, or I'll cut your heart out." When the whistle blew, Robeson dashed at the player and slammed him to the ground. "I touched you that time," Robeson whispered. "How did you like it?"[27]

In the first few decades of the twentieth century, the stifling sense of isolation and segregation at HWCUs and the moralized contraption at HBCUs contributed to a low retention rate, as it would for decades. At Cornell, none of the six students in the 1904 cohort returned the next year. Alarmed, the remaining African Americans formed a support group. It was an instantaneous sensation. On December 4, 1906, seven male students refashioned the group into Alpha Phi Alpha, the nation's first African American intercollegiate Greek-letter fraternal organization. It was the sunrise of black student organizing—not to change the racial constitution, but to endure it.[28]

The racist restrictions those seven men faced resembled the patriarchal restrictions women bore at Howard—emblematic of all HBCUs. By 1910, Howard had graduated a mere twenty-three women, compared to fifty-eight at Fisk and eighty-two at Shaw-U in Raleigh.[29] Incoming and outgoing mail passed through the matron, who sometimes acted as a censor. Going off campus alone without a chaperone was out of the question. Expulsions were a fact of life for any woman daring to smoke, drink, entertain the opposite sex in an unapproved manner, or escape the socially fortified campus. As late as 1913, Howard's board of directors decreed that any woman teacher who married "would be considered as having resigned her position." Estranged on some level from the teeming patriarchy and encouraged by Professor Ethel Robinson, a Brown-U alum who shared her sorority experiences, the thought of forming a sisterhood stirred junior Ethel Hedgeman into action. The St. Louis native, along with eight other Liberal Arts students, formed Alpha Kappa Alpha at Howard on January 15, 1908—the nation's first black sorority. It was "no accident," Paula Giddings observed, "that the first Black fraternity was established at a predominantly White university," where black men were socially ostracized, "or that the first Black sorority emerged at a coeducational one like Howard," where black women were socially hampered.[30]

In 1910, Indiana-U seemed eerily like Cornell in 1906 (and appeared to be like Butler-U, where Sigma Gamma Rho chartered in 1922). The ten black male IU students were disallowed from using recreational or entertainment facilities on campus. They could take up space on campus, but there was no place for them. They were socially homeless, invisible to the majority, with no virtual or physical dwelling. Elder Diggs had had enough. He brought the ten scattered men together to establish Alpha Omega. Eventually, the men gave their organization permanence by founding Kappa Alpha Nu on January 5, 1911. Soon, their house parties attracted isolated African American students from across the state who were in search of a community, even if for one joyous night. Three years later, presumably in reaction to a white IU student who nicknamed the new fraternity "Kappa Alpha Nig," the fraternity changed its name to Kappa Alpha Psi. By the time the Kappas took on their new moniker, three more Greek-letter organizations had formed at Howard—Omega Psi Phi (1911), Delta Sigma Theta (1913), and Phi Beta Sigma (1914)—and Zeta Phi Beta was established there in 1920 (Iota Phi Theta was founded in 1963 at Morgan State).[31]

Even though only three of the nine black fraternities and sororities were established at HWCUs, most of their early growth could be found at white colleges, where the need for social refuges and campus housing became vital in the early twentieth century. Like their white counterparts, black fraternities and sororities utilized Greek names and symbols, maintained an exclusive membership, and performed rituals. They were "not conceived to transform society but to transform the individual," explained Paula Giddings—an indication of their colleges' notion of ladder altruism.[32]

*   *   *

Stalled and actually pulled back for almost three decades, black higher education surged forward, pushed by the Great Migration, wartime mania, and the returning politicized New Negro filled with a newfound race pride, during and after World War I. A growing number of revolting nationalists and egalitarian elites were studying black life and uncovering the normalized mask of whiteness in the first decades of the twentieth century. This growing force of black scholarship was powered by revisionist and inventive literature on people of African descent, such as W. E. B. Du Bois's studies of southern African Americans, the formation of Carter G. Woodson's association in 1915 and Negro History Week in 1926, the introduction of black history, sociology, and literature courses at HBCUs, and the founding of black literary groups. Tougaloo, a LAC in Jackson, Mississippi, hired faculty who introduced the school's first courses in Negro history and literature. Two new electives were inserted at Howard in 1918—"Race Problems" and "The Negro in American History." Several HBCUs hired black presidents and professors, often pressured by revolting nationalists and white separatists who demanded the removal of whites from black institutions.[33]

Some (perhaps most) New Negro students in the early twentieth century did not welcome these developments. Poet Langston Hughes surveyed his fellow students on the matter at Lincoln (PA) in the late 1920s. He found that only a few objected to the absence of a black history or literature course and two-thirds of the 127 juniors and seniors did not want black professors. "The reasons given were various: that Lincoln was supported by 'white' philanthropy, therefore whites should run the college; that favoritism and unfairness would result on the part of Negro teachers toward the students; that there were not enough Negro teachers available; and that things were all right as they were, so why change? Three students even said they just didn't like Negroes. Two said they did not believe Negro teachers had the interest of students at heart. Another said members of his own race were not morally capable!" At the least, for these students, the racial constitution had achieved its subordinating mission, angering Hughes, a revolting nationalist. The college had "failed in instilling in these students the very quality of self-reliance and self-respect which any capable American leader should have."[34]

Nevertheless, at the same time, the first black student social movement, powered by students like Hughes, emerged during a drastic postwar modification of the collegiate composition. Public high schools were multiplying, yielding more students. Many HBCUs that had served as boarding schools for decades expanded to become bachelor's-degree-granting colleges—schools such as Prairie View (1919) outside of Houston, Spelman (1924), and Jackson State (1927). Talladega's ratio of elementary/secondary students to college students in 1907 was 180 to 1. The ration at Alabama's oldest HBCU tightened to three to one by 1927—five years later it was one to one. Tuskegee, Saint Augustine's (NC), Hampton, Voorhees-C (SC), Saint Paul's (VA), Oakwood-U (AL), and Stillman-C (AL) were also part of the upsurge in degree-granting HBCUs, the number of which increased from thirty-one in 1915 to fifty-four in 1954.[35]

Before the 1920s, black higher education was primarily a male phenomenon at private HBCUs—thus the obvious dominion of benefactors and patriarchy. Transformations came that decade. In 1914, for every public HBCU student, there were forty private HBCU students. By 1926, the ratio had dropped to three to one. In 1935, it was 1.5 to 1. More were attending public HBCUs in the 1950s. A mere two of every ten graduates were women in 1920. The number had doubled by 1930. In 1940, there were more black women graduating from HBCUs than men.[36]

In addition to demographic factors and first-wave feminism, the National Association of College Women (NACW), founded in 1910, played an important role in this upsurge. NACW president Lucy Slowe, who in 1922 became the first HBCU dean of women at Howard, impressed upon presidents the need to create similar positions. They did so when the female population skyrocketed in the 1930s and 1940s. The NACW joined students in censuring degrading rules. "When a college woman cannot be trusted to go shopping without a chaperone she is not likely to develop powers of leadership," Slowe wrote in 1931.[37]

During and after World War I, black higher education grew tremendously. From 1914 to 1925, the number of HBCUs increased 81 percent and their populations skyrocketed 533 percent. There was a massive rush of bachelor's graduates—more than ten times more from HBCUs in 1936 (2,130) than in 1914 (180), and about a fivefold increase at northern white colleges. More black students graduated from college between 1926 and 1936 than in the nation's previous 300 years combined. Changes to the institutional, gendered, and numerical configuration of HBCUs sometimes led to enhancing the moralized contraption. At Jackson State, for instance, a series of regulations came into effect in 1924 relating to female chaperonage, curfew, required attendance, and shopping days, and stated that "vulgar language and bad habits will be sufficient for exclusion from the school."[38]

To curb the surge of black students and satiate the rising tide of post-World War I white nationalism, some southern HBCUs welcomed black presidents and professors. Northern and border HWCUs maintained or instituted official and unofficial racial quotas and segregationist policies, and kept, with few exceptions, only white faculty, administrators, and staff in their ranks. The Ku Klux Klan (KKK) in Austin, Texas, played a role in the installation of Huston-Tillotson's first black president in 1924. Catholic-U implemented the color bar in 1919, and it remained for almost two decades. At UPENN, black students could not enter the cafeteria and were required to eat their lunch under the stairs of the library. Frederick W. Wells, a Columbia law student, received at least two death threats from the KKK and stomached a burning cross on campus in 1914. In the late 1920s, Adam Clayton Powell Jr. tried to pass for white at Colgate-U, where only five (at the most) of about one thousand males were African American. When the New Yorker pledged an all-white fraternity, members discovered his black heritage and publically rejected him. His white roommate, who had befriended Powell, demanded his removal from their room, with the backing of university officials. The maturing Harlem preacher and Congressman never again passed on the white side of the racial divide.[39]

In 1927, Butler-U officials issued a quota—no more than ten black students were to be admitted per year and they each had to have three letters of recommendation from "substantial," presumably white, citizens. African Americans were forced to take an extra history course to make up for the gym class they were forbidden from taking. "Nobody said anything ugly to us," said Mildred Marshall Hall, who arrived at the Indianapolis institution in 1929. "They just didn't see you—we were invisible." The quota was not lifted until 1948.[40]

Harvard accepted Ewart Guinier, but denied him a scholarship because it had already fulfilled its reported quota of one funded black student per class. Unlike other Harvard freshmen, who were required to live in the campus dormitories, Guinier was granted permission to live at home. "Men of white and colored races shall not be compelled to live and eat together," stated the *Harvard Alumni Bulletin* of 1923. At a freshman assembly in 1929, with upwards of one thousand people, Guinier stuck out, or more precisely disappeared, as the only African American. As students exited the hall, conversations sprang up all around him like sprinklers, but he stayed dry. "No one looked me in the eye: no one spoke to me," he said. "As I walked towards a group, they would move away." Not one Harvard professor ever called on him in class. Not one white student ever initiated a conversation. The first person to acknowledge his humanity, to voluntarily enter his island within, happened to be a black graduate student he met at the campus bookstore. "Welcome to Harvard!" shouted Ralph Bunche, the future educator, diplomat, and civil rights power broker.[41]

Ohio State, U-Michigan, and U-Iowa also sanctioned residential segregation in the 1930s. Several northern HWCUs excluded black students, using a paternal liberal justification: they do not want them "subjected to discrimination," as Williams-C (MA) president Tyler Dennett put it in 1935. Racial restrictions and social isolation coupled with the rising black enrollment led to the founding of sociocultural groups that resembled, in a less politicized form, the BSUs of the

BCM. The "Negro Students Club" at UC Berkeley hosted dances in the mid-1930s, and complained in 1935 when a black student was denied service at a student-run barber shop. The "Negro Student's Club" at SF State held "social meetings" in 1937. U-Chicago had a "Negro Student Club," critiqued as segregationist by a writer in the *Chicago Defender*, as BSUs were in the 1960s. "The aim of the 'Negro Student Club' is to immediately alleviate and ultimately to abolish...lamentable" campus conditions, explained John H. Johnson, future head of the Johnson Publishing Company, in defense of his organization in 1937. The club organized balls, participated in Negro History Week activities, hosted a lecture by Howard's William Leo Hansberry on ancient Ethiopia, and hosted dancer Katherine Dunham and her cast, which performed "Tropical Revue" in 1945.[42]

As black students steered through the stormy racial waters at northern HWCUs, the racial waters sometimes became more perilous for HBCU students in segregated, racially explosive areas. To many white Americans in the South clinging to a strict racial caste between the World Wars, black college students, in the vein of free blacks during slavery, embodied present racial displacement and future racial reordering. For many whites who did not attend college, and most did not, the presence of articulate, confident, polished black students oftentimes undermined their sense of superiority and thus their sense of self. Nowhere was this situation as galling as in Atlanta—one of the prime centers of black higher education *and* the southern white supremacist order—where the swelling of black students at its HBCUs in 1920s swelled the racial tensions in the city. In 1928, when a Morehouse student named Barnes went into a café to request payment for an overdue bill on papers he delivered, the proprietor shot him in the head to "teach him how to act when talking to a white man." A grand jury "justified" the murder. Two years later, white men shot and killed Dennis Hubert, a Morehouse sophomore and son of a local Baptist pastor, claiming he "insulted a white woman" at a public park on June 30, 1930. Morehouse secured the state's most successful white criminal lawyer, William Schley Howard. These six men became the first whites to be convicted for murdering a black person in Georgia.[43]

*   *   *

On campus, students still faced restrictive rules at segregationist white and paternalistic black colleges in the 1930s, and most curriculums remained culturally irrelevant. Few sets of coursework and even fewer courses discussed the Africana experience at HWCUs. HBCU curriculums, aside from maybe one course on Negro history and another on Negro literature, were hardly distinguishable from those at HWCUs, with the white mask on firmly. According to Horace Mann Bond, Fisk professor and later dean at Dillard, during that decade "Cicero, Livy, Horace, Quintilian, Tacitus, and Prose Composition afforded a rather full fare in Latin, while Greek could hardly be said to suffer neglect when every student was expected to read Xenophon's *Memorabilia*, Homer's *Iliad*, Sophocles' *Antigone* and other Greek tragedies, the New Testament in Greek, Thucydides, Plato's *Apology* and the *Crito*, and Demosthenes' *On the Crown*."[44]

The Great Depression of the 1930s proved a Greek tragedy for many HBCUs, replaying the dismal days during the panic of 1873. Some folded. Most weathered the economic tornado by cutting back and raising tuition—pricing out families held afloat by black farmers and domestics, who were not given the New Deal. Those HBCUs that survived saw a somewhat brighter day. Educators had finally convinced the Southern Association of Colleges and Secondary Schools to consider accrediting HBCUs in 1930. In 1933, the Association of Colleges and Secondary Schools for Negroes formed to promote the advancement of HBCUs. The critical mass of black students, aided by the National Association for the Advancement of Colored People (NAACP), started challenging the separate but equal doctrine in the 1930s, pointing to their inability to attend graduate school in the South. Refusing to desegregate, state legislatures and philanthropists appropriated funds to found new HBCUs, beefed up existing ones, and established graduate and professional programs at HBCUs over the next few decades.[45]

As the Depression ebbed in 1939, Congress instructed the Office of Education to study the state of black higher education. The agency reported in the 1942 *National Survey of the Higher Education of Negroes* that black K–12 students were allocated one-third the amount of funding that white students received and that the school years of African Americans tended to be one to three months shorter, resulting in many students' being poorly prepared for college. During World War II, HBCUs could do little about the predicament, as the male presence on black campuses fell by half. Along with this population reduction, certain funds customarily earmarked for HBCUs were diverted to the war effort. Together, they were a "double assault" on the livelihood of HBCUs, wrote Tuskegee president Frederick D. Patterson in 1943, appealing to his fellow presidents of private black colleges to kick off a "unified financial campaign." His peers obliged, and the next year twenty-seven member colleges founded the United Negro College Fund (UNCF) to raise funds for private HBCUs and provide scholarships for aspiring students. Four years later, another group of college presidents formed the National Scholarship Service and Fund for Negro Students to "increase and broaden opportunities for Negro students at interracial colleges."[46]

*   *   *

Black World War II veterans returned to the states with the G. I. Bill (Servicemen's Readjustment Act) in hand, looking to earn a college degree. Often their knocks on the doors of higher education only led to more knocks. Black colleges experienced a roughly 25 percent increase in the fall of 1944, maxing out their space, and many white colleges refused to admit blacks or increase their quotas. It was a travesty for black veterans to face this reality after putting their reality on the line for America.[47]

During the war, a partnership emerged between the federal government and higher education. It revitalized into a postwar partnership in which federal dollars poured into research coffers, producing scientific and technological knowledge that augmented the nation's imperial endeavors, industrial engine, and domestic patriotism. This fresh pool of funds allowed colleges and universities, mostly HWCUs, to expand rapidly over the next few decades. Meanwhile, the marginal manual-industrial versus intellectual debate reached a postwar consensus of classical liberal arts curricula *and* business, technology, or science courses that soothed both egalitarian elites and accommodating separatists, forming a corps of accommodating egalitarian elites.[48]

W. E. B. Du Bois materialized as an opponent of this postwar consensus, which the BCM would soon challenge. In fact, while the Pepsi-Cola Scholarship Board circulated a College Primer for Negro Students in 1948, Du Bois circulated his "memorial address" to the forty-five-year-old notion of the Talented Tenth and ladder altruism. "I assumed that with knowledge, sacrifice would automatically follow," he explained. "In my youth and idealism, I did not realize that selfishness is even more natural than sacrifice." As an alternative, he offered the "doctrine" of the "Guiding Hundredth," whose "passport to leadership" would be "expert knowledge of modern economics as it affected American Negroes" and the "willingness to sacrifice," imploring students to jump off the ladders, unveiling the notion of grassroots altruism.[49]

"The object of the world is not profit but service and happiness." Thus said Du Bois to the postwar generation of black students, who entered an almost wholly segregated academy. The days of Jim Crow flying over higher education were numbered, though, with black students and NAACP lawyers on the hunt, and the US Supreme Court increasingly siding with them. The 1940s and 1950s saw some northern HWCUs drop (or increase) their quotas, and border-state HWCUs were voluntarily, court ordered, or community pressured to desegregate. As the *New York Times* reported in 1950, "greater progress has been made in the last two years toward breaking down segregation in higher education than at any time since the Civil War." The walls continued to come down in the South throughout the 1950s, with the bulk of African Americans desegregating graduate programs. A few HWCUs even had hired black faculty. The Julius Rosenwald Fund subsidized the appointment of Allison Davis, a sociologist and anthropologist, at U-Chicago in 1941. In the 1940s, the NAACP disseminated a list of qualified black professors to HWCUs. A mere sixty black professors taught at white institutions in 1948.[50]

* * *

Many white students, professors, and alumni urged their Deep South college administrators to stick to tradition when the US Supreme Court threw out the separate but equal doctrine in its *Brown v. Board of Education of Topeka, Kansas* decision in 1954. The Universities of Mississippi, South Carolina, Alabama, and Georgia listened to students, rabid southern public opinion, and politicians, defiantly deepening the color line, particularly after UA publically demonstrated its insolence by admitting, mobbing, and then expelling Autherine Lucy in 1956. Despite the Deep South's recalcitrance, the collegiate desegregation carried on with a trickle of African American students. Clennon King was not one of them. For requesting admission to U-Mississippi in 1958, he was temporarily confined to a state mental hospital in order to evaluate his sanity. Ironically, the year before, black students thought this Alcorn State history instructor needed to be excluded from their campus after he published disparaging articles on African Americans.[51]

Many desegregated colleges and universities took down their white only signs only at the admissions offices. They stayed posted on dorms, either excluding the few black students outright, as at U-Texas in 1956, or segregating the students, such as at Northwestern and U-Illinois in the late 1940s. Or, as at Earlham-C in Indiana, the fresh handful of black students were forced to live alone until they found a roommate on their own. Then, when they found a place to live, some black students were terrorized, as at Harvard in 1952 (cross burning) and Louisiana State in 1953 (rocks thrown in their rooms). Black students at HWCUs far away from black population centers complained about the lack of black barbers and beauticians. They also encountered long-standing racist rituals. Those admitted to Missouri State in the fall of 1954 may have come across Delta Sigma Epsilon sorority's "Delta Darkey Minstrel Show...as one of the biggest events of the year."[52]

Like segregated southern HWCUs, some HBCUs felt they were under attack by the federal government in the late 1940s and 1950s. McCarthyism and the frenzied search for communists had zeroed in on Fisk—one of the citadels of African American intellectualism. In 1949, Fisk president Charles Johnson testified that communists had not infiltrated HBCUs before the House Un-American Activities Committee (HUAC). Two years later, another Congressional committee held hearings in Memphis, claiming that Fisk had formerly had two communist teachers and a communist student (Du Bois in the 1880s). Before the committee, Johnson calmly addressed the meaninglessness of former affiliates and assured the committee that there were no communists at the Nashville college. In 1954, HUAC traveled back to the area—this time in Dayton—and summoned Fisk mathematics chairman Lee Lorch to testify. Like other white radical professors in the 1950s, he had been blacklisted by HWCUs and welcomed by an HBCU willing to take the risk with his impressive credentials. Lorch refused to discuss previous affiliations. The next day, Johnson announced that his contract would not be renewed.[53]

While HBCU presidents were fighting off the anticommunist hysteria in the 1950s, they were acquiring their accreditation and removing the last of their elementary and secondary students. HBCUs were shedding their industrial veil and exhibiting a liberal arts identity in 1950s. HBCU presidents were also preparing for their annual "shows" for visiting white trustees and philanthropists, which still occurred into the 1950s. These shows dwindled in the 1950s though, as the UNCF increasingly aided private colleges and southern states boosted their public HBCUs to hold off the march of desegregation. HBCUs lost clientele as African Americans continued their twentieth-century mass migration to the North and West, and meager migration to newly desegregated HWCUs. Civil rights student activists in the early 1960s used black colleges as bases. Thus, the contradictions of the racial constitution at HBCUs were exposed when some college officials expelled or restricted protesters.[54]

*   *   *

In 1961, Georgia Tech peacefully opened itself to African Americans—the first Deep South school to do so without a court order. Yet peace did not reign at

U-Georgia (1961), U-Mississippi (1962), or U-Alabama (1963), as federal troops were needed to protect newly admitted students from white mobs. However, these violent desegregation sagas were the exception. Desegregation quickened in 1962 and only increased as civil rights activism peaked in 1963. Most institutions admitted students during summer sessions to lessen the anti-black reaction. Yet they were only allowing in a few, with student bodies in the South resembling faculties in the North and West in 1963. MIT and NYU had two black professors, Princeton and Notre Dame had one, Harvard had tenured none, Columbia had no black full professors, and Yale and Stanford did not have any black professors. Among prestigious institutions, two of the "sanctuaries" for black professors were U-Chicago and UCLA, with no more than six.[55]

Congress augmented the stream of black students by passing the Civil Rights Act of 1964 and the Higher Education Act of 1965, which provided financial assistance for students and increased federal funding. The Civil Rights Act gave government agencies the power to withhold federal money from discriminatory programs or institutions. In fear of this loss, many of the remaining holdouts cracked opened their doors. In April 1965, 1,830 colleges and universities out of around 2,100 had submitted signed assurances of compliance with the Civil Rights Act.[56]

Inspired and pressured by the CRM or campus activists, some institutions, such as Wesleyan-U in Connecticut, Los Angeles's Occidental-C, UCLA, and Rutgers, initiated programs to recruit a small contingent of black students as early as 1963.[57] Meanwhile, throughout the 1960s, private northern and western HWCUs and southern HBCUs toyed with desegregating their student bodies by launching student exchange programs, oftentimes through denominational ties. By 1967, southern HWCUs were not just desegregating but had also joined what became a recruiting rush, primarily for the brightest African Americans, offering four-year scholarships at colleges such as Wake Forest in North Carolina. NYU and Roosevelt-U in Chicago also established scholarship programs, and corporations and foundations such as the National Distillers and Chemical Corporation, Ford Foundation, and Rockefeller Foundation did the same. Because of the movement pressure, recruiting efforts, and scholarship offers, the number of black students attending HWCUs shot up 70 percent in 1965. There were about 200,000 black students in higher education that fall, about 4.5 percent of the total enrollment of 4.5 million. By 1967, the enrollment had increased to 5.15 percent.[58]

* * *

The history of black higher education prior to the BCM is a tale of debate and consensus among egalitarian elites, revolting nationalists, accommodating separatists, white paternalists, segregationists, and benefactors. Egalitarian elites joined with paternal liberals. They ideologically opposed accommodating separatists and paternal conservatives, both of whom were dictated by white capital. The four groups joined hands after World War II, opposed by a growing band of revolting nationalists. Black students resided on an island within at the center *and* periphery of this narrative of hugs and tugs. They were centered, since the dominating position at sea changed and dictated the nature of their island, their lives, more profoundly than any other group, and they were on the periphery—relocated from the sea—with nonstudents giving them little influence on the dictations and restructuring. Thus, Du Bois's island within was forced—serving as both the students' political position and their sociocultural place of refuge. Only through the LBSM did they endeavor to leave the island. Only through the BCM did they finally center themselves in the discourse of black higher education, appropriating the ideology of revolting nationalists.

2

"God Speed the Breed": New Negro in the Long Black Student Movement

Black student activists started to depart their politically, socially, and culturally exiled "islands within" decades before the 1960s. In a larger sense, African American activism did not abruptly burst onto the scene in the mid-twentieth century. In recent years, historians have provided new frames to chronicle this extended story, pulling the origin of the twentieth century black freedom struggle back to the 1920s and extending the purview of activism to the North and West. In 2005, Jacquelyn Dowd Hall termed this new historiography the "Long Civil Rights Movement," exposing the sea of activism throughout the country in the late 1930s, 1940s, and early 1950s. In Hall's conception, the Long Civil Rights Movement encompasses not only these formative struggles, but also the classical civil rights period (1954–1965) and the BPM.[1]

Peniel Joseph challenged this "master narrative," contending that black power should not be subsumed "under the all-powerful rubric of civil rights." In fact, Joseph introduced the concept of the "Long Black Power Movement" with roots in the New Negro Movement and the politics of Marcus Garvey in the 1920s. In sum, historians have elongated the two most storied black social movements of the twentieth century—stretching, complicating, and adding fresh voices, themes, and events to these stories.[2]

Weaving in and out of both the elongated civil rights and black power movements with roots in the 1920s strolled the LBSM. Just as the traffic for civil rights and black power did not begin in the 1960s, neither did the mass, concerted activism of black collegians. After almost a century of scattered, disconnected protest antecedents during the antebellum era, the post-Reconstruction period, and the early twentieth century, the LBSM began after World War I in the New Negro Campus Movement (NNCM) in the 1920s and early 1930s. The LBSM focused increasingly (though not totally) on accruing off-campus civil rights from the mid-1930s to the early 1960s, and then ventured to black power, reaching its pinnacle in the late 1960s and early 1970s during the BCM—all the while building on previous gains and recycling and erecting ideologies, tactics, and aims.

*　*　*

Black student activism had surfaced almost a century before the appearance of the *New* Negro on campus, in 1919, and the LBSM. Some of the initial black students activists participated in the antebellum abolitionist and colonization movements. With paltry numbers, fiery speeches were their main form of activism, initially speaking on colonization and eventually on abolition. John Newton Templeton, a former South Carolina slave, spoke at the 1828 commencement of Ohio-U on the topic "The Claims of Liberia." The fifth black graduate called for the "gradual" decline of "one of the greatest evils in our day," which had hindered "hapless Africa...in order that its total overthrow be permanent." He made the case that continental African people are capable of "intellectual improvement and self-government," as shown by the success of missionaries in teaching "multitudes" to read and write. Seeking donations for colonization, in closing, Templeton charged, "If there is then a true philanthropist or patriot in the house...let him evince it by his liberality and bounty, by undertaking the cause of the oppressed."[3]

When the abolitionist movement gained sway in the 1830s, galvanized by slave revolts and voiced in booming antislavery speeches and periodicals, students lent their crusading voices to this struggle. Templeton actually reversed his pro-colonization stance in 1834.[4] Seven years later, on January 27, 1841, Thomas Paul of Dartmouth delivered a forceful speech in Boston before the Massachusetts Anti-Slavery Society. The preacher's son had been schooled as an apprentice at abolitionist William Lloyd Garrison's newspaper and had studied at Noyes Academy before its institutional lynching. The antislavery society formed "to stay this torrent of vice that is rushing over us," he hammered home at the speech's height. "It is to lift up our perishing countrymen...It is to give opportunity for the development of the moral and intellectual powers of man...It is to save our churches and ministers...It is to wipe a foul blot from our country." But abolition is dying away, say the upholders of slavery, he recanted. "Dying away? Impossible! *Truth* never dies. Her course is always onward. Though obstacles may present themselves before her, she rides triumphantly over them; and the more formidable the enemy, the more terrible the encounter, and the more glorious the victory."[5]

Almost a decade after Paul's words galvanized abolitionists, Lucy Stanton gave "A Plea for the Oppressed" at Oberlin's commencement exercises on August 27, 1850. The first African American to complete the "ladies course" presided over the Oberlin Ladies Literary Society. The brave Stanton ridiculed slavery in Ohio, which bordered a slave state, in the midst of an unprecedented amount of abolitionist persecution, two weeks before the enactment of the chilling Fugitive Slave Act. "The Anti-Slavery pulse beats faintly," Stanton began. But "ye that advocate the great principles of Temperance, Peace, and Moral Reform...will you not plead the cause of the Slave?" She paused, then stoutly declared, "Slavery is the

Photo 2   *Lucy Stanton* (Courtesy of the Oberlin College Archives)

combination of all crime. It is War. Those who rob their fellow-men of home, of liberty, of education, of life, are really at war against them as though they cleft them down upon the bloody field." Stanton closed with words of hope, and from history's standpoint, words of prophecy. "Truth and right must prevail. The bondman shall go free. Look to the future! Hark! The shout of joy gushes from the heart of earth's freed millions!"[6]

The bondman and bondwoman did go free a decade later, as Stanton engaged in her itinerant teaching career. Meanwhile, some black students may have left their colleges to join the Union Army, just as John Copeland left Oberlin-C in 1859 to join John Brown's raid on the federal armory at Harpers Ferry (WV) that failed in its attempt to spark a mass slave rebellion. Before facing death at the gallows, Copeland dispatched a letter to his family in Ohio. "I am not terrified by the gallows, which I see staring me in the face, and upon which I am soon to stand and suffer death for doing what George Washington was made a hero for doing." Heroic black student voices continued to be heard when the Civil War ended, as they filled the refrain of the Reconstruction consensus on black higher education. And their sorrow songs were heard when the segregationist-Democrats disenfranchised their fathers and brothers and violently exchanged America's nascent interracial democracy for renewed white supremacy. Like their racial brethren in the community, black students were not immobilized by the fall of HBCUs from 1880s to the first decade of the twentieth century. From the nadir sprung the first black student protests.[7]

Hiram Revels, the first black US Senator, resigned his Mississippi post to become Alcorn State's inaugural president in 1871. He established a classical curriculum at the public HBCU supported by a generous appropriation from the ruling Republicans, like most HBCUs manifesting the Reconstruction consensus of education for advancement. By 1874, with Democrats asserting power, Revels intoned reverence for racist whites, infuriating students, who staged a crippling boycott of classes, filed complaints with officials, and triggered a mass exodus from the school and a short vacation for Revels.[8]

At Nashville's Roger Williams, later incorporated into LeMoyne-Owen, the paternalism and strict financial maneuvers of the white president and treasurer were "obnoxious" to the vast majority of the one hundred HBCU students who threatened to strike in 1887. They were seemingly led by Frank Levi Trimble, who in the early 1890s roomed at Brown-U with Morehouse's future president, John Hope. An indignant President William Stifler told reporters, "it is simply a war of the races, as there will always be when the negroes have a chance, but I tell you they have to submit this time." In the end, with local black community support, students did not submit.[9] Stifler and the treasurer were dismissed.

That summer of 1887, trade students at Hampton petitioned the faculty "as a discontented working class," James Anderson explains. The resentment and resistance had been building for years. According to students Perry Shields and W. H. Scott, "every apprentice of the school signed his name," grieving the menial level of training, hard labor, and meager wages and working conditions. "Four years at a trade like ours, working from 7 a.m. to 5:50 p.m., is enough to break down the constitution of a man, much less boys in the bloom of youth," Scott said. The protest petition and other forms of passive resistance were ignored or delegitimized during those years of student strife at Hampton, while Armstrong publically proclaimed that at his model institution "there was no begging except for more work."[10]

In the fall of 1887, a daughter of former South Carolina slaves enrolled at Barber-Scotia in North Carolina. Soon, Mary Jane McLeod (Bethune), the founder of Florida's Bethune-Cookman in 1904, became the "unacknowledged leader" of her peers and convinced the administration to give senior women the ability to serve as chaperones in place of teachers when students left campus.[11] Black student activism continued into the first decade of the twentieth century, although it stayed sporadic. Just as students did not idly take the excessive maneuvers of moralists or paternalists on their campuses, some did not take the regressive transformation in their communities either. After the Arkansas legislature segregated street cars in 1903, students at Shorter, an HBCU in Little Rock, released a protest publication, *The Voice of the Twentieth Century*. "The law was intended to humiliate negroes and every time a negro man, woman, or child goes to the back seat or sits on the cars while this iniquitous law is in force, the negro is humiliated. Simply stay off the cars. Stay off the cars." Galvanized by students, ridership plunged 90 percent in Little Rock and other cities, and remained at that level for weeks. But black communities could not sustain the boycott.[12]

What appears to be the first nationally renowned black student protest occurred two years later at Howard, where students demanded the removal of their "prejudiced" white president, John Gordon, who restricted the power of Howard's dominant black deans. On December 8, 1905, four hundred students assembled in the chapel at noon for the regular service. When Gordon appeared, a student near the front stood and yelled, "Down with Gordon!" In unison, students rose to their feet, waved their hats and coats in the air, and hissed and applauded as they marched out of the church and went on strike. By the end of the month, Gordon had resigned, becoming the first of more than one hundred college presidents over the course of the twentieth century forced out of their positions by the LBSM. The students demanded an African American, but the trustees selected another white minister, Wilbur Thirkield. Not even two months after the Howard strike, about two hundred Talladega-C undergraduates vacated their Alabama HBCU over the appointment of L. O. Parks, a "Southern white man," as assistant farm superintendent, saying it "was a blow at their manhood."[13]

That September 1906, some Talladega students may have crossed paths with people fleeing the Atlanta Race Riot. White fury toward African Americans had been inflamed by racially incendiary articles and politics, and by job competition. It exploded into an invasion of black Atlanta on September 22, lasting five days. Dozens of African Americans and two whites were killed. During the riot, most African Americans stayed and defended their communities, including those in Brownsville that adjoined Gannon Theological and Clark (Atlanta). Reportedly, armed Clark (Atlanta) students defended their campus too. When he learned of the riot in Alabama, W. E. B. Du Bois rushed to his home on the Atlanta-U campus. He had never handled a weapon but immediately bought a shotgun and two dozen rounds to patrol the campus and waited for a mob that never came. "I would without hesitation have sprayed their guts over the grass," the cofounder of the NAACP later said.[14]

Two years after the NAACP was founded, on October 21, 1911, none of the two hundred students reported for class after the faculty of NC A&T hung another rule on them: required Saturday courses. The senior and junior classes, the perceived leaders of the strike, were expelled. Up north that year at Cornell, Pauline Ray and Rosa Vassar had been denied dormitory rooms. Traveling a mile and a half from campus, they had "grown tired of climbing the hill or getting half frozen waiting for street cars." Learning of their predicament and that of others before them, in 1911 sophomore St. Lucia native James B. Clark passionately pleaded for justice in the *Cornell Era*, the student weekly. "Is that the way Mr. Cornell's ideals are being carried?" he asked. Gertrude Martin, advisor to Cornell's women, announced that the university did not have a racial ban. "I advised them to go somewhere else, as they would not find it pleasant for them living at Sage College," asserting a common justification at the time among paternal liberals for de facto campus segregation. The majority of Cornell's white female students (269 in total) petitioned the trustees in late March 1911 to officially bar African Americans. Within days, Ray and Vassar, still desiring campus rooms, issued a statement. "We don't seek social equality," they declared. "If we could live at Sage College, as far as convenience and comfort goes, we would be as one with the rest of the girls, but in all things social we would be as separate as two fingers on one hand," sounding like Booker T. Washington. A week later, Cornell president Jacob G. Schurman publicly unlocked the women's dorm for black students.[15]

In 1912, thirty-three Howard women, restless from the patriarchal campus rules and inspired by the budding women's movement, requested the appointment of a dean of women to "direct them in all womanly activities." The request was not granted for a decade. In 1913, two months after Delta Sigma Theta was founded at Howard, Osceola Adams rallied her sisters to participate in a suffrage march in Washington, DC, on March 3. They accompanied Ida B. Wells-Barnett and upwards of ten thousand women who marched down Pennsylvania Avenue, unfazed by the horror-faced walls of male policemen halting their progress at times or by the male onlookers throwing items or slurs. Back on campus, they were subjected to criticism for their engagement. "But we expected that," said Madree White. "Those were the days when women were seen and not heard. However we marched that day in order that women might come into their own...In those years Delta took a stand."[16]

In January 1914, students at Shaw and Clark (Atlanta) took a protest stand when one of their own was punished for defying a college rule. Shaw activists also demanded a black president. Seven hundred Howard students boycotted classes for a few days in April 1916 following the suspension of the senior class for unlawfully using the gym for a dance. In 1917, Morehouse men staged a four-day strike to annul required attendance at study hall.[17]

*   *   *

The eyes of African America were transfixed on East St. Louis, Illinois, the year Morehouse men eyed the end of compulsory study hall. White residents launched a vicious riot, incensed at the job competition in aluminum factories posed by southern black migrants and incited by businessmen, white nationalistic and corrupted union organizers, journalists, and politicians. Dozens of blacks were killed and thousands were driven from their homes by arsonists. Three weeks later, ten thousand protesters marched from Harlem to midtown Manhattan, blaring their resentment with their silence.

The East St. Louis riot and aftermath loomed as a dress rehearsal to what James Weldon Johnson termed the "Red Summer" of 1919. During a six-month period, northern whites in twenty-five cities and towns violently tried to stoke out their supremacy over the emboldened black residents, proud returning veterans, and the newly arrived southern migrants. African Americans stridently defended their humanity, urged on by Claude McKay's poem "If We Must Die," published in 1919. "Like men we'll face the murderous, cowardly pack, Pressed to the wall, dying, but fighting back!"[18]

A new mood stirred in the political and cultural pot of African America in the late 1910s and early 1920s—a mood that had become a conviction by the mid-1920s. Residue lingered from the stingingly racist 1915 film *The Birth of a Nation*. More than one million Great Migrationists tossed hope, ambition, impatience, heightened expectations, and the tangible and symbolic notion of black travel

Photo 3 *Zora Neale Hurston at Howard* (Courtesy of Prints & Photographs Department, Moorland-Spingarn Research Center)

to a better life into the pot. Many of the 400,000 or more black men who served in World War I injected into the pot their fighting spirit, a sense of urgency, the taste of interracial activity, and the seasonings of change, as did first-wave feminists and clubwomen. The self-determination slogans of President Woodrow Wilson were thrust into the pot, along with the parallel ideas emerging from the Russian Revolution in 1917. Scholars and artists accelerated their striving in African American self-discovery, self-examination, and self-inventiveness. African Americans downgraded political accommodation, cultural assimilation, and reverence of whiteness, allowing another ideology to rise in its place. The mood, then conviction, became encapsulated in two words: New Negro.[19]

Community nationalists, such as the venerable Pan-Africanist organizer Marcus Garvey, built organizations harnessing the newness, along with a young NAACP. Renaissance poets, novelists, musicians, and essayists, such as Langston Hughes, Zora Neale Hurston, Jessie Fauset, and Countee Cullen, gave African American culture its first sweeping tangibility apart from the everyday animation of African Americans. Some of these artists received their literary starts as students at HBCUs in the 1910s or the formative period of the movement. Hurston, for example, worked on the staff of Howard's literary journal, *The Stylus*, where she published her first short story in 1921.[20] Revolting nationalistic intellectuals, many of whom attended and oftentimes professed at HBCUs, gave the New Negro meaning in books, journals, and newspapers in the earliest concerted outpouring of literature on the African American experience. Shaw professor Benjamin Brawley, for instance, published his 1921 social history of African America a year before Carter G. Woodson did. "The Negro now loves his own, cherishes his own, teaching his boys about black heroes, and honors and glorifies his own black women," Brawley wrote. "A whole people has been reborn; a whole race has found its soul." E. Franklin Frazier discussed "New Currents of Thought Among the Colored People of America" in his 1920 master's thesis at Clark-U in Massachusetts. Frazier had an essay in the New Negro Movement's prime anthology, *The New Negro*, edited in December 1925 by Howard philosopher Alain Locke.[21]

Many black students enrolled imbued with the novel mood. With high schools finally planted widely across the American landscape, the black collegiate population jumped by 50,000 each year during the 1920s, quintupling over the entire decade. The number of women at HBCUs also doubled. The members of this Great Migration to mostly HBCUs did not form an ideological monolith, just as students throughout the LBSM thought in unique ways. Assertiveness and race pride swept up many New Negro youth minds. These independent, black nationalist inclinations collided with a moralized contraption of rules that restricted assertiveness and with benefactors, trustees, and presidents hostile to racial vanity, generating the first black student social movement.

"Old Negro" students succumbed to what Claude McKay, speaking of his Tuskegee experience in the early 1910s, called "the semi-military, machine-like existence."[22] But those were the Old Negro students. New Negro campus activists were a fresh breed—older and more diverse. Ideologically driven by New Negro literature and leaders, inspired by internationally circulating notions of passive resistance, the burgeoning African colonial civil rights struggle, and the domestic strike-laden union movement, shielded by their snowballing numbers, and moved by the atmosphere of postwar modifications, New Negro campus activists instigated a protracted assault on the harshest elements of moralized contraption of black higher education and standardization of exclusion and began uncovering the normalized mask of whiteness.

*   *   *

As white students enjoyed their "age of flappers and bootleggers, coonskin and bathtub gin, hot jazz and new dance crazes," the NNCM propagated slowly and steadily in 1919 and the early 1920s. In the spring of 1920, Wilberforce students learned that their Monday date time between sexes had been eliminated, and they had to walk the gendered pathways to classes. Soon after, a short rebellion gripped the campus until President William Scarborough relented. The suspension of seniors for insubordination prompted a strike in March 1921 at Johnson C. Smith in Charlotte.[23]

Most HWCUs overtly barred blacks or urged them to stay away from the dormitories "for their own sake" to maintain the standardization of exclusion. This happened at even the most diverse HWCU in the nation, Oberlin in Ohio.

In 1919, Beulah Terrell decided to rally her peers. She was the daughter of Mary Church Terrell, who in 1923 urged college students to "eradicate prejudice by starting a crusade" against racism and sexism. As would become standard operating procedure for HWCU activists in the NNCM, Beulah Terrell solicited the help of the NAACP, and together they forced the ban's removal. This aiding of the NNCM at HWCUs is one of the more notable, but unrecognized, feats of the teenaged NAACP.[24]

The NAACP assisted students when Harvard president A. Lawrence Lowell declined to desegregate freshman dormitories. "We do not owe it to him to force him and the white into social relations that are not, or may not be mutually congenial," Lowell paternalistically rationalized, as other liberals at the time had. In the spring of 1922, upperclassman Edwin B. Jourdain Jr., the world's best broad jumper, pleaded for the bar's removal. President Lowell did not jump at the suggestion. But in a year, NAACP officials, students, professors, alumni, and prominent newspapers were jumping with critiques over the bar. The high-pitched refrain touched W. E. B. Du Bois, a Harvard alum, who proclaimed it as "perhaps the most heartening sign of sanity on the race problem that has happened in fifty years. Not a single person of importance has yet dared to defend Lowell." In April 1923, Harvard's board of overseers stopped defending Lowell as well, unanimously repudiating his policy.[25]

As the press zeroed in on the Harvard dispute, in November 1922, a group of students at Storer-C in West Virginia, which closed in 1955, scrapped with local white youth. Utilizing the quick trigger of HBCU presidents to punish "insubordination" and possibly to curtail the rising racial tension in Harpers Ferry, President Henry T. McDonald expelled the three students, expelling the calm of the campus. Students briefly boycotted classes and withdrew. In 1923, the calm had receded at HBCUs more generally, as the NNCM agitated toward its climax. In May, students boycotted, and some withdrew from, the AME Zion's Livingston-C in North Carolina, while Ella Baker, the future civil rights organizing stalwart, petitioned nearby Shaw to allow females to wear the latest fashion trend—silk stockings. In 1918, the year Baker enrolled just short of her fifteenth birthday, applicants needed an "unblemished moral character" and willingness to "comply cheerfully with reasonable rules and regulations." By her senior year in Shaw's high school, around 1923, her docile willingness and cheerfulness to face the rules had subsided, if they were ever there. Grasping this, a group of women, mostly older and in college, who Baker said "didn't have guts enough," requested she lead the petition. Aghast, the dean of women not only denied the request but also gave the students extra chapel time to pray for forgiveness. She called Baker into her office. Expecting to see a remorseful girl, particularly after issuing a threat of expulsion, the dean was startled by Baker's resolve and fainted at one point. "But it didn't bother me," Baker said, "because I felt I was correct."[26]

* * *

Countee Cullen, a student at NYU already gaining notoriety for his poetry, spoke in the summer of 1922 in New York City during an event hosted by The League of

Youth. "The young American Negro is going in strong for education; he realizes its potentialities for combating bigotry and blindness," and it is "working a power-ful group effect." The group effect exhibited itself that summer at a black student conference down the eastern seaboard in New Jersey. Students in the Atlantic City group and possibly The League of Youth discussed the group effect—the need for a national black student organization—into the fall of 1922 and the win-ter of 1923. Ultimately, they decided to found the first national black student organization in American history—the American Federation of Negro Students (AFNS). Its founding conference convened at Howard in April 1923, attracting delegates from Oberlin, Yale, Cornell, Lincoln-U (PA), Tuskegee, Howard, and a few high schools. Students installed an executive committee of seven students, with I. J. K. Wells of Lincoln (PA) presiding. The AFNS selected the slogan "A more progressive people." The students were addressed by a few Howard fac-ulty members and administrators, including philosopher Alain Locke. AFNS resolved for the inscription of race relations and black history courses in the col-lege curricula and pledged to launch three drives: "business co-operation," "the stimulation of Race pride," and "the encouragement of education." That month, one of the organizers published a piece in *The New Student* entitled "The Negro Youth Awakening." The AFNS "seeks the fundamental weakness of the situation and proposes to work from the bottom up—a method which appears to be the reverse of that used by the present leaders," wrote Howard's J. Alpheus Butler, theorizing an early grassroots altruism.[27]

After studying black higher education, the AFNS executive committee injected marginalized black student ideas into the center of the debate over the function of higher education. Eschewing Du Bois and the late Washington, suggesting that black higher education had historically overemphasized manual, professional, and classical education, the AFNS in late 1923 contended that business educa-tion had been neglected. Then, in December 1923, the AFNS launched its first drive, "Bigger and Better Negro Business," to encourage business education and inspire students to become entrepreneurs, like Garvey at the time and Booker T. Washington before them, both of whom promoted black capitalism. Wells and company at Lincoln (PA) mailed out a torrent of folders outlining AFNS ideas to HBCUs and large HWCUs in the winter of 1923–1924, urging students to read them and pass them along. By March 1924, the AFNS had chapters at fourteen institutions, including Howard, Virginia Union, Morehouse, Atlanta-U, and West Virginia State (a HBCU), with a reported membership of six thousand, which if true, made this mobilization of black students the largest in American history up to that point. In April, the AFNS gathered for its second national conference in Nashville, welcoming students from U-Chicago, Northwestern, Meharry Medical, West Virginia State, Atlanta-U, and Lincoln (PA), and elect-ing officers from eight black fraternities and sororities. The students decided to focus all of their efforts in 1924 "upon the economic development of the Race," Wells said.

In addition to a letter Wells sent in June to the editors of several newspapers challenging students to start "selling goods instead of labor," the AFNS spear-headed a campaign in 1924 to name and honor the "ten greatest Negroes America has produced." The "mythical ten," as black newspapers termed them with glee, turned out to be George Washington Carver, Frederick Douglass, Madam C. J. Walker, James Weldon Johnson, *Chicago Defender* publisher Robert S. Abbott, painter Henry O. Tanner, Du Bois, Washington, Paul Laurence Dunbar, and Colonel Charles Young. The naming of the ten, which glaringly omitted quite a few great women, seemed to be the last major affair of the AFNS. After a failed attempt at fundraising for scholarships and a conference in August 1925, the AFNS had seemingly declined to relative obscurity by 1926.[28]

* * *

While the AFNS provided a deviation for off-campus activism in 1923, accommodating separatists and paternal conservatives drove the Florida A&M (FAMU) president of twenty-two years, Nathan B. Young, out of his position because he refused to place more emphasis on the subordinating agriculture and manual learning. The trustees then selected W. H. A. Howard, the dean of vocational studies, against the wishes of alumni and students who circulated petitions asserting he was "not qualified to be head of a college since he…held no degree." To segregationists and capitalists, however, his accommodating separatist ideology qualified him for the position.

On October 8, 1923, FAMU students deserted their classes. One-third of the college's 325 students returned home. Three days into the strike, campus activists firebombed Duval Hall, and over the next three months they burned the hated Mechanical Arts Building, Gibbs Hall, and three other buildings. Assigning white guards to restore order by enforcing an evening curfew and patrolling the main men's dormitory only led to more disorder. To the students, there hung a "reign of terror on the campus with white men standing over us with guns at their sides." Eleven young men were expelled during the uprising, but no one ever apprehended the arsonists. Order did not return until the trustees replaced Howard, in May 1924, with J. R. E. Lee, a former Tuskegee instructor, who presided over FAMU for two decades.

Another year-long campaign to push out Fisk president Fayette McKenzie succeeded the year-long struggle to eject Howard at FAMU. McKenzie had just netted the famed Nashville HBCU a $1 million endowment, unprecedented for a black college. But the money came with strings that interlaced Fisk with the conservative cravings of the donors. McKenzie terminated the SGA along with the oldest HBCU student publication, *The Fisk Herald*. He rejected a campus charter of the NAACP and tossed NAACP literature out of the library, while inviting Jim Crow entertainments and arrangements for benefactors. McKenzie forbade Fisk females from wearing the popular silk or satin dresses. They had to wear high necks, long sleeves, black hats, and cotton stockings. Officials had to be present for any meeting between the sexes. Students of the opposite sex were often sent home for walking together in broad daylight. Regulations mandated when students ate, slept, and studied. Students were summarily dismissed for any opposition to Fisk's moralized contraption. President McKenzie's favorite saying resounded, "If you don't like Fisk, then get out!"

W. E. B. Du Bois muted his thunderous voice as he heard criticisms of his alma mater in the early 1920s. He came for his daughter Yolanda's graduation in June 1924 and had the opportunity to speak to the alumni in conjunction with the festivities. With McKenzie and the trustees sitting nearby, undergraduates peering down from the gallery, and alumni ranging in the rows in front of him, the probably hour-long speech remains one of the most searing face-to-face attacks on a president in American higher education history. "I maintain that the place to criticize Fisk University is at Fisk University and not elsewhere," he said early in the speech. "Fisk is choking freedom. Self-knowledge is being hindered by refusal of all initiative to the students." He fearlessly urged students to boycott the institution. "Fisk will and must survive," he said in closing. "The spirit of its great founders will renew itself, and it is that Spirit alone, reborn, which calls us tonight."[29]

When Du Bois ended, it was only the beginning of his writing and speaking that summer and fall of 1924 to serve "an example either for the Power that furnish the Cash or for the awakening youth and their supporters." One of his more influential articles appeared in *The American Mercury* in October 1924. "It has gradually become a rule of philanthropy that no Negro higher school can survive unless it pleases the white South." To please the white South, HBCUs had to "train servants and docile cheap labor," Du Bois charged in the widely discussed essay.[30]

Fisk youth, like their peers around the nation, followed the example of Du Bois, who was to New Negro campus activists what Stokely Carmichael became four decades later to black campus activists—a guiding light of resistance. When trustees traveled to Fisk in November 1924, they were greeted by grievances posted everywhere and one hundred students chanting "Away with the czar!" "Down with the tyrant!" Seven students met with the trustees and demanded, among other things, a student newspaper, a student council, and an honor system to replace the dreaded Fisk Code of Discipline. In December 1924, students defied curfew and protested on two occasions. On February 4, 1925, more than one hundred male students again ignored curfew and stormed through campus—singing, yelling, smashing windows, overturning chapel seats to the tune of "Du Bois! Du Bois!" and "Before I'll be a slave, I'll be buried in my grave." At midnight, McKenzie allowed fifty white Nashville officers from a force complacent with recent lynchings to quell the rebellion, maddening blacks in Nashville and throughout the nation. Seven students were arrested—the same students who had met with the trustees in November—even though McKenzie had no proof of their involvement. "McKenzie, You're Through," the *Chicago Defender* shouted from its editorial page.

Nobody was more enraged than the Fisk student body, who unleashed a strike the next day that lasted ten tumultuous weeks. Many pupils withdrew. A large number tried to transfer to Howard. Nashville's white community rallied behind McKenzie, while Nashville's black community and Fisk alumni stridently supported the strikers. Five weeks into the strike, student leader George Streator proudly proclaimed, "We don't need to do anything except tell the students: 'Boycott this, or boycott that,' and believe me they do it to a finish!" Sensing his firing was imminent, McKenzie resigned on April 16, 1925, bringing to a close the paramount protest of the NNCM. Many of the proposals were thereafter instituted by a temporary leadership committee and the next president, Thomas Elsa Jones. In addition, Jones, a white Quaker, added courses in black history and literature and sponsored an annual conference with black scholars. Du Bois, in probably one of his happiest times in an almost a century of living, hailed the successful Fisk student "who hits power in high places, white power, power backed by unlimited wealth; hits it openly and between the eyes; talks face to face and not down 'at the big gate.' God speed the breed!"

In the midst of the Fisk strike, Baltimore's *Afro-American* took a panoramic look at the movement and its implications. "Student disturbances…may be traced to efforts…to win a larger measure of participation in college control," the editors noted on February 28, 1925. Two decades ago, the "strict military discipline" could be insisted upon, since "education came largely thru philanthropy" with many teachers giving free services. But today's college student "has grown to the stature where he knows the blessings of self-government and academic freedom and demands them. If rebuffed, he resorts to the strike method. The very appearance of a student strike in an American college may be taken as evidence of growth in intelligence and independence."[31]

Presumably inspired by their Fisk fellows, Howard students started a strike shortly after McKenzie resigned. On May 7, 1925, two days after the university suspended five students for skipping compulsory ROTC—another facet of the moralized contraption that bred docile discipline—Howard students voted to strike. With posters screaming, "Don't Be an Uncle Tom" or asking, "What Is This Going To Be—An Army or a University?" picketers lined the campus, sometimes blocking classroom buildings. After four days of bitter debate, the faculty issued threats of suspensions and failures. "Are we scared?" some students chanted in defiance. "No!" Fearing Congressional retaliation and facing the unlikelihood of an accord, local alumni convinced students to return to classes on May 14 with the five reinstated, amnesty, and the ROTC requirement suspended while a special committee studied the issue. After the summer vacation, the special committee abolished compulsory ROTC.

But some students and professors, and many alumni were far from pleased with J. Stanley Durkee's presidency and sought to remove him and compel trustees to hire Howard's first black president. With pressure swelling that summer of 1925 and into the next academic year, the trustees finally granted students, faculty, and alumni their wish, hiring Mordecai Johnson, a 36-year-old black Baptist preacher, in 1926.[32]

With the protest activity mounting, a few black newspapers published scathing editorials in May 1925, particularly unnerved by the Howard protest. After interrogating their growing list of grievances, the *Chicago Defender* mocked, "next we shall hear of students striking because they are asked to attend classes; they will insist on writing their own examination questions; they will demand free movies on the campus." Undeterred, New Negro campus activism hovered like a storm cloud above higher education. Amid the rain of the Fisk and Howard protests in 1925, Simmons-C students disrupted their Kentucky Baptist HBCU, and forty students, about half of the student body at Lincoln-I, east of Louisville, vacated the school Berea officials created when forced to segregate. In December, students struck against their "prejudiced" president at Knoxville-C (TN).[33]

*   *   *

On December 7, 1925, a group of black and white students gathered in Lane Hall at the U-Michigan to organize the Negro-Caucasian Club (NCC). Spearheaded by Lenoir Beatrice Smith, a Mississippi native, NCC became one of the first, if not the first, interracial student civil rights associations in American history. Smith became the first president of this group, which aimed for the "abolition of discrimination against Negroes." After a clerk at a lunch counter just off campus refused to serve Smith, she accompanied a sympathetic professor to visit Dean John R. Eiffinger. "My grandfather owned slaves in Virginia, but you mustn't think I'm prejudiced," he said. "I would do something for you if I could." It was the first of many grievances the club brought before the dean. Black exclusion from college dances and swimming pool were others, as desegregated HWCUs tended to bar African Americans from every venue, activity, or course that involved physical contact. Eiffinger claimed impotence if not outright hostility. NCC members implored area eateries to desegregate, but were told whites would walk out if the interracial band of students were served. On a few occasions after the group formed in December 1925, a small set of black and white NCC members tested this reason, sitting in at eateries despite not receiving service. Reportedly, white customers did not walk out during perhaps the nation's first student sit-ins.

NCC members (and New Negro campus activists more generally) also began to uncover the normalized mask of whiteness, challenging the racist ideas that had poured out of the academy since its founding. In the 1920s, academics tended to rationalize American and European colonization of nonwhite peoples and the political-economic plight of the African world as the natural order of civilization, reflecting a racial hierarchy. Lothrop Stodard's *Rising Tide of Color* had just been published four years earlier, and it saturated the scholarly mainstream. On U-Michigan's campus, NCC members were outraged at the lectures of A. Franklin Shull, who maintained Nordic superiority, and Ulrich B. Phillips, who classified slavery as paternal and humane. To challenge demeaning ideas and engage studies on African Americans, black students formed literary societies and clubs in the 1920s at schools such as Colgate-U, City College of NY, Harvard, and Howard.[34]

*   *   *

In 1925, Prairie View A&M students near Houston resisted the inappropriate sexual advances of professors, which led to the termination of President J. G. Osborne. He was replaced by W. R. Banks, who, serving in that capacity for two decades, "never forgot that the students were his 'children,' and that he must save them from themselves," according to a college biographer. Thus, as an alternative to giving them the freedom to mature, Banks regulated dress, kept the sexes separated, increased the number of religious gatherings, and when students objected, he ordered them to head to the highway and "grab the first thing that went by smoking."[35]

Students involved in a hazing incident at Johnson C. Smith (NC) were also told to grab the first thing smoking, spawning protests that led to the suspension of seventy-five students, mostly freshmen, in 1926. Nonetheless, with all the activism in the previous few years, the NNCM had new heights to reach. In her commencement speech at Shaw as valedictorian of her collegiate graduating class in April 1927, Ella Baker emboldened her peers. "Awake youth of the land and accept this noble challenge of salvaging the strong ship of civilization, by the anchors of rights, justice and love." Students awoke later that year at nearby Saint Augustine's, an Episcopalian affiliate, in a weeklong protest for a relaxation of rules.[36]

Presumably the first black collegiate athletic protest occurred that fall at Howard after officials, due to an athletic deficit, abolished free housing and food for its football team. Demoralized and underfed, the team suffered a heart-wrenching defeat to Bluefield State (WV). The loss ended Howard's storied three-year undefeated streak. The defeat started a weeklong strike in October 1927, which lasted until students and alumni pledged to fund the athletic amenities.[37] As Howard players boycotted practices that month, students at Lincoln-U (MO) fumed over the recent firing of their beloved president Nathan B. Young—just as FAMU students did in 1923. State authorities were hostile to Young's vision of an academically upgraded, accredited public institution of higher learning that did not school meekness. Young was replaced by Clement Richardson, well known for favoring submissive vocational education. "We are not interested in our lessons any more," one student announced. "We know that they are not running it for our benefit, but for their own." Lincoln's student council called a boycott, and roaming bands of strikers damaged property. Many left "in disgust, never to return again." Disruptions were quelled only when governor Sam Baker sent armed prison guards to police the campus.

The protests at Howard and Lincoln-U (MO) paled in comparison to what occurred at Booker T. Washington's alma mater. Hampton students assembled in Ogden Hall to view their Saturday evening movie on October 8, 1927. An administrator made a startling announcement: the lights were going to stay on at the rear of the auditorium above the seats of students with escort privileges. "Lights out," the students began to shout, stomping their feet, perplexed at the latest rule. "The matter of the lights was unusually small" to the students—no more than "the accidental puff of wind that touched off an already smoldering fire." After refusing to sing "plantation songs" for white visitors on Sunday evening, on Monday, what one student said "has been trying to happen for the last ten years" happened, as a protest fire smoldered at Hampton. Twenty-one men (and no women on the sexist campus) were elected to serve on the Student Protest Committee. It delivered seventeen requests to the office of Principal James Gregg on Tuesday evening, including a student council composed exclusively of students, resignation of trade teachers without high school degrees, and weighing of academic preparation above religiosity in selecting instructors.

Using the same draconian but effective tactic that HBCU administrators used forty years later during the BCM when faced with a student-body-wide rebellion, Gregg closed the campus, expelled all of the students, and told them that to regain readmission they had to sign a "loyalty, obedience and cooperation" pledge. Nineteen members of the Student Protest Committee—all of whom were some of Hampton's most promising male students—were suspended for the remainder of the 1927–1928 academic year. Hundreds were placed on probation. The only committee member not to be suspended was an informer. But the New Negroes wrecked his room.

Aside from a few voices, parents, alumni, and newspapers did not come to the aid of the Hampton strikers, no doubt influenced by Gregg's public relations machine, which he kept operating efficiently during the strike. Hampton reopened on October 25, 1927. No strikes were in the offing, but a protracted spontaneous, leaderless campaign of passive resistance against Gregg engrossed the campus, gaining momentum with each passing semester. Anarchy seemed to be on the horizon in 1929. Before catastrophe came, Gregg resigned in May 1929. He was replaced by George P. Phenix, a white New Englander, who ushered Hampton away from its vocational past.

"An epidemic of student strikes has been sweeping over the country of late," wrote the editors of the *Pittsburgh Courier* on October 29, 1927. One of the few editorials endorsing the Hampton strike, it presented the pulse of the NNCM. "Many of the rules and regulations in force in colleges and schools are archaic and should be scrapped. Often there is entirely too much restriction," and faculty supervision "too often borders on espionage." Morality "should be taught at home." Many HBCUs "are still run more like disciplinary barracks or reform schools than" colleges and universities attended by free people. "It is quite natural, then, that students should occasionally revolt."[38]

Students denied admission to dormitories and the physical education course revolted at NYU in 1927. Freshman Thomas W. Young insisted that his racial brethren must "keep striking back at every injustice and mistreatment," in a letter to the NAACP's head Walter White. "If New York University knows that for every offense there is a strong organization ready to 'strike back' she will not be so inconsiderate in her actions." Student pressure and the NAACP's publicity campaign and legal threat prompted NYU to change its official rhetoric, but discrimination continued.[39]

The NAACP also involved itself in a protracted struggle, spearheaded by Loren Miller in the 1920s and Wray Choat in the 1930s, "looking to the wiping out of the various discriminations in Kansas University." They persuaded the legislature to investigate the matter, but Chancellor Ernest Lindley defiantly insisted he was "not afraid of the courts or of publicity," exclaiming that the "University is a white school, built by white money for white students. If we want to get tough about it the Board of Regents could meet tomorrow and pass a ruling to exclude all out-of-state Negroes." In a rare occurrence, a HWCU chancellor took off the mask and exposed normalized whiteness, despite (or rather due to) having one of the largest black student populations in the nation.[40]

*   *   *

The arc of the NNCM encapsulated 1923 to 1927. Yet activism against tyrannical rules did not stop until it joined the early CRM in the mid-1930s. In 1928, two AME institutions (Kansas's Western and Kittrell-C in North Carolina) were disrupted by strikes. Before Langston-U students went on strike, they presented ten resolutions in November 1928 to their president, including the ability to form a student council at the lone HBCU in Oklahoma.[41]

Writing in the January 1929 issue of *The New Student*, John P. Davis explained that revolts had gripped "nearly every" HBCU in recent years. Students were rebelling against the "benevolent despotism" of white college presidents or trustee boards indoctrinating "pacifism and servility" through student codes that prescribed every moment of students lives and regulated practically all of their social interactions. "Imagine putting such a rule into effect at Dartmouth or Smith!" Furthermore, the Harvard graduate student reasoned that the gargantuan number of regulations had been bred on "two fallacies": that black students are "not prepared for the exercise of free will" and that "the white trustee and executive knows unerringly the best method of Negro education," viewing "Negro students as members of a child race, thinking they know just the kind of soothing syrup they need." After discussing the racist basis of paternal liberalism and conservatism, the revolting nationalist maintained that HBCUs headed by African Americans "suffer from the same fate" due to their dependence on white capital. "It is the old story of 'whose bread I eat his song I sing.'"[42]

Davis failed to add that some black educators imposed these rules not just because of the sway of white capital. Some accommodating separatists believed in the same paternal, racist ideas as their white peers. Usually conceptualizing themselves as extraordinary, a number of black educators believed African Americans were inferior to whites morally or academically, and it was their duty, as extraordinary African Americans, to lift them up—the crudest form of ladder altruism. Furthermore, to ensure that students were morally up to the task of proving racial equality and black humanity to whites, which to them would yield civil rights from whites, zealous egalitarian elites also maintained the moralized contraption.

*   *   *

Students at Howard rallied and broke up a basketball game when Dean of Women Lucy Stowe, a champion at the time of certain women's rights, expelled a woman for kissing her boyfriend in February 1929. "As women we should stand for our rights and if necessary go to the limit so as to protect the integrity of Negro womanhood," one unnamed black female leader told reporters. That month, as Langston-U students staged another protest, the *Chicago Defender*, citing the Howard "kissing" controversy, suggested that HBCU presidents and deans "hold a stock-taking conference" to "cure" the "problem" of "our college unrest." When a federal report revealed that a white dean at Benedict-C (SC) had lied about his doctorate degree, boycotters commanded his firing in March 1929. Two months later, a student at North Carolina's Brick Junior-C hurried home without notice at the urgent request of his father. Another refused to take part in a college play. Both were expelled. The students were reinstated "after the most riotous week in the history of this institution." The suspension of two students also caused a strike at Alcorn State that year.[43]

Even though HBCUs experienced profound hardships during the years of the Great Depression, the economic downturn did not depress student activism. President J. L. Peacock's barring of black newspapers from the library and halting of the showing of *The Millionaire*, a black motion picture, provoked an eight-hour strike at Shaw in early 1930. "He is a Northerner who has gone South and embedded himself in all the 'isms' of the South," wrote alumnus C. D. Jacobs, calling on fellow alumni to support the students in opposition to the paternal liberal. Students boycotted Georgia's Paine-C in April 1930, as the *Pittsburgh Courier* proclaimed, "The day of white presidents of negro colleges is far spent." "The strike fever spread" to NC A&T with a three-day walkout.[44]

The fever subsided in 1931, but it increased the following year. When in January 1932 Virginia Union fired a young Rayford Logan, on leave finishing his Harvard doctorate, for reportedly advocating for a black president and encouraging his students to think critically, students were imbued with a protest mentality. A mere 10 of the 316 Knoxville-C (TN) students did not strike that month when 40 students were punished for attending an off-campus dance. Striking Gannon Theological seminarians demanded the firing of a racist professor in March 1932, Langston-U students demanded the firing of their president in May, and Storer-C students demanded, along with the NAACP, the erection of a memorial tablet to John Brown on their Harpers Ferry campus.[45]

In 1933, students staged strikes to protest restrictions on class choice at Howard and poor food at Saint Augustine, against the Virginia-U of Lynchburg president (leading to his resignation), and to force the creation of a student council at Lincoln (MO). Bayard Rustin led a strike against the dorm's "bad" food—the sole academic year the music major and future civil rights organizer attended Wilberforce. In May 1934, the demotion of a popular school official, Howard Gregg, triggered a march of eight hundred Wilberforce students around their campus, shouting, "We want Gregg!" That year, Howard law students boycotted classes for a week to push out a professor. And a detail of "rough, brutal, and disrespectful" county police and the dismissal of twenty-eight students ended a four-day strike at Virginia State that decried, among other things, the separate gendered entrances to the library, dining hall, and chapel, and the annual "show" of spirituals performed for the governor.[46]

Thirty-one striking students were terminated at Alcorn State in 1935, a year that probably had the least number of protests since the beginning of the NNCM. In contrast, at least eight demonstrations rocked HBCUs in 1936. Howard students protested in January and November. A white Morgan State (MD) professor's telling of "Mammy" stories sparked a class walkout. In November, food strikes gripped NC A&T, Shaw, and Saint Augustine's. In addition to demanding better food, strikers at Langston-U (OK) demanded a student council, more guidance and fewer threats from administrators, and for women "to be treated as women and not as wards." "The wave of [New Negro campus activism]...sweeping the country," identified the *Pittsburg Courier*, hit Prairie View A&M and West Kentucky Community & Technical-C in Paducah, Kentucky, in 1936.[47]

* * *

The NNCM had battered the moralized contraption, which had been utterly fundamental to the racial constitution of higher education from the Civil War to World War I. Wardens of the academy, HBCU officials tended to seek to control every aspect of the lives of their students. The students' crimes were their blackness, their youth, their gender, their being born in a segregated society, and their being bred within a political economy that primarily desired them to teach or preach subordination, or their docile, manual labor. Their moral performance had to be pristine. Their moral "beasts" had to be restrained to attract white benefactors, to mold producers for white capital, to live in a segregated society, and to demonstrate black civilization.

Sometimes these justifications of the moralized contraption emerged from the mouths of white presidents, which gave them an overtly racial overtone and led to demands for the replacement of those presidents with African Americans. But they were no less racial, no less demeaning, no less dehumanizing coming from black HBCU presidents who unconsciously and possibly consciously believed African Americans were inferior, at least in a moral or academic sense. Therefore, HBCU students needed more policing than the morally and academically superior white college students, the racist myth stated. Black HWCU students detected a penitentiary too—from the standardization of exclusion.

In effect, the NNCM was a fight for *basic* social and academic freedoms for black students in higher education, which white students by the 1920s took for granted. The stress of *basic* cannot be understated. Without gaining—or placing themselves on the road to gaining—these basic freedoms to live on campus, eat tasty food, dictate their campus life schedules, socialize, publish a student newspaper, organize student governments, not face expulsion for breaking a rule, and file a grievance, as a few examples, the BCM would not have been possible. Their prime placement in the CRM in the decades between the New Negro and black power activist would not have been possible.

3

"Strike While the Iron Is Hot": Civil Rights in the Long Black Student Movement

The NNCM ebbed in the late 1920s and ended by the mid-1930s, while black student activism changed course, latching onto the commencing Long Civil Rights Movement. However, in the growing historiography of the formative years of the CRM, black students are rarely brought to light. Instead, New Dealers, community activists, populist politicians, Communists, unionists, anti-colonialists, NAACP and NNC members, and labor organizers are some of the groups often situated at the starting line in the late 1930s. Although there has been some notice of black student activism of the 1920s, the traditional historical lines reads [implies? asserts?] that black student protesters were marginal until the sit-in wave of the spring of 1960.[1]

In actuality, the LBSM encapsulated the lost years of the late 1930s, 1940s, and early 1950s. As participants of the civil rights struggle, African American students began a concerted battle to raze Jim Crow in the late 1930s, while also campaigning against war, fascism, capitalism, and the racial constitution on their campuses. Thus, after engaging mainly in campus activism in the 1920s and early 1930s, they developed a binary activist focus (campus and community) until the late 1950s, when they were swept up in the off-campus civil rights crusade until the rise of the BCM in 1965. Black student sit-ins in 1960 were not the *beginning* of any movement. They were the *crowning* of mounting civil rights student protest waves coming from the sea of American colleges and universities that slammed into the shores of Dixie throughout the 1930s, 1940s, and 1950s.

* * *

As the NNCM declined in the early 1930s, the three-decade student civil rights struggle started to lay its roots. James Jackson, who had joined the Communist Party by 1931, as a Virginia Union student helped establish the Cooperative Independent Movement (CIM) to "train leaders for the deliverance of our people, through militant action, from every semblance of racial and class oppression." The CIM joined white students at UVA and presented grievances to the Virginia legislature concerning fascism, war preparations, job discrimination, and educational retrenchment. At Fisk, a Denmark Vesey Forum stimulated racial discussions and picketed a local Jim Crow theater in the early 1930s, led mainly by Ishmael Flory, a graduate student. When white supremacists lynched Cordie Cheek, a black teenager living on the edge of campus, on December 15, 1933, the Forum organized a rally. Meanwhile, Fisk student council president John Hope Franklin decided to hand President Franklin D. Roosevelt an antilynching petition when he visited the campus in November 1934. However, Fisk president Thomas E. Jones cleverly convinced the future historian to do otherwise by deceiving Franklin about arrangements for a personal meeting with FDR. "I took from my disappointment one lesson: Jim Crow America was skilled at deflecting or ignoring appeals to justice and equity," Franklin later wrote.[2]

In 1934, the lone black congressman, Chicago representative Oscar De Priest, petitioned to abolish the unwritten rule barring black patrons from the House public dining room. After officials dismissed a waiter who was attending Howard for violating the rule, his peers joined the struggle. On March 17, 1934, about thirty students dashed to the Capitol but were stopped from entering the dining room "to test the legality" of the rule. "We are citizens and we can go wherever we want in the Capitol of the United States," the unnamed Howard leader insisted. Unmoved, the Capitol police ejected the students, who returned only to be repulsed again and again. De Priest called their attempted direct action protest "a serious mistake," since it "would do no good and only causes trouble." At the onset, students etched their "troublesome" position towards the left of the older civil rights center, where they remained for the entirety of the movement.[3]

* * *

While some civil rights scholars are not aware of the array of student activism prior to 1960, historians of student activism tend to locate America's first student movement in the 1930s—concealing the NNCM in the so-called "moribund" 1920s.[4] This prewar student social movement was not America's first student movement, nor was it wholly white. The American Youth Congress, a prominent organization during that period, had a sprinkling of black members and sometimes spoke out and campaigned against racial discrimination.[5] As an executive in the National Youth Administration, Mary McLeod Bethune founded the National Conference of Negro Youth in 1937, which took a conciliatory approach until 1942. Spurred by the wartime radicalization, it changed its name to the National Council of Negro Youth, compared fascism to racism, attacked lynchings, the biased judiciary, and segregation in the armed forces, and lobbied for anti–poll tax legislation. "We must strike while the iron is hot to end the poll tax once [and] for all, now," said Winifred Norman, the group's chairman.[6]

The American Student Union (ASU), the signature majority-white organization of the 1930s, formed in 1935, merging the socialist Student League for Industrial Democracy and the Communist National Student League, which had James

Jackson of Virginia Union in its national executive committee. The ASU mobilized hundreds of thousands students who feared another World War to boycott classes for one hour annually from 1936 to 1939. Although rarely illuminated, the ASU mobilized black student antiwar activists who often connected militaristic fascism in Germany, Japan, Spain, and Italy (particularly after its invasion of Ethiopia) with militaristic fascism in Georgia, Mississippi, Louisiana, and Alabama. Students at Howard and Virginia Union participated in antiwar conferences. Howard had the sole ASU-initiated strike in Washington, DC, in 1936, with nearly two hundred students peopling a parade and mass meeting. Shortly after the ASU strike in 1937, a young John H. Johnson declared, "Yes, students should strike for peace."[7]

"To speak of a powerful student movement without speaking of the Negro student is impossible," wrote Maurice Gates, challenging the ASU the year of its inauguration. The ASU did in fact speak to the Negro student, due to the Communist Party's directive in the 1930s to attack racial discrimination, and due to the influence of black ASU members and chapters at schools such as Virginia Union and Howard. At its national gatherings, ASU delegates resolved to fight against "discrimination against Negroes" and lynching, and objected to segregated amenities. "The very foundation of democracy cannot be made stable unless we root out minority discrimination," Bill Davis, a Howard delegate, told the fourth annual ASU convention in 1939. The ASU demonstrated and rooted it out when black students at Columbia (1936), U-Illinois (1938), and Temple-U (1940) were refused service at area businesses. In possibly the ASU's largest rooting-out operation, the Bennett-C chapter boycotted Greensboro (NC) theaters with all-white films in early 1938, mobilizing more than one thousand college students. With the Nazi-Soviet Pact of 1939, the refusal of some ASU Communists to criticize Soviet imperialism, pre-McCarthy efforts to "clean out communism" on campus, and the United States' entry into World War II, the ASU had collapsed by 1941.[8]

The year after the ASU faded, in 1942, the Congress of Racial Equality (CORE) was formed by white U-Chicago students, such as George Houser, along with James Farmer, a recent Howard law school graduate. Many of the founders were members of the Fellowship of Reconciliation (FOR), a pacifist civil rights organization inspired by Mahatma Gandhi's philosophy of nonviolence. White middle-class college students almost entirely made up the initial growth of the organization. Nathan Wright Jr., a student at Episcopal Theological School in Massachusetts, was one of CORE's few black student staffers, serving as the New England field representative in the late 1940s. Wright, who chaired the Black Power conferences of 1967 and 1968, traveled on the Journey of Reconciliation in 1947 along with eight whites and seven other African Americans, including Andrew Johnson, a black Cincinnati student, to test the recent court ruling declaring segregation in interstate travel unconstitutional. CORE declined after its famous Journey, but revitalized itself during the classical civil rights period (1954–1965).[9]

* * *

Black students were part of the unprecedented impetus for what Jacquelyn Dowd Hall termed "civil rights unionism," prominent in the seminal years of the civil rights struggle in the late 1930s.[10] Yet, as usual, their brand of civil rights unionism or, more so, labor politics looked to the left. More than four hundred black youth, including students from Virginia Union, Howard, Atlanta-U, Fisk, Spelman, Morehouse, and Morgan State, convened in February 1937 in Richmond under the auspices of the youth section of the National Negro Congress (NNC) to establish the Southern Negro Youth Congress (SNYC). "We are here to save ourselves and our people!" declared Edward Strong, a Communist who, as the NNC's national youth chairman, did much of the early planning for the SNYC. African American conditions are not caused by "the majority of white Southerners...but the few, those who profit by pitting white labor against black labor to the harm of both," the inaugural conference proclaimed. "We have a right to" free and equal schools, homes without poverty, recreational facilities, jobs, the right to organize with whites, suffrage, and the eradication of lynching. Delegates also resolved that "Negro history be added to history books," the maintenance of world peace, the freedom of the politically imprisoned Angelo Herndon and the Scottsboro Boys, and the support of the ASU and the NAACP. According to Robin D. G. Kelley, SNYC members articulated a "complex radical consciousness that simultaneously advocated interracial unity and black nationalism" or a "politics of inclusion *and* self-determination."[11]

At its peak, the SNYC reportedly claimed a membership of 11,000 in ten southern states, welcoming youth for about a decade to annual All-Southern Negro Youth Congresses, often held at HBCUs, beginning in 1937. Paul Robeson gave his first Deep South singing performance in 1942 at the fifth congress, held at Tuskegee. In 1944, Mary McLeod Bethune told SNYC delegates to "get ready in heart, in head and in hand, for the new world order which is coming." Honored as "the senior statesman of the American Negro's liberation struggle," W. E. B. Du Bois challenged the 1946 congress to stop "running away from the battle here in" the South and instead "grit their teeth and fight it out right here" using "white slaves of modern capitalist industry" as allies.[12]

In one of its initial campaigns, through the efforts of its leader James E. Jackson, the hardened Virginia Union activist, the SNYC helped unionize Richmond's five thousand tobacco stemmers, who in 1938 successfully struck for better working conditions. However, most of its activism emerged around Birmingham, Alabama, which had become SNYC headquarters by 1940 after its largest conference to date was held there—650 delegates, including students from Alabama HBCUs. Ester Cooper, an Oberlin (1938) and Fisk (1940) graduate who had participated in the ASU, politically tussled with Birmingham City Council members and Public Safety Commissioner "Bull" Connor in petitioning for the integration of a local park and playground. She kept the organization alive while her husband, James Jackson, fought in the war. The group involved itself in quite a few civil liberties cases concerning segregation and police and mob harassment and brutality in the 1940s. It launched a Free Nora Wilson campaign in Alabama that succeeded in stopping the railroading of this teenager, who sternly defended her sister, accused of stealing, to a white woman. (The SNYC was notified of the case by Caravan Puppeteers—a group consisting mostly of black college students—who in 1940 used puppets to amuse and clandestinely educate rural blacks about the poll tax, disenfranchisement, and labor disunity.) Like other groups with black students, the SNYC lobbied the government to investigate the revitalized KKK and to coerce defense contracts to hire blacks during World War II, and powered anti–poll tax, voter education and registration, and anti-Hitler campaigns. Nonetheless, by 1949, like countless other groups, SNYC had been red scared into oblivion.[13]

*   *   *

Unlike many civil rights organizations, the NAACP survived late-1940s and early-1950s McCarthyism. Black students gradually entered this group in the late 1930s, along with or aside from the ASU, SNYC, the Communist Party, church youth organizations, and other campus, local, and national groups. Sensing the strengthening activist impulse of students, the NAACP wisely established the "Youth and College Division" in March 1936, appointing Juanita Jackson national director. Jackson, who earned a master's degree from UPENN in 1935, had a storied past of youth organizing in Baltimore, having served as vice president of the National Council of Methodist Youth. "Discrimination and segregation are on the increase," Jackson told NAACP youth in 1936. "We cannot lose a moment. We must not falter a step. We must march forward!"[14]

Jackson terminated the "junior branches," reorganizing the youth division into junior youth councils (for those aged 12 to 15), youth councils (for those aged 16 to 25), and college chapters with new guidelines. In her first mobilization campaign, she hurried youth into the antilynching legislation struggle galvanized by a Senate bill first introduced in 1934 (and blocked every year by segregationists). In February 1937, working closely with the SNYC, NAACP college chapters held a series of antilynching radio broadcasts, demonstrations, and programs around the nation, wearing black armbands at most events to symbolize their mourning. Each November during the "American Education Week" in the late 1930s, Jackson encouraged protests against educational injustices. The NAACP's youngsters and students raised money for black labor struggles and initiated a few "Buy Where You Can Work" campaigns in states such as New Jersey and Indiana. They demonstrated against police brutality and set up "citizenship training schools" to ready black southerners to register and vote in the late 1930s. In 1938, Jackson resigned her post in order to marry. James H. Robinson replaced the venerable Jackson, one of the unsung giants of the LBSM whom the NAACP's Walter White unsuccessfully tried to retain.

Still, the youth division continued to grow, and students unremittingly formed college chapters, even at Hampton in 1940, and some studied "Negro" history, such as the chapter at LeMoyne-Owen. In March of that year, the NAACP convened the First Annual Student Conference at Virginia Union, at which students condemned the Roosevelt administration's expansion of the military budget at the expense of social programs, thereby opposing foreign war without domestic civil rights. It was the furthest left NAACP youth would go—mirroring the CRM the Cold War witch hunts intimidated back to the center. The NAACP as a whole claimed a record membership, stepping up its fight over the color line. For instance, in 1943, Howard's NAACP chapter picketed and desegregated a cafeteria near the college. One of the leaders of the mostly female and undergraduate group of activists was law student Pauli Murray, the future cofounder of the National Organization of Women (NOW). Howard president Mordecai Johnson squashed another demonstration the next year, since it threatened Howard's federal appropriation. At that point, according to Murray, students turned their "reform energies upon the administration of the school and called for a whole review and revamping of administrative procedure...so that students would have more say," similar to what happened two decades later.[15]

When World War II ended in 1945, many African American soldiers and migrants became students. And they gave birth during the next few years to baby boomers, groomed for two decades on far-reaching civil rights and black power activism before enrolling in higher education in the late 1960s. The mothers and fathers of BCM activists were dynamic as youngsters, too—a dynamism they imparted on their children. Fascism had been defeated. Now it was racism's turn. With many veterans joining and starting chapters at schools such as Cornell, Long Island-U, and Columbia, it is not surprising that in the years after the war, NAACP college chapters and youth councils created veterans committees. Aside from veteran matters, such as securing the G. I. Bill and ending segregation in the military, which President Harry Truman did in 1948, voter registration appealed to postwar civil rights workers after the white primaries were deemed unconstitutional in 1944.

Georgia students were particularly active in this arena. Arthur Johnson, who became a prominent Detroit NAACP leader in the 1950s and early 1960s, organized Morehouse's NAACP chapter as a freshman in the mid-1940s. The group attained a membership of fifty, holding meetings every month that drew a teen-aged Martin Luther King Jr., whose father was active in the Atlanta chapter. Under Johnson's leadership and at the urging of "Daddy King," the Morehouse NAACP launched a voter registration drive among black college students across the state in 1946. At around the same time, Coretta Scott (King) joined the Antioch-C NAACP chapter after not being allowed to hone her teaching skills in the segregated Yellow Springs, Ohio, schools.[16]

NAACP college chapters (and campus-based, usually interracial, organizations, such as the Council of Minority Equality at Indiana's DePauw-U) also launched direct action protests in northern, midwestern, and western states in the late 1940s and 1950s against area establishments that discriminated against black students. The Penn State NAACP chapter staged a demonstration against six campus barber shops that made African Americans travel twenty-eight miles for a haircut. Due to the national office's discouraging direct action protests in places where Jim Crow flew legally, external and internal red purges, the Korean War, and tension with the national office that did not help the reduced NAACP membership and the association's financial crisis, NAACP youth councils and college chapters hit their lowest point in the early 1950s.[17]

*   *   *

NAACP youth councils and college chapters were, on occasion, cradles for intrepid student activists whom civil rights historians have largely sidelined. One of the pivotal, protracted skirmishes of the Long Civil Rights Movement between the 1930s to the mid-1960s was the desegregation of higher education, especially in the South—first graduate and professional schools and later undergraduate programs. The NAACP's legal division, with the likes of Charles Hamilton Houston and Thurgood Marshall, has been placed at the axis of this history. Black student plaintiffs have been relegated to the margins in this story, rarely identified as central activists.

In reality, aspiring students thrust themselves into the center of the desegregation of southern higher education. Fueled by a forward-looking temperament, they applied in droves to segregated schools from the late 1930s to the 1960s, agreed to file lawsuits, served as the vulnerable center of the NAACP's cases, and if they won, stridently and *crucially* held open doors while weathering social seclusion, separate classrooms, hostile students and faculty, and white mobs. The NAACP brilliantly tried and won these cases, and history has praised their endeavors. However, lawyers cannot do anything without clients. Hence, just as significantly, would-be black students of varying ages handed the NAACP its cases and implemented the rulings by walking fearlessly into the fog of southern segregation. Black student activists, supported by NAACP lawyers, desegregated southern higher education.[18]

The first joint affair between hopeful students and the NAACP tried to cut the color line at UNC Chapel Hill in 1933, a university the *New York Times* categorized that year as "the most liberal State institution in the South in its attitude toward the Negro race." The *Times* added, "There is no likelihood that any other Southern college or university for whites will acquiesce in the admission of Negroes" so long as Dixie reigns in Chapel Hill. Thomas Hocutt, a 24-year-old graduate of NC Central in Durham and a Duke hotel waiter, applied for admission to the state's only school of pharmacy in March 1933. Denied on Jim Crow grounds, Hocutt solicited the assistance of local lawyers, who in turn contacted the NAACP. Eager to demonstrate the superiority of legal activism and curb the growing influence of the Communist Party (CP) among African Americans in the 1930s prompted by the CP's widely touted defense of the nine Scottsboro Boys charged with rape in Alabama, NAACP executive secretary Walter White happily grabbed the case. James Shepard, the accommodating separatist head of NC Central, fearing white retaliation or pursuing white propriety, refused to release Hocutt's transcript, dooming the case from the start. Yet, in throwing out the case, the judge also tossed out some hope. Judge M. V. Barnhill stated that the denial was due to Hocutt's race and that he could have ordered the university to review the application fairly. The NAACP proclaimed a moral victory for a new program. Aspiring black students gazed at the closed door.[19]

In 1935, two aspirant students visibly attempted to pry open Dixie doors in neighboring states. Alice C. Jackson, a graduate of Virginia Union, sought admission to her state's lone graduate program in French at UVA. Officials denied Jackson's application because of the racial bar and "other good and sufficient reasons." Advised by the NAACP, she mailed a letter to the rector and the Board of Visitors, asking them "to specify the 'other good and sufficient reasons' why you rejected my application." Sensing legal redress, they did not specify. But to hold off desegregation's advance, the Virginia legislature established a graduate school at Virginia State and provided scholarships for African Americans to attend out-of-state schools.[20]

The NAACP did not take UVA to court. However, in 1935, it did defend Donald Murray, a graduate of Amherst-C (MA), whom the U-Maryland law school told it "does not accept Negro students." The Baltimore City Court ordered U-Maryland to admit Murray and an appeals court agreed the following year. NAACP executive secretary Walter White encouraged the newly enrolled Murray to "work hard" because "by your very manner you will create...a new concept of the Negro." Egalitarian elites were willing to endure the burden of demonstrating the humanity of African people.[21]

These three aspiring students cracked the dam. Black applications started flowing into southern, lily-white admissions offices in the late 1930s. Then the student-NAACP coalition raised the stakes, taking to the US Supreme Court the case of Lloyd Gaines, who had been denied admission to the U-Missouri. In 1938, the Court ruled in *Missouri ex. rel. Gaines v. Canada* that Missouri had violated the equal protection clause of the Fourteenth Amendment of the recent Lincoln (MO) graduate since it did not have a separate but equal law school for African Americans, thus mandating Gaines's admission. The Court's first foray into the "separate but equal" clause vitalized the civil rights community to launch an all-out legal attack on Jim Crow.

Before that assault took shape, tragedy tempered this first victory. In 1939, the Missouri legislature created a law school at Gaines's alma mater. However, Gaines was not one of the thirty enrollees that year. In the meantime, Charles Hamilton Houston and NAACP lawyers had managed to initiate a second case to argue that Lincoln's law school dwarfed the flagship school, ultimately positing the fallacy of the "separate but equal" policy. The NAACP had moved Gaines to Chicago after he received death threats. When he needed to be deposed for the second case, he could not be found. Without a plaintiff, the court dismissed the case. Gaines, who had reportedly been saddened by Missouri's building of a black law school, thus prolonging his already three-year wait, was last seen in Chicago in March 1939. No one knows his fate for sure, but speculation pointed to suicide, self-exile, assassination, or a retreat into hiding, bribed or bullied by white supremacists.[22]

Still, hopeful black students constantly applied and stood up as plaintiffs in the 1940s, and by the end of the decade they had fissured a few nearly century-old walls. Silas Hunt decided to forgo his plans to attend U-Indiana and instead struggled to gain admission to U-Arkansas. Unexpectedly, the WWII veteran and graduate of U-Arkansas at Pine Bluff averted the snaillike court pace. Seeking to dodge the negative publicity they saw trouble other southern institutions, university officials announced on January 30, 1948, that they would admit qualified black graduate students, starting with Hunt. He enrolled in law school days later as the first African American to be admitted to a white public university in the Deep South since the handful during Reconstruction. Hunt attended segregated classes in the law school basement, some of which were attended by a few sympathetic white students, until tuberculosis cut his life short on April 22, 1949.[23]

The well-publicized trial of Ada Lois Sipuel (Fisher), who was attempting to enter the U-Oklahoma law school, inspired Hunt's activism. Following its *Gaines v. Canada* decision, in *Sipuel v. Board of Regents*, in 1948, the US Supreme Court finally ordered her entry. When the daughter of a minister and Langston-U graduate enrolled in 1949, the university assigned her to a restricted classroom area with a chair marked "colored." George McLaurin, a black doctoral education student pushing 70 years old, admitted by U-Oklahoma due to the Court's order in 1950, sat in a desk in a row reserved for blacks, had a designated space in the library, and ate at a different time than whites at a table with a sign overhead that read "reserved for colored only" until compassionate white students ripped it down. McLaurin and the NAACP challenged the legality of campus segregation, and the Court in *McLaurin v. Oklahoma State Regents* ruled in the coalition's favor. This latest ruling in 1950, along with *Sweatt v. Painter*, which required black admission to the U-Texas at Austin law school, hampered colleges that were forced to desegregate from inserting mechanisms to sustain the standardization of exclusion.[24]

The energy behind the student-NAACP coalition for the desegregation of higher education received a jolt from these rulings. The President's Commission on Higher Education's endorsement of the ban on educational discrimination in 1947 also blew the sails. Students were encouraged by their younger brothers and sisters who were desegregating high schools in the 1950s. It is not known how many African Americans applied to break down higher education's barriers. It is quite possible that thousands of aspirant black students stared grisly Jim Crow admissions policies in the face, including several prominent leaders of the 1960s, such as Pauli Murray of NOW and CORE black power director, Floyd McKissick Sr. To be sure, Ada Sipuel and George McLaurin inspired and invigorated many hopeful African Americans across the South who were engaged in multiyear battles to attend graduate school.

*   *   *

The activity of these student desegregationists has been marginalized in pre-1960s civil rights literature. But not nearly as much as the black campus activism that snatched headlines almost every year during the late 1930s, 1940s, and early 1950s. A three-year battle for the first black professor at City College of NY resulted in the hiring of Max Yergan to instruct "Negro History and Culture" in the fall of 1937. Upon the imposition of an earlier curfew for female students at Wilberforce-U in 1938, several hundred mostly male students boycotted classes and rampaged through campus, hurling rocks at windows and lights until sheriffs arrived and the nine "ringleaders" were expelled. In 1939, Allen-U students struck for two weeks, demanding the resignation of the "illegally" installed new president of the AMEC institution in South Carolina; a violent strike at NC A&T followed the dismissal of the football coach; and Hampton students vacated classes for five days, angered at the white president and English department chair's unexplained firing of a black professor.[25]

In 1941, activists at NYU and Harvard rumbled when black athletes were benched against Jim Crow institutions, and Howard women showed their discontentment with the recently installed dean of women, whom they labeled

Hitler, for her "walk-the-chalk-line" rules. However, the major campus protest that year disrupted Tuskegee, where nearly half of the 1,400 students went on strike. Dozens were arrested, suspended, expelled, or battered by policemen in remonstration of "despicable" food sometimes seasoned with flies, ants, roaches, and tacks. In the 1940s, large, spirited food strikes also unsettled Spelman (1942), North Carolina's Livingston-C (1946), Alabama A&M (1947), Alabama State (1948), South Carolina's Benedict-C (1944 and 1947), and Clark (Atlanta) (1944), where students complained that the food was "not fit for pigs." Students protested for the reinstatement of suspended and expelled students, and for more voice in college and disciplinary affairs at Johnson C. Smith in Charlotte and Morgan State (MD) in 1943, NC A&T (1945), Missouri's Lincoln (1948), Georgia's Fort Valley State (1949), Elizabeth City State in North Carolina (1953), and Kentucky State (1953). Strikes to run off or reduce the power of presidents, who usually prevented student movement, fraternization, and organization, battered Maryland's Bowie State in 1941 and Delaware State in 1942 and 1949, and Saint Augustine's and Morris-C in South Carolina in 1943. Stringent regulations for women prompted strikes at NC Central in 1942 and Virginia Union two years later.[26]

In 1944, the Baltimore *Afro-American* asked some HBCU presidents, "Should College Students Have the Right to Strike?" A few said no outright. Most were like Kentucky State's R. B. Atwood, who said, "Students have the right to strike although in my twenty years of experience with students I have known of very few strikes which I have felt were justified." Up north, feeling their causes justified, seventeen student waiters boycotted the racially restrictive faculty club at U-Chicago in 1945, and public campaigns pushed nearby U-Illinois into granting dormitory space to black women. Mid-1940s campus activism, just like civil rights struggles more generally, were often waged by veterans aghast at the rules and restrictions that mirrored their aborted military lives. In 1946, Charles Evers and his younger brother Medgar, fresh from fighting in World War II, which Charles Evers said, "woke up a lot of Negro GIs," enrolled at Alcorn State (and later registered and tried to vote). The 23-year-old Charles assumed the class presidency and led a food strike and a campaign "to get the deans to stop treating us like babies." A "bunch of Uncle Toms installed by the white power structure" ran Alcorn State at the time, he recalled, and they allowed the use of "the same old white racist textbooks that described us as savages and Reconstruction as a terrible evil."[27]

A similar state of affairs prompted a four-day strike in 1947 at Wiley-C in Texas, with picketers, some with signs that read "Down with Dictatorship." Wiley-C students forced amnesty, the resignation of a dean and two professors, the ability to establish a student council, and the elimination of campus separation between men and women. Students not only coerced professors, but progressive, activist, and outspoken professors were terrorized by HBCU administrators, seeking to clean their campuses of those deemed to be Communists or to prevent faculty radicalism, disloyalty, or clout. Student strikes followed the "unjust" firings of popular professors at Johnson C. Smith in 1942, and Knoxville-C and Langston-U in 1949.[28]

African American and Jewish students conducted a strike at City College of NY in 1949, demanding the ouster of an anti-Semitic professor and a racist residential hall director, while administrators tried to isolate the students by playing the Communist card. NAACP chapters at U-New Mexico and Columbia protested against exclusionary clauses in campus clubs in 1949 and 1953, respectively. In addition, black students, sometimes through newly organized NAACP chapters, continued their multidecade struggle against segregated housing and faculty at institutions such as the UW Madison and Cornell. With McCarthyism breeding conservatism, campus activism slowed in the early 1950s.[29]

∗   ∗   ∗

On May 17, 1954, the US Supreme Court ruled in *Brown v. Board of Education* that "separate educational facilities are inherently unequal," trashing the "separate but equal" doctrine that had been the law of the land for roughly six decades. Black students rejoiced on their campuses. Some, in the midst of their elation, immediately realized the historic mandate. "We should not look on this decision as merely something we have to obey," said Duke's Jolee Fritz and David W. Stith, a NC Central law student. The two vice presidents of the North Carolina State Conference of NAACP youth councils and college chapters urged the youth of their state and the nation to look upon the decision as a challenge "to make Democracy work." For southern white supremacists, federal legal cover for segregation and the standardization of exclusion in higher education had been removed. State rights and hawkishness became their last major recourse. As the LBSM accelerated away from the political pit stop of *Brown*, violence stayed on its tail.[30]

Emmett Till became southern aggression's most notorious post-*Brown* victim. For hissing at a Mississippi white woman, white supremacists tortured and murdered the Chicago teenager. They beat in his face so ruthlessly that he was unrecognizable. His mother, Mamie Till Mobley, one of the unrecognized engineers of the classical civil rights period, decided to have an open casket funeral and allowed the gruesome pictures of her battered son to be seen around the nation on the cover of *Jet* magazine. No African American was the same after the seeing Till's bludgeoned face. If *Brown* gave African Americans hope, the Till lynching packed them with rage—a hope and rage that fueled the CRM over the next decade. The murder kicked Till's black peers presumably the hardest, and they then turned around and kicked off a stretch of seventeen years of fresh, forceful, and oftentimes front-page civil rights and black power activism on and off campus.

Civil rights activists first tried to rock the "cradle of the confederacy." Although rarely illuminated, some of the first arms in Montgomery came from black students. In October 1954, a little less than half of the two thousand Alabama State students rallied, boycotted classes, and burned a campus building in their effort to gain a stronger voice in student affairs. The following fall, they directed their activism off campus. Late in the evening of the day Rosa Parks was arrested in Montgomery for refusing to give up her bus seat, Alabama State professor Jo Ann Robinson, a colleague, and two of Robinson's "most trusted senior students" gathered on campus to pull an all-nighter. For four hours, they cut stencils and mimeographed 52,500 leaflets announcing a bus boycott on December 5, 1955.

Then, for another four hours, Robinson and the two students mapped out the distribution routes for the notices, arranged bundles in the appropriate sequence, and loaded them into her car before arriving at her morning class. After the 8 a.m. class, in which the two seniors were enrolled, and working on no sleep, the trio circulated the notices to Montgomery's black community. Black students supported the 381-day Montgomery bus boycott and the women like Robinson who rode the boycott instead of the buses.[31]

However, in 1956 the epicenter of the LBSM was in another Alabama city—Tuscaloosa. A few months into the Montgomery bus boycott, when Americans did not widely know the name Martin Luther King Jr., many heard the name of youngest of ten children born to farmers from Shiloh, Alabama. With the NAACP's help and a court order, on February 1, 1956 Autherine Lucy enrolled at U-Alabama as a graduate student in library science. Three days of volatile demonstrations from mobs ultimately led to Lucy's suspension because U-Alabama claimed it could not keep her safe. When she audaciously filed suit to reverse the suspension, U-Alabama cried slander and expelled her—a tragedy that "enlisted world-wide sympathy for a civil rights cause that was yet to be called a movement," wrote E. Culpepper Clark. The episode galvanized the American resistance to and for *Brown*.[32]

It incited black student crusading as well. In March 1956, food strikes at Cheyney-U (PA) produced a new food facility. Early the next month, five hundred SC State students, encouraged by the local NAACP, declined to eat dinner in the cafeteria because Jim Crow distributors supplied some of the products. Students at nearby Claflin-C, South Carolina's oldest HBCU, joined the boycott. Soon after the strike began, SC State students brought up long-standing grievances with President Benner C. Turner, including his selection of student leaders based on loyalty to his administration instead of merit. The failed strike lasted six days, after which the all-white trustee board expelled several students, including student council president Fred Moore, a month away from his graduation.[33]

On a crowded Saturday bus in Tallahassee on May 27, 1956, less than two months later, Wilhelmina Jakes and Carrie Patterson, two Florida A&M students, sat down on a three-person seat next to a white woman they knew. "Get up or get off," ordered the bus driver, who had pulled over to enforce the racial code. "I'd be glad to get off," Jakes retorted, "if you'll give us our money back." The driver spurned the offer and waited for the police to arrive, who arrested and charged the students with inciting a riot. The next evening, Klansmen burned a cross on the lawn of their apartment. Word of the incidents traveled through the FAMU campus like the sound of its marching band. On May 28, students boycotted classes and city buses, boarding every bus at the main bus depot on campus to pressure riders off. Eventually, all the buses were like those in Montgomery—practically empty. Three days into the boycott, black community leaders created the Tallahassee Inter-Civic Council to facilitate the boycott and organize crucial car pools.[34]

As Tallahassee buses limited their racial codes in February 1957, 40 percent of the student body walked out of Mississippi Valley State for thirty-six hours, demanding an SGA to replace the faculty-student committee. It ended with an assurance, but the students did not receive the right to organize for four years.[35] The next month, student activists were again on the rampage in Mississippi at the Evers brothers' alma mater, Alcorn State. Clennon King, a black minister and history instructor, published a series of articles with student pictures in a Mississippi newspaper linking the NAACP with communism, criticizing black leaders, soothing American slavery, and admiring Uncle Tom. On the third install-ment of his series, students supported by President Jesse R. Otis boycotted his classes and demanded his termination. The all-white trustee board, who arrived in Alcorn on March 7, 1957, to address the matter, ordered the students back to their classes, threatening to close the institution. "I don't give a damn if you burn [Alcorn] down!" one student announced, reflecting his peers' wrath. The next day, student body president Ernest McEwan read a statement, supported by 489 of 571 students, on the chapel steps, after students filed out from a rally. "At 11:55 a.m. the oldest land-grant college in America for Negroes, which was founded in 1871, died." The trustees did temporarily close the college, fired President Otis, replaced him with John D. Boyd, who the students dubbed the "white man's tool," renewed King's contract, and forced all of the students to vow to bury their activ-ism before they reenrolled. It was an indisputable message to Alcorn State stu-dents and to students across the state and nation who followed the affair closely. Whites and "white tools" still dominated public black higher education.[36]

This was a contradiction black students did not address until the BCM, as in the late 1950s southern desegregation touched them the dearest. Editorialized in the *Chicago Defender* in March 1957, "Negro college students are alive to the issues of the day, and feel an identity with the Negro masses off campus who are fighting for equality and recognition in the South." Black students did not merely feel an identity—they were an intricate part of the fighting force, the civil rights infantry, shedding their notion of ladder altruism. Applications rushed into the last remaining segregated academic holdouts. Eleven Allen-U students, for example, sought entry to U-South Carolina in 1958.[37] Later that year, about five hundred students saturated the nation's capital during the "March for Integrated Schools." The next year, more than 30,000 black and white youth—13,000 were members of NAACP youth councils and college chapters—returned to lobby congressmen and were joined by Martin Luther King Jr., A. Phillip Randolph, and Roy Wilkins.[38]

In the fall of 1958, John Lewis, a student at American Baptist Theological and future SNCC chairman, noticed a "sense of urgency and awareness spreading among...black students throughout" Nashville. "There was a growing feeling that this movement for civil rights needed—no, *demanded*—our involvement." Their consciousness and sagacity of grassroots altruism had been fortified with each newsflash of student strikes, bus boycotts, school desegregation struggles, and even decolonization movements in the 1950s. They were taught the basics of nonviolent resistance by attending FOR workshops on their campuses and reading the main FOR pamphlet, titled *Martin Luther King and the Montgomery Story*, and King's *Stride Toward Freedom: The Montgomery Story*. Black students nurtured on profoundly Christian and patriotic HBCU campuses with officials who had been crusading on morals since their arrival were not surprisingly enthralled by FOR, Gandhi, and King's moral philosophy and by the budding moral crusade against segregation.[39]

In the 1950s, African Americans were thrusting de jure segregation out the door, along with its guard—unpunished hawkishness. In May 1959, when FAMU students learned that four white youths who confessed to abducting and raping a 19-year-old FAMU woman might get off, a body of angry, armed students started making plans for a massive march. Student government leaders intervened and organized a one-day class boycott of six hundred. Students sang, prayed, listened to speeches, and picketed with banners that hollered, "Justice is all we want. Silence is not our motto." Possibly trying to avert the power students displayed three years prior in the bus boycott, county officials announced that a grand jury would be reconvened. The four youth became the first whites to be convicted for raping a black woman in the Deep South.[40]

*   *   *

The 1959–1960 academic year has been the most celebrated of the LBSM due to what occurred in the spring semester. Yet students built the base for the spring launch during the previous summer and fall. Collegians on some HBCU campuses trained in nonviolent direct action in the summer and fall of 1959. Some learned in FOR and NAACP sessions. Activists attended the Institute of Nonviolent Resistance to Segregation at Spelman in Atlanta in the summer of 1959, at which Bayard Rustin and Ella Baker spoke. More than six hundred attended CORE's first southern interracial institute in Miami that summer. Some of the attendees, such as Patricia and Priscilla Stephens, took these ideas back to their HBCUs. The Stephens sisters, who were FAMU students, founded a Tallahassee CORE chapter, holding their first meeting in October 1959 with thirty FAMU and Florida State students. On November 11, the chapter staged its first sit-in at a "white-only" lunch counter. But members spent most of their time building the small organization, dissecting Tallahassee segregation, and attempting to negotiate.[41]

The late-1950s sit-ins happening in Oklahoma City, Tulsa, and Stillwater, Oklahoma; Wichita and Kansas City, Kansas; Miami, Florida; Durham, North Carolina; and Marion, South Carolina were local affairs, not nationally reported spectacles quickly inducing activism in other towns.[42] In Nashville, James Lawson, a Vanderbilt seminarian and FOR veteran, had run weekly justice workshops in a local church since the fall of 1958. The handful of Nashville students had surged to twenty by the fall of 1959. Lawson and John Lewis had been joined by two future SNCC leaders, Marion Barry and Diane Nash. The group staged their first sit-in at a downtown department store on November 28, 1959, as "a test, nothing more." Soon, the prepared team, like others across the South, would be in the struggle of their lives against Dixie.[43]

After being denied service at the bus terminal in Greensboro, North Carolina, Joseph McNeill discussed the incident with his NC A&T roommate, Ezell Blair Jr., and eventually Franklin McCain and David Richmond joined the discussion about the slow pace of desegregation. "We've talked about it long enough,

Photo 4   *Four African American college students sit in protest at a whites-only lunch counter during the second day of protest at a Woolworth's in Greensboro, North Carolina. From left: Joseph McNeil, Franklin McCain, Billy Smith, and Clarence Henderson* (by Jack Moebes, News & Record Staff)

let's do something," McNeill declared, prompting quietness. From the quietness sprung the beginning of the loudest battering of segregation in American history. The next day, in the late afternoon of February 1, 1960, with the covert blessing of the local NAACP, Richmond and McClain walked into a Woolworth, accompanied by Blair and McNeill, two former NAACP youth council members. The four North Carolina A&T freshman sat down at its restricted counter, unaffected by the refusal of service, and remained until the store closed. The next day, William Smith and Clarence Henderson joined McNeil and McCain in a replay of day one. Spearheaded by the newly organized Student Executive Committee for Justice, within five days hundreds of students from area colleges were "sitting in." News reports of these sit-ins flashed nationally. Television lounges in black college dorms across the South were so quiet when these reports flashed that "you could hear a rat pissing on cotton."[44]

The Greensboro Four rang the liberty bell of protest, and legions of students heard it—in Durham and Winston Salem (NC) on February 8, 1960, Charlotte on February 9, and Southern Virginia two days later. And on February 13, the already organized students were demonstrating in Nashville and Tallahassee. By mid-March, student protests disrupted Atlanta, and by April student demonstrations were rocking seventy-eight southern and border communities. Police tried to stop the surge with thousands of arrests. Parents tried to stop their sons and daughters with threats. Local communities tried to stop them with their violent rigidity. But once these students got going, desegregation became the only brakes that slowed them down.[45]

Some administrators, politicians, and trustees tried to slow them down, which sometimes prompted campus activism at schools such as Jackson State and Voorhees-C in South Carolina. When Alabama governor John Patterson ordered the suspension of any Alabama State student who sat in, students rallied and were addressed by Martin Luther King Jr. One thousand threatened to vacate the college if punishments followed their activism in late February. In April 1960, President Atwood at Kentucky State unrecognized the campus CORE chapter and terminated eleven students and two instructors during a week of protests against his administration, which restricted civil rights activism. Soon after, the student gymnasium was firebombed, probably in retaliation.[46]

It became apparent to Ella Baker, the former student activist and now first executive secretary of King's Southern Christian Leadership Conference (SCLC), that these lively students needed coordination. She organized a conference on April 15–17, 1960, at her alma mater, Shaw, in Raleigh. Nearly two hundred students from more than fifty colleges and high schools from thirteen states heard Baker encourage them in her opening address to develop their own organization with "group-centered leadership." Not long afterwards, the attendees organized the Student Non-Violent Coordinating Committee (SNCC). This new group committed itself to nonviolence and the "politics of direct action."[47]

∗   ∗   ∗

Deep South desegregation of higher education had barely moved until the court forced U-Georgia to matriculate Atlantans Charlayne Hunter and Hamilton Holmes. After Georgia Tech narrowly defeated U-Georgia's basketball team, a crowd of white students mobilized outside of the new students' dorm on the evening of January 11, 1961. With KKK members present and a large banner that read, "Nigger go home," the crowd tossed bricks into Hunter's room and set matter on fire—rioting at U-Georgia. Rioters succeeded in replicating the 1956 Autherine Lucy episode, as the university withdrew the students and state troopers took them back to Atlanta that night. Their triumph was short-lived though. Two days later, a federal judge ordered U-Georgia to readmit the students.[48]

Later that spring semester, CORE repackaged its 1947 Journey of Reconciliation, went freedom riding on buses through the South, and desegregated interstate bus terminals. John Lewis and Howard's Stokely Carmichael were two of the many students who got on the buses. The widely reported viciousness of the white mobs, who violently curtailed these "Freedom Riders," even blowing up a bus in Alabama, riled up black America, causing another wave of students to inundate CORE, NAACP, SNCC, local civil rights associations, and new groups, such as the Northern Student Movement. In the Deep South, students organized clandestine civil rights groups, such as the Mississippi Improvement Association of Students in Jackson.[49]

After hesitating in the summer of 1961, SNCC and CORE joined the NAACP, SCLC, and the National Urban League in the well-financed and Kennedy-administration-initiated Voter Education Project in the South. SNCC entered the depths of segregation—rural Mississippi—to register a group of people who had been disenfranchised for nearly one hundred years. In northern and western HWCUs, black students in the political mainstream joined NAACP and CORE chapters, Friends of SNCC groups, and new interracial civil rights campus organizations that raised money for southern campaigns, staged sympathy demonstrations, welcomed popular activist speakers, such as Malcolm X, rallied against segregationist speakers, and occasionally protested against campus and community discrimination.[50]

While black students hacked away at segregation in 1962, sometimes with little success in places such as Albany, Georgia, federal officials whisked Air Force veteran James Meredith, the grandson of a slave, in an unmarked federal car into Oxford, Mississippi, on September 30. Ole Miss had been court ordered to desegregate. Angered by the arriving federal police force of 536 to protect Meredith, segregationists rioted on campus that night, leaving a French reporter and a maintenance worker dead, 375 injured, and more than two hundred arrested. The mob defied President John F. Kennedy, who addressed the nation earlier that evening. "In a government of laws, and not of men, no man, however prominent or powerful, and no mob, however unruly or boisterous, is entitled to defy a court order." At the highest count, 20,000 soldiers occupied the campus during Meredith's two semesters, which were doggedly filled with death threats, hate mail, and taunts. He graduated in 1963 after existing as "the most segregated Negro in the world," he said.[51]

Since the mid-1930s and the fall of the NNCM, black students in groups such as the ASU, SNYC, NAACP, CORE, and SNCC waged the LBSM, a usually leftist feature of the civil rights struggle. Over the course of the twentieth century, black students did not stop striking while the iron was hot, warming to grassroots altruism. As this struggle entered its climax year, 1963, African Americans were on the cusp of amassing civil rights they had desired for almost three decades: the federal elimination of de jure segregation, social equality before the law, and the franchise for southern African Americans—rights off campus they soon would be demanding on campus. Higher education seemed headed toward complete desegregation. Those last three years of the CRM, 1963 to 1965 (narrated in the following chapter), were crucial in finally winning these rights. These years—actually the first half of the 1960s in general—were also critical in nurturing the BCM, a struggle several years in the making.

4

"March That Won't Turn Around": Formation and Development of the Black Campus Movement

Civil rights and black power activists in the 1960s typically sought to raise the consciousness of white and black Americans, respectively, regarding the debilitating and oppressive exigencies of mid-twentieth-century African American life. Said differently, the CRM to primarily affect the moral conscious of white America to advance African Americans—or *white suasion*—gave way to *black suasion* to develop the moral, cultural, and political consciousness of African Americans toward the necessity of black unity, power, and agency through the Black Power Movement (BPM). Guided by the leading youth organization, SNCC, black students started hastily leaving civil rights in the mid-1960s, entering the ideological orbit of black power. In effect, the failures (and successes) of the CRM prepared the stage for the BPM, and its arm in academia, the BCM.

After showcasing the lead-up to the BCM in the early-1960s civil rights period, this chapter delves into the forces that continuously generated and energized the BCM in the late 1960s. Traveling activist-speakers continually praised, motivated, challenged, and developed that energy and student critiques of the academy. Furthermore, through their marathon informal campus discussions, widespread reading, cultural weeks, conferences, and newspapers, black students profoundly developed their own movement ideology and force. Alongside activist-speakers, black campus activists circulated black power ideas that enhanced their self-determination, self-love, and sense of black solidarity, and raised their consciousness about the irrelevant racial constitution of higher education.

* * *

After decades of dual activism, the LBSM primarily moved off campus from 1959 to 1963. Spurred by African liberation struggles, NAACP outcast Robert F.

Williams in North Carolina, Malcolm X, and other radicals and black national-ists, some students organized outside of civil rights norms during that period. They created study-turned-protest groups, such as UHURU in Detroit (1962) and the Afro-American Association in the Bay Area (1961)—where early black power cultivated—a "crucial prelude to the better known tale of Black Power after Watts," writes Donna Murch. The "African American Club" formed at NYU and facilitated a speech by Malcolm X in 1962, which stimulated "countless corri-dor conversations." During the 1961–1962 academic year, Central State students voted into office a slate of officers known as the Reform Action Movement (RAM) wielding a black nationalist, students' rights platform. Before long, RAM became the Revolutionary Action Movement, relocated to Philadelphia, and under the stewardship of Max Stanford Jr. (renamed Muhammad Ahmad), provided an organizational base for young revolutionary nationalists in the mid-1960s.[1]

The juniors and seniors who launched the BCM in 1965 peopled these progres-sive organizations as well as civil rights outfits in the early 1960s as freshmen and sophomores. Herman Carter, the architect of Southern-U's 1965 protest, deseg-regated New Orleans movie houses, travelled on CORE freedom rides, and saw the inside of several Louisiana jails after enrolling in the fall of 1961. Even more BCM leaders tasted activism in high schools and grade schools in the early 1960s. Edward Whitfield, the president of Cornell's Afro-American Society (AAS) dur-ing an (in)famous building takeover in April 1969, presided over Arkansas's NAACP Youth Council in high school before being estranged from the national office's aversion to SNCC's brand of direct action. A 12-year-old Ben Chavis desegregated his local public library in 1960. In the mid-1960s, Chavis affiliated with SCLC, SNCC, NAACP, and CORE, keeping his hair short, sporting a sport coat, shirt, and tie. By the fall of 1968, the UNC Charlotte student's hair stretched in an Afro, and he donned a field jacket, sunglasses, and black boots, often carry-ing Mao's red book, like thousands of black campus activists. In February 1969, he led his peers in their campaign to racially reform UNC Charlotte. Chester Grundy desegregated his Louisville high school before becoming a student leader at U-Kentucky. In 1965, he participated in its black social club, Orgena (Negro spelled backwards). "We talk about it now, it's like, we were a bunch of backward Negroes," Grundy remembered, "but [laughing] you know that's what we had." By 1968, they had organized a BSU.[2]

Future black campus activists participated in the CRM, but even more were aroused by watching the struggle that reached its apex in 1963. The signature protest confronted the South's most lethal center—Birmingham. The ferocious-ness of southern segregationists and hesitations and refusals of the federal gov-ernment to hold them off troubled black youngsters. That May, they watched on television, like most Americans, as thousands of Birmingham youngsters their ages were being clubbed with nightsticks and ripped to pieces by vicious blood-hounds, and saw fire hoses breaking limbs, snatching clothes off of bodies, and slamming children and teens against store walls. They heard about the urban rebellion there. "The racists' tactics of using dogs, tanks, and water hoses on women and children was too much for African-Americans to stomach," recalled Stanford, who traveled on weekends that spring building RAM. "Within months mass demonstrations had occurred all over the south. The movement seriously began to gel as the mood of African American people in the North became angry." They were angry in Birmingham too. The bombing of the home of A. D. King and the Gaston Motel (SCLC's headquarters) in retaliation for the desegregation accord between SCLC and city leaders unleashed the first major urban rebellion of the decade on May 11, 1963. When King aides tried to disperse the mob, "Tell it to 'Bull' Conner," someone yelled. "This is what nonviolence gets you!"[3]

Like these rebels, some black youth began to seriously rethink whether the civil rights platform—ostentatious nonviolence, desegregation, uniting with white liberals, and white suasion—was the most effective road to progress. One idea steadily gathered ground—African American solidarity (or black nationalism), and in the context of higher education, the need for black students to band together and discuss the movement, their history and culture, and their lives. In late April, days before the most vicious assaults in Birmingham, thirty-five students at Harvard formed the African and Afro-American Association, inspired by the southern movement, Malcolm X, and African independence struggles. Nicknamed Afro, it sought "to promote mutual understanding," to provide "a voice" by publishing their ideas, and to develop leaders to cope "with the various problems of our peoples," the preamble to its constitution expressed. At the study group's founding meeting, students discussed the desirability of desegregation, African Americans at Harvard, and black nationalism. Afro's most articulate spokesman, George Armah, championed the notion of "anti-racist racialism," another term for black nationalism, as the group barred from membership all students not of African descent. During the ensuing controversy over the racial bar, senior John Butler announced, "There is nothing malicious in our desire to be ourselves."[4]

That summer, Alabama segregationists planned a replay of the 1956 Autherine Lucy affair. The Kennedy administration had other plans. Hundreds of National Guardsmen, state troopers, and city police militarized U-Alabama when Vivian Malone and James Hood entered on June 11, 1963, upon a court order. Governor George Wallace, in a televised symbolic display of resistance, stood in the doorway of Foster Auditorium to prevent the duo from registering in de jure segregation's last public stand in higher education. That evening, after Wallace moved aside and Malone and Hood registered, President Kennedy spoke to the nation. It ought to be possible "for American students of any color to attend any public institution without having to be backed up by troops," he said. "One hundred years of delay have passed since President Lincoln freed the slaves, yet their heirs, their grandsons, are not fully free." Later that night, Byron De La Beckwith, a member of the White Citizens Council, shot and killed NAACP field secretary Medgar Evers in front of his house in Jackson, Mississippi. No, African Americans were not free. "With their mentor now dead, several students started quietly humming a tune laced with contempt for a system that could suddenly and unapologetically snatch Medgar Evers from their midst," Jelani Favors noted. In three years, everyone heard the tune's title: Black Power.[5]

As the body bags started to pile up, alongside them amassed the number of black youngsters contemptuous of America and questioning the civil rights program. At least ten civil rights workers were killed during that fateful summer of 1963, and an untold number were injured. Still, the March on Washington in late August provided a boost for civil rights, as did the money from corporate America to moderate the maturing radicalism. Yet on September 15, 1963, a bomb from white supremacists shattered the Sixteenth Street Baptist Church in Birmingham, leaving four girls deceased, shattering the civil rights ideological fortress where a declining number of black youth resided. Three of the girls were 14, one was 11—the age-range of the future agents of the BCM. A 7-foot-2-inch, skinny, and reserved high schooler named "Lew" Alcindor (later renamed Kareem Abdul Jabbar) attended mass with his mother when the girls were killed. The news of the massacre hit this basketball star in New York City like a bucket of water. It woke him up to black nationalism, as it had other youngsters, through the cold coverage of the white mediums and the posturing of the Kennedy administration. Alcindor decided that "nobody cared," nor would anybody defend and enrich "black people except black people." He embraced black suasion. In five years, Alcindor headlined the black collegiate boycott of the 1968 Olympics.[6]

Ann Beard (Grundy), the future wife of the aforementioned Chester Grundy at U-Kentucky, already knew that her hometown's moniker was "Bombingham." She heard bomb threats growing up as the pastor's kid in the Sixteenth Street Baptist Church. Her father arrived to pastor the historic church in 1944 (and passed away in 1960). Congregants called Grundy the "Sixteenth Street Baptist Church baby." She was attending high school in New York at the time of the tragedy. One of her teachers handed her the *New York Times* with the news. "I was too shocked to cry. I was just—I didn't know what to feel." The next year, she knew what to feel when she enrolled at Berea-C in Kentucky. "We had no black faculty and staff. We didn't even have parent figures." She gathered with other black students who felt the same sense of isolation, and formed one of the early BSUs.[7]

Four days after the Birmingham bombing, a group of African American students, "upset going out of their minds" at SF State, petitioned the student government to establish a Negro Students Association (NSA), the predecessor to the first known BSU, which formed in 1966. According to the NSA's constitution, the study group sought to "engage in the study of Negro history and life; to foster the growth and dissemination of Negro cultural contributions." NSA members agreed on the need for civil rights but were divided over the issue of integration, according to one college official. A group of students organized at U-Memphis in 1963 and a black study club materialized at Roosevelt-U in Chicago. John Bracey Jr., one of the developers of the Roosevelt group, also participated in the Amistad Society, a Chicago-wide black history club. (Five years later, Bracey, then a graduate student, was one of the ten student signers of the agreement that ended a thirty-six-hour takeover of Northwestern's bursar's office.)[8]

The year 1963 proved to be the seminal year of black nationalist organizing at prestigious and urban HWCUs, with moderately large African American populations stimulated and angered by the southern civil rights atrocities, colonial struggles, and northern and western racism. Meanwhile, HBCU students moved away from off-campus demonstrations and civil rights that year as well. By 1964, they were noticeably headed toward campus activism and black power, with campus protests at Jackson State, Alcorn State, Norfolk State, and Howard. From May 1 to 4, the Afro-American Student Movement, a radical affiliation of SNCC headed by Michele Paul and Betty Rush, convened the first Afro-American Student Conference on black nationalism at Fisk. To RAM's Stanford, who attended and helped plan it, the conference "was the ideological catalyst that eventually shifted the civil rights movement into the black power movement."[9]

* * *

After a white cop killed a black teenager and the police department refused to concede guilt in July 1964, a protest turned into an explosive five-night rebellion in Harlem. At the time, Lew Alcindor was participating in the journalism workshop of the Harlem Youth Action Project. With the editorial board that produced the workshop's weekly paper, Alcindor (and presumably other future college students) interviewed rioters and their supporters. Cries about Harlem's powerlessness in the face of the regular killing of blacks by cops soaked these interviews and the special issue his workshop published on the rebellion. Since his youth newspaper whispered as one of the few media voices reviling the police, the fury he felt about the Birmingham blast the year before resurfaced—more robust than ever. Like other black youngsters across the nation who would soon be rebelling against the racial constitution of higher education, Alcindor was radicalized by the underlying causes of the rebellion. A similar cacophony of rebellion eventually spread to Brooklyn and five other cities that summer, including Rochester, Chicago, and Philadelphia. For four straight years, black urban rebellions erected a soil of protest that cultivated the necessity of grassroots altruism during the BCM. To black students, grassroots altruism became the solution to what became known at the time as the "urban crisis."[10]

Ideologies also proceeded to the left that summer, when three more activists (all college-aged) had to be buried in the cemetery of the CRM—Michael Schwerner, Andrew Goodman, and James Chaney. They were SNCC organizers of the Mississippi Freedom Summer of 1964, which, among other things, organized the Mississippi Freedom Democratic Party (MFDP), triggering a wave of violence that compelled many activists to sequester nonviolence. The MFDP demanded that its delegation be seated in place of the racist state party at the Democratic National Convention in August 1964. The Johnson administration, not wanting to alienate its fleeing southern contingent, rejected the MFDP appeal and offered a compromise—two nonvoting seats accompanying the racist delegation. "We didn't come all this way for no two seats!" bellowed Fannie Lou Hamer, an MFDP leader from the buckle of Mississippi's black belt.[11]

Hamer and company defied civil rights leaders, the Johnson administration, and segregationists in Atlantic City in 1964. In a larger sense, the vanguard of LBSM rapidly accelerated its pace away from the CRM, abandoning white suasion—seemingly as crucial to the CRM as nonviolence. "Things could never be the same," Cleveland Sellers of SNCC recalled. "Never again were we lulled into believing that our task was exposing injustices so that the 'good' people of

America could eliminate them. We left Atlantic City with the knowledge that the movement had turned into something else. After Atlantic City, our struggle was not for civil rights, but for liberation." The left wing of the CRM started planting its own black power roots.[12]

The women from the MFDP who came to Atlantic City donning natural hair styles enthralled Robin Gregory, a Howard student and SNCC staffer in the Washington, DC, office. "I was really turned on by that statement," she said. When the aspiring painter left Atlantic City that summer, she left the perm on its beaches, along with her civil rights ideology. "I felt it was an affirmation of being who we were," Gregory explained. She did not get affirmed when she returned to Howard in the fall of 1964 though. Yet, in the fall of 1966, the cultural climate had warmed and Gregory received the ultimate affirmation. Students elected her the first homecoming queen in Howard's one-hundred-year history with a gleaming Afro, the first (perhaps) of many during the BCM.[13]

When Gregory first returned to Howard with her visual statement in the fall of 1964, returning white UC Berkeley students who had participated in the Mississippi Freedom Summer desired to radicalize their peers, only to be rebuffed by administrators. Black students carefully scrutinized the widely publicized Free Speech Movement at UC Berkeley that accelerated white campus activism around the nation, which by the late 1960s supported the BCM. "It provided watchful black militants with an excellent practical education in the tactics of disruption," explained Roger A. Fischer. "They discovered the awesome secret of student power, that the university was pathetically vulnerable to the pressures that could be brought to bear upon it by a relatively small cadre of well organized, deeply dedicated student revolutionaries." Some students, aware of the four decades of crippling campus protests by black students since World War I, did not learn any secrets from UC Berkeley students.[14]

In the meantime, black students continued to unite. Columbia and Barnard students, including Hilton Clark, the son of psychologist Kenneth Clark, established the Students Afro-American Society (SAAS) that fall of 1964 as a forum for black students to discuss African American problems "and hopefully have the individual come up with some answers for himself." Two years later, a politicized Clark and his fellow SAAS members had come up with answers to whether their college aided them in that process. In their newly released magazine, *The Black Student*, editors proclaimed that universities do not prepare black students to cope with their problems "as well as the schools seemingly prepare white students to cope with theirs."[15]

*   *   *

In 1964, societal circumstances ripened for the BCM. The "white only" signals on campus became more discernible since they were taken down in the federal law books with the summer passage of the Civil Rights Act. Black nationalists and student rights activists organized groups and steadily accrued more campus influence with their peers. State authorities and college administrators had become progressively hostile to progressively militant civil rights activities. The steadily increasing numbers of black students walking into hostile academic doors at HBCUs and HWCUs were increasingly likely to be veterans of the movement who participated in direct action protests and registration drives in junior high and high school in the early 1960s. These movement veterans formed a small, highly trained, associated, and politically astute force that gradually considered the college campus the next battleground as the decade reached its midpoint. The victories, tragedies, and outliers of the CRM, which started its decline after its apex in 1963, inspired and alienated this "new generation." The civil rights debacle at the Democratic National Convention in August 1964 and SNCC's subsequent move to black nationalism were decisive in the LBSM's release from paternal liberalism.

Nevertheless, the BCM, like any social movement, needed a societal trigger. It received three in 1965. The assassination of Malcolm X and Bloody Sunday within weeks of each other in early 1965 first did the job, then the Watts rebellion in the summer completed the spawning triad. Malcolm X's death did not impact students like King's murder did in 1968. Student interest in Malcolm X in early 1965 could not compare to the widespread love of the Muslim martyr in 1969 at the acme of the toil for black power, with his autobiography, *Malcolm X Speaks*, iconic posters, and recordings of his speeches in mass circulation. But a rapidly growing loose federation of alienated civil rights veterans and movement outliers had followed Malcolm closely when he lived.

In the late 1950s and early 1960s, as the national spokesman for the Nation of Islam (NOI), Malcolm became a controversially popular leader, particularly after the 1959 CBS documentary, "The Hate that Hate Produced." Black youth were not initially attracted to the breadth of his ideology, since Malcolm wrapped it in NOI theology, which deified Elijah Muhammad, evaded civil rights activism, preached a strict moral code, articulated "traditional" roles for women, espoused whites as inherently evil, and demanded complete separation of the races. As each year passed in the 1960s, Malcolm's rhetoric secularized and matured politically. Consequently, with each year, his appeal to students skyrocketed, impressing youth with his booming but clear voice, fiery speeches, quick wit, striking analogies, historical knowledge, glorification of African people and African anticolonial struggles, audacious denigration of white liberals and racism, and down-to-earth yet scholarly expressionism. In 1964, he left not only the NOI but also its theology, increasingly sharing and refining his ideas of black national and international unity, self-determination, self-defense, distrust of white liberalism, socialism, and cultural pride. Other than James Baldwin or Martin Luther King Jr., no black voice attracted students more than Malcolm X in the early 1960s. Malcolm probably lectured to more students in 1963 than in any other year, which presumably influenced the outbreak of nationalistic campus organizing that year.[16]

In his most critical speaking engagement concerning the production of the BCM (aside from his two speeches to Alabama youth weeks before his death), Malcolm faced off with Bayard Rustin on October 31, 1961, at Howard. With the fifteen-hundred-seat Crampton auditorium filled to capacity, sociologist E. Franklin Frazier moderated the debate, titled "Integration or Separation."

Howard's student government and the Nonviolent Action Group, a Howard SNCC affiliate, hosted the event. "The black man in America will never be equal to the white man as long as he attempts to force himself into his house," Malcolm argued at one point. "The real problem is that the anemic Negro leader, who survives and sometimes thrives off of gifts from white people, is dependent upon the white man whom he gives false information about the masses of black people." Malcolm's captivating performance deeply impacted many of the attendees, including Stokely Carmichael. At the time, a "European theoretical context" anchored Carmichael's political worldview. But what "Malcolm demonstrated that night…was the raw power, the visceral potency, of the group our unarticulated collective blackness held over us. I'll never forget it."[17]

It is no wonder that the assassination of Malcolm X on February 21, 1965, devastated thousands of black youth. Upon hearing the newsflash, Merritt-C's Bobby Seale, a future founder of the Black Panther Party, went to his mother's house, picked up six loose bricks, walked to the corner, and hurled them at every cop car he saw. Like scores of black students across the country, Seale's sorrow overwhelmed him, forcing out tears. Black students mourned their fallen icon in services and rallies at schools such as Southern Illinois and SF State.

Adding fuel to their fire, some black youth immediately suspected that the US government had a role in the assassination. The American media "right from the beginning have intimated that the Black Muslims killed him, which is so easy to believe because of his rivalry with them," one black youngster wrote in a statement published in Harvard's student newspaper. "There are several fishy things that make it difficult for any honest person to believe anything." In addition, SNCC circulated an essay two years later on, "The Murder of Malcolm X," that questioned the official story of three NOI assassins. Malcolm's death motivated a small grouping of black students to carry out his mission. Within a few years, a critical mass of black campus activists would be motivated to actualize Malcolm's teaching, as his name, face, and ideas became the poster elements of the BCM. Practically all black campus activists adored Malcolm X, and one at U-Texas at Austin even apparently renamed himself after his idol.[18]

Still, in 1965, more students were stirred to campus activism by what occurred in Selma, Alabama, on March 7 than by the death of Malcolm X two Sundays prior. Since the beginning of the year, SNCC and SCLC had been engaged in a fierce battle for black suffrage. Martin Luther King Jr. called and then cancelled a march from Selma to Alabama's statehouse in Montgomery. Some SNCC and SCLC members proceeded without King, who believed the march jeopardized the Voting Rights Act that passed that summer. At 4 p.m. on March 7, the six hundred marchers, many wearing their Sunday best, formed two lines and set out on the roughly fifty-mile trek to Montgomery. They reached the Edmund Pettus Bridge on the outskirts of Selma. When the marchers reached its crest, they saw an army of state troopers and Selma police at the bottom eerily flanked by a hundred white Alabamians waving Confederate flags. They bravely pressed forward.[19]

"Troopers, advance!" Sheriff Jim Clark roared when the marchers did not turn back upon a state trooper's order. With news cameras rolling, the soldiers

Photo 5 *Gwen Patton as a teenager (Dr. Gwen Patton Collection, Trenholm State Technical College Archives, Montgomery, Alabama)*

of segregation slung tear gas and darted forward like a Confederate infantry, pouncing on the six hundred marchers with clubs and whips. The marchers retreated, and the small, mounted army chased them into Selma's black communities, battering, bruising, and beating them along the way. It was a televised "Bloody Sunday" on March 7, 1965.[20]

Within days, students from Howard delivered a petition with hundreds of signatures to the White House, urging President Johnson "to take any and all necessary measures to stop brutality being done to the Negro people in Selma, Alabama." Tuskegee students were irate, as almost everyone had viewed the ambush on the bridge. The black and white images were like piercing shots of activism. When members of the newly organized Tuskegee Institute Advancement League (TIAL), a SNCC affiliate, rushed into the dorms that Sunday evening to mobilize, just about all the students attended the meetings. TIAL heeded King's directive to join another group of marches in Montgomery on Wednesday, March 10, from a march set to begin in Selma the day before. Three thousand lined up behind King as he left Brown's Chapel on March 9. King halted the march before it reached the valley of the shadow of Bloody Sunday, prayed, and led the singing of "We Shall Overcome." Then King, who had secretly made a deal with federal officials to not force his way through the troopers, turned and walked back to the church, followed by the mystified crowd.[21]

Gwen Patton, like many Tuskegee students, felt outraged and betrayed when she learned of the about-face. Born into a "race family" in Detroit in 1943, Patton regularly visited relatives in Montgomery in the 1940s and 1950s. In April 1956, about five months into the bus boycott, Gwen Patton moved to Montgomery (where she eventually graduated from high school). At 13 years old, she raised money for the Montgomery bus boycott, attended its Monday mass meetings, and listened in on the popular citizenship classes her grandparents held in their homes.[22]

Patton, TIAL's direct action chair, and her peers resolved to defy King and federal and state officials and show up the next day in Montgomery anyway. King telegrammed Tuskegee, asking the students to cancel. The Tuskegee administration joined in King's pleas, threatening expulsion, claiming students needed parental permission. As Tuskegee students entered the dining hall for dinner the night before their march, they saw copies of King's telegram on every placemat. "March, March, March!" the students chanted as they banged on their tables and disdainfully read the telegram. That night, they accumulated more than $1,000 to charter buses to Montgomery, and the next day they waged what they boldly termed, "the march that won't turn around."[23]

When Tuskegee students arrived back on their campus, it did not take them long to realize that the same forces they fought in Montgomery dictated to them from the administration building. As SNCC's James Forman attested, Tuskegee students asked themselves, "Is it enough for me just to get an education so that I can join (or remain in) the professional middle class? Does the administration of my school stand for progress or the status quo?" Hundreds of Tuskegee students left civil rights behind to become committed members of the rising BPM. They wanted their black college to be just as committed, exhibiting grassroots altruism.[24]

"After the march, a lot of people couldn't take Tuskegee any more," Gwen Patton said. Its "contradictions could no longer go unattended." Patton decided to lead her peers in resolving the contradictions, declaring her candidacy for student body president. Against her four male competitors, Patton's platform beckoned "Total Representation for the Total Student Body." When the candidates were ordered to take down campaign signs for a board of trustees meeting, Patton refused and circulated a petition, raising questions about the "great white fathers" on the board. The stand against the administration and her queries about white paternalism and power generated a current of support in April 1965 that carried her into the presidency—the first woman SGA president in the school's history. She was also one of the first (if not the first) students enamored with burgeoning black power ideas to gain control of an HBCU student government in the mid-1960s with a radical restructuring in mind.[25]

*   *   *

The summer after Patton's election, students were politicized by the thousands of African Americans in Los Angeles who in August 1965 rebelled against police brutality, economic exploitation, dilapidated housing, and poor health care, damaging $100 million worth of property. Police officers killed more than thirty rioters and observers and arrested about four thousand people. Jimmy Garrett, 19, spent most of the riot in his parents' home in the middle of the riot zone on Vernon between Central and Broadway. He had an impressive resume of activism—sit-ins at 14 in 1960, Freedom Rides in 1961, and work with CORE. He joined SNCC in 1962 and relocated to Los Angeles in 1965 to head SNCC's fundraising efforts. On Saturday, August 14, 1965, after three nights of rioting, Garrett interviewed rebels, just as Lew Alcindor did after the Harlem rebellion the year before. "If I put a pillow over your face, and try to smother you and you want to live bad enough you've got to come up breathing quick and fighting hard," one man told Garrett. "That's just what we're doing." That Saturday night was the first of the 8:00 p.m. curfews. Garrett sat on his front porch. He turned his radio down when he noticed a police car. "Get your black ass back into your house!" screamed an officer. He grudgingly and slowly got up. The car circled back around. As he entered the house, he detected the long barrel of a shotgun aimed in his direction. With the door slammed and him scampering up the stairs, he heard three thunderous bursts. "I ran to my parents' empty bedroom and lay shaking on my back for the rest of the night like the spider in Kafka's *Metamorphosis*."[26]

As the smoke cleared from the Watts Riot, Garrett climbed out of the puddle of sweat and anxiety on his parents' bedroom floor, dripping with a renewed commitment to the movement. Garrett was one of the SNCC members who that summer after the rebellion tossed around the idea of the college as a next site for struggle. In the spring of 1966, Garrett enrolled in SF State and in a few months helped organize the first organization to use the term Black Student Union (BSU).[27]

Before Garrett enrolled at SF State, in the fall of 1965, one of the major black power organizations responsible for the surge of black consciousness organized. Out of a study group in Los Angeles led by Maulana (Ron) Karenga emerged the influential US Organization. "Anywhere we are, US is." The organization pledged to serve the interest of us—the black community. Karenga, the creator of Kwanzaa, served as one of the primary voices that inspired black campus activists, principally their sense of cultural pride and awareness. While high schooler Robert Lewis labored in the hospital in San Diego recovering from car accident injuries in the fall of 1965, his aunt brought him *The Quotable Karenga*. This book, widely read by black youth, particularly on the West coast, "was talking about black," Lewis remembered. "It was talking about Black people, concepts, ideas—like I had never heard it being talked about before." It left such an impression that he became a member of Karenga's US Organization after his recovery and eventually became an activist at CSU Northridge, receiving one of the nation's stiffest sentences for a building takeover in November 1968.[28]

In addition to his writings and organizing, Karenga most intensely impacted the ideology of students through his speaking in the late 1960s. In the fall of 1967, for example, Karenga gave a series of lectures at UCLA titled "Black Student/Alienation." Karenga suggested a three-point program for survival—self-determination, self-respect, and self-defense—in the initial speech on October 17. It was well received by Harambee, UCLA's black student group, which in a few

months made demands on the administration. Karenga delivered a similar message in February 1968 as the featured speaker at the first annual Oklahoma
Conference for Black Collegians at U-Oklahoma. It was "emotionally engulfing,"
recalled George Henderson, an activist-professor. "One minute we were laughing;
the next, we were grimacing. The overall effect was consciousness-raising."[29]

As Karenga fashioned US, Gwen Patton tried to radicalize Tuskegee during
the 1965–1966 academic year. She made headway with campus protests in the
fall of 1965, but her spring 1966 administration had to manage a tragedy. Because
popular Tuskegee student and SNCC activist Sammy Younge Jr. demanded to
use an indoor "white-only" bathroom, Marvin Segrest, a 67-year-old gas station
attendant, shot and killed him on January 3, 1966. His death injected vigor into
the already vitalizing campus movement. Students, such as Hampton's Nancy
Regina Hooten, dispatched letters to President Johnson. A native of Tuskegee
who knew Younge "very well," Hooten wrote, "It hurt me very deeply when I
learned of his violent death. Must all people die who are fighting for what rightly
belongs to them?"[30]

The murder helped further radicalize SNCC, a group that in turn radicalized
campus activists. Soon after Younge's death, SNCC released its first official statement opposing the Vietnam War. "The murder of Samuel Younge in Tuskegee,
Alabama, is no different than the murder of Vietnamese peasants, for both Younge
and the Vietnamese sought, and are seeking, to secure the rights guaranteed them
by law. In each case the United States government bears a part of the responsibility for these deaths." Moreover, SNCC members helped local African Americans
in "Bloody Lowndes" County, Alabama, organize the Lowndes County Freedom
Organization, choosing the black panther as the mascot of this independent
political party. In May 1966, the party had its primary, while SNCC members
elected Stokely Carmichael (renamed Kwame Toure), a recent Howard graduate,
their new leader. A striking thinker and speaker, the courageous, captivating, and
charismatic Carmichael embodied the new defiant young black generation that
Malcolm X had seen approaching around history's corner.[31]

By the summer of 1966, Carmichael had become a national black power youth
icon during the Mississippi March Against Fear, which SNCC used to politi-
cize, organize, and register Mississippi blacks in each town the march entered.
During an impassioned speech in Greenwood, Mississippi, on Thursday, June 16,
Carmichael hurled the term "black power" into the American rhetorical mainstream. To Carmichael (and Charles Hamilton), black power was "a call for black
people in this country to unite, to recognize their heritage, to build a sense of
community. It is a call for black people to define their own goals, to lead their
own organizations. It is a call to reject the racist institutions and values of this
society." Blown by the fans of the American media, the slogan whisked through
black America, among present and future black campus activists.[32]

Many black students viewed Carmichael in person. He spoke at dozens of community rallies and no less than twenty-five colleges and universities in the late
summer of 1966 and the 1966–1967 academic year, while raising much-needed
funds for SNCC. Toward the end of August, Carmichael brought his poignant
oratory to Boston. "It's time for all black people in Boston to get together and

move to gain control over your communities," Carmichael insisted at a rally. In Boston, Carmichael inspired Howard's Adrienne Manns, who was attending a summer school program at Harvard. She enrolled at Howard in 1964, looking for a black environment. Coming from a majority white town and high school, she was struck by the bourgeois, Eurocentric setting. Her roommate needed an extra dorm-room closet. Only opera and (European) classical music boomed from the Fine Arts building. There was one course on "Negro History," and only history majors or upperclassmen could take it.

A case of a Howard student being expelled for violating curfew politicized Manns, as did her attending a rally for the Selma affair at the White House in the spring of 1965. But Carmichael's speech in Boston in 1966 proved pivotal in Manns's leap into black campus activism. Manns thought the CRM had a "passive kind of beggar mentality." And she detested it. "The speech changed me," she said, "because when I realized that what I had been feeling and thinking was not just personal, it wasn't just me—somebody else, in fact someone of prominence and stature, felt the same way and could articulate it. I really felt encouraged."[33]

After speaking at schools such as Princeton, Howard, U-Michigan, Dartmouth, Hunter-C (NY), and UC Berkeley in the fall of 1966, on January 16, 1967, Carmichael challenged fourteen hundred Morgan State (MD) students to adopt grassroots altruism. "Until you begin to help your black brothers in the ghettos, I'll blame you for the rebellions of the past summer and for the ones which will happen this summer." On April 11, 1967, he addressed Tougaloo-C students for two hours. A student newspaper editor reported "a new awareness in the minds of the students. There has been a lot of thinking going on since he left, and these have been profound thoughts about US Black People." Two days later, he urged U-Houston students to regain their history from the "cultural terrorism and degradation of self-justifying white guilt." That spring he urged Fisk students to "take over the administration" of their school. And he spoke to four thousand people at a Seattle high school, urging black unity. "The way I looked at myself and America changed" during that speech, said Aaron Dixon, who in 1968 led U-Washington's BSU. With H. Rap Brown assuming the mantel of SNCC chairman in May 1967, the policing community hot on Carmichael's tail (specifically since campus activism, sometimes violent, followed some of his appearances), and his exile to Guinea, Carmichael's speaking surge slowed during the rest of the decade. However, by the time of his departure from the collegiate speaking scene in 1968, the movement was in full swing.[34]

* * *

As Carmichael first started making his college rounds in the fall of 1966, two students at Oakland's Merritt-C, dismayed that its black student group was not acting on Malcolm X's mission, founded the Black Panther Party for Self Defense, in October 1966. Huey P. Newton and Bobby Seale developed a ten-point program of what they wanted and what they believed. The fourth point in particular would soon captivate black campus activists. "We want education for our people that exposes the true nature of this decadent American society. We want education that teaches us our true history and our role in the present-day society. We believe in an educational system that will give to our people a knowledge of self. If a man does not have knowledge of himself and his position in society and the world, then he has little chance to relate to anything else."[35]

By 1968, particularly through its Free Huey campaign, the Oakland-based Party had become a national sensation, subsuming a groundswell of chapter creations across America, usually with college-aged black youth. Along with its revolutionary nationalist philosophy, assiduously shaped by the contours of black nationalism and Marxism, black students were enthralled by the Party's confrontational posture, actualization of the principle of self-defense, grassroots altruism, cool dress (black berets, pants, and leather jackets), street credibility, community service programs, and charismatic, articulate leaders, including Kathleen and Eldridge Cleaver, Fred Hampton, and Elaine Brown. Some black students affiliated with both the Black Panther Party and with BSUs or SGAs.

Quite a few BSUs were modeled after the Black Panther Party. In 1969, the Dickinson-C (PA) Afro-American Organization (AAO) changed the title of president to prime minister in order to show support "for the ideals of the Black Panther Party movement," according to AAO prime minister Mike Floyd. The BSU at U-Washington and the AAS at Duke both developed ten-point programs. Moreover, BSUs aided Panthers in their service programs. At Roosevelt-U, members solicited funds from faculty members and administrators to support the breakfast for children program. BSU members held a Free Huey Day at U-Georgia in May 1969, as black students around the nation rallied feverishly against Panther repression. Yet most profoundly, Panthers inspired (or were involved in) black campus activism. Panthers in the BSU instigated the renaming of Chicago's Crane Community-C to Malcolm X College in 1969. The inspiration was obvious at Franklin & Marshall (PA), where in April 1969 the BSU "proposed EDUCATION, COUNSELING, HOUSING, FINANCE, [and] TEACHERS [to] SUPPORT the FREEDOM AND POWER to determine the destiny" of black students. Shortly after a delegation of Panthers appeared at Lake Forest (IL) that spring, the BSU demanded black faculty and the right for students to be involved in the interview process. The faculty complied. Ultimately, as Jeffrey Ogbar explains, "despite the Panthers' emphasis of organizing the lumpen, the party was incredibly active on college and high school campuses."[36]

*   *   *

A number of African American speakers graced stages at colleges and universities, motivating black campus activists and formulating their ideologies. It may be the case that more radical black speakers and speeches could be heard on college and university campuses in the late 1960s and early 1970s than during any other period in higher education history. Martin Luther King Jr. occasionally spoke. Days after coming out against the War in Vietnam at Riverside Church on April 4, 1967, King discussed the "illegal and unjust war in Vietnam" at Occidental-C in Los Angeles. H. Rap Brown of SNCC championed Black Studies at City College in NY in October 1967, and then in November at Columbia he criticized American universities as "propaganda mechanisms for white national-ism." He called on black students to apply their education to changing the world and advancing Black America.[37]

Coretta Scott King replaced her slain husband as Harvard's commencement speaker in June 1968. "In struggling to give meaning to your own lives, you are preserving the best in our traditions and are breaking new ground in your rest-less search for truth. With this creative force to inspire all of us we may yet not only survive—we may triumph." More than one thousand people sprung up from their seats as she finished. Shirley Chisholm, the first black congresswoman and presidential candidate, appeared at more than a half of dozen campuses for commencement exercises in the spring of 1969. At Howard, which had been embroiled in protests most of the semester, she gave a ringing endorsement of the movement. Fight the system that "has been denying you the opportunity to be a total man or woman," she resounded. Activist-poet LeRoi Jones (renamed Amiri Baraka) intermittently lectured at institutions. The "black man must finally have the power to govern his life," he said during his forty-five-minute address at Carthage-C (WI) in February 1969. Joe Trotter, president of Carthage's AAS wrote afterwards that "the campus has a Jones hang over."[38]

Fannie Lou Hamer induced at least two hangovers that stimulated protests. "A turning point for all of us was Fannie Lou Hamer being there," said Bertie Howard, who helped take over a Duke building on February 13, 1969. "For a lot of us it caused us to stop and pause and think about what we were going to do." The following February, Hamer spoke closer to her home, at Mississippi Valley State, while students combated their president. At one point, she implored President J. H. White to "go home, and be quiet." "I've seen some of the world's greatest Toms in service," she added, "but this man must be a Nuclear Tom." A few days later, the students marched on campus, still sizzling from Hamer's speech.[39]

Muhammad Ali made the rounds during the crucial politicization period. "The truth makes you free—not integration," Ali said in April 1968 to 750 stu-dents at Fairleigh Dickinson in New Jersey. Also formulating black student ide-ologies through college speeches were Betty Shabazz, who often spoke at the opening of Black Cultural Centers (BCCs), former NFL running back Jim Brown, usually pushing black capitalism, Angela Davis, CORE's Floyd McKissick, Adam Clayon Powell Jr., historian John Hope Franklin, poet Sonia Sanchez, Georgia politician Julian Bond, James Farmer from the Department of Health, Education, and Welfare (HEW), feminist "Flo" Kennedy, author Ralph Ellison, and SF State professor Nathan Hare, to name a few.[40]

Carmichael's speeches may have been the most important in growing an infant movement, but without question comedian Dick Gregory gave the most speeches during the BCM. One report says he spoke at five hundred institutions during the 1967–1968 academic year alone. "I spend about 98 percent of my time today on college campuses—and for a reason," he said at Pittsburg State (KS) in September 1968. "I feel that you young folks in America today are probably the most morally committed, ethical group of dedicated young people that have ever lived in the history of this country."[41]

In addition to these national voices, local black power leaders often roused students. "We have started to be what we are," declared John Barbour, Hartford's Black Caucus spokesman at Trinity-C (CT) in October 1967. Father James Groppi, a white Catholic priest and one of the stimulators of the Milwaukee BPM, spoke at institutions in the Midwest, including Michigan Tech and Clarke-U in Iowa, where in January 1968 he said, "black power is good, and not anti-Christian." Seemingly the most productive local ideological engineer was Howard Fuller, a community organizer in Durham and the founding director of Malcolm X Liberation University in 1969. He lectured on black power and grassroots altruism at most of the black and white institutions helping to make central North Carolina the hotbed for the BCM in the South.[42]

*   *   *

Many of these speakers spoke during Black Cultural Weeks or Weekends (termed a variety of names), organized annually by BSUs seemingly wherever they existed during the late 1960s and early 1970s. Speeches, films, panel discussions, socials, and artistic events usually comprised these weeks—with an affair each night. The week usually gave black students and the campus community the first concerted systematic explication of African American history and culture, exposing the normalized mask of whiteness. Sometimes protests for Black Studies departments and courses were inspired by these weeks. But in most cases, students demonstrated through these weeks the need for Black Studies. They were even observed at black colleges. From December 10 to 13, 1968, at Fayetteville State (NC), the Black Awareness Week comprised a kickoff speech by Howard Fuller, a play titled "The Word is Given Black Liberation," a panel discussion on "The Role of Black Students," a black cultural program, another panel discussing religion, and a social gathering.[43]

Most profoundly, black campus activists molded their own ideologies through these weeks. The influence of traveling black speakers could not compare to the influence black students had on each other. During these weeks and the movement in general, black campus activists constantly discussed black power, black nationalism, Pan-Africanism, self-defense, nonviolence, violence, guerilla warfare, racism, black capitalism, Marxism, Maoism, culture, Africa, Asia, Latin America, Europe, war, poverty, white liberalism, white conservatism, black conservatism, the black middle class, segregation, integration, assimilation, colonialism, Third World liberation movements, pedagogy, educational philosophy, the function of education, protest tactics, patriarchy, the man's role, the woman's role, and the role of students in the struggle. They debated the writings of Malcolm X, James Baldwin, Mao Zedong, Ernesto "Che" Guevara, Audre Lorde, W. E. B. Du Bois, Booker T. Washington, Frances Beal, and Frantz Fanon, among others, as no generation of students read more political literature than these black campus activists. They incessantly deliberated over the function and direction of the campus, local, national, and global movement in their dorm rooms, libraries, social gatherings, black houses, Greek houses, cafeterias and, eventually, BSU and Black Studies offices and BCCs.

Black campus activists were like their thoughts—constantly on the move to other campuses. They visited to party, hear black speakers, attend BSU and SGA meetings, support BSU and SGA events (and protests), give speeches, and organize BSUs and radicalize SGAs. The appearance of black Oberlin-C students compelled students at Thiel-C (PA) to organize a BSU in December 1968. Two Texas Southern students visited St. Andrews Presbyterian (NC) in February 1969 to aide in the establishment of the BSU.[44] When students at Creighton-U (Omaha) were organizing the Black Coalition in the spring of 1968, they contacted the nationally renowned BSUs at SF State, Stanford, Yale, and Columbia "for information on their constitutions." BSUs also informed their peers about their progress. Shortly after their BCC opened in January 1970, the AAS at Bowdoin-C in Maine wrote to more than four hundred organizations encouraging them to establish similar centers.[45]

Formally, campus activists connected through a series of conferences they organized during the movement. Aside from the socializing, they proved to be politicizing, motivational, networking, and tactical minicamps. Groups of students left conferences and soon after organized BSUs, unleashed protests, and intensified their campus struggles for racial reform. In late 1966, several groups of college representatives from the region came to Columbia to hear national leaders speak about black student empowerment. Several contingents were inspired to organize, including students from Rutgers and Wellesley. Crammed in the back seat of a taxi, riding back from the conference, five Wellesley women founded Ethos—a story now fabled at the women's LAC in Massachusetts.[46]

"It was very powerful to see the number of black students there and to hear what was happening on other campuses," recalled Elmer Freeman, a Northeastern-U activist who attended a conference of black students in Boston in March 1967. "We came out of that room with a broader agenda because we knew other folks were doing similar kinds of things." On the other side of the country, in Los Angeles, dozens of high school and college activists took part in the West Coast Black Youth Conference during Thanksgiving weekend in 1967. "We must begin to institute programs that speak to the needs of Afroamericans and not programs that are a reaction to white definitions," read the conference's manifesto.[47]

During the weekend of April 13, 1968, about two hundred students, many representing BSUs from forty-two colleges along the eastern seaboard, convened at Princeton for three days. "People don't talk revolution," Charles Hamilton declared in the keynote address. "They make revolution." The next weekend, seventy-eight delegates from thirty-seven HBCUs traveled to Shaw, in Raleigh, where they had met eight years earlier at the height of the sit-in movement. Shaw president James E. Cheek had issued an announcement to all HBCUs shortly after the death of Martin Luther King Jr. on April 4, 1968.[48]

Quite possibly the most activism-inducing was the "Towards a Black University" conference at Howard in November 1968. Carmichael said to some two thousand students, "you've got to quit talking and start acting." Karenga suggested that there were seven types of students: the forced student, the integrationist, the professional student, the athlete, the career student, and the nationalist. The nationalist "is the ideal student," Karenga explained. "He realizes his first

Photo 6   *Front cover of* The Harambee *at Tougaloo College (MS) on December 7, 1970* (Courtesy of Tougaloo College)

commitment is to his people," and a true Black University would produce this type of student. HBCU students left with a clear concept of a "Black University." One Fayetteville State (NC) student attendee explained to his campus community that the concept "emerges out of the frustrations of" African Americans "who recognize that the present institutions of higher learning have no relevance to the total Black community." Over the next few years, black student conferences were held at institutions such as Augustana-C in Illinois, Stanford, Jackson State, Princeton, UTEP, and the Universities of Minnesota, Oklahoma, North Dakota, Missouri, and South Carolina.[49]

Finally, black student newspapers influenced the construction and circulation of their ideology. Urban rebellions, black power, gender issues, and the notion of a Black University were a few of the many topics columnists discussed in HBCU newspapers, just as writers carried stories on the demands and protests at their schools (and other institutions). In many cases, the editors of HBCU student newspapers were activists—specifically at the movement's height in 1969. Sometimes campus newspapers were the voice of the struggle at HBCUs, resulting in some administrators clamping down on them with the same ferociousness as they did on protests. In 1971, soon after a story in the *Campus Echo* questioned whether NC Central was "a Black School," President Albert Whiting pulled the newspaper's funding.[50]

At white institutions, BSUs founded, to give a few examples, *NOMMO* at UCLA, *Watani* at U-Montana, *The Black Expression* at Western Carolina, *Harambee* at New Mexico State and Duke (after the US Organization's publication title), *Black Explosion* at U-Maryland, *Pamoja* at U-Georgia, *Black Fire* at SF State, *Uhuru* at CSU Fresno, and *The Grapevine Journal* at Michigan State, which reportedly had the largest circulation. Usually funded through their student government allotments, named after African terms, and printed at a high quality, these BSU periodicals, which had their HBCU counterparts, like Tougaloo-C's *Harambee*, publicized the ideas and activities of the BCM. BSU journalists reported on their demands and protests (on their campuses and other schools), challenged the campus community on its racism, and discussed the major black stories of the day, specifically the repression of black power leaders in 1969 and the early 1970s. Poetry, short stories, book reviews, essays, announcements, tributes to black women and men, and drawings accompanied the articles. BSU newspapers also provided white students their first lessons on African Americans, amassing new allies. A presumably white Duke student from Washington, DC, wrote the editors of *Harambee* in February 1969. "I have been reading Harambee and have not been able to put it down!" Lynne Anderson expressed. "I have gained a much greater understanding of Blacks. Thank you, Harambee, for one of the most rewarding learning experiences I've had since I've been [at] Duke."[51]

* * *

According to surveys in 1968 and 1970, most black students in college were women, grew up in cities, received little or no financial support from their financially strapped homes, majored in the social sciences, were the sons and daughters of parents who had not graduated from high school, expressed racial pride, were usually older than their white peers, blamed the system for the plight of their people, and were interested in collective black mobility. Black students were far from monolithic during the BCM though. Black student communities comprised collections of minigroups ordered by charismatic students, fraternal connections, artistic talents, hometowns, and mutual interests and friendships, to name a few distinguishing factors. A large number of black students at HWCUs entered remedial or special programs, such as Educational Opportunity Programs (EOPs), and joined (or rejected) the BCM. Many conservatives or liberal white suasionists steered clear of the movement—students whom Harry Edwards termed "conforming Negroes." At the same time, on most campuses with large black populations, it was simply cool to be sporting black power garb, challenging "whitey" and the institution. At colleges and universities with small black populations, it was socially, politically, and culturally expedient to be in the movement.[52]

It is impossible to pinpoint exactly how many students were involved in the BCM. Drawing from empirical and anecdotal data at the time, presumably about a quarter (a conservative estimate) of black students on college campuses in the late 1960s and early 1970s participated in the BCM by speaking out against the racial constitution, regularly attending BSU or radicalized SGA meetings, or participating in a single protest. Roughly another quarter seldom attended meetings and never protested, but sympathized with and supported the struggle in their own way. The rest of the "conforming Negroes" (a quarter or potentially one-half) opposed the BCM with their silence and sometimes public rebukes.[53]

Black campus activists were usually moderate or radical black nationalists. The movement became the primary aim of many radical students who were often shrewdly loyal to their conception of "blackness" or Africanity, hated imperial white supremacist capitalism and liberalism, considered African American culture viable in its own right, embraced self-defense or violence, envisioned new black institutions, were unafraid of protesting and dramatically challenging their colleges and universities, and attempted to fuse their social and academic interests with their political and cultural activities. However, most activists seem to have been moderates, juggling (and separating) the politico-cultural struggle with their academic and social lives, while also ideologically juggling radical and liberal thoughts, socialist and capitalist ideas, the desire to work in and outside of the "system," protest tactics with negotiations, profound fear and intense courage, higher educational reforms and structural changes, and optimism and pessimism for American institutions. Many black moderates flocked to BSUs or activist SGAs (often momentarily, sometimes permanently) when they felt personally threatened, a campus or societal issue intrigued them, campus social norms thrust then into a campaign, or due to a community or campus tragedy, such as Bloody Sunday, urban rebellions, assassinations, or an act of harassment on campus, all of which were rampant in the late 1960s.

Black capitalists and Marxists ideologically battled, patriarchs and feminists clashed, cultural nationalists and revolutionary nationalists tussled, heterosexuals and gays and lesbians were at odds—the ideological divides were endless in this politically and culturally charged movement residing in America's centers of ideas. On many campuses, black women had to fight sexism in their BSUs and SGAs while they fought the racist academy. By the early 1970s, some black women participated in the BCM and the Black Feminist Movement, organizing panels, festivals, and conferences to discuss black womanhood and feminism. They brought to campus speakers such as Michelle Wallace of the National Black Feminist Organization, who charged that "many men feel a need to prove their masculinity. Black men find this very necessary," in a speech at Ramapo-C (NJ) in 1973. Challenging the idea that black women and white men were emasculating black men, Wallace asked, "How can somebody take away your manhood?"[54]

Throughout the BCM, black feminist students questioned and rejected sexist sentiments, specifically in the movement, which numerous men considered a male terrain, suggesting women activists were supposed to support men and reproduce and raise the black nation. In 1971, Gerry Whitted at NC Central wrote, "I (a young, black woman) am told that this man is going to change me from matriarch to woman. In my 'new definition,' I find myself on some African pedestal/stool, bound and gagged (for my protection, they say)...So I stand there and every now and then my gag is removed so that I can scream

'Black Power! Justice! Freedom! Africa, unite!'" Fortunately for the corps of the BCM, most women refused the gag and used their resounding voices to demand the racial reconstitution of higher education. In a letter to Wellesley-C (MA) president Ruth Adams in 1969, the black student group named Ethos declared, "A propensity for forgetting our names has often been demonstrated. For those who have difficulty distinguishing us, we have a suggestion. Call us merely Black Women. For that is basically what we are, that is the basis upon which we operate as a group. That is the basis of our ethos."[55]

* * *

The CRM directly and chiefly spawned the BPM of the 1960s and 1970s and all of its movements, including the BCM. Many of the early black power activists were trained during the civil rights era. Furthermore, desegregation had to preface the striving for diversity. New Negro and civil rights students eliminated most of the regressively overt institutional regulations at black and white colleges. In 1965, after protest knocking for a half a century, black students were finally residents in the house of the academy—some measure of freedom at HBCUs, some measure of place at HWCUs. Like any new resident, black students then began a movement to clean up the last overt vestiges of racist and paternal discomfort and just as importantly move in vestiges of relevant comfort for African America. Inside, but on the margins, they placed the entirety of the racial constitution of higher education on their list of renovations: the moralized contraption, the normalized mask of whiteness, the standardization of exclusion, and ladder altruism. Since the New Negro Movement, black students had pecked away at the moralized contraption and the standardization of their black exclusion from power at HBCUs. The CRM provided enlightening lectures in the standardization of exclusion at HWCUs after they enrolled. At both, activists began to uncover the normalized mask of whiteness. They increasingly grew disturbed by the overwhelmingly high number of white trustees, presidents, and faculty—demanding blacks in their stead.

Moreover, during the classical civil rights period (1954–1965), the example of SNCC, CORE, and other left groups compelled black students to marginalize, in unprecedented fashion, ladder altruism. The old idea that my personal success advances black America no longer held nearly as much weight. In addition, early-1960s striving for civil rights in the community allowed students to clearly view their unsupportive, often restraining colleges as their longtime ladders, removing them from the masses. Fueled by grassroots altruism, they instead wanted to break down the ladder and replace it, reforming or revolutionizing their colleges into organs of grassroots change, organs producing grassroots agents. These hacks over the course of multiple decades on the racial constitution of higher education came down on the academy with the most unbridled level of black student energy and focus in American history during the BCM.

5

"Shuddering in a Paroxysm of Black Power": A Narrative Overview of the Black Campus Movement

Similar to the hostility that greeted their racial brethren when they migrated to majority white urban centers throughout the twentieth century, a poisonous white backlash hit African American students when they entered HWCUs in the mid-1960s. Higher education may have desegregated, but many of the new African Americans still felt excluded, removed from the academic, social, and cultural milieu of the campus with few (if any) relevant courses or social and cultural outlets, particularly at nonurban HWCUs. "A solitary man, a foreigner in a strange land" was the language used by Stan Herring, the vice president of the Association of Black Collegians (ABC) at Gannon-U (PA) in November 1968; a student at St. Andrews Presbyterian (NC) used the phrase "a rat in a maze." At Lawrence-U (WI) "you are alone—stranded in the middle of white culture," said an unnamed student. "This university is an oasis in the desert, surrounded by vultures who are only waiting to pick up a crumb, a smell, a taste, and a feel of black nitty-gritty substance," wrote the Afro-American Students Association at U-Iowa in May 1968. Meanwhile, a few Michigan Tech students in an "alien white atmosphere" felt that the black student had two choices: "give up his black identity or perish."[1]

At many HWCUs, campus police officers continuously harassed African Americans. Some white students demeaned them by using derogatory names and sayings, making insulting phone calls, waving Confederate flags, singing "Dixie," organizing minstrel shows, and defacing their flyers, posters, doors, and campus property. On some occasions, they poured lighter fluid under black students' doors and set it on fire. When walking across campus, black students were hit with objects or nasty stares. Drive-by insults were rampant, along with offensive bathroom poetry. When black students reached their cars, on occasion they founded them damaged, or worse, set ablaze, which occurred at the U-North Dakota in September 1968. Some trainers and nurses seemed surprised they could get hurt. Several white professors notoriously assumed that African Americans were unintelligent and spewed bigotry in the classrooms, such as the Cornell economist who reportedly said in the spring of 1968 that urban African Americans "play sickly and perverted games stressing cunning and survival, as in the jungle." Campus publications proclaimed black inferiority. In the spring of 1967, Columbia's humor magazine satirized the formation of a black fraternity as "trying to provide Negro students with a home away from home, a sort of haven for the noble savages in this world of chrome and glass."[2]

Then there were the endless litany of questions. Part of the black experience at Trinity-U in San Antonio, according to Reggie Butler, was "being asked questions like 'why do Blacks want so much and do not want to work?': a question so naïve it is only surpassed by the nerve of the person asking it." Even more naïve were the questions that came after tragedies. "I was terribly sorry to hear about Dr. King," said a white student to a grieving black student in the Yale cafeteria the morning after King died. "But I'm interested to know how all this affects a Negro. Would you mind telling me just how you reacted to it?" The black student just glared at the white student for a few moments. After answering the question silently, he left the dining room, leaving his half-eaten breakfast behind. The questions kept many black students in a perpetual emotive bind. Am I here to educate or gain an education? Usually, they tried to do both, while the racism leaking from the questions drowned them in fury. Charged a Yale activist, "I came here to be a student not to educate whites about blacks. I'm tired of being an unpaid, untenured professor."[3]

At HBCUs, the conditions were not any better in 1965. At quite a few (usually private) HBCUs, the faculty bodies were mostly white, and included many conservative African Americans. At Tougaloo in 1968, 60 percent of the professors were still white. "The whole direction of the college is set and controlled by white supremacists," said Political Action Committee leader Howard Spencer that year. Most of the professors at Clark (Atlanta) were white, and *none* of the shared art and psychology instructors at the Atlanta University Center were African American in 1968.[4]

The vast majority of HBCU boards of trustees were either all-white or majority white, and they employed African American presidents that were often conservative and paternalistic. Therefore, many HBCUs still had compulsory class, ROTC, and chapel attendance in 1965. They usually prohibited smoking, drinking, cross-gender dorm room visitation and student franchise on college matters, and mandated curfews and dress codes (usually for women). For instance, Grambling officials, as late as 1967, did not allow women to wear pants and locked the dorms at 10 p.m. Students there ate breakfast at 6 a.m. in a dining hall with large hanging signs ordering them to "take bite-size mouthfuls" and "break bread before eating." There was not a single Africana Studies program or department in 1965, and at both HBCUs and HWCUs, courses studying Africans Americans were rare. Although weakened by the LBSM and recent civil rights measures, the moralized contraption, standardization of exclusion, normalized mask of whiteness, and ladder altruism still dominated the racial constitution of higher education in 1965.[5]

*   *   *

Like any social movement, the BCM started slowly. The day after Bloody Sunday, on March 7, 1965, two black student protests crippled a historic HBCU and a HWCU with a storied history of enrolling a relatively large number of black students. In late February, saying it would alienate white benefactors, Hampton officials refused to allow students to conduct a sympathy demonstration for the ongoing Selma campaign in downtown Hampton. On February 25, students called for the freedom to speak, demonstrate, and determine the college's curriculum and student code. In a passionate letter, Hampton student leader Donald Hughes pledged that his peers were no longer "cottoning to the White man" or "eating cheese for the White man's money. Do we need funds that only serve to perpetuate the things that the Negro is trying to get rid of once and for all—non-self-reliance, subordinating due to fear and feelings of inadequacy? No!"

Still reeling over administrators' intransigence and outraged by the carnage on the Selma bridge, about two hundred students rallied outside Hampton's administration building on March 8, 1965, with signs that read, "We want freedom" and "Hampton a Reformation or College." Three days later they staged a sit-in, blocking the entrance to administrators' offices. President Jerome Holland met none of the demands and eventually expelled the student leaders. Nevertheless, the Hampton affair became one of the pioneering first calls of the movement for their Negro University, controlled by white benefactors, to be refashioned into a Black University dictated by and for African Americans. Gwen Patton and her comrades at Tuskegee would be making a similar call in a few weeks, after their Montgomery "march that won't turn around," as narrated in the previous chapter. Although neither group initially used the term Black University, the two HBCUs that formed the model for all four elements of the racial constitution over the last hundred years at HBCUs were among the first to experience the thralls of campus activism. It signaled the prospect of a new day for black higher education, brought about by a fresh social movement. If the historically ultraconservative Hampton and Tuskegee could be radicalized, anything seemed possible.[6]

The day after Bloody Sunday, students also disrupted U-Kansas, which had annually amassed one of the largest HWCU black student populations for more than a half-century. Hundreds of campus activists demonstrated inside and outside of the president's office, demanding the abolishment of segregation in Greek organizations and housing. About 110 students were arrested, including soon-to-be NFL running back "The Kansas Comet," Gayle Sayers. During the early years of the BCM at HWCUs, the removal of the standardization of exclusion in student enrollments, clubs, and housing galvanized activists. In contrast, HBCU activists, during the initial years, sought to complete the removal of the moralized contraption. Actually, that March 1965, campus activists pressed to drive out the contraption, upgrade their facilities and services, and increase student power at Winston-Salem State and present day NC Central where picket signs shouted, "Human Rights! Civil Rights! What about Student Rights?"[7]

*   *   *

"You do not take a person who, for years, has been hobbled by chains and liberate him, bring him up to the starting line of a race and then say, 'you are free to compete with all of the others,' and still justly believe that you have been completely fair." Thus declared President Lyndon B. Johnson to Howard's graduating class on June 4, 1965, sounding like a proponent of affirmative action. Yet, on many campuses, black students were still hobbled by chains. The racial constitution of higher education stymied academic freedom. Even at Howard, two months before Johnson's commencement address, students protested administrative fetters.[8]

When black students returned in the fall of 1965, animated by the scorching Watts Rebellion, "symbols of slavery" still adorned newly desegregated southern campuses, including festivals with racial caricatures, Confederate flags, and the singing of "Dixie" at school events, prompting protests at schools such as U-Texas at Arlington. In November 1965, Herman Carter grieved that "Southern University perpetuates academic slavery, not freedom" before leading hundreds of his peers in rallies and marches. At Tuskegee that month, Gwen Patton and fellow activists marched on the president's home, boycotted the vesper service, walked out of a required chapel meeting, and organized a "turn-over-your-plate" protest in the cafeteria—all for more student rights, freedom, and power. Meanwhile, the Ivies made the concept of "diverse campuses" a fad that fall. "We don't want the well-rounded boy so much as the well-rounded student body," a Columbia admissions officer announced. Soon, black students would be requesting a racially well-rounded body of scholarship, a well-rounded faculty, a well-rounded curriculum, and a well-rounded scheme of services and facilities.[9]

*   *   *

Those well-rounded requests were voiced at quite a few campuses in the spring of 1966, as the movement intensified after a gas station clerk murdered Tuskegee freshman Sammy Younge Jr. BSUs were established or took on a new political posture. Marianna Waddy assumed the presidency of the nation's first organization that used the term Black Student Union at SF State. After asserting that the college had tried to "white-wash them," Waddy declared, "We will now strive to incorporate the eminent and profound concept of blackness into a new and positive image of black students on this campus." SOUL at NC A&T complained about cafeteria food, and the first of several campaigns during the BCM to oust a HBCU president reached its zenith at Alcorn State. NAACP state field director Charles Evers, the former student activist, aided the protests for the ouster of President John D. Boyd, whom he described as "only concerned with pleasing white folks."[10]

After the summer debut of the catchphrase "black power," black student activism started focusing primarily on campus issues, as in 1965 students (particularly at HBCUs) engaged in dual, campus and off-campus, activism. Marquette faced its first protest that fall of 1966, and senior women demonstrated for more rights at Tougaloo-C. BSU members introduced the Black Studies idea at SF State. The idea of a Black Studies department, studying the lives of African people from their perspective and for their benefit, emerged logically out of the minds of BSU members brewed with black power ideas of self-determination, black pride, and criticism of white thought and institutions. They had carefully uncovered the mask of scholarly whiteness and saw White Studies taught from the perspective of white people primarily for their advancement. Additionally, the concept of a Black Studies department surfaced when BSU members realized that students should be receiving credit for courses in their Black Arts and Culture Series, which they ran in the fall 1966 in the Experimental College, since they were absent in the curriculum. The idea at SF State quickly metamorphosed into a crusade for a new discipline.[11]

Additional BSUs materialized that fall, such as at NYU, where the organizers pledged to find "ways of making white middle-class NYU more meaningful to the black student." At Wesleyan, collegians founded a study group that read, among other things, Franz Fanon's *The Wretched of the Earth*, *The Autobiography of Malcolm X*, and *Up From Slavery* by Booker T. Washington.[12] By the spring of 1967, James Baldwin and Richard Wright had become their literary saints, and *The Autobiography of Malcolm X* had become required reading for anyone who claimed on campus the new, hip, progressive, and sometimes exclusive identity—black.[13]

The SF State BSU had established and was controlling the first Black Studies program in American history by the spring of 1967, taking courses out of the Experimental College and convincing departments to sponsor them for credit. But this was not enough for the BSU. They wanted complete control over their courses, organized in a department so students could receive a degree from their Black Studies. On March 1, 1967, BSU president Jimmy Garrett officially presented "A Proposal to Initiate an Institute of Black Studies at San Francisco State College" to the Instructional Policy Committee of the Academic Senate. "There is no such thing as an integrated institution when the educational process is geared towards one group of students," he wrote. For the rest of the spring and summer, ideologically unnerved SF State faculty played academic football with the proposal, nitpicking on minor issues, and frustrations mounted among BSU members regarding traditional channels, a sign of the prospects for those demanding Black Studies departments.[14]

Most of the other BSUs and SGAs around the nation advocated, through traditional channels, a few black courses. In addition, there were protests in the spring of 1967 to undo the standardization of exclusion and racism in student clubs, athletics, and academics at schools such as Illinois Wesleyan, Vanderbilt, and Wichita State. The April affair at Wichita State led to the organizing of a black student group, the activity of most black campus activists at HWCUs that spring.[15]

Propelled by SNCC organizers who had returned to organize black colleges, students at quite a few HBCUs, including Texas Southern, Fisk, Lincoln (MO),

SC State, and Howard, waged protests and violent rebellions to demonstrate their displeasure with their "Negro" universities (with the first demands for a "Black" university), student powerlessness, police brutalizers, poor food, racist professors, and administrators who fired popular professors in the spring of 1967. Shouts of "We are in slavery" echoed during the Howard protests. To sociologist Nathan Hare, who was fired from Howard for his activism, black students were seeking to overthrow the "plantation milieu" and the "missionary mores" under the "supervision of an outmoded generation of Negro overseers. They are no longer willing to cry 'Uncle' to Uncle Sam or Uncle Tom." Hare urged college administrators to keep pace with and channel "this new student vigor" so that black colleges could become a "vanguard of a brave new spirit of social change. If they "fail to meet this challenge," then "it is going to be a long, hot fall."[16]

They did fail, and consequently students scorched black and white colleges. A rapidly growing minority of the black student population were becoming more organized, more vocal, more active, more committed, and more determined to modify higher education. Black journalists took notice. "The Black student is demanding...a shaking, from-the-roots-up overhaul of their colleges," stated a December 1967 report in the *Chicago Defender*. *Look* senior editor Ernest Dunbar reported on the "birth of 'Afro' or all-black clubs and societies" in his magazine, a piece republished in several student newspapers that fall. "Time was when the occasional Negro accepted at an Ivy League school...worked fanatically to become what he imagined was a proper college gentleman," Dunbar wrote. "Today a new breed of black cat is tearing up white campuses." In the fall of 1967, Black students tore up many institutions, including San Jose State, Berea-C (KY), Grambling State (LA), Central State (OH), and SF State—forcing campus closures at the latter two colleges.[17]

In the spring of 1968, BSUs had either heard about the development of Black Studies at SF State or had conceived of a similar need on their own campuses. After the death of three black students in the Orangeburg Massacre at SC State in February 1968, during a campaign to desegregate a nearby bowling alley, the number of protests dramatically increased. Black power icon H. Rap Brown demanded revenge. "If it takes twenty to thirty million Blacks to tear up the country, we'll do it," he declared. Most of the campus activists did not tear up the country. However, the Orangeburg Massacre did tear up some passive minds, and activist ones formed in their stead. It was the first of two events that spring that hurled legions of students to the left. The major protest in reaction to the massacre occurred at the main incubator of the movement at HBCUs—Howard. Students issued the Orangeburg Ultimatum, which demanded, among others things, the creation of a radical Black University, and took over the administration building for 102 hours in a nationally renowned protest in March 1968 that inspired demonstrations at other HBCUs.[18]

In the first three months of 1968, black campus activists also met with campus officials and submitted grievances, usually through BSUs recently established at a number of institutions, such as Northeastern-U, Occidental-C, U-Mary Washington (VA), UCLA, and New Mexico State. If the BCM received a nudge from the Orangeburg Massacre, then it received a shove from the murder of

Dr. Martin Luther King Jr. on April 4, 1968. Once hesitant moderate students volunteered for the conflict for diversity and relevancy, and radical campus activism started to reign supreme. Central State student Jaribu Hill "got as serious as the time we were living in," he said. "I never looked back on the meaningless life I had lived before. I lived a life of conviction, resistance and protest on my college campus."[19]

As cities burned after King's death, some black students at Florida A&M, Tennessee State, Lincoln (MO), and Jackson State joined in the riots, but most black students attended and spoke at memorial services held at practically every college in America. Some boycotted services in protest, such as the eighty at Harvard who stood on the church's steps having their own commemoration. "If they come out of there with tears in their eyes," said Jeff Howard, the president of Afro, pointing to the church, "we want it to be plain that we don't want their tears. We want black people to have a place here at Harvard." A few days after King's murder, Vassar's black women issued a thunderous statement. "White America…has plainly demonstrated that the only tactics that can move its violent heart is violence. Force only responds to force and power to power. Pretty soon this nation will be shuddering in a paroxysm of black power."[20]

Higher education shuddered in a paroxysm of what Stefan Bradley termed "black student power" for the rest of the spring 1968 semester. Campus activists usually formed BSUs (or took over SGAs) at schools where black students were unorganized or marginal before King's death. Infant BSUs forcefully and often publically submitted their first formal sets of demands—seemingly the most prevalent occurrence in April and May 1968. Protests were more likely to disrupt the minority of institutions with older BSUs that had demanded racial restructuring for years. Requests for Black Studies courses had been elevated to demands for programs and departments. Entreaties to reduce white prejudice had expanded to demands for BCCs. Pleas for a few more black students and professors were now demands for dozens of faculty and student quotas. The paroxysm shuddered colleges and universities in almost every state—Iowa, California, Michigan, Connecticut, Wisconsin, Illinois, Massachusetts, Oregon, Alabama, New York—just to name a few.[21]

While black students crafted their demands, some were mystified as they watched the deluge of diversity flood into the academy. Through his death, King dramatically appealed to the moral conscience of white America, particularly those in the academy, as dozens, probably hundreds of institutions succumbed to students' requests, or often on their own accord established scholarships, recruiting initiatives, race committees, and other memorials in King's honor. Colorado State, for example, started a memorial fund "to produce a thousand Martin Luther Kings for the one we lost."[22]

Influential protests hit Tuskegee, where students took trustees and the president hostage in early April, and Northwestern, where in early May activists led by James Turner and Kathryn Ogletree cleverly gained a department and black dorm, among other things, by means of a building takeover. Initially demonstrating in opposition to the building of a gymnasium in a nearby Harlem park against the wishes of residents, black and white students seized five buildings in late April at Columbia. Black students occupied Hamilton Hall, placing a cardboard sign on its door proclaiming "Malcolm X University, Founded 1968 A.D." Students welcomed into the occupied buildings famous journalists, who received lectures on American imperialism and racism before leaving and making this the most publicized campus demonstration of the 1960s student movement.[23]

On April 30, after seven days of negotiations between the students and the administration, with the faculty trying to mediate, the administration dispatched the NYPD to end the demonstration, probably confident that Harlem would not destroy the campus in vengeance. With no resistance, the black students quietly walked out of Hamilton and into the police vans. NAACP executive director Roy Wilkins, the movement's major antagonist, even praised these black students. While the NYPD cleared the four buildings with white students on the South side of campus, about a thousand mostly white students watched, some of them jeering, taunting, and ridiculing the police. When the police finished, they walked back into formation, broke from their line and flailed away at the students. The clouds of police nightsticks unleashed a rain of student blood. All told, 148 were injured, and 707 were arrested (charges were later dropped) in the crowd and from the buildings. Enraged, more than five thousand Columbia students spent the rest of the semester protesting for the right to "restructure the university."[24]

*   *   *

After the politically tumultuous summer of 1968, the largest and most radical incoming class of black students in history walked into the academy in the fall of 1968, many from the sweltering urban African America. Eight hundred members of Howard's freshmen class identified themselves as militants. At white colleges, dozens of critical masses formed BSUs, including at Catholic-U and Wake Forest. Black students hardly felt like aliens, needing to recede to islands within as their contemporaries had done. As an unnamed Yale student said, "When there were just a handful of us here we felt isolated and defenseless in a white world, so we just went along, I guess. But with more black kids coming in each year we've started getting together and we have a lot more confidence."[25]

Enrollees were able to find comfort in BCCs, take the nation's first Black Studies courses, or seek advice from the growing assemblage of black administrators and professors. An English professor taught a new black literature course at Northeastern-U (MA). "I wanted to see the fruits of our labor," said enrollee Jim Alexander. "I've read all the books, long ago. Most black students have." However, black students were far from satisfied. Several officials forecast an upsurge of black campus activism. Before classes began in the fall, some administrators took precautions, while others simply ignored the warnings.[26]

Throughout the BCM, the early fall had the lowest levels of activism, since the influxes of students compelled BSUs and SGAs to reorganize, while leaders and their political ideologies jockeyed for control. Usually after BSUs and SGAs modified, their new managers began asserting themselves. After controversy bristled through California concerning Black Panther Party member Eldridge Cleaver's teaching a course that fall at the UC Berkeley, and after a prominent protest at U-Illinois, the protest activity was raised when two San Jose State students, Tommie Smith and John Carlos, raised their fists in protest at the Olympics in October 1968. "Black America will understand what we did tonight," said Smith at a press conference after the event.[27]

Black America understood, and possibly no segment of it more than their peers. Black students started clenching their fists and lowering their heads during the playing of the national anthem at collegiate events. At SF State, the BSU started the longest student strike in American history on November 6, 1968, for a series of demands, including an autonomous Black Studies department. With most of the school's 18,000 white students behind its cause in a broad multiracial coalition, the strike lasted almost five months, inspiring black campus activists around the nation.[28]

Dozens of white colleges were consequently disturbed by blacks demanding a more relevant education in November and December of 1968—schools such as UMASS-Amherst, West Virginia's Bluefield State (where students firebombed a building), Fordham-U (NY), Brown/Pembroke (RI), and UW Oshkosh, where about ninety black campus activists were arrested and expelled on "Black Thursday." Even more groups of students, at Case Western Reserve and U-San Francisco for instance, issued demands and usually engaged in marathon negotiating sessions with administrators. Before 50,000 people at the Astrodome on November 23, 1968, Lynn Eusan, sporting an Afro, put on the crown of homecoming queen at U-Houston, becoming a source of pride for activists on campus and in the city until her tragic murder in 1971. (A campus park is now named after Eusan.)[29]

In December 1968, Robert Smith, the recently fired president of SF State, told *The Chronicle of Higher Education* that higher education "is at a serious and crucial turning-point." The academy still largely refused to racially reconstitute higher education. The bonanza of demands issued after King's death had only been partially addressed on some campuses and hardly addressed at others. Consequently, even though the SF State strike waned in January 1969, the movement as a whole surged, beginning its climax semester with a rash of protests, usually to force home those post-King-assassination demands. Brandeis-U, Queens-C, U-Pittsburgh, Wilberforce-U (OH), Shaw (NC), Wittenberg-U (OH), and UC Berkeley were all sites of protests that month. On King's soon-to-be birthday holiday, twenty-five black campus activists at Swarthmore-C outside of Philadelphia were engaged in the seventh day of their siege of the admissions office, demanding active recruitment of black students, faculty, and administrators. Like his peers throughout the nation, Swarthmore president Courtney Smith had been severely strained those seven days. On the eighth day of the siege, shortly before he was to meet with a faculty committee studying the demands, Smith suffered a fatal heart attack. Shock and sadness unsettled the campus, and in sympathy, the twenty-five students ended their protest. Death continued to reign the next day. Two UCLA students, John Huggins and Alprentice "Bunchy" Carter, leaders of the Los Angeles Black Panther Party, were gunned down by members of Karenga's US Organization at the end of a BSU meeting of 150 students. The students had deliberated over the selection of a director for the recently created Afro-American Studies Center, a selection the two groups had quarreled about since the fall. They also battled ideologically, a clash doggedly intensified by the divisive work of the FBI.[30]

In early February 1969, academics attended the American Association of Colleges conference, where almost every speech, panel, and discussion started or ended in a debate concerning the BCM and its implications. Meanwhile, the BCM quickened its activities—wreaking havoc at UVA, NC A&T, U-Dayton, and Huston-Tillotson (TX), reaching its pinnacle on February 13, 1969. On February 21, 1969, thousands of students memorialized their fallen leader, Malcolm X, slain four years earlier on that day. During the next month, headlines from black student protests became an everyday occurrence, with the most notorious demonstrations ravaging U-Texas at Austin, Mills-C in Oakland, Rutgers, Pepperdine-U in southern California (after a white security guard killed Larry Donnell Kimmons, a black high school student, during a confrontation over Kimmons's desire to play basketball on campus), and students took Morehouse trustees (including Martin Luther King Sr.) hostage to press for their demands for a "Black University." In the midst of this turmoil, the *Wall Street Journal* reported that "Black power is the force causing the greatest schizophrenia on the campus at the moment."[31]

*　*　*

Even though there had been several violent protests, specifically the mildly publicized affairs at small rural HBCUs, the academy did not link the movement with violence nor did it give the students' more radical demands legitimacy until students strutted out of an occupied Cornell building with guns and Harvard established a Black Studies department, respectively, within days of each other in late April 1969. Ironically, as their demands were legitimized, the academy grew more insensitive to them, with the hovering specter of violence. Still, the activism did not ebb. In late April and May of 1969, among other protests, black students took over an entire City College campus for fourteen days, which contributed to the installation of a widely touted (and censured) open admissions policy at the City University of NY, twelve hundred seized a Hampton administration building, students gained control over a Voorhees building with arms, barricaded themselves inside six buildings at Howard, forced the closure of Alabama State for two weeks, and shot it out with police at NC A&T for three days, an exchange that killed a student. This apex academic year of the movement led to massive repression and substantial reforms.[32]

Gwen Patton, who had joined the staff of the National Students Association since leaving Tuskegee, led about one hundred of her peers out of its convention in El Paso, Texas, in late August 1969. "We no longer can be part of a racist" group, as the leaders use "black problems for their own purposes to gain financial grants from foundations," Patton explained to the media. Urged by Nathan Hare and under Patton's leadership, black collegians formed their own group— the National Association of Black Students (NABS)—which became the major national network for campus activists during the final years of the movement.[33]

As Patton devised the NABS, black students and HWCU officials launched the greatest recruitment of black students, faculty, and staff in American history.

Photo 7 *Howard Fuller talking to a student in front of Malcolm X Liberation University, October 1969* (Photo by Bill Boyarsky)

Nevertheless, the staffing boom had its downside. HWCUs amplified their raiding of HBCUs for professors, leading to massive turnover. Miles in Birmingham, for instance, with a faculty of sixty-one in 1969, had to replace forty-five teachers the previous three years. "Every black Ph.D. who has his name mentioned twice, or has published in the slightest review, is besieged by Northern as well as Southern white institutions—most often in response to militant, urgent and often threatening demands by their black students," Spelman history chairman Vincent Harding explained to the *New York Times* in 1969.[34]

Aside from the new reforms and policing tactics, when higher education opened its doors in the fall of 1969, everything seemed out of whack. Black students, professors, administrators, and government leaders were still at odds over some of the core demands of the movement. There were fierce tug-of-wars for power over newly established Black Studies programs among African Americans themselves and between them and campus officials. Students and their allies were divided over ideology, tactics, and goals, marking the beginning of the end of the BCM. Black campus revolutionaries who wanted to escalate the movement to another level were combating activists who wanted to protest for reforms colleges had not yet instituted, and both of those groups were confronting students who wanted to nurture the gains won in the spring of 1969 (or off-campus matters). They all scurried around campuses picking the unparalleled crop of students that enrolled in higher education institutions in the fall of 1969.[35]

As hundreds of new initiatives, such as Black Studies programs, diversity offices, and black cultural centers, were unveiled in the fall of 1969 and black leaders such as the NAACP's Roy Wilkins questioned their efficacy, many of the progenitors of the reforms faced serious judicial repression, slowing the movement. Yet California's

Nairobi-C, North Carolina's Malcolm X Liberation University (MXLU), and a few other colleges that students built to provide a relevant and socially responsible education opened their doors. Betty Shabazz, the widow of Malcolm X, spoke at MXLU's opening ceremonies. Painted in black on a peach-colored wall just inside the door of its building was a Malcolm quotation, proclaiming that this was a school for members of "a new generation of black people who have become disenchanted with the entire system and who are ready now and willing to do something about it." Upon its founding, Director Howard Fuller said, "This university will provide a framework within which black education can become relevant to the needs of the black community and the struggle for black liberation."[36]

The revolt of the black athlete picked up at schools that fall, most prominently in the series of protests and refusals to play in contests against Mormon-controlled and what the activists deemed theologically racist BYU. Although much of the national attention focused on the revolt of the black student-athlete and on the UC regents' second crusade in successive years to oust a radical professor (this time Angela Davis of UCLA), black campus activists made demands and protested at colleges, such as Central Connecticut State, Marshall-U (WV), St. Ambrose-U (IA), Fairfield-U (CT), and Vassar-C (NY), where critical masses had just been reached. Protests still occurred at institutions where critical masses had long dotted the landscape, including at Fisk in December 1969, where students called for a Black University "controlled and administered by black people," devoted to their cultural needs, identified "completely with blacks," teaching "skills necessary for black existence," and void of white employees.[37]

Some administrative reactions to protests became more militant that semester. They met threats of demonstrations with counterthreats of prison time, and stood up to the force of protests by swiftly using the force of the newfangled enormous campus police state. It was now up to the students to change tactics. Black campus activists largely did not, and the growing ineffectiveness of proven tactics propagated disillusionment. The mounting number of retaliatory demonstrations to decry attacks on their communities also contributed to the decline.

Black students at UNC at Chapel Hill, Tufts-U (MA), and Harvard fought for the rights of black campus nonacademic workers that fall. For once, the *New York Times* affirmed their efforts. "Racial discrimination in the building trades must not be allowed to benefit from the vast expansion of construction programs on college campuses all over the country." During the Harvard protest campaign in December 1969, "Masai" Hewitt of the BPP, NAACP's Roy Wilkins, SCLC's Ralph Abernathy, and CORE's Roy Innis shared the stage for the first time that decade at Boston-C. Wilkins in particular, the major antagonist of the BCM, had grown more sympathetic to black power and sought to create some "common ground" with the Black Panther Party (BPP) in 1969, as Yohuru Williams documents. Like black students across America, the speakers were enraged about the recent police onslaught against the Panthers headquarters in Los Angeles and the vicious police murder of Chicago Panthers Fred Hampton and Mark Clark. "The Panthers today, next week CORE or the SCLC, the week after it may be the NAACP," Innis roared. The murders and Panther repression added to a year of political assassinations, harassment, raids, and unjust imprisonments of black power activists, which increasingly attracted the attention of students—another phenomenon that slowed the campus movement.[38]

* * *

"As Lafayette heads into the 1970's, there is a new awareness of the 'black problem' on the campus," wrote *Lafayette Alumnus* editor Ronald R. Parent, to begin the winter 1970 special issue on the movement at the Lehigh Valley college. It contained an interview with Roland Brown, Lafayette's first black graduate, who had graduated in 1949. "When I was young we took the view that the white man has that which you want, so you pacify him until you get what you want from him and then you do not have to pacify him any longer. The black student today says, the dickens with pacifying the white man, we're going to get what we want now."[39]

In the spring of 1970, the waning of the BCM continued, but there was still a rash of activism against the "white man." New campaigns at suburban and rural usually white LACs with recently enrolled multitudes of blacks were the new sites of activism that spring. Institutions such as Bowdoin-C and Colby-C in Maine, where students occupied a chapel for a week, Mount Holyoke (MA), Southern Oregon, Heidelberg-U and U-Mount Union in Ohio, and Cedar Crest-C, Kutztown-U, Elizabethtown-C, and Rosemont-C in Pennsylvania faced the BCM. Students thumped some universities, including U-Michigan, U-Toledo, Florida State, Creighton-U, and U-Northern Iowa. HBCUs were not exempt— Bishop-C (Dallas) and Mississippi Valley State were disrupted.[40]

That spring, black students saw some of their hard-fought gains dismantled, as the defensive struggle to maintain diversity strengthened, which would eventually supersede the BCM to gain diversity. SF State president S. I. Hayakawa fired six Black Studies professors on March 2, 1970. It was one of the largest political firings of black professors at an HWCU in history, until eight of the twelve Black Studies instructors at CSU Fresno received similar notices that spring. Four hundred students discussed the fact that their advances were being rolled back when they attended a "Black Unity Conference" at Stanford in early May 1970.[41]

Days before, on April 30, 1970, President Nixon announced the escalation of the Vietnam War, ordering troops into Cambodia. His announcement escalated a vanishing antiwar movement. On May 4, during an antiwar protest at Kent State in Ohio, National Guardsmen killed four white students. Black students did not enthusiastically join the outbreak of strikes following the Kent State murders, angering some white students. African Americans did protest against the war *and* racism at a few institutions.[42]

Not even two weeks after the Kent State tragedy, another tragedy struck Jackson State. After a night of violent disorders, in part stemming from the discovery of a bell in the campus warehouse that used to summon students to class and chapel like slaves, President John Peoples met with student leaders about the causes of the riot, and for nearly two hours on May 14, 1970, they complained about the bell, the lack of a bridge-walk over the dangerous Lynch Street, the women's curfew, poor cafeteria food, and the irrelevant, bourgeois "Negro" university. That night, a small group started tossing rocks at automobiles driven by

Photo 8   *Two students at Jackson State peer from a dormitory window that was shot out by police on campus, May 15, 1970* (AP Photo/Jack Thornell)

whites on Lynch Street, a major Jackson thoroughfare that ran through campus. The disruption intensified. Just as on the night before, the Jackson police and state patrolmen, many of whom were known Klansmen, stormed onto the campus with the order to "go in there and scatter them damn—those Negroes." In addition, a Jackson lieutenant assembled a group of officers to disperse more than one hundred students in front of a women's dormitory, Alexander Hall, on Lynch Street. It was about midnight, and some of the female students had just entered the dorms before curfew, after being escorted by their male friends, who were still milling around. The lawmen stopped in front of the dorm. "You white pigs!" "White sons-of-bitches!" The students were irate at the police presence. A bottle smashed loudly into the Lynch Street pavement in front of the frightened officers. "They're gonna shoot!" a student screamed.

Officers let off round after round at the crowd of students, who quickly fell, tried to take cover, and raced into the dormitory. They even shot at the dormitory. Female students scurried about in the dorm to other rooms and under their beds, dodging bullets. Chips of brick, concrete, and glass fell like an avalanche on students taking cover below. Thirty seconds later, the patrolmen stopped shooting, sent for all of the city's ambulances, and approached the dormitories,

checking the student bodies that lay sprawled in front of them. Near a small mag-
nolia tree in front of the hall, they found two young men, dead. One was 21-year-
old Phillip L. Gibbs, a junior at Jackson State and father of a young son, and the
other was James Earl Green, 17, a senior track star at a local Jackson high school.
Scattered about, they also found at least eight students and one community member injured. The next day officials closed the campus for the rest of the semester.
Klansmen donning badges instead of sheets had killed African Americans.[43]

An outcry of sadness and fury came from black America when it woke up to
the news that morning of May 15, 1970. Investigations and punishments were
demanded of these officers, who claimed they were defending themselves against
sniper fire. No group was more upset than black students, in Jackson and across
the nation. As white colleges had erupted after Kent State, so too did black colleges after Jackson State. According to Howard president James E. Cheek, the
resentment of his students neared the "breaking point." Rallies and demonstrations occurred at HWCUs too. When several black students at Ohio State tried to
lower the American flag to mourn the deceased, they fought off a group of white
students who tried to stop them.[44]

Fifteen HBCU presidents met with President Nixon and urged him to recom-
mend that police officers not carry guns on campuses and to make a national
televised address to affirm the "government's resolve to protect the lives of black
citizens." President Nixon demurred, but as a palliative he did offer more money to
HBCUs. Charles Evers, the venerable Mississippi leader, started to reconsider nonviolence. "I've preached nonviolence because I don't think blacks can win the other
way, but there comes a time when a man doesn't care anymore about winning.
The day of killing niggers is gone to hell." Shunning white suasion, CORE's Floyd
McKissick observed "the conscience of America was not even pricked" when the
two black students and six Augusta (Georgia) men were killed (in an urban rebellion days before the Jackson massacre), unlike the Kent State murders. "We must
all learn from this. For it is further evidence that there is no way for Black men to
reach the conscience of white America." Despite the President's Commission on
Campus Unrest's finding that bigotry, not self-defense, led to the slaying of the
students, in the fall of 1970, a Mississippi grand jury found the police "were justified in discharging their weapons," and in April 1972, an all-white Mississippi jury
ruled that neither state officials nor police were liable for civil damages. The *New
York Amsterdam News* editorialized, "This decision is simply another nail in the
coffin of America's system of justice and equal treatment in the courts."[45]

Usually repression either slows or accelerates a social movement. It often depends
on whether it is decelerating or quickening before the repression. The Orangeburg
Massacre and King's assassination in the spring of 1968 caught the movement
when it was accelerating, compelling militants to slam the pedal of the movement.
On the other hand, the Jackson State tragedy occurred when the movement was
slowing, and thus it proved to be yet another cause of the demise of the BCM.

*   *   *

The level of activism noticeably dipped in the fall of 1970. The calm on "most of
the country's campuses" that fall had "been so pervasive as to have been almost

unsettling," according to the *New York Times*. Ideological divisions had widened, particularly due to the growing sway of Pan-Africanism, feminism, black capitalism, and Marxism. Black Studies courses had been introduced in colleges across America, which blunted the thorniest issue of their activism. Scores of student leaders had been removed from the campus before the fall of 1970, either voluntarily or involuntarily, and the achievements of the movement were regularly assaulted. "We have to constantly fortify our position," said an Oberlin student.[46]

During the 1970–1971 academic year, protests to keep movement reforms became more prominent and the students grew more interested in off-campus issues, specifically political repression, including the Free Angela (Davis) campaign. Yet, black students, who were more likely to attend college outside of the South for the first time, still waged offensive protests to demand novel measures—sometimes athletic—that academic year at numerous institutions, including Syracuse, Fontbonne-U (St. Louis), Western Connecticut State, U-South Alabama, Norfolk State, St. Mary's (TX), Prairie View A&M, Bluffton-U (OH), TCU, Colorado State-Pueblo, Providence-C, U-Georgia, and U-Florida ("Black Thursday")—keeping the BCM alive.[47]

As the movement decelerated in 1971, black students did not have the living voices that galvanized their activism, as most of them had been killed, jailed, or exiled. The pendulum continued to shift among black students during the 1971–1972 academic year from offensive to defensive protests and from on-campus to off-campus concerns, such as the Attica Prison massacre in New York in September 1971. Officers killed and injured unarmed prisoners when they took back the upstate New York penitentiary from prisoners who seized it to demand better conditions. But offensive protests for new reforms still prevailed, manifesting once again at HBCUs and institutions with new critical masses, such as IUPUI, Tougaloo-C, Wartburg-C in Iowa, Eckerd-C (formerly Florida Presbyterian), Wilberforce-U, U-Hartford, U-Nevada, and Murray State (KY).[48]

Benjamin E. Mays, the former Morehouse president, noticed in his travels in the spring of 1972 that the "campuses—on of the whole—are much calmer." The assessment was not because higher education had responded to the needs of black students. The racial constitution had almost completely changed on the surface, in the public academic rhetoric, but that does not mean the new creeds—moral freedom, standardization of inclusion, a multicultural curriculum, and grass-roots altruism—were totally implemented. "Much is said" about aiding black students, but "little is being done," found an Indiana researcher who surveyed more than one thousand colleges. *The Chronicle of Higher Education*'s report in the spring of 1972 on "Higher Education and the Black America" further assessed that "the black studies programs...now fill a standard, if insecure, niche in the curriculum." But the struggle still had one more semester.[49]

In the fall of 1972, the declining specter of black campus activism affected higher education, including negotiations at Franklin-C in Indiana, Angelo State in Texas, and U-North Alabama, and an almost total boycott at U-Arkansas at Pine Bluff. The movement tragically left the academy at the school with the largest collection of black students in the nation—Southern-U in Louisiana. In the fall of 1972, President G. Leon Netterville ran the university like a feudal lord, one of remaining ultraconservatives still manning an HBCU. Nothing of significance went down without his approval, which was why psychology chair Charles M. Waddell resigned in mid-October 1972 when the president did not allow him to fire a professor who sexually harassed women. Disturbed, students formed a coalition of groups, Students United, and drew up a list of demands for more student and faculty power.[50]

In a gathering with more than five thousand students, on October 24, President Netterville rejected the students' proposal for power. Shock quickly transformed into fury. The five thousand students rushed out of the gymnasium like a pack of bulls and trudged five miles to the state board of education's office to see State Superintendent Louis Michot. But Michot was away in Atlanta, and when one of his subordinates came out to speak with the students, they called for the resignations of President Netterville and two other administrators. They were not finished marching that day. Numbering a reported seven thousand, they walked over to the state capitol in one of the largest black student marches in American history to meet with Governor Edwin Edwards, who told the students he would be willing to help. Activists returned to campus and compelled 80 percent of roughly 8,000 students to boycott classes. On October 31, President Netterville closed the Baton Rouge campus, while activists at the New Orleans campus had initiated their own boycott and eight-day building takeover the day before. On November 6, the Baton Rouge campus reopened with more than three hundred heavily armed sheriff's deputies and city police ready to stamp out the class strike. But it persisted.

On the morning of November 16, in an attempt to curtail the strike, the Baton Rouge police arrested four Students United leaders and charged them with "disrupting the normal educational process." Retaliating later in the day, students stormed into the administration building—three hundred strong—and up to Netterville's office. Hearing the leaders out, Netterville made a phone call and allegedly instructed the police to come and clear out the campus. He bolted out of his office and left for a meeting with the state board of education.

Not long after, on November 16, 1972, the assembly of students, now numbering three thousand, started to leave, when they saw a wave of sheriff's deputies, state troopers, and city police splash hard onto campus. They gave the students five minutes to disperse. It was a standoff—the students were not going anywhere. When the five minutes passed, a state trooper tossed a tear gas canister into the crowd. It did not explode. A student picked it up and tossed it back over the line of state troopers and near the sheriff deputies. The canister exploded and sent the deputies scurrying wildly for their masks. When they got them on, they turned towards the crowd of students and opened fire with more tear gas canisters. One officer reportedly emptied a single shotgun blast that killed 20-year-old Leonard D. Brown Jr. of Gilbert, Louisiana, and Denver A. Smith, a 20-year-old computer science major from New Roads, Louisiana.

The campus immediately closed, and soon after the disliked President Netterville, whom Students United blamed for the tragedy, resigned. In a statement released to the press, the group said the murders were "premeditated, plotted, and implemented." Louisiana governor Edwards tried to deflect blame from landing on his administration and the Southern officials he allowed to stay in power. He said over and over again, "It was the students who initiated the confrontation" by throwing the tear gas canisters first. Southern reopened on January 3, 1973, with campus guard forces tripled, loyalty oaths signed, and student leaders barred, harassed, or disciplined.[51]

This tragedy was too much for the national student community to endure. They still had not recovered from Jackson State. In contrast to the previous killing of black campus activists, sadness eclipsed fury when students around the nation heard about the shootings. The reaction was "scattered and subdued," according to one report. Only at nearby Grambling did students aggressively reply to the killings. Memorial services were more popular than protests. The BCM was clearly history.[52]

*   *   *

"We, the students of Langston University, have fallen into an abyss of apathy, where our only resolution is the condemnation of the institution." Condemnation had not been producing activism as in years past, irritating Leanear Randall, as he watched the BCM recede into history at his lone Oklahoma HBCU in May 1972. The cry of apathy had been heard since 1970, but it had not been this loud. In two issues of *The Afro-Times Newsletter* in the fall of 1972, students at Mississippi State added to the chorus. "Perhaps our biggest enemy is apathy," Edward R. Robinson wrote in September. In the November-December newsletter, Coleman Wicks alleged that MSU was "rapidly earning the unheralded distinction of being one of the nation's most apathetic." Up north at Lehigh-U in Pennsylvania, Nathan Harris, a black administrator, attested in December that the "belligerently angry black student" who pressured the "University through overt actions has faded." To the west, CSU Long Beach professor and former black campus activist J. K. Obatala asked in *The Nation*, in 1972, "What happened to the black campus revolution? Whatever happened to the gun-toting nationalist, the uncombed hair, the demonstrations, the handbills, the placards, the protests, the black leather jackets and Malcolm X sweat shirts that came to be symbols of black student militancy in the 1960s."[53]

With reports of apathy emerging from every region, the age had passed, even as black students detested higher education with new contradictions—substance not matching the new ideals. Derisively, on January 19, 1973, the white editors of *The Collegio* at Pittsburg State in Kansas awarded black students "first place in the age-old category of apathy. This infamous honor is presented to those with the most anger and the least action." The BCM had indeed faded, but not necessarily black student anger or action. Beginning in 1973, defensive, disconnected black student activism to maintain the gains of the BCM eclipsed the offensive, connected activism that instituted a slew of new racial reforms and rewrote the racial constitution of higher education during the previous eight years. Said differently, African American students no longer held the academy in the creative clutches of a social movement in 1973. In that sense, they were apathetic. However, they were far from apathetic in the rearguard, defending their humanity, defending their gains—a defense that continues to this day.[54]

6

"A Fly in Buttermilk": Black Campus Movement Organizations, Demands, Protests, and Support

Shortly after molding the Organization of African and Afro-American Students at American University (OASATAU) in 1968, Walker "Moose" Foster clarified the group's function. "All our lives, we've been told that niggers ain't nothing." But "it does mean something to be a Negro," said the 19-year-old son of a maid and butler. "We want to appreciate our cultural differences." Since first stepping on the Washington, DC, campus, "I felt like a fly in buttermilk. I was stranded in a wasteland, in affluent Spring Valley. The only Negroes we saw up here were janitors. I mean, it could be me or my parents." In the fall of 1969, the University of Tennessee BSU circulated an orientation booklet that exclaimed, "The Black student must realize that, here at U.T., he constitutes what is analogous to the 'fly in the buttermilk.'"[1]

African American students borrowed the James Baldwin adage and habitually used it to characterize their experiences in the mid-to-late 1960s and early 1970s. The application could be heard more at white colleges and universities, where aside from black service workers buttermilk tended to flow everywhere. Buttermilk gushed around at black colleges too—the white benefactors, politicians, education bureaucrats, trustees, literature, rules, overwhelmingly white faculty bodies, and presidential black puppets controlled by white strings. Long before the 1960s, African American students felt like flies in buttermilk, stranded in "academic wastelands." However, the contradiction had never been this pronounced. The flies were never this black. The buttermilk never seemed so white. Black campus activists, emboldened by the contradictions, fashioned SGAs and BSUs to reform the racial constitution by issuing a series of demands and forcing their institutions through a variety of protests.[2]

Organizing

Before they could transform their colleges and universities, black campus activists first had to build organized campus bodies to wage the struggle—the chief striving during the early years of the BCM. At HBCUs, these organized bodies were usually SGAs led by moderate nationalists or, to a lesser extent, radicals. By the 1967–1968 and certainly 1968–1969 academic years, most student bodies of HBCUs had elected black campus activists as SGA presidents. Ewart Brown Jr., a native of Bermuda, gave his opening remarks as president of Howard's student body in September 1967. Sounding a cord heard from other SGA presidents at the time, he declared, "black leadership must be developed in a black university. This is the kind of leadership the movement needs now."[3]

NC A&T students elected Vincent McCullough (president) and Nelson Johnson (vice president) in the spring of 1969. "We got elected on a pretty militant platform," said Johnson, who also helped organize and become the first national chairman of Students Organized for Black Unity (SOBU) that spring. "We took to the students as straightforward and honestly as we could, like what we felt was going on in the society and the whole question of Black Power." The whole question of black power dominated the platform of Earl Hart, Winston-Salem State's SGA president during the 1970–1971 school year. Upon announcing his candidacy, a campus reporter styled Hart "the little man from Rocky Mount, N. C. who has been a constant thorn in the side of the administration since he has been here."[4]

Hart had continuously pricked the administration as president of the BSU, with a mission "to help make Winston-Salem State University a mentally Black university." Historical memory and scholarship places BSUs solely at HWCUs. However, HBCUs were not void of BSUs, an umbrella term for all of the groups *with multiple names* imbued with a black power ideology that united and served the academic, political, social, and cultural interests of students during the movement. Although more prominent at HWCUs, BSUs were also organized at HBCUs, where they were often more radical than SGAs, and thus jockeyed with them for the direction of the struggle. Some HBCUs, including Tougaloo, had more than one BSU of differing ideological persuasion, or they had BSUs that were coalitions of many of the student groups, such as Howard's *Ujamma* or Students United at Southern. In the initial years of the movement, in the mid-1960s, BSUs were more likely to lead the movement, such as the Students for Academic Freedom and Black Power Committee at Howard, SOUL at NC A&T, Central State's Unity for Unity, and the Informers at Grambling State (LA). By the end of the decade, some former directors of BSUs had been elected to run SGAs, sometimes pushing BSUs to the margins. Paine (Afro-American Alliance), Kentucky State (Black Student Unity), Alcorn State (Black Culture Society), and Fisk (Students for a Black University) are a few of the many HBCUs that had BSUs during the movement.[5]

Nevertheless, BSUs were more ostensible at HWCUs. Black campus activists were most likely to name their BSUs Black Student Unions—thus the reason for the use of this general appellation. The first known group to be named "Black

Student Union" materialized at SF State in March 1966, led by Marianna Waddy, Jerry Varnado, Benny Stewart, and Jimmy Garrett. SF State's Tricia Navara came up with the name "Black Student Union," which spread (sometimes through SF State organizers) to other institutions in California, including CSU Dominquez Hills, CSU Fresno, Mills-C, UC Santa Barbara, UC Davis, UC Riverside, and USC. The term moved along the Pacific Ocean into Oregon and Washington and then made its way east, appearing in Utah, Kansas, Kentucky, and upstate New York. Presumably Columbia's Students Afro-American Society, founded in 1964, popularized the name Afro-American Society, which many organizers along the Atlantic Ocean borrowed, particularly in Massachusetts and Rhode Island. Generally, black campus activists were likely to name their BSUs after existing prominent groups in the area. Black Student Association was trendy in Illinois (Illinois Wesleyan, North Central, Roosevelt, Southern Illinois, Edwardsville, and U-Illinois) and Michigan (Michigan State, Northern Michigan, and Eastern Michigan). In the St. Louis area, most BSUs were named the Association of Black Collegians, a popular title in the Lehigh Valley of Pennsylvania as well.

Black campus activists publically announced the founding of BSUs at press conferences, campus forums, on circulars, and in student newspapers, disturbing white colleges and universities. Ten weeks after students founded the Carleton-C (MN) BSU in the fall of 1967, two college officials claimed that "a major change, some might call it a revolution, has taken place on campus." The change was a growing awareness of the "Negro's presence," as black students sought to end the standardization of their exclusion. Organizers often knew they were part of a national social movement. The founding of the Afro-American Association at U-Alabama emanated from a "national trend," executive Angela Jones explained in 1968.[6]

The spokesmen and spokeswomen and their founding constitutions proclaimed eight interrelated but distinct functions for BSUs at black and white institutions. A minority of BSUs contained only one or all eight of these functions. Most expressed a few, usually determinant of the ideology of the organizers, the number of black students, and the nature and location. First and most often, BSUs were guided by black suasion, like other black power organizations at the time. Students founded BSUs to unite and raise the consciousness of the black student body, which was why many started as study groups. Monmouth's BSU in Illinois sought to "unite the black students on campus" and discuss and make them aware of the problems of the day. At Kentucky State (an HBCU) in 1972, the BSU endeavored to "create black awareness, promote black pride, and maintain black unity."[7]

Second, and most practically, students established these BSUs at HWCUs to help them "survive the white college experience," as articulated at Franklin-C in Indiana in 1970. Students who "could find no security in the white cotton fields of Claremont Colleges" founded the BSU, said President Franklin Peters in 1969. U-Northern Iowa students "banded together to make it easier to survive on this malevolent campus," wrote Dwight Christian in 1969. Third, solving the black student identity crisis emerged as the major inaugural purpose of a few groups. This crisis took on different forms. At American-U, this crisis stemmed from a yearning for self-love and self-awareness, which related to the initial purpose. "For Negroes, the trend has been assimilative integration...the sponge theory," Foster posed. "We're trying to ring the sponge out." In the process of exploring their blackness and Africanity through black power principles, literature, and speakers, another identity crisis oftentimes surfaced: the contradiction of the contemporary ideas of blackness—socially responsible, working class centered, politically and culturally nationalist—and the hypothesized historic notions of student identity—bourgeois, socially irresponsible, and politically and culturally assimilationist. The Black Capitalism Movement escalated the identity crisis, along with those activists who regularly told black students that their campus activism was either irrelevant to the black struggle or not as relevant or revolutionary as community activism. Grassroots altruism resolved this crisis for many black students—the attempt to make their colleges vehicles of grassroots community change (with them at the steering wheel). Thus, they called for politically radical, culturally oriented, socially responsible Black Universities at HBCUs and Black Studies at HWCUs.[8]

BSUs also strove to "perpetuate the interests of blacks on campus," as the founders of a group at U-Arkansas at Monticello stated. Impregnated with the black power principle of self-determination, black campus activists based this fourth function on the assumption that no one on campus—not administrators, faculty, staff, or other students—no one had their interests in mind or could address them like they could. Twenty-two black students at Franklin & Marshall (PA) unanimously voted in the spring of 1967 to form a group to "speak for our collective interests," according to their leader, Ben Bowser. Correlated to the fourth function, but taking an activist step, a fifth function of BSUs was to create a relevant collegiate experience through the institution of "black reforms," which the BSU at Marietta-C (OH) announced in its circular in March 1969.[9]

Sixth, black campus activists formed BSUs to serve as an instrument of incorporation into campus life, usually at institutions where they had a small number of African Americans. This organizational mission initially guided the BSUs at Utica-C in upstate New York and Morningside-C (IA). Utilizing the civil rights code of white suasion, some BSUs formed to promote and enlighten their HWCUs about African American history and culture so as to decrease prejudices and racism. This seventh purpose imbued BSUs at colleges with relatively small black populations, such as C. W. Post Campus of LIU, Clarke-U in Iowa, Thiel-C (PA), and Guilford-C (NC), where founders struggled to get "the white student to know the Negro and his problems" in 1968. Finally, pioneers of BSUs at institutions near large black populations functioned to relate to, support, and serve off-campus black communities, such as Case Western Reserve's AAS in Cleveland.[10]

Each BSU tended to give prominence to different functions. Similarly, each black campus activist gave his or her attention to the functions that mirrored his or her ideology. The radicals often gave their energies to the BSUs' community projects and campus activism, while many militant moderates spent their time educating whites and addressing their identity crises. Black campus activists of differing ideologies were generally united on the BSU duties of black suasion, serving black student interests, and effecting relevant campus reforms, although they sometimes differed on the tactics and goals. Initially, these points of unity eclipsed the areas of divisiveness. However, there were always internal ideological conflicts in BSUs that only grew as the BCM rose in stature and tenure.

Although there were some city-wide, state-wide, and region-wide alliances, BSUs were fervently autonomous, focused on the campus and local community. As Marshall-U (WV) junior John Shellcroft explained in March 1969, "The Black United Students organization is a local campus group with no national ties other than the bond of black skin." There were a few national black student organizations in the late 1960s and early 1970s, most prominently SOBU and NABS, formed in the spring and summer of 1969, respectively. SOBU, which eventually changed its name to Youth Organization for Black Unity, focused (not totally though) on off-campus matters, particularly Pan-African projects, and the NABS provided a "national and international forum...to articulate the legitimate demands of blacks students," explained its national coordinator Gwen Patton.[11]

As BSUs at HBCUs have been historically overlooked as components of the BCM, so too have black SGA presidents at HWCUs. They were elected at Occidental (Don Cornwell) and St. Olaf in Minnesota (Lee Oliver) for the 1968–1969 academic year and at Ursuline in Ohio (Renee Jones) for the following school year. Probably the most heralded (and most improbable) SGA president at an HWCU was Harry Walker, who sported a large Afro, adored Malcolm X, and had been a BSU president at U-South Carolina. Walker became the first black SGA president at a former confederate school in March 1971.[12]

Demands

Demands were as varied as the prime functions of BSUs and the ideologies of SGA presidents. Nonetheless, most of the BSUs and activist SGAs in the early years of the movement (1965 to 1967) issued requests, concerns, and grievances through normal academic channels. The racist remarks to their requests, the slow pace of academic change, or rejections alienated many students from traditional channels by 1968 and 1969. As a preface to their list of demands in December 1969, the BSU at U-Pacific (CA) quoted the US Declaration of Independence: "In every state of these oppressions we have petitioned for redress in the most humble terms: our repeated petitions have been answered only with repeated injury." In the demands at Duke in February 1969, black campus activists shouted, "WE HAVE EXHAUSTED THE SO-CALLED 'PROPER' CHANNELS." Quoting Frederick Douglass in their demands, who said the "limits of tyrants are prescribed by the endurance of those they oppress," U-Houston students proclaimed, "our endurance is exhausted." In March 1969, Sally Smith of Mills-C in Oakland told reporters, "we felt we weren't getting anywhere, so we decided to turn our requests into demands."[13]

Demands did not merely surface due to the BSU members' or SGA leaders' growing conception of the irrelevant and racist constitution of higher education. Black campus activists were inspired to issue demands by hearing about other demands, traveling speakers, conferences, and Black Cultural Weeks. They materialized after an off-campus African American tragedy, such as Bloody Sunday or King's assassination, or an on-campus act of racism. The attack on black students at an ROTC demonstration at New Mexico State prompted the issuance of demands in April 1969. Two crosses were burned at U-Mount Union (OH) in March 1970, sparking demands from black students. Most of demands of the movement were presented from the day after King's assassination through the end of the spring 1969 semester.[14]

Almost all administrators despised the term "demand," which asserted a level of black student power they were unwilling to concede in highly hierarchical academia. Black campus activists usually wrote out their demands in essay format or as a simple numbered list. At HWCUs, they regularly addressed the demands to the president. The demands were more likely to be targeted to the trustees and governors at HBCUs, since black campus activists were adept at speaking directly to power. Sometimes they announced their demands at a press conference, campus rally, in a campus forum, in the student newspaper, or during a protest.

*   *   *

Demands at HBCUs were very similar. It was not rare for students to submit fifty-page reports, such as at U-Maryland-Eastern Shore, or more than fifty grievances, such as at Virginia Union. First and foremost, HBCU activists demanded some derivative of what came to be known as a "Black University." Generally, they asserted that whites controlled the existing "Negro University," which was the enemy or unsupportive of the struggle for black power. It merely graduated bourgeois conservative students removed from African American culture. Instead, a Black University would connect students to African American culture, imbue them with a social responsibility to aid or lead the black masses, and be a chief institutional participant in the BPM.

"The black student is being educated in this country as if he were being programmed in white supremacy and self-hatred," began Ernest Stephens, a Tuskegee student, in a spring 1967 article. "How long will it be before black leaders and educators take hold of Negro colleges and transform them from 'training schools for Negroes' into universities designed to fit the real needs of black people in this nation?" Also, that February 1967, a recently formed Black Power Committee at Howard presented the "Black Power Manifesto," which called for the "overthrow of the Negro college" and its replacement by "a militant black university which will counteract the white-washing black students now receive in 'Negro' and white institutions." Suggesting that Howard be renamed after Nat Turner or Marcus Garvey, they wanted it to emphasize "subjects more pertinent to the present and future demands of the black struggle in America and the world."[15]

HBCU activists demanded the firing of paternalistic, dictatorial presidents who they felt were controlled by southern segregationists. They desired presidents who would lead the transformation of their colleges into Black Universities. Students demanded the desegregation of all-white trustee boards that reigned over most of their colleges like colonial officials at the dawn of the BCM. As their white peers at HWCUs did, HBCU activists wanted student power. They demanded more-powerful SGAs and student involvement in decision-making bodies. Black Studies courses, programs, departments, and curriculums were demanded. They wanted their dorms, dining halls, classroom buildings, athletic fields—everything on campus—to be renovated, at least to the level of facilities at HWCUs. As they had for the last forty years, they wanted better food and service in the cafeteria. They demanded improved recreational, transportation, and medical services, and enhanced campus offices, such as the registrar's and financial aid office. At many HBCUs, activists wanted extended library hours, and they also demanded more black books. Some black campus activists required the rehiring of fired progressive white faculty, while at other HBCUs, including Fisk, they desired the ejection of all whites. Generally, they demanded better credentialed black faculty, whereas also demanding faculty power and a clear system based on merit (as opposed to loyalty to administration or religiosity) for their hiring, firing, and tenure.[16]

* * *

During the formative years of the movement at HWCUs, as civil rights shifted to black power, black students requested the desegregation of white Greek organizations, desegregation of nearby campus businesses that did not cater to black students, and open campus and community housing measures. However, their most notorious demand, their most impassioned demand, their most concerted demand was for more black students. Every other desire pivoted off of this one at HWCUs, in the same vein that every demand at HBCUs encircled the Black University. Practically every single set of demands (and there were hundreds issued at HWCUs) listed a demand for more black students. "The unusually small number of black…students here frustrates our attempts to obtain a meaningful liberal arts education relevant to the society we live in today," Skidmore-C (NY) activists said in 1971. Some BSUs wanted their collegiate composition to represent the racial demographics of the city, state, or nation, such as at CSU Fresno and Stetson-U in Florida. Others directly demanded quotas, including Brown and Pembroke activists in 1968, who demanded 11 percent, equivalent to the national black population. Related to this demand, black campus activists also demanded the active recruitment of black students and that they be involved (or in control of) that process.[17]

Demonstrating their grassroots altruism, BSUs frequently demanded students from "hard core, poor areas," to use the language of Illinois Wesleyan activists in 1969. Sometimes BSUs resisted calling these students "disadvantaged," such as at U-San Francisco in 1968. They demanded special remedial programs, financial aid, and scholarships, sometimes based not on academic performance, but on need, including at Goucher-C in Baltimore in 1970. Collegians at institutions such as UVA and Providence-C (RI) wanted application fees to be waived for blacks. Asserting that standardized tests were culturally biased, they demanded that the "SAT be waived for all black applicants," as activists at Wilmington-C of Ohio stated in 1971. At some institutions, radical BSUs demanded a special admissions criteria for black students, asserting, as Duke students did in 1970, that the present "criteria for entering black students are oriented toward white middle class students." Militant moderate BSUs were more likely to demand the hiring of a black admissions officer, who would not only review files from black applicants, but also effectively "sell" their colleges to black students, as Millsaps-C (MS) activists desired in 1970. They also requested student exchange programs with HBCUs (John Hopkins and St. Cloud State were examples), funds for recruiting weekends to host and convince potential applicants, and black orientation programs for entering freshman.[18]

After black admissions, the next two most popular demands were for BCCs and Black Studies in the form of courses, programs, and departments. It appears that Black Studies, specifically programs and departments, were more likely to be requested if an institution resided near a black population center or if it had a relatively large population of black students. In contrast, BCCs were more likely to be requested if the colleges were removed from black population centers or if they had a relatively low enrollment of African Americans. So even though historians have generally labeled Black Studies as the major programmatic demand, in reality BCCs were demanded nearly as often, if not more often. And students fought just as fiercely for them.

Black students envisioned BCCs as becoming the spatial nexus of black student life that would give them a social and cultural refuge—a place to cultivate their culture, display their culture to white students—or would run programs for the area black community. Its purpose depended on the guiding ideology of the BSU. To DePauw students in 1970, a BCC would serve as a "place to establish our cultural identity," while Middlebury students needed a place in 1972 to develop their "sense of community and solidarity," and UW Oshkosh activists desired that it "be a place apart" in 1968.[19]

Lying at the core of demands to bring literary relevance was Black Studies. Depending on the spectrum of their ideology and how much they uncovered the normalized mask of whiteness, students conceptualized their total curriculums as White Studies, or the departments, courses, or literature as Eurocentric. In 1969, Colorado State students described their education as "tragically irrelevant and vulgarly whitewashed," and they deplored the blatant white nationalism and a curriculum that taught all aspects of European civilization, while dismissing people of African descent. "When the focus in these classrooms is almost exclusively Western and white...and almost never black, dissatisfaction among those students with historical and cultural roots which are not white and European is inevitable," wrote Barbara Smith of Mount Holyoke (MA) in 1968.[20]

Black Studies would not merely have materials "relevant to their culture," as expressed by Roosevelt's BSA in 1969. Pioneers wanted it to "recognize the validity and the uniqueness of the new black perspective," according to U-Maryland-Eastern Shore activists in 1970, and to "equip us with the essentials necessary to combat the particular programs of black people," said the U-Houston group. Courses were more likely to be demanded by moderates from 1965 to the spring of 1968, while departments and programs were more likely to be demanded after the assassination of King, when radicals gained control of many BSUs. Radical

BSUs not only demanded Black Studies departments on the same level of existing departments, but periodically they demanded BSU (or black community) control over the new department, including hiring and firing faculty at schools such as Creighton-U (NE) and Reed-C (OR). Or, as at U-Akron, black campus activists wanted a department "independent of the university hierarchy." Students argued for control based on the argument offered by SUNY Stony Brook student leader Calvin Canton. "A program for black [people] cannot be run by people who have oppressed us," he said in February 1969. Quite a few groups of BSUs, including that at Vassar, demanded Black Studies facilities situated off campus in black communities. At Stetson-U (FL), Beloit-C (WI), and Emerson-C (MA), black campus activists wanted a Black Studies course to be required of all students to "dispel the myths about the black man," asserted Stetson students.[21]

Some pressed against interdepartmental programs in which Black Studies faculty and courses would be cross-listed between Black Studies and another discipline. Nevertheless, many radical BSUs demanding departments had to settle for these interdepartmental programs with formally or informally cross-listed professors and courses with a Black Studies director. Even more activists had to settle for (or were satisfied with) the intrusion of black courses in existing departments.[22]

In practically every case, students demanded Black Studies courses taught by black faculty. That emerged as the ideal across the nation, even as they settled for white professors. Many thought the "validity" of those courses "taught by whites" was "questionable," to use the language offered at Saint Peter's (NJ) in 1969. Some, like the SF State BSU, thought it was impossible. Therefore, those BSUs that considered this impossible demanded the firing of white professors who taught some of the original Black Studies courses. At U-North Dakota, for instance, students disrupted a black history course in February 1969, pronouncing that it should not be taught by a "honkie." In July 1969, Stanford's BSU demanded that its new Black Studies program be black led and black taught. Even at HBCUs, more black faculty were demanded, including at Howard, where students asserted in 1970 that white faculty "stifle thoughts, stagnate imagination or curtail analysis of and by black students."[23]

Black faculty, aside from teaching Black Studies courses, became a key demand, since professors dictated the academic direction of a university, they could serve as advisers, and students wanted their presence to "set the stereotype of black people straight," expressed the BSU at Xavier-U in Cincinnati in 1969. Just as many BSUs wanted to control Black Studies programs and departments, they also wanted "a recognized, responsive, and representative voice in the hiring and dismissal" of black professors, as the Providence-C (RI) BSU indicated in 1971. Sometimes they demanded a voice in the personnel decisions of all faculty and often requested that professors they deemed "bigoted" be terminated, as at Chicago's Roosevelt. Black campus activists also listed in their demands the termination of racist HWCU presidents, while habitually demanding the firing of prejudiced nonacademic staff, such as financial aid counselors, secretaries, store clerks, and security officers. Routinely, when they demanded the firing of racist whites, they wanted them to be replaced by African Americans. Police harassment prompted many demands for black officers (or no officers at all).[24]

In addition to faculty changes, black campus activists regularly demanded black administrators. Black students, such as those at Wilmington-C of Ohio, felt that they "would be able to relate to black administrators with greater ease" and that black administrators comprehended black "students' needs and desires." Sometimes they simply preferred that an African American fill one of the existing administrative positions. More often, they demanded the creation of a new administrative post—vice president for minority affairs (Eastern Michigan), dean of black student affairs (Western Connecticut State), or a black ombudsman (Coe-C in Iowa)—generally what today is called a chief diversity officer. The BSA at Rensselaer Polytechnic Institute (NY) wanted the "black dean" to "have the final word on all black affairs on campus and [be] responsible only to the VP," echoing their peers across the nation. More likely they wanted the black dean responsible only to the president or the BSU.[25]

At HWCUs, black students demanded a few black trustees, including at UMASS Dartmouth, while at HBCUs they desired for the boards to be controlled by blacks. Black campus activists demanded one or several black counselors because, as an Angelo State student said in 1972, black students have no one that will sympathize with them and know the way they feel. Some BSUs, as at Duquesne-U in Pittsburgh in 1969, reported that they spent too much time counseling each other, and therefore full-time counselors for black students were needed so the BSU could shift its focus from "academic programs to community problems." Based on reasoning similar to that supporting their demand for black counselors, some groups of students demanded a black psychologist, including the Allied Blacks for Liberty and Equality in 1969 at Knox-C in Illinois, "in order to help in the adjustment of Black students."[26]

To ease the adjustment, collegians demanded black residence areas, usually black floors, as at U-Akron (OH), and sometimes an all-black, majority-black, or African American culturally themed dormitory. "As it is your duty to secure the physical and mental well being of every student at Chatham-U (PA), allow us our physical and mental well being by permitting us a separate residence for Black students" in order to avoid the "mental cruelty perpetuated against us in interracial dormitories," wrote the BSU in 1970. They often desired and received office space for BSUs, as at U-Nevada, decorated with African fixtures and posters of their icons, such as Muhammad Ali and Malcolm X.[27]

As HBCU students wanted longer library hours, HWCU students craved something of relevance to read in their libraries. Less likely were the demands for a black library, which occurred in 1971 at Grinnell-C in Iowa. Defiance-C (OH) activists asked for 15 percent of the library budget for black literature in 1970, while they demanded a portion of the library at Saint Peter's (NJ). Black students often requested (and were given) a role in the selection of black books. As black campus activists desired mental food in the library, they craved soul food and black cooks in the cafeteria at schools such as Roger Williams in Rhode Island and Pennsylvania's Slippery Rock. In order to sustain their diets and their livelihood, some BSUs, including the one at Truman State (formerly Northeastern Missouri State), demanded campus jobs for black students.[28]

Due to reports of professorial racism and knowledge that members of their groups were underprepared, BSUs demanded an overhaul of the grading system.

This overhaul included the mass termination of racist professors, a pass-fail system, or even the establishment of an inquiry committee to supervise grading, to be controlled by black students. Activists demanded the appointment of a BSU representative to the SGA, or a senate vote (or bloc) allotted to black students, as at U-South Alabama. BSUs demanded higher appropriations for their ambitious and expansive campus and community projects. Some groups demanded a separate budget allocation or financial autonomy, requesting the depositing of all black student fees into their accounts. Activists at U-Houston and Kalamazoo-C (MI) demanded fiscal independence; as the Colorado State students explained in 1969, "the concerns of the black student...will not be met by the monolithic student association."[29]

BSUs, including at Case Western Reserve, tried to support the Black Capitalism Movement, demanding that their colleges and universities buy goods from black firms. At Harvard and Princeton, they commanded divestment from South African companies and colonizers. BSUs almost always demanded amnesty for its members and frequently appealed for the honoring of black holidays, specifically the birthdays and death-days of Martin Luther King Jr. and Malcolm X. They demanded that their colleges supply relevant social activities, cultural events, speakers, and black grooming products. Like their fellow white students, black campus activists wanted representation on college committees, particularly those that impacted black student life, and disciplinary committees at schools like Northeastern Illinois State, Cedar Crest (PA), and East Tennessee State. They also desired the creation of committees to address their demands and the dissolution of those committees if they did not meet their expectations. In March 1968, Indiana-U students demanded a new discriminatory practices committee "composed and approved by Black students and faculty members."[30]

*　*　*

Particular black student groups made special demands. Initially, at institutions such as U-Texas at Austin, students demanded more black athletes, while at Grambling State, one of the smoothest NFL pipelines in the 1960s, students requested the reduction of athletic attention. For decades, the athletic departments at HWCUs had had a miniscule number of African Americans who frequently were great players. In the 1960s, as black students in general began enrolling in unprecedented numbers, so too did black athletes. But those athletes, like black students generally, found themselves in "brutally dehumanizing, educational and athletic environments," wrote Harry Edwards, a former athlete turned activist-professor. Black athletes faced incredible pressure to succeed, holding the weight of the coach, the school, and the black race on their backs. Vociferously racist coaches assigned black athletes inferior housing and amenities, racially derided them, forced them to play injured, ordered them to trim their Afros and beards, herded them into "black" positions and sports, and misled them on scholarships.[31]

Calvin Murphy, an All-American basketball player, seriously considered leaving the U-Niagara in March 1968. He hated being called "boy." "The guys in the dorms—even the priests—call me this and don't realize what they are saying," said the future NBA Hall of Famer. "To me it's worse than being called nigger." White athletes called them niggers, coons, and jiggaboos six days a week, but on game day they wanted there to be team spirit. "In the social and educational areas of college life, the Black athlete is expected to function at a sub-human level. In athletics, he is expected to be super-human," Edwards disclosed. Obstructed by these two opposing expectations, black athletes dodged them repeatedly and scored athletic demands, supported by BSUs. They wanted more black athletes, cheerleaders, counselors, and especially coaches. They commanded equal treatment with their white teammates. They advocated for the firing of racist coaches.[32]

Athletic directors and coaches were usually highly resistant to the demands, and in many cases they refused to acknowledge that discrimination existed. At Michigan State in April 1968, black athletes gave their list for black coaches, cheerleaders, athletic employees, and a black academic counselor to Athletic Director Clarence "Biggie" Munn. He scanned the list, chuckled, and crossed the demands out one by one. When Munn finished, he smiled and said, "Ho, ho, I guess you want a black ticket manager or something." The black athletes boycotted practices—the common protest tactic (along with boycotting games) used by athletic activists—until the administration took positive steps to address their concerns.[33]

Seminary students demanded and protested for a relevant and socially responsible seminary experience with more black-oriented courses and black professors, inspired by James Cone and the Black Theology Movement. Fifty seminarians took hold of the administration building at Union Theological Seminary (NY) on May 12, 1969, in support of SNCC international affairs director James Forman's call for reparations in his 1969 "Black Manifesto." Twenty-four hours later, the students exited the building with officials having agreed to invest $500,000 in the Harlem community and raise another $1 million to be put at the disposal of the seminary's black community. Black medical and law students formed campus and sometimes national organizations to improve their lot in the academy, while psychology students established the active Black Student Psychology Association. Black graduate students organized and demanded more of their own at schools such as UCLA, John Hopkins, and U-Oregon. In general though, black campus activists tended to support the particular demands of their subset, while not losing sight of the larger black student challenge to higher education.[34]

* * *

With booming endowments and student populations in the 1960s, urban HWCUs continued to expand, encroaching on nearby black communities that resisted the expansion. Either community members approached BSU leaders or black campus activists independently became aware of the discord. Most BSUs formally or informally requested or demanded the termination, slowing, or altering of this encroachment, and improved community relations, facilities, and services for locals. Sometimes guided by the student-labor coalition fomented by student

Marxists at the time, but more often guided by a black campus nationalism, students demanded better conditions for black nonacademic workers and campus construction workers, and aided them during their strikes.

BSUs even demanded that their white colleges and universities produce a public statement acknowledging their institutional racism and pledging to eliminate it, the origin of the now popular diversity statements. Ohio's Wittenberg faced this request, along with Emory, whose president did announce that "racism exists" and pledged to cooperate with students, faculty, and administrators to "openly commit themselves to its eradication." In Northwestern's thirteen-page agreement in 1968, signed by seven school officials, the university confessed that "it has had in common with the White community of America the racist attitudes that have prevailed historically in this society."[35]

*   *   *

BSUs made sure to emphasize the urgency of their demands. They often gave administrators a week, two weeks, a month, a year—some timeline to respond to or implement their requests. Sometimes, the demands were classified as "non-negotiable," which, on top of the term demand, particularly unnerved administrators. Some BSUs refused to negotiate or to settle, feeling their academic freedom was at stake. "We will not sit here and submit. We will not sit here and conform. We will not sit here and be controlled," the BSU at St. Benedicts and Saint John's in Minnesota declared in its demands in 1970. "We know what we want and we are fighting for our survival. THEREFORE, WE WILL NOT ACCEPT A SLICE OF BREAD BECAUSE WE WANT THE LOAF."[36]

However, administrators habitually forced them to accept the slice, arguing the loaf was impossible, too expensive, against the law, reverse discrimination, or in opposition to academic freedom or the values of the colleges. Usually before the deadline imposed by BSUs and SGAs, presidents responded to the demands, sometimes with line-item replies after a marathon of faculty and administrative meetings. On other occasions, presidents and trustees requested meetings with BSUs, in which they deliberated (sometimes peacefully, more often combatively). Most presidents and faculty members responded to demands with the creation of diversity task forces or black student or Black Studies committees. BSUs usually contested the composition of these task forces or committees.

Customarily, administrators and BSUs exchanged letters on their demands. This occurred at Colby-C in Maine during a weeklong takeover of the college chapel in March 1970. Colby-C president Robert E. L. Strider dispatched a letter saying the college had made progress on their concerns through existing channels, demands closed rather than open doors, and the college could not engage in useful kinds of discussion during a takeover—the standard tripartite response of administrators. "Obviously, we would not now be in the CHAPEL if we were confident in the administrative mechanisms that you have instituted to bring about change," the black students responded. They took issue with the president's classifying of their demands as "complex problems." "There is nothing at all complex about the five demands," they wrote. "The complexity lies in your inability to free yourselves from the administrative paternalism and red tape which might unduly complicate a matter that is quite simple." They also argued that "the perpetuation of racism 'occasions disruption' of normal human development," which is why they felt justified in their disruptive occupation. "The matter of illegal trespass in the Chapel is pitifully irrelevant when compared to the matter of man's illegal trespass against human dignity."[37]

The issuance of demands during protests was more the exception than the rule, as BSUs tended to only protest as a last resort. HWCU presidents usually gave in to the demands for more black students, administrators, counselors, faculty, library books, office space, and Black Studies courses. When they did, they regularly claimed that they acted with more haste for a plan they had already devised to publicize noncoercion. HBCU presidents and trustees often agreed to extend library hours and curfew, and to offer more Black Studies courses and books, and better campus services and facilities. Administrators typically rejected demands for quotas, a separate admissions or grading criteria, firing of racists, Black Studies departments, black dorms, discontinuing expansion, requests relating to campus workers, black holidays, divestment, financial BSU or SGA autonomy, or black student control of anything.

Usually, BSUs and SGAs refused to let administrators' rejections end their struggle. Their language in letters and statements became more forceful, but they were frequently using a different language than administrators were. Administrators spoke about illegality, rationality, gradualism, and hope. Black campus activists shouted moral validity, racism, immediacy, and tangibility. Both sides usually hunkered down in the trenches. Not for long though. BSUs and SGAs regularly dashed out of their trenches and charged forward with protests.

Protests

BSUs and SGAs not only set deadlines as to when they wanted demands to be addressed. They frequently issued indirect or direct threats of protests if they were not satisfied with the responses. Deadline days or days when negotiations fell apart were some of the tensest days on college campuses from 1965 to 1972. Students, faculty, and administrators with urban rebellions and protests on other campuses in the forefront of their minds braced for the inevitable, braced for the academic apocalypse, braced for the end of the beginning.

If a dramatic act of campus racism had not stirred up the moderates to protest or a deadline had not committed them, then the "doubletalk," lying, paternalism, racism, or condescending posture of negotiators did the trick, to the pleasure of the radicals. Most protests, though, seemed to be relatively spontaneous affairs decided within minutes, hours, or days. But some, usually the more effective ones, such as those at Cornell and SF State, were planned for weeks and months in advance. The building takeover became the most famous type of protest associated with the campus activism in the late 1960s and early 1970s. On a few occasions, black students took over multiple buildings, as at Howard in 1969. Black campus activists seized an entire campus at LeMoyne-Owen in November 1968 and at

City College of NY in the late spring of 1969. Nevertheless, they were more likely to barricade themselves inside an office or floor than a building or campus.[38]

Black campus activists, often in the early morning, snuck into campus buildings carrying books, sleeping bags, records, and food, and forced out workers with threats and sometimes small fights and weapons. Then they barricaded all of the doors and announced to the campus community that they would not leave until their demands were met. They did not allow anyone into the buildings and took their posts at windows and doors to ensure safety for the occupiers. Often, the students plastered the inside and outside of the buildings with signs of resistance. While inside occupied buildings, black students usually did their homework, played cards, read, listened to music and speeches, debated, debated some more, laughed, laughed some more, grew nervous and more nervous. During the Howard takeover of the administration building in March 1968, the twelve hundred students controlled the university switchboard and served a "heavy diet of Black culture ranging from...African chants to *The Autobiography of Malcolm X* and the contemporary blues of Aretha Franklin." Often "traditional" gender roles played out—with the men on guard and the women preparing food. Or gender divisions were executed, as at Hampton in April 1969, when female and male occupiers stayed on different floors. BSU and SGA members spent more of their time drawing up demands, manifestos, and press releases, occasionally stepped out of the buildings for press conferences or rallies, and deliberated with their negotiators or negotiated with administrators. Takeovers lasted a few hours, days, or weeks.[39]

Students not only changed higher education by means of building takeovers. Building takeovers changed students. Before participating in the takeover in April 1968 at Columbia, one tense, unnamed sophomore from the South had been a regular in the university's counseling office, discouraged academically and estranged socially. She had made few friends and walked around campus with a straight and dejected face, and even straighter hair. A month after the building takeover, she looked almost unrecognizable to the counseling therapists. She had a large Afro. Her face was bright and alert. She looked completely at ease. She had been "completely swept up by the sense of friendship, closeness and belonging which prevailed in the occupied building," wrote a therapist. Paula Giddings, a participant in the building takeover at Howard in March 1968, "got a new sense of self, a new sense of my black self, in terms of culture, in terms of politics, in terms of the rights to demand certain things, the right to feel good about yourself."[40]

*　*　*

Black students employed their early 1960s tactic of a sit-in during the BCM, demanding to be served a relevant education at many institutions, including Radcliff-C in December 1968. Unlike during the takeovers, during sit-ins black campus activists did not close off buildings, floors, or offices. They simply sat there and commanded movement on their demands before they moved, generally allowing normal activities to continue.[41] When they were not taking over campus spaces or employing the sit-in, they were using the tactic campus activists had used throughout the LBSM. They struck at the heart of the racial constitution. The most notable and longest student strike in American history disrupted SF State for almost five months beginning on November 6, 1968. During quite a few strikes, black campus activists did not merely stay away from classes. They held campus rallies, picketed, negotiated with administrators, kept up with their class work, and often disbanded classes. Similar to a strike was a campus walk-out, which protesters utilized at Kent State and Clemson. Most of the black students dramatically left the campus in unison, pledging to stay away until their demands were addressed.[42]

Black campus activists staged numerous campus protest rallies and marches at places such as Marshall-U (WV) and George Washington (DC). They picketed campuses and disrupted athletic games at Lehman-C (NY) and Northern Michigan. Bowdoin-C (ME) students engaged in a silent protest for a few days in February 1970, while some BSUs silently sued universities. Students disrupted convocations, services, registration, concerts, and faculty meetings, often to recite their demands. For example, days after King's assassination, Stanford held a racism convocation, a common occurrence at the time. Suddenly, seventy black students rose up in unison and walked on stage, and one of them snatched the mike from the shocked provost. "Put your money where your mouth is!" BSU chair Kenny Washington yelled and then gave the mike to another BSU member who read ten demands.[43]

Sometimes students took school officials hostage for several hours. Often, they would not allow the president, administrators, or trustees to leave their offices or meeting places until they gave in to their demands. Activists burned remnants of what they considered campus racism. A dozen students at Wesleyan soaked four copies of the college's 1968 yearbook in gasoline and set it on fire. "The Olla Pod reflects the white Western racist orientation of Wesleyan which seeks to deny the existence and unique expressiveness of the black world," the AAS wrote in a statement. As other activists had, Beloit-C (WI) students burned an effigy of the president and other items on successive days in spring 1969. During their December 1969 drive to rid Fisk of whites, black campus activists burned the automobile of historian Theodore Currier, who had been at the college for so long he had taught John Hope Franklin in the 1930s. Years later, Franklin torched the students in his memoir. "At Fisk, of all places, some students were involved in some of the shoddiest activities imaginable, all done in the name of the students' rights and civil rights."[44]

However, that was not the extent of the burnings. Activists started fires at Lane-C (HBCU in TN) in March 1969 before burning a building to the ground. And they inflamed three buildings at Paul Quinn (HBCU in TX) in the summer of 1970. Bombs destroyed property at Bluefield State (WV) in November 1969 and at Hampton in May 1971. Violent disruptive rebellions, or riots, gripped many historically black institutions, such as Prairie View A&M in February 1971. Rampaging students also gutted offices. On January 13, 1969, about fifteen students at Queens-C (NY) ransacked the office of Joseph P. Mulholland, the director of the college's Search for Education, Elevation, and Knowledge (SEEK) program. Around 3:25 p.m., they brushed by four employees in the outer office, who swiftly left, and charged into the main office. The Black and Puerto Rican activists picked up the director's desk, a metal conference table, and eight chairs, carried them out of the room, and down a long corridor. They exited the building with furniture in hand and dumped the pieces between two parked cars on the asphalt like it was trash. Meanwhile, other students tore out phones and ripped down pictures. When the fifteen students were done, they left the room almost completely empty except for the green carpet littered with their debris.[45]

One of the most popular movies among black campus activists was the 1966 film *The Battle of Algiers*, which was based on urban guerilla warfare used during the recent Algerian revolution. Some students read Ernesto "Che" Guevara's *Guerilla Warfare* or Robert Taber's *The War of the Flea* on rural guerilla warfare in Cuba. Therefore, it was not surprising that activists utilized disruptive guerilla tactics during the movement. They demonstrated that campus normality would not proceed until their desires were granted. In May 1968, CSU Fresno students verbally harassed the president, uprooted parking lot trees, set small fires, jumped into public fountains, and painted classroom doors black. During the Brandeis-U (MA) building takeover in January 1969, five black women wearing bandanas paced into the reserve room at the library. One activist told the students there to sit down and "nobody will get hurt." Another went to guard the door with a piece of wood. After closing the window drapes and ripping out the phones, the students scattered more than two thousand books and periodicals before a library worker forced them out. A little over a month later, about fifty black men at Rutgers and a slightly larger number of women at Douglass entered their dining halls, stacked their trays with food, dumped the food on the floor, and left. The next day, Douglass women abruptly walked out of classes, yelled insults at instructors, ignored white students, locked bathroom doors, and stuffed toilets, while Rutgers men vandalized property, sent in bomb threats, and set minor fires.[46]

*   *   *

It was a rare occurrence that a protest did not lead to some promise of reform. Nevertheless, campuses that experienced protests also became virtual police states. Thus, reform and repression followed protests, diminishing their likelihood of reoccurrence and forever altering the racial *and* policing mechanisms of the institutions. It is not known how many protests were waged during the BCM. There is no available tally of the early years of the movement. Black campus activists disturbed more than 150 campuses during the 1967–1968 academic year with the vast majority of the disturbances occurring after the death of King. There were more than 250 protests during the climax year of 1968–1969, and more than 150 incidents the next year. Usually the more violent and the longer the student protest, the more successful. A protest at one college inspired a protest at another university and motivated administrators to pick up the pace on demands to prevent a protest. Said differently, not every institution experienced protests, but it is quite possible that administrators instituted the vast majority of racial reforms due to protests at their schools or at others, nearby or on the other side of the nation. Presidential files across the nation are beleaguered with reports on protests from other institutions.[47]

With several groups lined up in opposition, as discussed in the next chapter, black campus activists established their own support system. In addition to each other, BSU members usually had the support of white radicals, often in the campus chapters of the Students for a Democratic Society (SDS). White campus activists, whom SF State BSU members called "white mother country radicals," formed picket lines in front of seized buildings, educated white students on the demands through flyers and forums, and brought BSU members food and supplies, not to mention the staging of their own BCM protests. For example, in May 1968, about forty white students at Brooklyn-C were expelled, arrested, and charged with criminal trespassing for a sixteen-hour takeover of the registrar's office, during which they demanded one thousand more African Americans and Puerto Ricans by September. At a news conference, Brooklyn League of Afro-American Collegians president Orlando Pike, sporting a dashiki, said the demonstrators highlighted "the role that White people must play in the struggle for the emancipation of black people—to confront white racism wherever it may exist." Along with antiwar and student power activism, this confrontation and support for the BCM stood as a major pillar of the White Student Movement in the 1960s.[48]

Black campus activists received vital sustenance from black professors. No black professor contributed more to the BCM than young sociologist Nathan Hare, who was fired for his activism at Howard in 1967 and SF State in 1969, where he directed the nation's first Black Studies program. Most black professors, specifically younger faculty and those hired as a result of student activism, tended to be sympathetic, if not supportive, of the movement, pressuring colleagues to concede to demands, writing explanatory press statements and open letters, and joining protests. African American and Puerto Rican students banded together for joint programs and initiatives in demands and protests in New York. Thus there emerged Africana and Latino Studies programs and departments at institutions like SUNY Oneonta, and Baruch and Hunter of CUNY. In the Midwest and West, African Americans formed activist coalitions with Chicana/o, Asian, and Native American students. Black and Native American students issued a stinging statement of demands at South Dakota's Augustana-C in November 1969. "When the Red brethren tried to resist you called him savage and an animal. You brought the Black man from his native land to develop your ill-gotten gains. Yet we ask now for a little payment for our land and labor, and you set up committees! You, the good Christian people, did not form a committee to take the Red man's land or the Black man's labor." The most notorious actualization of these coalitions, what Jeffrey Ogbar terms "rainbow radicalism," occurred at SF State and UC Berkeley, where Third World Liberation Fronts formed in 1968, uniting the progressive black, Chicano/a, Latino/a, Asian, and Native American groups into factions that waged multimonth student strikes for colleges of Ethnic Studies.[49]

A sympathetic white administrator sometimes carried through with their demands or diffused protests. Radical and some liberal white professors aided black campus activists, as at Colgate-U (NY), where forty white professors joined a black student sit-in at the administration building in April 1968. "Why, that is, have we used this method to eliminate discriminatory practices from our fraternities? The answer is simple: Because no other methods have succeeded in eliminating these practices." Sometimes white alumni demonstrated support for the movement. For instance, three alumni of Marietta-C (OH) approached their president in May 1968 about recruiting more black students and faculty, and instituting Black Studies courses.[50]

The support of nearby black communities cannot be understated. Throughout the Brandeis-U (MA) takeover in January 1969, Boston community organizations, local schools, and parents supplied the students with food. "Now if we only had as much freedom as we have food," said one of the student leaders during the occupation. Possibly as focal as community support was the aid BSUs and SGAs received from each other. Tougaloo students raised money for jailed Tuskegee activists in the spring of 1968. On December 9, 1968, the BSU at U-Hawaii sponsored a rally in support of the SF State strike. Students dispatched letters of protest from Fort Valley State (GA), LSU, Paine-C (GA), and Xavier (LA) to the president of U-Texas at Arlington during the campus campaign to terminate the flying of the confederate flag and the singing of Dixie.[51]

The support from other students, nearby black communities, alumni, faculty, and administrators provided some refuge for the BCM. Because as soon as black students started complaining about the racial constitution of higher education, opposition and repression boomed in response. That opposition and repression only compounded as they organized BSUs and made demands, and exponentially expanded as black campus activists protested at hundreds of institutions across America. While black students shook higher education with the arms of protests, black students and their reforms were shook by the pairing arms of opposition and repression.

7

"Black Jim Crow Studies": Opposition and Repression

Minutes before the Cornell judicial board decided to reprimand three of the six black students involved in an earlier protest, the first of eleven fire alarms in nine dorms and two halls awakened the campus. In between alarms, at around 2:00 a.m. on April 18, 1969, a frantic black student called the police to report a six-foot-high cross burning on her dorm's front porch and the rock someone tossed through her front window. Black students were livid about the attacks on Wari, the black women's cooperative. For the rest of the day, rumors swirled about what they were planning. Everyone knew the racial bubble, which had expanded with each new cohort of black students over the previous few years, was about to burst. They just did not know when or where.[1]

It happened early the next morning. Members of Cornell's AAS seized Willard Straight Hall, the student hub of Cornell. By 7:00 a.m., AAS controlled the building, and white students in the Cornell SDS chapter were picketing the hall, chanting "the revolution has come…time to pick up the gun," echoing the popular mantra of the Black Panther Party. Settling in, AAS members called their parents, studied for upcoming exams, slept after a night of planning and partying, and contacted friends and urged them to join the occupation. Calls were coming into the hall, too, primarily from Cornell's vice provost, Keith Kennedy, who at around 9 a.m. made his way over to the hall along with Eugene Dymek, the head of campus security, and Cornell legal counsel Neal Stamp. They navigated through the SDS picket line. With a bullhorn, Dymek commanded the students to leave. During the exchange, black students heard a commotion from the rear of the hall. Everyone raced to the scene.

About ten white Delta Upsilon International Fraternity (DU) members had snuck into the Straight through unguarded rear windows to "liberate" the hall. As they reached the main lobby area and announced their intention to open the hall's front doors, AAS members sprinted out of rooms and corridors and ambushed them. "We're coming back! We're going to burn it down next time!" screamed a DU brother, as his small army retreated through rear windows. "If you do, then we will fill y'all with lead," replied a seething black student. During

Photo 9 *Heavily armed African American students leave Straight Hall at Cornell on April 20, 1969* (AP Photo/Steve Starr)

the next few hours, while a stream of telephone reports about copycat invaders unnerved them, AAS members smuggled guns into the hall for protection. What was planned as a festive, peaceful, and brief building takeover became an extended, apprehensive, and vehement seizure. DU students pushed Cornell student opinion behind the AAS occupiers, who in the early afternoon issued four demands: nullify the three reprimands, reopen the question of housing, and conduct thorough investigations of the cross burning and the DU attack.

The next morning, April 20, the national media arrived and calls by reporters kept a constant tune in the information office. Everybody wanted to verify leaked reports of the guns. The minds of Cornell officials were elsewhere though. It was Sunday, and all they could think about was forcing those students out before classes resumed on Monday. AAS and Cornell officials reached an agreement that afternoon: amnesty, a faculty motion for nullification of the reprimands, twenty-four-hour protection of the occupiers and the AAS's office, legal action against DU, a list of the invaders, and university assistance in securing legal help for AAS. During the final negotiations, students informed the administrators that they wanted to sign the agreement at their headquarters after a procession across campus. The administrators tried to disarm the black students. In the era of ostentatious self-defense, it proved impossible.

Eighty students lined up in military formation with women in the center, so they could be "guarded." "Breeches open, no ammo!" AAS president Edward Whitfield shouted. When word sprinted through campus that they were coming out, reporters and photographers sprinted to the entrance. Within minutes, the two hundred outside became two thousand. The heavy, wooden, rambling doors flew open. SDS members safeguarding the entrance scattered to the sides. One by one, at 4:10 p.m. on April 20, 1969, black students, brandishing their rifles, shotguns, knives, clubs, spears, and expressions of seriousness, victory, fear, and wonder, trotted out of the dark Gothic structure into a sea of bright cameras that latched onto their seventeen rifles and shotguns like leeches. "Oh, my God, look at those goddamned guns!" shouted Steve Starr, an *Associated Press* photographer, before snapping "The Picture," a Pulitzer Prize winner in 1970.

When the procession crossed the large porch of the building, SDS members raised clenched fists and cheered, while hundreds of onlookers watched, stunned into silence. They marched across the rolling Arts Quadrangle, over a gorge, and across a bridge to 320 Wait Avenue—the home of black students. People in cars and on foot abruptly stopped as the marchers approached, intoxicated with shots of amazement, confusion, and anger. When they reached the house, most of the students congregated on the porch. Riflemen took strategic positions on the steep lawn and steps, staring viciously at onlookers and reporters.

After hammering out some final details, Whitfield read the signed agreement to the press. When he finished, it was Eric Evans's turn. He pulled out a prepared statement, fixed his glasses, and faced the reporters. With his bandoliers crossing his chest and waist, his shotgun cradled in his left hand, and dozens of armed black students scattered on the lawn surrounding him, he proclaimed, "We only leave now with the understanding that the University will move fairly to carry out its part of the agreement that was reached. Failure on the part of the University to do so may force us to again confront the University in some manner."

The next evening, still reeling over the spectacle of guns, the Cornell faculty refused to sanction the "coerced" agreement. Many students rallied around the AAS, who lashed out with incendiary threats toward the professors. Several campus groups were armed or arming. There was talk about taking another building. With excruciating pressure coming from students, and the specter of police and student violence, the faculty reversed its earlier decision two days later, while also giving students more power and establishing an autonomous Black Studies department.[2]

The Monday morning after students exited the building, "The Picture" appeared on front pages around the nation. Although guns had been used by previous groups of black campus activists, it had never been displayed so publicly. State and federal politicians censured the AAS. Several Cornell professors resigned in protest, including Thomas Sowell, one of the college's few black faculty, saying he could not be a part of a college that was so "interested in its image—anything to keep the black students happy." The *Chicago Defender* characterized it as the most "frightful and damnable" demonstration of the year. Syracuse's daily newspaper worried that Cornell "provided the green light for similar groups on other campuses." The *New York Times* amazingly compared the AAS to the "jackbooted students" of Hitler's Germany.[3]

* * *

Black students at Cornell had to withstand opposition and repression seemingly coming from everywhere. The black and white press, African American professors and leaders, white administrators, students, faculty, politicians, campus judiciary, and security personnel all clamped down at some point on black campus activism at Cornell in the spring of 1969. Opposition and repression generated the protest in April 1969, and opposition and repression doggedly stalked the protest.

Black campus activists around the nation also had to face criminal courts, arrests, suspensions, expulsions, and police brutality during their effort to racially reconstitute higher education. White, Latino/a, Chicano/a, Asian, and Native American supporters and spectators were sometimes arrested, expelled, and brutalized by police seeking to end a black student protest. The storm of student activism that forever racially transformed the ideals of the academy had to endure a storm of opposition and repression that forever politically and culturally transformed the activists and established the academy as a policed state. Tens of thousands of students were rebuked, derided, suspended, expelled, harassed, beaten, arrested, jailed, injured, or killed in their determined effort (or as bystanders of the struggle) to change the racial contours of higher education. Many put their collegiate lives on the line and lost or nearly lost them. Some put their actual lives on the line and lost or nearly lost them. At the same time, though, black campus activists fought stridently against the opposition and repression alongside their fight to modify the academy. Thus, their activism persisted on two fronts—offensive protests to erect novel measures to diversify higher education and defensive protests against the reaction their activism produced. No depiction of the movement is complete without a discussion of this all-important rearguard, and the trauma and brutality black campus activists suffered, the way they sacrificed, the way they gave their lives to the struggle.

*   *   *

Early in the movement, HBCU students faced the bulk of the repression and opposition. For instance, one of the first black campus protests to become national news was headlined by what would become a familiar occurrence during the movement—brutality by Mississippi state troopers, many of whom, like other troopers and policemen across the South, were suspected KKK members. Troopers threw heaps of tear gas at one thousand protesting students and community members at Alcorn State in April 1966, and clubbed them with nightsticks and rifle butts. "Brutality! Brutality! Brutality!" a woman shouted at one point. The shout would reign throughout the BCM.[4]

It was particularly deafening in 1967, when students, engaged by an act of police harassment or brutality, rioted or battled it out with the police on or near at least three HBCUs, including a four-day urban rebellion in Nashville, a skirmish at Jackson State (where community activist Benjamin Brown, a 21-year-old bystander was killed), and an hour-long clash at Central State. At Texas Southern, after a three-hour stalemate with student snipers that lasted into the early morning of May 17, the police fired more than two thousand shots into the dormitory with rifles and carbines. After forty minutes of gunfire, which wounded at least one student, the police officers stormed the dormitory. One officer was shot and killed and two others were wounded during the swarm. The officers then ripped apart the dorm, hospitalized several students, and found three guns. With guns pointed at their backs, almost five hundred students were compelled to lie face down on the cold, wet ground before being arrested. In the morning, resentment resonated from the student body. "What can you expect?" one student told reporters. "To them we're just apes." Another indignantly said, "I'm sorry there wasn't but one of them killed." In June, the NAACP defended and got the charges dropped for the "TSU Five"—Trazawell Franklin Jr., 20, Floyd Nichols, 25, Charles Freeman, 18, Douglas Wayne Waller, 21, and John Parker, 20—who had been charged with first-degree murder and assault to murder, despite evidence of friendly fire. As it had throughout the LBSM, the NAACP came to the legal aid of black student activists, expelled or charged at schools such as Bluefield State (WV).[5]

Critics rebuked the student violence in 1967. The ACLU condemned activists for encroaching on the academic freedom of nonparticipants. The *Pittsburg Courier* editorialized in June 1967, "No amount of demonstration can take the place of good sound academic performance." Meanwhile, black campus activists at HWCUs were not immune. The NAACP executive director Roy Wilkins began his sequence of criticism in May 1967 upon hearing about the organizing of BSUs, calling it self-segregation and "puzzling, indeed."[6]

Throughout the movement, white students and faculty used similar language to censure BSUs as segregationist or isolationist and halted (or questioned) the founding of BSUs at numerous institutions, including Morningside-C (IA) and Boise State (ID). A campus newspaper editorial in May 1967 told the newly organized Trinity-C (CT) Association of Negroes to beware of "establishing an atmosphere of group separateness and confrontation." After the Cornell AAS formed that spring, one professor said, "There are many people here...who felt they had been fighting for integration so long, and they just couldn't turn themselves around that fast." Often these nascent BSUs produced even more controversy when they barred whites from speeches by black power activists, such as when Muhammad Ali spoke to only black students at UPENN on October 31, 1967. *The Daily Pennsylvania* labeled the white bar "flagrantly totalitarian behavior" and compared the Society of African and Afro-American Students (SAAS) to Nazis. "Equating Black societies in America with Nazism is a poorly constructed analogy," SAAS chairman pro tempore Billy Riley responded, "because the Nazis were oppressors, and we as Blacks are the oppressed."[7]

More often, BSUs organized two events for speakers: a publicized, open, formal speech to an interracial audience, and a clandestine, closed, informal discussion with black students. Opponents rebuked these closed meetings too, as they did any affair that prohibited whites (or was open, but clearly designed for blacks). Sometimes white students and faculty forced their way into these meetings. In September 1968, two Tulane-U (New Orleans) professors and twenty students staged a "reverse sit-in" of a black first-year orientation facilitated by the Afro-American Congress.[8]

Black nationalism and black power faced critiques as well, even from black students. To rebut Primus J. Mootry's piece at Chicago State declaring "we are

Afro-Americans," Chuck Riley claimed "this recently popularized term is a clever but inaccurate substitute for Negro," which "comes originally from Latin, a language used a couple thousand years ago." To Riley, "soul brother" and "black" were also "misnomers." Black and white students at HWCUs debated black power in newspapers in the early years of the movement. In November 1967, for instance, Madelyn Clark at Wilson, a women's LAC in Pennsylvania, declared her support for "black unity, identity, pride, and growth." Within a week, a "Wasp student" responded, "After having accepted the Negro as a 'thinking, creative HUMAN,' I have not been accepted by him." Many HBCU presidents and professors tried to distance themselves from black power. Spelman president Albert E. Manley, who gave a series of anti-black-power lectures in the fall of 1966, reasoned that "radical exponents of black power" were attempting "to substitute one form of racism for another."[9]

In effect, the fists of reaction lodged at black campus activists initially stemmed from their ideology and organizing. Some blacks were "puzzled" by this rejoinder from white students who had isolated and alienated them. On quite a few campuses, when BSUs did not bar whites, they did not come. When BSUs barred whites, they were critiqued. Often, these detractors conflated segregation, an involuntary domineering relationship, with separation, a voluntary act of solidarity. Black campus activists sometimes erringly used this language, undercutting their nationalistic arguments.

∗   ∗   ∗

1970s were seemingly conflated with HBCUs, having spent so much time on those campuses. In late October 1967, five hundred National Guardsmen descended onto a protest-ridden Grambling State (LA) campus, and twenty-nine students were dismissed—crippling the demonstrations and boycott. Guardsmen arrived in Orangeburg, South Carolina, after SC State students, embroiled in a battle to desegregate a nearby bowling alley, rioted and battled police on February 5, 1968. By February 8, roadblocks had been set up surrounding SC State, and students were urged not to leave. That night, students built a huge bonfire on campus, separating them and a massive line of hundreds of guardsmen, state troopers, and police officers. As Henry Smith, a tall sophomore, standing in front of the crowd attempted to put something into the fire, the officers began shooting for an unknown reason. Smith spun and crumbled to the ground. When the officers finally stopped shooting, three students— Smith and Samuel Hammond, both SC State students, and Delano Middleton, a local high school student—were dead and at least thirty-four were wounded, mostly in their backs.[10]

As when officers killed students at Jackson State in May 1970 and at Southern-U in November 1972, both covered in Chapter 5, upon hearing of the "Orangeburg Massacre," African Americans were furious. The presidents of six HBCUs in Atlanta wrote a letter to President Johnson, Attorney General Ramsey Clark, state governors, and law enforcement agencies urging them "to stop these invasions of college and university campuses by the American version of storm troopers." It did not stop. Two weeks after the Orangeburg Massacre, Mississippi police wounded six students at Alcorn State during a protest. Even though hundreds of students were jailed for nonviolent activism, the "storm troopers" in Mississippi and South Carolina did not have to pay for the killing and wounding of the students in criminal or civil court.[11]

*　*　*

On April 7, 1968, thirty-five members of Colgate's ABC occupied the Sigma Nu fraternity house for seven hours after residents shot at a black student. Still mourning the death of King, they threatened to "burn" the house "down," until the president agreed to close the fraternity house and investigate the shooting. It was just one of numerous occasions on which black campus activists faced harassment. A few nights after a black student protest at Bradley-U (IL), a DU member spit on Renee Grant as he drove by her in early May 1969. Not long after, all three hundred BSA members descended on the DU house "ready to burn it down." The perpetrator hid for two days, until he mustered up enough courage and swallowed enough pride to apologize to Grant. In late April 1968, reports of an Ohio State bus driver's mistreatment of two black women compelled seventy-five allegedly armed black students to hold various officials and secretaries in the administration building hostage for eight hours. Within a year, thirty-four protesters were each indicted on eleven felonies and one misdemeanor, including five counts of unlawful detention and conspiracy to unlawfully detain. It marked one of the most serious sets of charges ever filed against a group of student protesters—what Julian Bond called "an old Southern practice—lynching." As in the BPM more generally, many male black campus activists thought their masculinity rested on whether they defended "their women" from white racism. Harrassing a black woman became one of the quickest ways to arouse black male campus activism.[12]

Some black leaders were particularly loud in their condemnation of the BCM in the summer of 1968. Benjamin E. Mays, for one, rebuked black dorms, Black Studies, and demands for more black faculty as "working against Negro colleges" because they "would take away the best professors" and students. "I hope black students will ponder this." Black students did not have much time to ponder this. They were bombarded by the strengthening recoil from educators, newspapers, and politicians who were passing measures to curb their activism. As part of the now well-studied Counter-Intelligence Program (COINTELPRO), FBI director J. Edgar Hoover dispatched a message in 1970 to his staff. "Increased campus disorders involving black students pose a definite threat to the nation's stability and security and indicate need for increase in both quality and quantity of intelligence information." Active BSUs were investigated by the FBI, and the FBI kept a running list of prominent activists. Organizational, personal, and ideological conflicts within BSUs were exacerbated by the FBI. It sent forged letters to endanger BSU affairs and manipulated the press. The Bureau (as well as local and state police) recruited, employed, and deployed an army of spies (students and college employees) that collected data on student groups or thwarted their activities. A mole at Widener-U (PA) reported to the FBI that BSU members were "not engaged in any militant type of activity on campus." Administrators also had their spies and trackers. "Mary" reported on a black student dance attended by officers from area ABCs to the U-Missouri-St. Louis chancellor in September 1968. CSU Fresno officials apparently planted plainclothes officers on campus to follow black and Chicano activists in the spring of 1969.[13]

BSUs officers received hate mail and their dorm rooms were sometimes ransacked, which occurred at Luther, an Iowa LAC, in March 1969. Phillita Carney, after becoming the U-Utah's first black homecoming queen in October 1971, was happy "to see the shock on those sorority bitches' faces" and termed it an "opening for minorities." The story (and Carney's vulgar words) went national. "Better make that black bastard, bitch, take back what she said or she will be crowned, but not a QUEEN of any Homecoming event, we can assure you of that," stammered a white Chicagoan in one of many nasty letters mailed to the university. A "loyal Tennessee fan" teased, "This evidently was a tree climbing contest. This is the only possible way *it* could win" (italics added).[14]

In a letter addressed "to the NIGGERS," the "silent majority of Cal State Long Beach and the surrounding cities" expressed, "if this verbal harassment of white people does not stop, the B.S.U . . . will be exterminated." Sometimes the foes of the BSUs acted on their violent declarations. Three white students attacked Gene Locke at U-Houston on the morning of March 17, 1969. In retaliation, several students rampaged through campus and were later charged for the property damage. With mass opposition, charges against the UH Fourteen were eventually dropped (or they pled out). In revenge of five white students jumping a black male student in the presence of university police, about 250 Northern Illinois students went on a rock-throwing, window-breaking charge through campus on March 22, 1969. All of DeKalb's available policemen were brought in to restore order. In a statement, the black students declared, "The black student body wishes to serve notice . . . it will not tolerate or let go unnoticed any acts of violence committed on black people."[15]

After fielding threatening phone calls and dodging a bullet the week before, BSU vice president Paul Whiteurs was shot in the arm at U-South Alabama on March 9, 1971. "In my life, I have never had time to be afraid," Whiteurs avowed after the unsolved shooting. "My philosophy is like many people—if you have nothing worth dying for then you are already dead." Law enforcement officers also continuously harassed BSU leaders with some of the force they used to abuse black power figures off campus. According to an undated BSU flyer, a local assistant district attorney declared, "We are going to get those black students" at UC Santa Barbara.[16]

Similarly, the day before William Garrett of the Lawrence Police Department shot and killed Rick "Tiger" Dowdell, 19, on July 16, 1970, Garrett allegedly told his brother he was going to "get one of you Dowdells." Dowdell, a U-Kansas rising sophomore, walked out of the Afro-House, the BSU's new black cultural center, and soon after Garrett was chasing him in his car and then down an alley, where he discharged the fatal shot. In the small college town of Lawrence, the Dowdell black power activists were respected by the activist community and despised by the policing community, leading to many altercations. Rick Dowdell entered the struggle as a student activist at Lawrence High, staging a walkout there in September 1968 (around the time the KU-BSU developed). Paralleling the BCM, a similar movement emerged in high schools across America, in which many black campus activists received their first taste of black power.

Garrett claimed Dowdell shot first, while activists dubbed it a racist murder and gave the student activist the funeral of a martyr (just as students did for the other twelve youths killed during the BCM). The BSU vowed that the exonerated Garrett "shall reap what he has sown," and the death sparked a weeklong student uprising that eventually led to the police killing of a white KU student, Harry Nicholas "Nick" Rice, and the wounding of a black chemistry graduate student, Merton R. Olds. Unlike those at Orangeburg, Kent State, and Jackson State, the Lawrence tragedies flew under the national radar.[17]

* * *

When black campus activists were not being harassed, injured, or killed, they were being expelled and arrested, as at UW Oshkosh in late November 1968. For ransacking the president's office, nearly the entire black enrollment (about ninety students) was arrested and expelled in one of the largest mass expulsions of the movement at an HWCU, touching off several unsuccessful student protests for their reinstatement. Instead of using their hands to damage a building, students at Bluefield State in West Virginia let a bomb do the damage that month, leading to a few arrests.[18]

Arrests were often clamored for by white community members and alumni. When administrators showed restraint, as did Washington-U chancellor Thomas H. Eliot, who ended a ten-day sit-in in December 1968 with a peaceful agreement, they usually received a stack of fuming letters. "Put your foot down," ordered one commenter from his message. C. L. Husbands of Littleton, Colorado, declared the university was "no longer...worthy of the name Washington" due to its "ignoble surrender to the forces of riot and anarchy." An alumnus in St. Louis condemned Eliot's "outrageous concessions to inarticulate and illiterate Negroes."[19]

These writers probably desired someone like SF State president S. I. Hayakawa, a Japanese American semanticist, who took over for the more liberal Robert Smith in late 1968 as the embattled college's third president that year. Hayakawa instituted new rules for the college, including the banning of amplification equipment and noon rallies. Strikers ignored the rules on December 2, 1968. When Hayakawa heard the usual early morning strike refrains amplified from a sound truck, he stormed out of his office with mimeographed copies of his "emergency regulations," followed by police, photographers, and reporters. He leaped onto the top of the truck, tried unsuccessfully to snatch the microphone out of the white students' hands, then he looked around madly until he saw the wires of the amplifier. He grabbed at them until the sound stopped. Some students tried to remove Hayakawa. "Don't touch me, I'm the President of this college!" A crowd hurriedly gathered to watch their odd new president before the police arrived and hustled him back to his office. The national media caught and reported the entire scene. With that single spontaneous act, Hayakawa became the symbol of presidential sturdiness, the most popular reactionary president of his day, who projected himself as a pillar that could not be pushed or swayed by the BCM. BSU leader Jerry Varnado would later say, "He would never have dared to do that to us. We would have trampled all over him."

The next day—December 3, 1968—turned out to be even worse at SF State. On Bloody Tuesday, as it has been designated, the police had a new directive—prevent any large congregation on campus. In the morning, officers arrested and clubbed fifty picketers and chased one of them into the cafeteria, where they smashed more students. A white male student was hauled out with blood streaming from his face. When an enraged crowd mobilized at the administration building upon hearing about the cafeteria brutality, the police scattered and clubbed them too. After the regular noon rally, students marched on the Behavioral Science building. Hundreds of police officers stopped their advance with batons, impelling a colossal battle at the center of campus. Students used pieces of campus furniture as weapons. Over the campus loudspeaker, Hayakawa ordered students to disperse. "If some of you want to make trouble, stay right there. The police will see that you get it." Hayakawa was not lying. Four officers jumped Don McAllister, a black student, creating a gash that bled profusely and almost killed him. Collegians caught so savagely by police clubs that they could not get up were thrown into paddy wagons. Two ambulances made runs to the hospital. At an afternoon press conference, after the ferocious melee, Hayakawa praised the police for their "restraint and professionalism" and declared, "This has been the most exciting day of my life since my tenth birthday, when I rode on a roller coaster for the first time!" The press stood stunned. Conservatives applauded. Sore strikers were enraged. Hayakawa's quote symbolized the unapologetic militarism of some presidents in 1968.[20]

*   *   *

Weeks later, during a twenty-four-hour takeover of the U-Minnesota administration building in January 1969, activists turned a fire house on counterdemonstrators who had brandished white supremacist signs and shouted epithets such as "go home and take a bath." White students ridiculed protesters or tried to end protests at UC Santa Barbara in October 1968 and at UW Madison in February 1969. Some of those counterdemonstrators at UW Madison were members of the right-wing Young Americans for Freedom (YAF) and wore "H" armbands to identify with Hayakawa, a former student. YAF members and conservative students in other groups, such as the Young Republicans and the John Birch Society, tried to slow the BCM at several other institutions, including CSU Stanislaus and Marquette in Milwaukee. At Delta State (MS), white students cheered and sang "Dixie" on March 10, 1969, when the police arrived to arrest rebelling campus activists.[21]

Hayakawa probably cheered on January 23, 1969. During an illegal campus rally, police arrested more than four hundred SF State strikers, including Nathan

Hare and almost the entire leadership of the BSU and its allying groups, and charged them with at least three misdemeanors. Police used every paddy wagon in the city for the biggest single arrest in San Francisco history. Meanwhile, threats from the BCM detractors rose in volume in early 1969. The House Special Education Subcommittee held hearings on student unrest in February. Roy Wilkins threatened to sue institutions that established separate dorms or "autonomous racial schools within colleges and universities"—ironic, since local, more left-wing NAACP chapters were defending black campus activists. For CORE's Roy Innis, Wilkin's latest reproach became "the last straw. If Wilkins can use funds supposedly earmarked for black people to fight against those same people, then CORE will commit its resources to defend and safeguard the students in their demands."[22]

Nathan Hare continued Innis's assault on Wilkins in *Newsweek* in February 1969. As part of a larger spread on the "Black mood on campus," Hare made "the case for separatism," and Wilkins presented "the case against separatism." In the "Black Perspective," Hare wrote that he was appalled by "the sneaky way in which critics like Roy Wilkins accuse us of 'separatism.'" He added, somewhat accurately, "Our cries for more black professors and black students have padded white colleges with more blacks in two years than decades of whimpering for 'integration' ever did." Wilkins sympathized "with the frustration and anger of today's black students." But "in demanding black Jim Crow studies…and exclusively black dormitories or wings of dormitories, they are opening the door to a dungeon."[23]

* * *

Shortly after black students at Duke opened the door and walked out of their barricaded building on February 13, 1969, hundreds of mostly white supporters and spectators started to disperse. To accelerate them, police drove cars through them, driving students into a frenzy. The students banged on the cars and tried to set them afire. Officers launched a barrage of tear gas, which ignited a social fire on campus, with police clubs fanning the flames. Students defended themselves. One black student even lashed at the police with a chain. When the police finally retreated into the administration building (and ultimately left the campus), the students numbered three thousand. Forty-five people, including two officers, needed medical treatment. Mostly white students were also brutalized a week later at UC Berkeley during the notorious strike for Ethnic Studies.[24]

By late February and early March 1969, the oppositional rhetoric had reached a fevered pitch. There were the campus critiques. Instituting the demands would be "like levitating the University Tower 30 feet off the ground," a dean at U-Texas at Austin told students. After the BSA issued its demands, Eastern Michigan professors mockingly circulated eleven similar demands "for the Welsh Minority on this campus." (In 1968, white students wrote similar lists at William Penn in Iowa and UW Oshkosh). President Nixon endorsed a tough stand against disrupters, and so did many professors and the majority of Americans. NBC News' Chet Huntley called the ferment for Black Studies departments another "college fad" that he hoped did not get out of hand. Bayard Rustin, the executive director of the A. Phillip Randolph Institute, condemned the "separatist demands" of the struggle. The National Governors' Conference passed a resolution pledging to keep colleges open and safe. In the name of academic freedom, or more appropriately, academic power, faculty unrelentingly slammed protesters "who would subordinate intellectual freedom to political ends," as Cornell professors wrote in March 1969.[25]

On March 5, 1969, HEW warned all colleges and universities receiving federal assistance not to institute separate Black Studies programs, "separate housing," or "separate social activity" spaces that excluded white students. In particular, in late February, HEW told thirteen private institutions, including Ohio's Antioch, that they could be violating the Civil Rights Act of 1964. HEW gave Antioch president James P. Dixon two weeks to explain how its Afro-American Studies Institute for black students was not against the law. A literal interpretation of the Civil Rights Act in this "deliberate and crucial question" might deny black students rights that white students long have had at Antioch, President Dixon wrote back to HEW. In most cases, activists did not demand total white exclusion as much as white exclusion from control of their black programs. Therefore, they did tend to believe in separate but equal power relations, access, and organizing ability.

This interaction between HEW and Antioch was leaked to the press. "In defending the 'Crow-Jim' policy, Dr. Dixon gave HEW the greatest line of double talk I have ever read," stated a *Chicago Defender* columnist. Psychologist Kenneth B. Clark resigned from his trusteeship at Antioch. "It is whites who need a black studies program most of all," he said, echoing a view of white suasionists, who mildly supported Black Studies. Liberals, like the Antioch president, had to satisfy the wishes of black campus activists and reactionary conservatives. They castigated African American students for forcing them into this untenable position, saying their protests prompted the conservative reaction that curtailed their efforts at reform. Paradoxically, some liberal presidents did not enact reforms until protests took place.[26]

*   *   *

On April 9, 1969, seven Southern-U New Orleans students walked to the flag pole with their Pan-African flag and a sizeable police force watching. They opened up their flag, reported its meaning, read their demands, pulled down the American flag, and raised their Pan-African flag in a seamless series of motions and words. When it was lifted, the police had to fight through a crowd of two hundred observers and supporters to make twenty arrests. Black students, in the late spring of 1969, were also arrested at Memphis State (109), South Carolina's Voorhees-C (25), Howard (21), Brooklyn's Pratt (11), and Alabama State (365), where they were hauled away like cargo in three trucks for demonstrating at the state capitol for the termination of their president.[27]

When not fighting white policemen, black campus activists were usually fighting white students, which occurred at City College of NY when it reopened on May 6, 1969, after a two-week takeover by black and Puerto Rican students. Students also brawled at Queens-C (NY) in early May. As black and Puerto Rican students ran from building to building smashing windows, jeering white students chased them, shouting "animals," "criminals," and "get back to the jungle." While the NYPD mobilized a small army of five hundred in six busses, seven paddy wagons, and a dozen patrol cars, more than one hundred angry whites converged on twenty black students. Outnumbered, the black students stood their ground. Punches and rocks were thrown until security guards closed a chain-link fence between the groups.[28]

In the late spring of 1969, Bayard Rustin, once again deriding the movement, implored college officials to "stop capitulating to the stupid demands of Negro students" and "see that they get the remedial training that they need." At a two-day law institute sponsored by the NAACP in May 1969, Columbia's Leon Denmark was not at all surprised at Rustin's criticism. "Given his hookups and where he gets his money, he can't do anything else but come out against black student demands." Charles Duncan from Cheyney could not understand why Rustin had been calling them stupid. "We're the most educated black generation" this nation has had, he said. Activists in particular were usually the smartest students, as the US commissioner of education James E. Allen Jr. announced in late May.[29]

Down south, after police drove out building occupiers (eight of whom were expelled) at U-Louisville in early May, Kentucky governor Louis B. Nunn told reporters, "I'm damned sick and tired of this kind of thing." The tactic of taking over a building had steadily lost its effectiveness, as more presidents used court orders and the police to force out students they refashioned as "militants." Apparently, the words of President Nixon in late April, who said "it is time for the faculties, board of trustees and school administrators to have the backbone to stand up against this kind of situation," his strongest public comments on to date, had been fully digested.[30]

The backbone produced what some administrators feared—a tragedy. The campus that accelerated the LBSM early in the decade by patterning nonviolent protests concluded the decade with violence. Under the cover of nighttime, in late May 1969, policemen and National Guardsmen descended on a protest-imbued NC A&T campus only to be met by sniper fire from a dormitory. The officers fired back. "It's just like guerillas in Vietnam," said Greensboro mayor Jack Elam. The battle scene grew more intense when activists found 20-year-old honor student Willie Grimes dead in a clump of bushes with a gunshot wound in the back of his head. Students believed the police had executed him.

The next day, May 24, students got their revenge. Seven police officers were shot by snipers, the worst critically injured in the back and lung by a .45-caliber slug. A student was shot that day, too, in the groin. On the third day of the shootout, Police Major E. R. Wynn resolved to end it. He declared a state of emergency and told the students they had five minutes to "get out of here." The students answered with a spatter of gunfire, wounding a sergeant. Guardsmen returned fire, while a plane and helicopter flew low over the dorm and executed one of the government's new counterinsurgency techniques, tried for the first time three days earlier on white campus activists at UC Berkeley. The plane and helicopter unleashed swirling clouds of tear gas into the dorms. Coughing and choking, the students spilled out like bugs gassed out of cracks. The police swept the building and found nine rifles, and arrested two hundred students. Soon after, the students were all set free when the police could not compel any of them to disclose the snipers, ending one of the most horrifying demonstrations waged at a college in the nation's history.[31]

Not surprisingly after all of this violence, many of the remarks from leaders that summer were unfavorable. Supreme Court Justice Thurgood Marshall said, "Many of us are not going to let [the nation] go down the drain and stand for anarchy, which is anarchy, which is anarchy." Andrew F. Brimmer, the sole black member of the Federal Reserve Board, suggested focusing on traditional courses, rather than advocating for Black Studies, if students wanted a future career. Harvard government professor Martin Kilson said at the annual NAACP convention that summer of 1969 that he was "opposed to proposals to make Afro-American studies into a platform for a particular ideological group." In early September, Kilson described Black Studies as "a frightful experience of strangeness and alienation," sordidly and indirectly positing that the overwhelming white curriculum did not (or rather should not) alienate. Another Ivy League black professor, Arthur Lewis, called Black Studies a "folly of the highest order," because "employers will not hire the students who emerge from this process, and their usefulness even in black neighborhoods will be minimal."[32]

White opponents used these ideas from ladder altruists to legitimate their opposition on their campuses and to remove the cloak of racism from their critiques. Citing Lewis, Rustin, and Brimmer, Robert H. Mills, a white accounting professor, asserted in September 1969 that "under no condition should Lehigh establish" a Black Studies major, suggesting it will not prepare African Americans to live in an integrated society. Responding to a black student request for more black history courses, U-Missouri-St. Louis chancellor Glen R. Driscoll explained his personal bias against a "proliferation of Afro-American courses...I am impressed that American development is the result of an intertwining and interacting of many streams, and I would prefer that each course reflect this fact." As the Black Studies idea soared from desegregation of existing courses, to courses, to interdepartmental programs, to autonomous departments, to colleges, to a unique discipline, the grander the white (and to a certain extent black) opposition. Black students on many occasions were forced to settle for new courses in interdepartmental programs—a massive nonstructural transformation of many curriculums, which before the movement had zero Black Studies courses.[33]

BCCs, the other major demand of BSUs, were opposed too, though with less intensity than Black Studies. BCCs were designated as a form of segregation. More than two hundred students at Morningside-C (IA) signed an oppositional petition in early 1970. In November 1968, an anonymous St. Cloud State (MN) student asserted that the center indicated "reverse discrimination." "As they slink into their black sanctuary...they alienate all but a few well-chosen whites," another anonymous student proclaimed at St. Olaf (MN), as if white groups were not doing the same. "The door is open, from 10 a.m. to 10 p.m., to us and our blackness," the Cultural Union for Black Expression (CUBE) responded. The vast majority of BSUs kept their BCCs open to all members of the campus community, placing the onus on white students to keep them interracial. Usually, they did not.[34]

* * *

While black leaders and academics censured the BCM in the summer of 1969, Congress, spurred by their inflamed constituents, continued writing and passing laws to slow the campus activism of all races. The laws regulated student codes of conduct, revoked funds from protesters, illegalized specific tactics (such as building takeovers), and empowered governors and presidents to declare a state of emergency if students threatened campus property (Oregon) and to proclaim "closed periods," barring people from setting foot on university property (Wisconsin). Campus officers seemed to be preparing for war that summer. At the annual convention of College and University Security Directors, some 180 campus law officials sought the latest riot-control equipment. They advocated a hard hand to squash protests. That is "the only way to handle disruptions," said Wayne O. Littrell, the association's president. "This view is shared by other security directors, but unfortunately not by many administrators," who realized, like many police departments that summer, that police brutality invigorated student activism.[35]

Administrators greeted the incoming class in the fall of 1969 with stern warnings against disruption, as they would for the next few years. Many colleges adopted or revised their disciplinary codes and circulated them widely for the first time. Colleges increased their police forces, increases that continued in the early 1970s. For example, Temple-U formed its own 125-man security force after previously relying on an outside detective agency, and Ohio State doubled and Southern Illinois almost quadrupled its number of officers, as academia became a policed space. Universities let it be known that they would seek injunctions against protests. Ohio-U president Claude R. Sowle informed students in the early fall of 1969 that "unlawful force is not an acceptable substitute for reason. It must be met with lawful force—promptly and without hesitation." Administrators received training during the summer of 1970 on how to deal with protests. The US Army ran one of the programs.[36]

* * *

In the fall of 1969, many black campus activists could not return to their institutions. Some protesters left because their financial aid was cut off as a punishment for their activism. The courts and prisons further deprived the BCM that summer and fall, as hundreds of black students faced criminal charges and were jailed, including students at U-Minnesota and SF State. For their role in seizing the administration building in November 1968, ten women and fourteen men at CSU Northridge went on trial in September 1969. They faced seventy-five felony counts of "willfully, unlawfully, feloniously and knowingly" conspiring to commit kidnapping, robbery, false imprisonment, and burglary. In total, they were charged with 1,730 felonies—a record for the BCM. The NAACP retained a Los Angeles law firm to defend the students. The case received national exposure, since the government attempted conspiracy convictions for the first time, which, according to the students' lawyers, "has significant ramifications for the entire nation. If the district attorney is successful in arguing that a conspiracy existed, the black protest movement is in serious difficulty."

In January 1970, twenty students were convicted of conspiracy, kidnapping, and false imprisonment. In announcing his verdict, Judge Mark Brandler said, "We dare not and will not sanction or tolerate the use of force, violence, or other illegal acts to effect desired changes." In effect, negotiating had not brought the desired changes and now *effectual* protesting became virtually illegal. Archie Chatman (the BSU leader) and Robert A. Lewis, both 22 years old, and 21-year-old Eddie Lee Dancer were sentenced from one to twenty-five years in state prison— the stiffest prison punishments for nonviolent campus activism in American history. Eight other students were assigned to the county jail for periods ranging from three months to a year, seven students were fined, one was placed on probation, and the final student had her charges dismissed. One of the students' lawyers described the sentences as a "judicial lynching," the *Chicago Defender* designated it as "an OUTRAGE."[37]

* * *

The major work of athletic activism that fall and spring of the 1969–1970 academic year occurred in the Western Athletic Conference (WAC). For suggesting they would boycott an upcoming game against BYU, which was affiliated with what the students deemed the racist Mormon church, U-Wyoming football coach Lloyd Eaton revoked the scholarships of fourteen black players. He kicked them off the team in October 1969, all the while ridiculing them, saying they now had to go on "Negro relief" or back "on the streets hustling." Six of the athletes were starters on U-Wyoming's undefeated and twelfth-ranked team. At a press conference a week after dismissing the "Black 14," President Bill Carlson told reporters that football was more important than civil rights. With NAACP assistance, the Black 14 filed an unsuccessful civil suit against Coach Eaton and the University. Ten graduated from other colleges, and four played professional football.[38]

In the midst of the Black 14 affair, black students, demanding more well-paid black construction workers, shut down a construction site in December 1969, leading to campus disciplinary charges, to the delight of the *New York Times*. Thirty-six Harvard students did not report to the hearings and conducted their own "fact finding hearing" in January 1970. Several university officials were invited to defend themselves. None attended. LeRoy Boston of the New England Consulate of the Republic of New Africa served as judge and found Harvard negligent and racist.[39]

In February 1970, police arrested 896 Mississippi Valley State activists, the largest mass arrest in higher education history, 89 at Ole Miss, and 351 students at Bishop in Dallas. Mississippi Valley State president White did not file criminal charges, but he did expel the students—close to a third of the student body—and required them to sign a statement pledging to not take part in protests in order to reenroll, a tactic also used at Tuskegee in April 1968 and throughout the LBSM. By late February 1970, only a few dozen had signed the pledge. One student leader announced, "Anyone [who] signs this should be enslaved."[40]

Sometimes the suppression came from parents, prompted by media coverage of protests or letters from administrators. On February 23, 1970, a dean of students at Pennsylvania's Thiel-C sent a letter to the parents of black campus activists. "We are certain that you wish your child's education to continue uninterrupted. Your advice and counsel to your child will be greatly appreciated." In this case, the parents stood behind their daughters and sons, and were reportedly aggravated by the condescending letter. In other cases, parents were incensed when they learned that their kids were throwing away (or from the students' perspective gaining) their education. On January 14, 1969, a mother heard that her child was in the occupied building at Brandeis-U outside of Boston. She raced to the campus, walked up to the hall, and pounded on the doors with her fists and umbrella. "Christopher Carombo, come out! Christopher Carombo, come out! I don't believe in black power!" she screamed. A few moments later, a student hurried down the fire escape and ran into his mother's wrath, and car, which quickly sped away.[41]

During the 1970–1971 academic year, suspensions or expulsions of protesters led to campus activism and often police retaliation at Norfolk State (VA), Syracuse, U-Florida, and Hampton, where administrators suspended five activists, including SGA vice president Roxanne E. Sinclair. The "Hampton Five" freedom campaign compelled a 90 percent effective class boycott, and by early May the historic institution became a war zone. President Roy Hudson cancelled commencement and closed the campus because he "didn't want to wait until someone was killed."[42]

Hudson had ample reason to think someone would be killed, as black youths were slain at Tuskegee, South Carolina State, NC A&T, Jackson State, U-Kansas, Pepperdine-U (CA), and Southern-U. At least thirteen youths (nine collegiate, three high schoolers, and one community activist) were killed by police during the BCM—thirteen tragedies on or near campuses that have largely receded from America's memory. Absent from historical consciousness are the dozens of students injured by police bullets, the hundreds arrested and jailed, the thousands brutalized, suspended, expelled, and tracked by the intelligence community, and the millions who opposed the movement and endorsed these atrocities. Black egalitarian elites, liberals embracing their goals and disparaging their methods, conservatives hollering for their heads, professors clamoring for academic freedom to maintain academic white supremacy—it is remarkable black students were able to win so much, were able to change the racial constitution of higher education. Put simply, these baby boomers boomed with determination. It's like what SF State BSU chairman Benny Stewart constantly told his members during their 134-day strike, "The only way a people can be defeated is when they lose their determination to fight."[43]

8

"Black Students Refuse to Pass the Buck": The Racial Reconstitution of Higher Education

Two days after armed black Cornell students marched out of their occupied building, professors at Harvard paced into a faculty meeting prompted by the BCM. In January 1969, a Harvard committee recommended the establishment of an Afro-American Studies major in an interdepartmental center. The *New York Times* praised the "important step in depoliticizing an issue that has become enmeshed in unnecessary controversy at many colleges." Harvard's black students were not nearly as pleased, especially in early April when they came across an outline of the new program. They were dismayed that Afro-American Studies majors had to combine their studies into one of the existing, and to the students' thinking, "racist" disciplines. The setup presupposed "Afro-American Studies is less than a legitimate and valid intellectual endeavor," said sophomore Fran Farmer. In turn, African and Afro-American Association (AAAS) members demanded an autonomous department to give the academy's latest intellectual endeavor that legitimacy and validity.

As Harvard professors walked into the meeting room to decide the fate of Black Studies on April 22, 1969, a black student greeted them waving a meat cleaver. Terrified, some professors thought "he would run amok, loping off heads" if they voted against the department. Others saw it purely in symbolic terms. Nevertheless, most did trust the ultimatum broadcast by AAAS president "Skip" Griffin in one of the meeting's first talks. "Not to make a decision in favor of the proposal that we have put here before you is to commit a serious mistake... creating a tragic situation which this university may never be able to recover from." As the professors hissed, rumors were already circulating about the impending doom coming to the campus. Officials stood guard at the library and the museum. According to one Harvard professor, "the shadow of Cornell was spreading to Cambridge, Massachusetts."

A zealous debate followed Griffin's threat. Two hours later, the time to decide had come. "All in favor, please rise," Harvard president Nathan Pusey requested.

"All opposed." It was too close to judge. A head count ensued, as more than seventy-five nervous black students huddled together around their radios outside the meeting room. "The motion is carried by a vote of two fifty-one for, one fifty-eight against..." Before the president could finish, a cheer drowned him out. "I consider this a great victory for black students and for American education," senior Clyde Lindsay told reporters. Indeed, it was one of the greatest victories of the BCM—the planting of a radical idea at arguably the leading HWCU.

Black students partied the rest of the night, letting out collective sighs of joy, while the faculty let out collective sighs of relief. Some of the professors voted in favor of Black Studies due to their sympathy for the budding discipline. With the Cornell guns and AAAS threats on their mind, others were scared into voting. Whatever the reason—the debate on the legitimacy of Black Studies—the signature intrusion of the BCM—received a boost in favor of the discipline's progenitors with that Harvard vote. Furthermore, the faculty placed six students on the thirteen-member committee to develop the department, the first time in the university's history that students had ever been given a direct role in the selection of faculty.[1]

Two weeks after the historic decision at arguably the most illustrious HWCU, students forced a historic decision at arguably the most illustrious HBCU. On May 8, 1969, what Harvard professors feared became a reality at Howard during the student fight to reform their "Negro University" into a "Black University." Six buildings were occupied by black campus activists, compelling President James Nabrit to close the college. The students not only barricaded themselves inside the buildings but also barricaded the main gate with boards, chairs, and desks to repel a police invasion. Students who were not inside buildings broke into the campus restaurant and smashed doors, windows, and vending machines. Litter pervaded the campus. A fire gutted the ROTC building.

The university had a temporary restraining order against building takeovers. The Howard students did not care, defying the order and Nabrit's threats to "call on outside forces." The warning actualized on May 9. More than a hundred federal marshals sporting riot gear charged onto the campus and smashed, sawed, and cut their way into buildings to drive out the remaining students. In their first target, Frederick Douglass Memorial Hall, seventeen students were holed up in a second-floor office with a sign on the door that read, "This is a black struggle." Two husky marshals had to kick the locked door in unison before it caved in. Seventeen students were led out to police cars shouting, "Black Power!" The marshals moved onto Locke Hall and entered through the frame of a plateglass door they smashed. No one was there. A note was. "Welcome pigs...Unity is the Way."

In all, during the sweep of the six buildings, twenty-one students were arrested and charged with "criminal contempt of court." Two of those students ended up serving two weeks in jail. But that did not stop their activism. At the end of the month, twenty Howard students pushed past two policemen into a trustees' meeting and suggested they appoint Kwame Nkrumah, the deposed president of Ghana, as Howard's next president. The *Chicago Defender* endorsed the students' suggestion: "He would bring dignity and leadership of the highest order to embattled Howard." The trustees passed on Nkrumah. But they did replace the disliked Nabrit with James E. Cheek, who endorsed aspects of the Black University concept. In the summer, Cheek outlined a program for the future of

Howard that included "creative and imaginative ways to deal with the problems of the cities, the economically disadvantaged, health care, black Americans and black people throughout the world." He presented his "new humanism" at the opening convocation in the fall of 1969, as Harvard opened its Black Studies department with Ewart Guinier as chair.[2]

The weekend after the Howard protests, the *New York Times* reported that "colleges and universities across the county are hurriedly instituting changes and reforms, as administrators attempt to deal with student restiveness and to avoid the kind of demonstrations that have shaken Ivy League and other major universities," the story opened. With a team of correspondents issuing reports from forty-two campuses, the newspaper found that one of the most significant changes and reforms was the establishment of "Black studies programs and increased effort to recruit Negroes and other minority groups." American Council on Education (ACE) vice president Kenneth Roose informed the *Times* that "even in areas where faculty resistance was strong, the walls are crumbling." This assessment was not new. Educational pundits and officials had seen the walls crumbling in 1968. Black campus activists (along with other activists) had stoked a crisis of "educational authority." F. Champion Ward, the Ford Foundation's vice president for research and education, declared in 1968 that the crisis "has strained the institutional fabric of American universities and colleges. Strengthening that fabric is now the first order of business if higher education is to make its aims clear and quicken its responses under stress." Moreover, in July 1969, the *Wall Street Journal*, after surveying educators from forty leading colleges and universities, reported that "black students are an identifiable, relatively cohesive group... [that] have become the cutting edge for much of the academic and social experimentation sweeping the schools these days." Researchers, who studied innovations in 1969 at almost one thousand LACs, found evidence "from every quarter...suggesting that the 1970s will see vastly different colleges and universities than those of the 1960s."[3]

These vastly different colleges and universities did not come about as a result of the 1954 *Brown* decision or the Civil Rights Act of 1964. It was the BCM that forced the rewriting of the ideals of the four elements of the racial constitution and a massive implementation of those ideals that is without parallel in higher education history. Academics started conceiving of grassroots altruism as foundational to higher education's function, as opposed to ladder altruism. Diversity and the standardization of professed inclusion eclipsed the long-held standardization of exclusion. Some scholars started to remove the normalized mask of whiteness, conceding that nonwhite ideas, assumptions, perspectives, methodologies, methods, and scholarship were academically legitimate or on par with Euro-American tradition. Moral freedoms for HBCU students have in many cases replaced the moralized contraption.

Moralized Contraption

At HBCUs in the mid-1960s, there were still remnants of the moralized contraption that students furiously strove to decimate throughout the LBSM. The contraption of rules and regulations was based on the racist, sexist, and ageist paternal notion that these black students were incapable of acting responsibly with academic, social, and political freedom. HBCU activists began to conceptualize in unprecedented fashion the totality of the contraption and its ideological basis in the mid-1960s. The ideas undergirding the rules became just as germane to their activism. In his "State of the Campus" address on February 24, 1966, SGA president Charles E. Daye of NC Central declared, "We are engaged in great revolution on this campus." He referenced the previous year's strike against the rules. "We seek to overthrow the system of ideas that refuse to permit us to grow into adulthood. If our college administration spent greater time administrating and less time trying to baby-sit for grown men and women, Negro colleges would not be so far behind." A booming applause from student congress members interrupted this speech, one that SGA presidents and BSU presidents at HBCUs across the South replicated throughout the early years of movement.[4] As Joy Ann Williamson revealed, "Their arguments mirrored the burgeoning black freedom struggle's demands for participatory democracy."[5]

By the end of the BCM, the moralized contraption as exhibited in a series of rules and regulations was largely history at many HBCUs, aside from cross-gender room visitation. Women, at least on paper, began to be regulated somewhat equally. Chapel, class, and ROTC mandates had been abolished on most campuses. The efforts of faculty and administrators to raise the academic acumen of students surged ahead of moral advancement. Many of the dictatorial, paternalistic, conservative presidents, who openly treated students as their children, were driven from office by black campus activists.

Standardization of Exclusion

"The freedom to learn depends upon appropriate opportunities and conditions in the classroom, on the campus, and in the larger community, which we have been denied," said one of the organizers of a building takeover by two hundred students (a third of the body) at Bowie State (MD) days before King's death in 1968. Like the speech from the NC Central SGA president, the avowal from the Bowie State organizer echoed from the lips of most black campus activists at HBCUs during the movement. Calvin Matthews, SGA president at NC A&T, mourned his school's "archaic and dilapidated system" in February 1969, while students the following year at U-Maryland-Eastern Shore called their HBCU a "poor attempt at an institution" in their roughly fifty pages of "demands and recommendations."[6]

In addition to conceiving of their lack of freedom due to the moralized contraption, black college students recognized that poor campus facilities and services at HBCUs standardized their exclusion from adequate learning environments and thus their "freedom to learn." Collegians grieved over inadequate housing, understaffed campus offices, short operating hours for campus facilities, including the library and student center, and meager medical, transportation, laundry, and telephone services. HBCU students faulted their faculty, administrators, governors, education bureaucrats, trustees, and benefactors. Public HBCU activists regularly compared their campus facilities and services to those at historically white colleges and universities and demonstrated the white supremacist intentionality of the inequalities. In 1966, Alcorn State had one professor for every twenty-two students, compared to the Ole Miss ratio of thirteen to one, and fourteen library books for each student, while there were sixty books for every Ole Miss student. "This state of affairs," wrote a member of the Southern Student Organizing Committee in a pamphlet on Alcorn, "is only the final step in a totally inferior and almost totally segregated education system for Mississippi Negroes." The writer classified Alcorn State as a "plantation college," the same label sophomore Guinnevere Hodges latched on to U-Oklahoma in 1967.[7]

American institutional racism produced the inequality of HBCUs and HWCUs—the historic and present inequality of state appropriations, private credit lines, and wealth of alumni, the deliberate appointment of incompetent administrators, and administrators and faculty benefitting from their accommodation of the white supremacist order that mandated a bottom-tier position for HBCUs, campus activists charged. During the era of black pride and self-love and its concomitant psychological attack on black inferiority complexes, HBCU activists distanced themselves from the commonly held conscious or subconscious conception (among whites and many African Americans) that the inferiority of African Americans produced the inferiority of HBCUs. As opposed to reasons, black campus activists deemed excuses the prominent justifications for the inferior quality of HBCUs: financial mismanagement, administrative incompetence, alumni giving, and student comportment. If HBCUs were failing, trustees, politicians, and presidents wanted them to fail, since failure and inferiority reckoned their proper places in the academy and in society, students argued. The "guardians," as Matthews called them, endeavored to keep the standardization of HBCU exclusion from an equal academic playing field, from achievements, and from progress.

Yet the guardians failed to keep black students from producing change. Echoing the demands of black students, although for not quite the same reason, the Southern Regional Education Board in the early summer of 1969 circulated a report to trustees, foundations, and government agencies proposing that HBCUs needed special operating funds in addition to their regular allotments. As black campus activists asserted, black colleges were deficient in faculty salaries, administrative services, curriculum change, and a range of remedial and compensatory education programs. "It is essential that a systematic procedure be adopted for removing these deficiencies over a period of years," the report stated. Nevertheless, the impetus among the task force members was probably propelled as much (if not more) by corporate capital's desires to smooth out HBCU pipelines as they were by the BCM.[8]

By the early 1970s, the standardization of exclusion of HBCUs from adequate learning environments equal to HWCUs stayed in place, an exclusion that largely continues into the second decade of the twenty-first century. However, there was a shift in the early 1970s due to the BCM. HBCU officials had largely reversed the century-long acquiescence of most (though certainly not all of) their prede-cessors to the exclusion standard. Funding discrepancies were at its heart, and by the early 1970s officials were making demands of their own upon the federal government for more funds. Representatives from forty-six institutions came to Washington, DC, in May 1971 to criticize the Nixon administration during a salute to black colleges sponsored by the Capital Press Club. Even though not even two decades had passed, it seemed like ages ago that HBCU officials were putting on campus shows of humility for public and private benefactors. Their begging had turned into decrees. Lincoln (PA) president Herman Branson called it "immoral" and "dirty" that black colleges had received a mere 3 percent of the $4 billion in overall funds for higher education that year. This is what black students had demanded for several years—aroused, assertive, and aggressive administrators unwilling to allow state and federal institutional racism to hold back their HBCUs.[9]

Black students also demanded the elimination of their exclusion from cam-pus decision-making bodies, such as university committees, and the desegre-gation and black domination of trustee boards. Many HBCUs gave students an unprecedented amount of power in newly written student constitutions, and the trustee boards were made over racially, oftentimes with student trustees. Clark (Atlanta) named student trustees and placed students on policy-making com-mittees "with the clear understanding that these were not short-term responses to the national campus crisis, but ideas whose time had come," wrote President Vivian W. Henderson in 1974. The administration and student body at Alabama A&M agreed in 1969 to establish a faculty-student evaluation committee in order to assess teaching performance. At NC A&T, trustees unanimously voted John S. Stewart, the president of the Mutual Savings and Loan Association, chairman of the board in the fall of 1969. He became the first black chairman since the Greensboro institution had opened in 1891. A&T trustees also approved the cre-ation of a student legislature, a student judicial system to handle disciplinary cases, and a new student code of conduct. They even allowed 21-year-old students to have alcohol in their rooms—a striking allowance, since a decade earlier alco-hol consumption probably led to immediate expulsion.[10]

*   *   *

On December 1, 1969, Case Western Reserve president Robert W. Morse responded to a few concerns voiced by AAS president Raymond A. Henry, including a concern regarding racism at the university. "There has been injustice to minorities and denial of equal opportunities in many institutions of American life, including universities. With your cooperation, we have been trying to make advances at this University to create a more responsive atmosphere for all, and to redress those inequities which particularly affect Black students on this cam-pus." Morse proceeded to list the "record of some of the developments in this University during the past year." The black student population had nearly qua-drupled, from twenty in the fall of 1967 to seventy-two in the fall of 1969. There were six and seven more black professors and administrators (respectively) than the previous December. A "large number of new books" on African Americans had been added to the library.[11]

The change at Case Western reflected higher education in general at HWCUs. Black students poured into the academy at a growth rate of 50,000 per year between 1965 and 1973—what two scholars called the "golden age of black educational opportunity." Tuition increases, financial aid decreases, and the end of the BCM in the fall of 1973 reversed the rate, as the percentage of black freshman dropped from its peak in the fall of 1972 at 8.7 percent to 7.8 percent. However, it increased again for the fall of 1974, marking the first time the number of African Americans in the academy reached the 800,000 mark, at 814,000. That fall, African Americans made up about 9 percent of the total student body (compared to 5 percent in 1964), and 12 percent of the freshmen class, comparable to 11 percent of blacks in the country's population. The black student enrollment would reach 10.3 percent by 1976. But the number of incoming black students started to come down from their mountaintop of the mid-1970s, such that they accounted for a mere 4.9 percent of the fall class of 1978.[12]

During the apex academic year of 1968–1969, more than three hundred schools established special admissions programs for African Americans. By 1970, after the three most scorching academic years of the movement, almost one thousand colleges had adopted more open admissions policies or crafted particular adjustments to admit blacks, had a tutoring program for black students, were providing diversity training for workers, and were actively recruiting black professors and staff. Almost three hundred colleges were providing financial aid for African Americans and had developed diversity policy statements. In addition, during the 1970–1971 academic year, almost two hundred institutions hired black professors, and more than one hundred established special admissions programs. Almost every college with a substantial black student population hired black counselors, admissions staff, and administrators—often black deans or diversity officers. BCCs were opened at hundreds of institutions. Usually, public colleges and universities, western and northeastern institutions, higher ranking, and large urban institutions were the most responsive to the demands of the BCM. Meanwhile, the private church colleges, the southern colleges, and the lower ranking schools were the least responsive.[13]

In sum, the BCM forced the academy at HWCUs to demean the standardization of exclusion. In its place emanated diversity statement after diversity statement and professed presidential commitment after professed presidential commitment as the twentieth century became older—demonstrating new ideals, a new constitution. The gains from the movement are immense. However, individual gains do not necessarily mean institutional progress, just as writing a new racial constitution does not mean that constitution has been implemented.

Normalized Mask of Whiteness

As campus activists conceptualized the standardization of exclusion, they also uncovered the mask and challenged normalized whiteness, which had concealed racist or Eurocentric thought as the norm in American higher education since its colonial conception. American higher education had a dominant political persuasion, cultural expression, and class position, many students contended. Black campus activists usually termed institutions White or Negro Universities—with curriculum, programs, and personnel that indoctrinated and socialized assimilation into a politically docile bourgeois whiteness. They were no longer willing to stay in the academy "dislocated" on "borrowed European terms." They wanted to think on their "own terms," to use Ama Mazama's recent words. They wanted something of relevance to their sociocultural experience.[14]

"We feel that the University of Houston is a White Anglo-Saxon Protestant institution," read a statement by Afro-Americans for Black Liberation (AABL) on February 7, 1969. In 1970, New Mexico State BSO president Hardy Murphy said the curriculum prepared them for the life as a middle-class white man. Meanwhile that year, a student in the Howard SOBU chapter said that from the institution's "inception," it had had "a calculated program of assimilation and degradation for Black people." Hampton had been "geared to fitting us for a 'nice, comfortable, middle-class' existence with a nice-paying job in some huge impersonal corporation—that is unobtrusive assimilation into White bourgeois society (Booker T. rides again)—rather than teaching us to think...and to preserve our cultural integrity in a hostile society," said sophomore activist Sharon Masingale. All the U-Georgia offers its black students is indoctrination into white society, making "honkies" out of black folk, read a BSU news release in 1969. It continued, "Neo-slavemasters have declared that it is illegal, unnecessary and educationally unsound for black people to obtain a meaningful education." According to Fisk's Students for a Black University, the storied HBCU "had been known to cater to 'Negro' scholars who have aspired to assimilate." At the height of a movement, in 1969, Paul E. Wisdom and Kenneth A. Shaw captured the black student presumption in the *Educational Record*. "What the universities have failed to realize in almost every case is that the American educational experience is a *white* experience, an experience based on white history, white tradition, white culture, white customs, and white thinking, an education designed primarily to produce a culturally sophisticated, middle class, white American." In the "Black Challenge to Higher Education," the two collegiate deans added that "the key word to black students today is the same one most often used by white critics of our universities: *relevance*."[15]

Curricular relevance was nonexistent for many African Americans in 1965. Nonracist content was rare at white colleges and universities, while Africana Studies courses were rarer, and programs and departments nonexistent. Until black students called this into question, the paucity of courses and literature dealing with African Americans was *normalized* for higher education. Normalized as opposed to normal, since these lily-white curriculums were deliberately created and recreated over the years, ignoring black scholarship from W. E. B. Du Bois, Anna Julia Cooper, Zora Neale Hurston, J. A. Rogers, Cheik Anta Diop, and Alain Locke—to name a few. It was no coincidence or oversight. To white and quite a few black academics, scholars had not been reading and discussing "white" literature over the years. A basic assumption was that these "objective" professors were reading and discussing the best or the only literature.

The same conceptions rationalized the exclusion of scholarly blackness at HBCUs until black campus activists uncovered the mask. A graduate dean at NC A&T knew of few courses "oriented to the Negro" at HBCUs in 1968. Most HBCUs merely had one "Negro history" and "Negro literature" course at the most. Activists constantly brought to light this glaring contradiction of few black courses at institutions with practically all black students, including Earl Hart at Winston-Salem State (NC) in 1969. In the physical education department, they only teach the "fox-trot and all those other European dances," he said. "In the music department we are still fooling around with Bach and the rest of those pigs when we have soul musicians." Ultimately, "black students emerge after four years of college completely Europeanized." Some did, but during the movement black campus activists also endeavored to make European thinkers relevant, by ascertaining their utility to the struggle. "Like a Black Midas' wand, this movement imbues everything it touches with an ebony hue," revealed Robert Goodman, a Morehouse instructor in 1968. "A discussion of Descartes in Western civ is likely to wind up in heated debate over how Descartes would have analyzed Black power or whether white philosophers are relevant to black people anyway."[16]

The Black Studies idea conceived and injected into the academy by black students challenged head-on the normalized mask of scholarly whiteness at both HBCUs and HWCUs. In one of the first issues of The Black Scholar in 1970, its editors wrote that black campus activists had blasted the "archaic illusions of scholarly objectivity, of the sanctity of the ivory tower, of the almost church-like serenity of the college." Black students "demonstrated that American colleges were as racist and oppressive as any other of this country's institutions." Black students, as will be discussed more in the section on ladder altruism, also challenged the notion of knowledge for knowledge's sake. Black campus activists drew a line in the academic sand and claimed that all knowledge either reinforces or challenges the status quo. And therefore, knowledge for knowledge's sake has been utilized to justify scholarship that maintains the normalized mask of whiteness in academia and white supremacy in the community.[17]

Race specificity replaced purported race neutrality in the scholarly exercise for many. Racist mainstream scholarly ideas, which had long been disproven by black scholars, were refuted with a new vigor by students—ideas such as the historical and cultural backwardness of Africa, African American incompetence during Reconstruction, the humaneness of slavery, and the docility of slaves. In addition, black campus activists' notion of a black perspective challenged the idea of a universal scholarly perspective, at the time almost wholly drawn from European thinkers. It deuniversalized the European ideas that had been cast over much of the globe. Like Third World revolutionaries stopping imperialists dead in their tracks in the 1960s, so too did students challenge imperial ideas. "Through perspectival elimination you have necessarily de-emphasized some aspects of reality," wrote Genna Rae McNeil of the BSO to the faculty and administration of Kalamazoo-C (MI) on May 19, 1969. "You do not focus on total reality. No human being or social group does. Black people are not demanding the impossible. Black people are affirming the need to look at reality again. For in looking more closely with us you, too, may build a construct of more details from which you, too, may see new patterns of possibilities."[18]

Black students provided the vision for Black Studies. Their activism led to its institutionalization. By 1970, after the three most scorching academic years of the movement, nearly one thousand colleges had organized Black Studies courses and more than two hundred had interdepartmental programs or autonomous departments. Although interest waned and attacks increased from "color blind" conservatives, egalitarian elites, and liberals, by mid-decade the discipline of Black Studies thrived. In 1972, the *New York Times* reported that "although divided on what black studies are, what they should be and whom they should reach, a number of black educators, social scientists and intellectuals agree that the discipline has forever changed some aspects of American higher education." Continuing, the report stated that "the adherents of black studies have questioned and broken a number of long-accepted academic rules." The United Press International, the American Association of State Colleges, and Nick Aaron Ford's groundbreaking study on the discipline all demonstrated the success the Black Studies. Even *The Chronicle of Higher Education*'s report on "The State of Black Studies" in late 1975 reported that the demise of the discipline proved to be exaggerated. The programs and departments "are not where they thought they would be by this time, but they're slowly becoming more established," said the report's author, Elias Blake.[19]

The Black Studies idea and the BCM generally (along with student activism from other races and the loud voices of usually younger, progressive faculty) profoundly affected the existing disciplines. Five dissident factions—Psychologists for a Democratic Society, Psychologists for Social Action, Women's Consortium of Psychologists for Social Action, the Association of Black Psychologists, and the Association of Black Psychology Students—actively sought to reform their discipline and its affairs at the American Psychological Association's annual convention in 1969. The newly organized Association of Black Psychologists and a group of twenty-five black psychology students raised concerns about the discipline's relationship to the black community and wanted the association to actively recruit black students and faculty into the area of inquiry. Delegates established a committee to study the issue and provide funds for students to travel to campuses to discuss problems.

The American Sociology Association convened the "most politicized meeting" in the organization's sixty-four-year history in 1969. A black caucus condemned it as racist, saying the "association has profited parasitically by victimizing the black community, by using the black community as a research laboratory for white experimentation, by using black people as human guinea pigs for publishing books, surveys, and the earning of Ph.D.'s for whites, and for gathering data on blacks for the purpose of oppression, exploitation, and control." To revamp the association, the black caucus demanded, among other things, that it appoint black members to its decision-making bodies.

Activist members of the American Political Science Association formed a caucus and won several victories at their annual conference that year. African Americans received more influence in the association's affairs, while David Easton of U-Chicago devoted his presidential address to the "revolution in political science" based on the "credo of relevance." He proclaimed that the revolution does not seem to be a passing phenomenon, "but rather...a specific and important episode in the history of our discipline, if not in all the social sciences." A progressive caucus formed at the annual convention of the Association of American Geographers to make their discipline more relevant. "We're changing from just looking at the way man uses the land to trying to figure out why he uses it the way he does," said one geographer. Similar shifts and caucuses were formed in several other social sciences, with their activity coming to a head at the 1969 conventions.[20]

*   *   *

Their college administrations, their presidents—were they relevant to black people? Aside from the curriculum, it was another question HBCU campus activists debated in the mid-1960s. They had reached a general consensus by the end of the decade. Many of their African American presidents personified the normalized mask of whiteness on their HBCU campuses. Deeply immersed in colonial literature and news, they compared them to the white-controlled "puppet presidents" who had "sold out" their people in the Third World in the mid-twentieth century. Activists had long demonstrated against these "puppets," since conservative African Americans increasingly took the helms of HBCUs in 1920s. Yet by the 1960s the mask had been completely exposed, with some of these HBCU presidents furiously clamping down on civil rights protests, as if they were white segregationists. To Charles Daye, the SGA president at NC Central, HBCUs in 1966 were propagated by a coalition of white southerners and African American elite who gained "personal aggrandizement and social prestige." The deplorable conditions persisted at Prairie View A&M (TX) because a group of black administrators were "willing to do the bidding of their white mentors" for "authority and affluence."[21]

By the early 1970s, many accommodating separatist HBCU presidents had been replaced by liberal egalitarian elites and a few progressive revolting nationalists, as previously stated. One example was the forced resignation in 1969 of J. D. Boyd, who served as president of a protest-riddled Alcorn State for a dozen years. Students staged major protests calling for his termination in 1964, 1966, 1968, and 1969. Walter Washington took over for Boyd and proclaimed that he would create "The New Alcorn." In July 1969, Washington's administration met with student leaders on the list of forty grievances they had drawn up for Boyd in the spring. He agreed to improve the dining hall, extend library hours, and grant dancing privileges, and he brought in two physicians, beautified the campus, requested more capital for the restoration of facilities, and most importantly, from the students' perspective, yielded "the responsibility of young adulthood to the student of Alcorn." He was not like Boyd, who "maintained a conservative view point to retain his empire," explained Alcorn student Ervin Barnes Jr. in October 1969. "Suddenly, out of despair there came hope, out of confusion there came logical reasoning, and out of unfairness there came justice. This was all a realization as a result of a new president Dr. Walter Washington."[22]

Ladder Altruism

In its totality, the BCM critiqued the suggested purpose of higher education. Black campus activists on almost every campus indicted higher education for perpetuating the maintenance of the status quo. The rebuked status quo revolved around inequality and black powerlessness for the more moderate militants, and capitalism, institutional racism, imperialism, and sometimes patriarchy for the radicals. The university has a "large responsibility" in "influencing the creation of an equitable society for all," proclaimed the BSU at Indiana Northwest in 1969. The ABC at U-Missouri-St. Louis described colleges and universities as "wholesale producers of a designated mentality conducive to the perpetuation and continuation of America's present national life—a national life which we have witnessed to be in total and complete contradiction to the wholesome development and survival of our people." Students, including those at Mississippi State and Michigan State, continuously argued that their colleges programmed or indoctrinated them into a Eurocentric, capitalistic, patriarchal, liberal, or conservative ideology. Robin Gregory, Howard's first homecoming queen with an Afro, who spoke out against gender issues during her 1966 campaign, particularly despised the special assemblies for women. "We had this lecture on etiquette, and how we were supposed to dress, and how we were supposed to behave. And we were supposed to be ladies [*laughs*]." Barbara Garrison of the Alliance of Black Students at UW-Milwaukee declared on February 13, 1969 that "black students refuse to pass the buck and become the colonial buffer-zone niggers emasculate reincarnation."[23]

Their colleges were like ladders, removing them from the struggles of their people, many black campus activists claimed. At a mass meeting concerning their twelve "non-negotiable demands" at Stetson-U in Florida in May 1970, an elder professor advised black students to focus their energies on competing in the professions. A leader "rejected the idea vociferously," according to a university biography, and instead announced that their chief purpose at the school should be to prepare to "work for justice" in black communities. The pervasive notion of ladder altruism, as projected by Stetson's elder professor, resulted in black collegians leaving their communities, spatially and psychologically. "His community has thereby been left without the element most essential to its regeneration and construction—its aware young people," asserted U-Missouri-St. Louis's ABC in its Black Studies proposal. "Henceforth, our education must speak to the needs of our community and our people. We can no longer prostitute our minds to the vain and irrelevant." Serving as professional role models on the ladder of success did not speak to the community's needs as much as it satiated the conscience of the professional black person who believed the community's livelihood rose as he or she trekked up the ladder, black campus activists insinuated.[24]

Graduates in the 1950s and early 1960s were not interested in relating to the poor black community and instead strove to be "as 'middle class' as possible," according to Black United Students (BUS) at U-Akron in 1970. Carrying on the point, Roosevelt's BSA attested, in its 1969 "A Minority Report," that black students were disallowed from studying matters of housing, relief, social welfare, education, and other matters germane to their people. Expressing an ideology of grassroots altruism, participants in the BCM asserted (and were supported by many black power speakers across the ideological spectrum) that they must become the "dominant force in improving the conditions of the poor black community," U-Akron's BUS exclaimed. Shortly after the Orangeburg Massacre, the killing of two SC State students in February 1968, the U-Chicago BSA, "as the future leaders of the American black community," felt "compelled to go on record that our primary commitment is to our people" in a letter to President Johnson. "Blacks no longer want college degrees to escape from the black community," said Ken Blackwell, president of the Afro-American Student Organization at Cincinnati's Xavier-U in March 1970. "We want degrees to aid it." The weight of this aid rested on the "shoulders of young black Americans in our colleges and universities," since Eldridge Cleaver was in exile, Huey P. Newton was in jail, and both Martin Luther King and Malcolm X were dead, read a 1969 pamphlet created by the NABS, coordinated by movement pioneer and Tuskegee alumnus Gwen Patton.[25]

Black campus activists were fairly united on the idea of education for liberation. To be relevant, the liberation pedagogy must allow them to intensely study and figure methods to improve the complex condition of people of African descent, ultimately training them to be socially responsible leaders (or servants) of the masses of blacks. That was the practical rationale black students usually laid out for Black Universities and Black Studies. The Claremont Colleges BSU proclaimed in their demands in May 1968 that an "adequate education will provide them with the tools to combat racism, discrimination, and inequality."[26] "Our first goal should be to obtain an education relevant to the needs of the mass of Black people in this country," asserted Tougaloo's Irma Watkins in February 1969.[27]

Before the BCM and the student activism of nonblack students in the late 1960s and early 1970s, ladder altruism thrived as a constituent element of the racial (and for that matter nonracial) constitution of higher education. Colleges were like ladders, disassociating from the communities and professing to serve as enlightened models for the development of society. African American college graduates utilized these ladders to individually make their ascent in society, while also claiming that they were helping the entire race by smashing ceilings and by serving as positive examples. This situation did not surprise BCM students. They theorized that if colleges and universities were like ladders, or tools of removal, then students would use them accordingly. However, if higher education tossed the ladder aside and directed itself openly to grassroots community advancement, then students would follow. This was the most unyielding aim of the BCM (and student activism generally during this period)—switching the function of the academy from ladder altruism, which largely maintained the status quo, while giving a few blacks sustenance, to grassroots altruism, which students speculated would make the academy an organ of racial reform or revolution.

Black campus activists were unable to totally alter the function of higher education, but they did help rewrite the racial constitution of higher education, replacing ladder altruism with grassroots altruism. Many HWCU officials and academics, particularly at public, Christian, and prestigious institutions, said higher education had come down from the tower (or ladder) and began to assume a social responsibility in the late 1960s and early 1970s. "No longer is it possible to separate the world of scholarly pursuit from the world of reality," wrote Marquette president John P. Raynor in 1967. "The two have firmly inter-twined, and we (Marquette University) would have it no other way." Marquette's Students United for Racial Equality praised Raynor's words, but then challenged him to turn his words into action in a November 1967 letter. He did not, so black campus activists stepped up the pressure with weeks of protests in May 1968. After the campus crisis was finally resolved, a widely circulated Associated Press story reported that many were saying the Catholic institution would never be the same. "Some say it was a permanent sense of 'Christian commitment' that will make unmistakably clear that Marquette as an urban institution has an inescap-able need to help find solutions to Milwaukee's social problems."[28]

In a spring 1969 speech at the forty-ninth annual meeting of the American Association of Junior Colleges, William M. Birenbaum, president of Staten Island Community-C said, "Those who cry out most loudly now against politicization of the university are really making a last-ditch defense of the present political rigging of academic privilege and vested interest." In the early fall of 1969, SUNY chancellor Samuel B. Gould gave three lectures on "The Academic Condition." "We can no longer consider the university as an enterprise largely removed from the main concerns of society, but now must see it as one part of a complex web of social institutions, each of which is rapidly and perceptively changing in charac-ter and direction, while [at] the same time interacting with all the other forces," he explained at Colgate-U. The "conscience of the academic community has been aroused, and in small towns and big cities our institutions are searching for ways to be 'part of the action,'" elucidated Cleveland State president Harold L. Enarson in a prepared paper for ACE's 1969 Annual Meeting. HEW secretary Robert Finch, in a paper for the same meeting, suggested new expectations and respon-sibilities for higher education. As "great equalizers of opportunity," they should "exercise a sort of providential influence over people's lives" and tackle "the most intractable problems of our society."[29]

During the movement, black campus activists at HWCUs and HBCUs did not merely project a new grassroots vision for the academy. They led the way through their scholarship, initiatives, and programs. Using BSU, SGA, Black Studies offices, and BCCs as bases, black students entered black communities and lectured on Black Studies, launched food drives, organized tutoring programs, sickle cell anemia campaigns, and student recruitment programs, initiated Kwanzaa cele-brations, helped establish day care centers, lent their money and time to the series of urban and rural black political campaigns, and campaigned to free political prisoners. They engaged in all forms of reformist and revolutionary community activism, peopling most of the local and national black power organizations, including SNCC, CORE, RAM, National Black Feminist Organization, Congress of African People, US Organization, and the Black Panther Party.

*　*　*

Many HBCUs were drowning with dwindling lifelines, due to the fact that black students were increasingly choosing white colleges, and government and corporate funds followed them in the late 1960s. They were searching in those treacherous, ever-changing waters for a new identity, since the academy had desegregated. HBCU officials heard the deafening calls for their elimination. They heard their alumni and students match that volume with avowals for their existence. The new crop of HBCU administrators planted by the BCM found a fresh identity in 1969. They had to look no further than to what their students had been requesting, demanding, and protesting for since the spring of 1965. Once some of the fiercest opponents of the Black University concept, in 1969 HBCU administrators started crafting an identity, a function for HBCUs out of its main tenet—grassroots altruism—void, at least initially, of the racial rhetoric. As Miles-C (AL) president Lucius Pitts explained in October 1969, "We're taking students whom no one else will take, and we're designing programs for the whole spread of students." The following march, Betty Gates, a Miles-C professor, stammered, "White people do not belong on any black campus in positions of power and decision-making because we now have to determine our new direction. No one can define us for ourselves anymore."[30]

Morehouse started a project in 1969 in an Atlanta storefront to enable residents to become good consumers. Termed Project CURE, it endeavored to organize credit unions and buy clubs, and to form cooperative stores. Most HBCUs enacted grassroots altruism by supporting arguably the most conservative facet of the BPM, the burgeoning Black Capitalism Movement. Yet they were in the black power orbit, a drastic shift from just a decade prior. There were other grassroots experiments at HBCUs, which, according to the *Boston Globe*, "are symptomatic of larger shift in emphasis at black schools to train students for a wide range of functions that will aid in the uplifting of black communities. It is not scientists that are needed, but social workers, community organizers, teachers." Clark (Atlanta) moved to strengthen focus on urban and rural problems in its curriculum "when student pressure built," according to President Vivian W. Henderson. And, with the help of the Voter Education Project, Clark (Atlanta), Talladega-C (AL), Miles-C (AL), and Southern-U established instructional and technical assistance centers for black elected officials in the early 1970s. "Students and professors became more systemically involved in the voting, political, and policy processes and in providing technical assistance to public officials," Henderson added in 1974. NC A&T president Lewis C. Dowdy, like many during his day, also articulated elements of the Black University concept. "We want you," speaking to the students in 1969, "to assist us in making our programs relevant. I think some of our programs are obsolete and should be replaced with courses that are relevant to us. Change is inevitable and we must face it with perseverance and responsibility."[31]

Epilogue: Backlash and Forward Lashes of the Black Campus Movement

Malcolm X, the ideological father of the BCM, once reasoned, "You don't stick a knife in a man's back nine inches and then pull it out six inches and say you're making progress." The BCM pulled out the knife several inches. The new ideals, the new racial constitution gave higher education the tools to fully extract the knife and heal the wounds inflicted by one hundred years of the moralized contraption, standardization of exclusion, normalized mask of whiteness, and ladder altruism. Forty years have passed since the demise of the BCM. Has the knife been fully removed? Have the wounds healed? Has higher education racially advanced? Are we making progress?[1]

Most would agree that the new ideals put forth by the BCM, exemplified now in one catch word—diversity—echoes from higher education. Almost every college and university in America has a public statement or mission on its web site or in its literature declaring a commitment to diversity, a public commitment unheard of fifty years ago. There are "signs" the knife has been removed. Nevertheless, the debate lies in whether the statements are merely statements, ideals remain ideal, or whether they have been (or are trying to be) implemented; whether college and university presidents are truly devoted to diversity, or whether their public commitments simply satiate the political order of the day.

There are without question new racial ideals, but some of those new ideals have been used to discriminate against African Americans (and Chicanos, Latinos, Asians, Native Americans, women, LGBTs, and some whites) over the last forty years. Ideals are rhetoric. The rhetorical tools that students forced onto the academy to pull out the knife have been used to keep it in higher education. The BCM created new contradictions in the racial constitution of higher education—the use of new ideals, supposedly to eliminate the old, to maintain the old.

We live in an era in which pleas of (reverse) discrimination are used to discriminate. Integration segregates. Color-blindness blinds us from racism. The Civil Rights Act and the Fourteenth Amendment are used to extinguish African American rights on campuses. Standardized testing standardizes the class of students.[2] Racial affirmative action is labeled as racial warfare. Meanwhile, class affirmative action (parental wealth, legacies, networks, superior K–12 schools) is not seen as class warfare. Black college athletes generate billions for white universities, while the HBCUs that some of them socialize at flounder financially. The racist claims that an institution must lower its standards to draw legions of black students and faculty remain popular mythology. The titled champions of diversity sometimes limit diversity. Corporate capital, not ingenuity, guides many research agendas. Some black boards of trustees at HBCUs have become as paternalistic, class conscious, and accommodationist as the white boards of trustees they replaced. Cries for academic freedom help to enslave free academics. White cries of racism maintain white privilege. Cries for present equality preserve past inequality. Some African Americans (let alone whites) classify HBCUs as inferior using false claims, and demean HBCUs for complications that regularly occur at similarly funded HWCUs. Black egalitarian elitism still fuels remnants of the moralized contraption. The professed standardization of inclusion excludes. The mask may be off, but normalized whiteness still regularly shows its face. Grassroots altruism operates as and veils ladder altruism.

These contradictions—this egalitarian or inclusive exclusion or color-blind racism or multicultural whiteness—appeared during the BCM. Most of the campus activism of black students over the last forty years has been defending the gains of the BCM and fighting the new contradictions, a drive that began during the movement (covered somewhat in Chapter 7). While white students were members of exclusive groups, barring or limiting African Americans, they audaciously criticized the racial makeup of the BSUs in the late 1960s, calling them discriminatory, separatist, and forms of reverse discrimination. White students at Dickinson-C (PA) called the AAO racist and segregationist when it formed in 1967. Mike Floyd, AAO prime minister, replied, "When we organize ourselves, when we direct our actions towards racism, it is a defense mechanism."[3]

When white organizations desegregated and allowed in a handful of African Americans, black organizations had no reason for existence and certainly no reason to form, the argument went (and continues to go). Black organizing restrictions also operated at HBCUs in the late 1960s and early 1970s. As soon as HBCUs—propelled by student appeals for a "Black University"—started reforming into institutions geared toward the development (as opposed to submission) of African America, white liberals supported by black egalitarian elites (usually trained at HWCUs) questioned their need to exist, since HWCUs had desegregated. These questions (and all-out calls for their destruction) occurred during the BCM and still occur even while the majority of American colleges and universities remain lily-white. Existential critiques of predominantly black institutions, specifically those that are struggling, have been constant. But where are the similar condemnations of the hundreds of subpar lily-white institutions? Based on the integration argument, why is America not questioning their right to exist?

During the BCM, one of the major rearguard actions of HBCU activists was their defense of HBCUs, as threats of mergers and closures were steady in the early 1970s (and continue today). Believing that North Carolina governor Bob Scott's proposal to merge all state institutions under one centralized board could lead to the phasing out of the five public HBCUs, more than five thousand black students met at Shaw-U in Raleigh on October 25, 1971. They marched to the state capitol, where they heard passionate pleas to "Save Black Schools." SOBU members spearheaded this defense, preparing a report earlier in the year on the "crisis" with the heading "Save Black Schools." The creation of a centralized board in Arkansas that year also sparked a capitol invasion, specifically by students from U-Arkansas at Monticello (formerly Arkansas A&M). SGA president Woodson Walker argued that other state institutions were just as white as his college was black, but they were not in the hot seat. Depriving students of voices "in the future of AA&M is an unethical and insidious act that demonstrates aggression against the welfare of Black people in this state," Woodson penned in a letter to Arkansas governor Dale Bumpers. Students in the "Save Black Schools" struggle contended that the inclusion of HBCUs in centralized state systems controlled mainly by whites may have led to more forms of equality between white and black public schools, but at the same time it standardized the exclusion of blacks from power over HBCUs. This egalitarian exclusion of HBCUs within state systems endures to this day.[4]

At HWCUs, egalitarian exclusion—*the prohibition or limiting of nonwhites, nonwhite authority, or race-specific initiatives using derivatives of equality or "reverse" discrimination as justifications*—first rose to prominence in the spring of 1969, when the federal government threatened to pull funding from institutions that agreed to the most radical brand of black student demands. In order to not violate the "compliance requirements of Title VI of the Civil Rights Act of 1964," HEW ordered that housing, social activity spaces, and Black Studies units "must be available to all students without regard to race," and that assignments must be made "in a nondiscriminatory manner." Activists classified HEW's directive for color blindness in an extremely racialized society as absurd, just as students and BCM supporters did when presidents used this mantra to reject demands. For instance, UNC at Chapel Hill chancellor J. Carlyle Sitterson responded to the Black Student Movement's (BSM) demands in late January 1969, saying, "the University cannot, in policy or in practice, provide unique treatment for any single race, color, or creed; to do so would be a step backward." In reaction, the seemingly multiracial student and faculty New University Conference at Chapel Hill argued that "discrimination is a meaningless term unless one considers the intention and results of discriminatory practices. Discrimination which results in the subordination of one group to another is a far different thing from discrimination which leads to the equality of all people." Meanwhile, BSM chairman Preston Dobbins, announced that he hoped "Sitterson is not foolish enough to think that this is the end of the line." It was not. On February 21, 1969, about thirty-five black students marched across campus chanting, "We're going to burn this place down."[5]

The HEW edict, to a certain degree against what became known as affirmative action, has been increasingly used by champions of egalitarian exclusion and white privilege over the last forty years, including privileged African Americans who resent white perceptions cast on them as affirmative action babies. Most people agree that inequality has been apparent, and a problem. But many attempts to affirmatively act to eliminate the inequality, the focal drive of the BCM, have been classified as discriminatory. The noble intent of those who opposed black student demands was not to actively level the unequal score. At the most, it was to equalize the playing field—all the while probably knowing (or being ignorant of the fact) that merely equalize the playing field will merely stop the inequality from growing, will merely stop the knife from going in deeper. Demands for present equality have preserved past inequality.

The use of egalitarian exclusion came to a head in 1978, after five years of mainly defensive black student activism to resist cuts to their programs at schools such as Macalester-C in Minnesota, U-Michigan, Harvard, UC Santa Barbara, and U-Alabama. Allan Bakke believed that a special admissions program that set aside sixteen seats for nonwhites at the UC Davis medical school reversely discriminated against him and violated his civil rights when he was denied admission. He appealed to the courts. In 1978, the US Supreme Court mandated the thirty-seven-year-old white male's admission to UC Davis, ruling in *University of California Regents v. Bakke* that race can be a factor, but only one of many, to achieve a racial balance. The medical school discriminated against whites because it disqualified them from sixteen seats due only to their race. The court deemed this "quota" unconstitutional under the Equal Protection Clause of the Fourteenth Amendment. The court severely weakened the legality of affirmative action to heal the *present* manifestations of *past* discrimination.[6]

Many black students, particularly those studying law, did not need to have the long-term effects of the *Bakke* decision explained. They were livid, rising up around the nation. They often perceived the ruling as an "attack on" their "civil rights," as a poster shouted from a demonstration organized by the BSU at Roosevelt-U in 1978. Even before the ruling, on April 15, 1978, upwards of 30,000 mostly black students from along the eastern seaboard marched down Pennsylvania Avenue in Washington, DC, chanting, "We won't go back. Send Bakke back!" The DC coordinator of the demonstration was Jimmy Garrett, who organized the first BSU at SF State in 1966 and at the time taught political science at Howard. He gave a thrilling speech. "We said no to racism. We said no to sexism. We said no to Carter. We said no to those eight old white men on the Supreme Court." Carrier Fairley, a student at Rutgers-Newark, asked the press, "How can there be reverse discrimination when minorities aren't free now? That (Bakke) thing is crazy."[7]

According to Mary Frances Berry, who served as the assistant secretary of education from 1977 to 1980 in the Carter administration, the climate had shifted by the late 1970s. The "reaction" came from "everywhere, the backlash against the progress that had been made" with "rationales for why nothing more needed to be done." These rationales for nothing or for equality or to reverse "reverse discrimination" amplified in the 1980s and eventually became standardized by the end the century. The professed standardization of inclusion now too often excludes the champions of diversity from instituting race-specific programs, the primary way to eliminate past (and not to mention present) inequities. Nevertheless, these programs have continued to emerge. Mirroring operating procedures of racists in the twenty-first century, the shrewdest diversity workers create initiates for African Americans that do not exclude whites and are void of any public racial language. In effect, we live in an age in which both racism and the programmatic fight to undo its effects are tragically placed on the same demeaning plane, as both racists and racial reformers are similarly scared to broadcast race-specificity in fear of a virulent reaction. The public racial wars of 1960s are waged in private in the twenty-first century—a removal from the public sphere that many label progress. We do in fact live in a "colorblind society" where people purposely blind themselves from racism and disgrace those who force them to see.[8]

* * *

Aside from the underchronicled mass antiapartheid activism in the late 1970s and 1980s, the zealous support for the presidential campaigns of Jesse Jackson in 1984 and 1988 (and opposition to the Reagan administration), the resurgence of black student nationalism in the 1990s, the antiwar proclamations of the last decade, the current occupations and resistance to educational cuts in the midst of American military abundance, and the short-lived eruptions to societal scandals or tragedies—most recently the Jena 6 affair in Louisiana in 2007—black student activism has continued to defend the gains of the BCM from the conservative and liberal backlash. At the same time, as the 1960s and the BCM have grown older and more distant, the avowals of black student apathy have grown louder. However, vital to the generation of any new social movement is a consciousness of the prevailing conditions. Twenty-first-century higher educational racism (aside from demography) seems to be largely unknown to black students, largely unknown to many of us. In addition, when compared to students in the LBSM, they seem to be more bourgeoisie, more fearful with their knowledge of 1960s repression, and more imbued with a sense of freedom, since they do not see "white-only signs." Many seem to have bought into the notion that there is something progressive, selfless, and grassroots-oriented about ladder altruism, the idea their personal success as distant role models generates black community success. As the BCM has faded further into history, so too has the widespread student ideal of grassroots altruism, the drive to organize and create progressive community programs and leadership. Numerous black students have fused the two disparate notions into their ideology.

* * *

The extremely paternalistic pre-BCM moralized contraption may have been refashioned into the operation of the "familial environment," a principal element of the twenty-first century HBCU brand. Is this "familial environment" due to a genuine black solidarity or concern of administrators and professors willing to provide a home away from home, willing to share their wisdom with students they consider sovereign adults? Or is it (also) a result of a racialized paternalism from the pre-BCM idea that black students need extra help, care, and supervision due to their inferior blackness (in addition to their sometimes poor academic preparation)? Moreover, quite a few HBCUs still do not have coed dormitories or cross-gender room visitation for freshmen, and some schools still try to regulate more than the academic lives of their students. Hampton, for example (as of 2011), a university with many inventive initiatives, nevertheless turns students away from various functions for inappropriate dress and prohibits "at all times... except in the privacy of the student's living quarters... do-rags, stocking caps, skull caps and bandanas." This, and other elements of the dress code, "is based on the theory that learning to use socially acceptable manners" is a critical factor "in the total educational process."[9]

As some HBCUs still try to vindicate paternalism, and to moralize and civilize their students into "socially acceptable manners," diversity workers have become staples at HWCUs in the post-BCM era. However, these diversity workers have been placed in jobs they will eliminate the need for if they truly succeed. Said differently, they have filled positions in which it is in their self-interest to *not* do an exceptional job. They are working in staff or administrative posts, often close to (and only reporting to) presidents, in which it is sometimes in their self-interest to diffuse the very campus activism that once brought measurable diversity to their institution. And yet black students and higher education have given them the keys to the diversity movement during the last forty years. Some diversity officers have boldly challenged their institutions over the years, usually confident that students will revolt if they are dismissed. Most try to toe the treacherous line, keeping marginalized students and administrators pleased with their work. However, some do not have (nor desire) student support, and therefore find backing from the very people who are sometimes against true integration and real inclusion—upper administrators and trustees of institutions who may not support (although they would never say so publically) their curricula, programs, and student, faculty, and administrators bodies' reflecting the physical, cultural, and ideological diversity of the regions, states, or national spaces from which colleges draw students and onto which they project their identity. They can quickly picture the exodus of white alumni funding, students, and capital. Therefore, too many diversity officers are administrators performing administrative duties, representing the interests of the college or university and defending it against charges of racism, while occasionally ruffling feathers with serious questions and programs. They do not represent the interests of real diversity any more than an American politician represents the interests of her or his constituents. As a politician's primary aim is reelection, so too is career advancement the primary function of many diversity officers.[10]

At the same time, the ridicule must not be placed on the diversity officer any more than one can ridicule a politician for satisfying benefactors to fund her or his reelection. The ridicule needs to be placed on their paradoxical position, as many are doing the best they can in their positional anomaly, one that black students did not envision when they secured these black administrators and staff, some of whom were former black campus activists. It is the responsibility of the students (and faculty) to create a political atmosphere that compels the upper administration to empower the diversity officer with the freedom to truly institute meaningful diversity. This is what occurred when diversity officers were first hired at HWCUs during the BCM.

*   *   *

Progress is vibrant at HBCUs in the twentieth-first century. While some remain havens for black subordination, and many are toiling to stay afloat, quite a few are progressive sites of innovative, socially responsible, concerned learning, magnificent African American cultural production and refinement, and relevant, didactic scholarship with talented faculty, administrators, and students who constantly and consciously turn down HWCUs for HBCUs. Amid the criticism, many have a fertile love for HBCUs, growing from enriching social, cultural, and political experiences. In addition, somewhat meaningful diversity has been clear in terms of nationwide undergraduate black enrollment. After doubling during the BCM, between 1976 and 2008, black enrollment rose from 943,000 to 2,269,000, and the share of the overall enrollment increased from 10 percent to 14 percent (13.6 percent for graduate schools in 2009), slightly exceeding the overall black population of 12.8 percent in 2008. Still, it must be noted that too many African Americans are being herded into community colleges and for-profit institutes, a growing number of "black" college students are not from America, professors are steering African Americans, particularly women, away from STEM (science, technology, engineering, and mathematics) careers, men are vanishing from cohorts, and three times as many African Americans live in prison cells as in college dorms (as of 2007). It is a "mass incarceration" that Michelle Alexander labels "The New Jim Crow," leaving many young impoverished African Americans believing that prison cells are more incorporating than higher education. Then again, it makes sense, given that California spent 45 percent more on prisons than universities in 2010, a far cry from thirty years ago, when the state expended three times more on higher education.[11]

African Americans remain woefully underrepresented in the fairly permanent positions—administration (9.4 percent in 2001), trustee boards (8.8 percent in 2005), and full-time faculty (5.3 percent in 2009)—that comprise and guide the car of higher education that momentarily taxis students. Thus, in this inclusive exclusion (opening a limited amount of space for nonwhites and restricting them from everywhere else), African Americans can ride, but rarely drive, the academy. The faculty figure, barely one percent higher than its mark of 4.4 percent in 1975, is alarming, since faculty diversity directly leads to diverse academic leadership, curricular diversity, and an assortment of ideas and scholarship—vital to keeping off the mask and denormalizing whiteness. If faculty growth continues at this rate, then it will take more than two centuries to correspond with the current black student percentage. These poor numbers are partly due to the low number of doctorates, as African Americans earned 5.2 percent of all doctorates in 2004 (in fields other than education, which mainly produces K–college administrators). However, the faculty underrepresentation is also the result of white networks that clandestinely exclude African Americans, and *black lines*, specifically in the humanities and social sciences. Many departments at HWCUs have a set line (or number of lines) for African Americans (as they do for other under represented groups). It is usually the line(s) that treats the African American experience and is cross-listed with Africana Studies programs, a minute percentage of the faculty. It is difficult for African Americans to receive positions in nonblack lines, such as general Americanist positions, specifically when faculties have no pressure to diversify. Thus these black lines, forced on the academy by the BCM, have created an inclusive exclusion for African Americans professors.[12]

Using black lines to ostensibly diversify is not a new pattern or policy. In May 1968, the Yale BSA organized the nation's first Black Studies symposium, welcoming several scholars to provide a well-defined charge for the academy's newest discipline. The Ford Foundation's McGeorge Bundy, an alumnus of Yale, advised that "the strength of Black Studies was...in its ability...to desegregate the faculty and curriculum of traditionally 'white' disciplines." Using this "integrationist rationale," Bundy and the Ford Foundation granted ten million dollars to support two dozen interdepartmental programs over the next two years. As Robert Allen noticed, "With hundreds of such programs competing for limited funds, effective control of the future of Black Studies was thereby shifted away from black scholars and students, and instead...to the funding agencies—college administrations, government and foundations."[13]

Financed by white capital, interdepartmental programs arose with cross-listed professors in conflicting positions, like the diversity officers. Their "traditional" departments and Africana Studies programs have often competed for majors, prominence, and resources, while also having some opposing ideas. Black campus activists were aware of this paradox, compelling them to habitually demand autonomous Black Studies departments. "Cross listing may be better described as academic double cross," said activist Robert McCray at U-Illinois at Chicago in March 1973. Many black professors and interdepartmental programs have remarkably toed the line to make lasting contributions to the academy.[14]

At the same time, though, with their doctorates, supervision, tenure, and often institutional legitimacy in the existing disciplines, it is not hard to figure out where some of these cross-listed scholars' academic loyalty lies. More important, students during the BCM posed the discipline of Africana Studies as different than studying blacks using the assumptions, perspectives, methods, and methodologies that scholars in the existing disciplines had long used to validate black exclusion and inferiority. Many scholars have managed to carve out a space in the "traditional" disciplines and have used traditional methods to produce scholarship that has exposed and removed the mask and challenged normalized whiteness. But some who study African Americans have merely added a multicultural subject guise as the new colorful mask of normalized whiteness. In sum, this contested normalized whiteness has persisted alongside a contested Africana Studies, which Fabio Rojas terms a "counter center," or a "formalized space for oppositional consciousness." This "counter center" has inspired the carving out of other counter centers that are removing the mask and denormalizing whiteness (Chicana/o Studies, Latina/o Studies, Native American Studies, Asian Studies, and Whiteness Studies), patriarchy (Women's Studies, Men's Studies, and Gender

Studies), and heterosexuality (Queer Studies). In addition, Africana Studies has increasingly engaged in the all-important disciplinary process of reproducing itself through its more than ten doctoral programs founded in roughly the last twenty-five years, first in 1988 at Temple-U by Molefi Kete Asante and most recently at UPENN, Indiana-U, Brown-U, and UW Milwaukee.[15]

* * *

One of the dominant assumptions in this analysis of the reactionary racial reconstitution of higher education by conservatives, liberals, and black egalitarian elites is the idea that conditions of inequity usually demonstrate intent. In the twenty-first century, popular notions of racism, and more important, what proves racism, have not caught up with the performance of racism. In other words, we are using racism's spectacles from the 1950s to see racism in 2011. We are looking for racist public statements, laws, and policies, like the ones that harnessed the educational mainstream before civil rights and black power, to prove racism at a time when racists rarely make racist statements, and racist laws and policies rarely use direct racial (i.e., blacks, whites) language.

For higher education, a lily-white condition *does* prove intent, incompetence, or acceptance. Intention and acceptance are virtually the same when it comes to diversity work. There is no major difference between a college that intends to keep a college faculty below 5 percent black and a college that accepts a proportion of black faculty that is perpetually below 5 percent. By acceptance, the college or university chooses not to divert resources to dramatically change that figure, to truly become diverse, to live up to the diversity statement it keeps broadcasting. Astute administrators speak regularly about diversity, say they want to be diverse, say they are trying, but send little money and power in that direction, demonstrating their acceptance.

One of the first to discuss these empty avowals, this conserving egalitarian or inclusive exclusion, was SF State's Nathan Hare in his groundbreaking Black Studies proposal of April 29, 1968. "It will be an irony of recorded history that 'integration' was used in the second half of this century to hold the black race down just as segregation was so instigated in the first half." With the second half of this century now recorded, Hare's irony has come to fruition. While the ideals put forth by black students have been somewhat implemented, the ideals of a countermovement to the BCM have kept the "black race down" in the name of equality and integration. The contradictions will not be confronted by an imitation of the BCM (1965–1972)—the collective black student thrust of radicalized SGAs, BSUs, BSAs, AASs, of blackness, of Africa, of demands, of deadlines, of black power shrieks, of strikes, of building takeovers by five or five hundred, of ten-person student meetings, of ten-thousand-student marches, of arrests, of expulsions, of students feeling emboldened by the sights and sounds and words and pulse of their living and deceased heroes. These black students stood high on the shoulders of the LBSM and for eight long years forced higher education to look upward to raised fists, Afros, Pan-African flags, and educational change. Likewise, the future probing ideas and protest tactics will build on the Black Campus Movement.[16]

Abbreviations Used in the Notes

The following abbreviations are used in the notes.

College and University Archives and Special Collections

AAMU Archives	Alabama A&M University Archives, Normal, Alabama
ACSD Archives	Augustana College Archives, Sioux Falls, South Dakota
AU Archives	American University Archives, Washington, DC
ADU Archives	Adelphi University Archives, Garden City, New York
ALSU Archives	Alabama State University Archives, Montgomery, Alabama
ASU Archives	Alcorn State University Archives, Alcorn State, Mississippi
BERC Archives	Berea College Archives, Berea, Kentucky
BOW Archives	Bowdoin College Archives, Brunswick, Maine
BSU Archives	Boise State University Archives, Boise, Idaho
BRWU Archives	Brown University Archives, Providence, Rhode Island
BUTU Archives	Butler University Archives, Indianapolis, Indiana
CARC Archives	The Staubitz Archives, Carthage College, Kenosha, Wisconsin
CWRU Archives	Case Western Reserve University Archives, Cleveland, Ohio
CATU Archives	American Catholic History Research Center and University Archives, The Catholic University of America, Washington, DC
CHU Archives	Chatham University Archives, Pittsburgh, Pennsylvania
CLAC Archives	The Claremont Colleges Archives, Claremont, California
CLAU Archives	Clarke University Archives, Dubuque, Iowa
CLEU Archives	Clemson University Archives, Clemson, South Carolina
COC Archives	Colby College Archives, Waterville, Maine
COLU Archives	Colgate University Special Collections and Archives, Hamilton, New York
CSTU Archives	Chicago State University Archives and Special Collections, Chicago, Illinois

CSU Archives	Colorado State University Archives and Special Collections, Fort Collins, Colorado
CSUFRES Archives	California State University, Fresno University Archives, Fresno, California
CSUP Archives	Colorado State University Pueblo Archives, Pueblo, Colorado
CSUSTAN Archives	California State University, Stanislaus Archives, Turlock, California
CU Archives	Creighton University Archives, Omaha, Nebraska
CWPLIU Archives	Archives of C. W. Post Campus of Long Island University, Brookville, New York
CWRU Archives	Case Western Reserve University Archives, Cleveland, Ohio
DARC Archives	Dartmouth College Archives, Hanover, New Hampshire
DEC Archives	Defiance College Archives, Defiance, Ohio
DEPW Archives	DePauw University Archives, Greencastle, Indiana
DICC Archives	Dickinson College Archives, Carlisle, Pennsylvania
DKU Archives	Duke University Archives, Durham, North Carolina
DKU SC	Rare Book, Manuscript, and Special Collections Library, Duke University, Durham, North Carolina
DQU Archives	Duquesne University Archives and Special Collections, Pittsburgh, Pennsylvania
DSU Archives	Delta State University Archives, Cleveland, Mississippi
EMU Archives	Eastern Michigan University Archives, Ypsilanti, Michigan
ETSU Archives	East Tennessee State University Archives, Johnson City, Tennessee
ECSU Archives	Elizabeth City State University Archive, Elizabeth City, North Carolina
F&MC Archives	Franklin & Marshall College Archives and Special Collections, Lancaster, Pennsylvania
FARU Archives	Fairfield University Archives, Fairfield, Connecticut
FASU Archives	Charles W. Chesnutt Library Archives and Special Collections, Fayetteville State University, Fayetteville, North Carolina
FC Archives	Franklin College Archives, Franklin, Indiana
FU SC	Fisk University Special Collections and Archives, Nashville, Tennessee
GAU Archives	Gannon University Archives, Erie, Pennsylvania
GC Archives	Guilford College Archives, Greensboro, North Carolina
GOC Archives	Goucher College Archives, Baltimore, Maryland
GWU SC	George Washington University Special Collections Research Center, Washington, DC
HARU Archives	Harvard University Archives, Cambridge, Massachusetts
HEIU Archives	Heidelberg University Archives, Tiffin, Ohio

HEC Archives	Hendrix College Archives, Conway, Arkansas
IIT Archives	Illinois Institute of Technology Archives, Chicago Illinois
ISU Archives	Iowa State University Archives, Ames, Iowa
IUN Archives	Calumet Regional Archives, Indiana University Northwest, Gary, Indiana
IWESU Archives	Tate Archives and Special Collections, Illinois Wesleyan University, Bloomington, Illinois
JHU Archives	The Ferdinand Hamburger University Archives, The John Hopkins University, Baltimore, Maryland
KAC Archives	Kalamazoo College Archives, Kalamazoo, Michigan
KC Archives	Special Collections and Archives, Knox College, Galesburg, Illinois
KSU Archives	Kentucky State University, Frankfort, Kentucky
KUP Archives	Kutztown University of Pennsylvania Archives and Special Collections, Kutztown, Pennsylvania
LAFC Archives	Lafayette College Special Collections and Archives, Easton, Pennsylvania
LGU Archives	Langston University Archives, Langston, Oklahoma
LAWU Archives	Lawrence University Archives, Appleton, Wisconsin
LEHIU SC	Lehigh University Special Collections, Bethlehem, Pennsylvania
LUTC Archives	Luther College Archives, Decorah, Iowa
MAC Archives	Marietta College Archives, Marietta, Ohio
MARU Archives	Marquette University Archives, Milwaukee, Wisconsin
MARSU Archives	Marshall University Archives, Huntington, West Virginia
MHC Archives	Mount Holyoke College Archives and Special Collections, South Hadley, Massachusetts
MIDC Archives	Middlebury College Archives, Middlebury, Vermont
MILLC Archives	Millsaps College Archives, Jackson, Mississippi
MITU Archives	Michigan Technological University Archives, Houghton, Michigan
MMC Archives	Marymount Manhattan College Archives, New York, New York
MONC Archives	Monmouth College Archive, Monmouth, Illinois
MORC Archives	Morningside College Archives, Sioux City, Iowa
MSSU Archives	Mississippi State University Archives, Mississippi State, Mississippi
MSU Archives	Michigan State University Archives and Historical Collections, East Lansing, Michigan
NATU Archives	North Carolina A&T State University Archives, Greensboro, North Carolina
NCCU Archives	North Carolina Central University Archives and Records, Durham, North Carolina
NCSU Archives	North Carolina State University Archives, Raleigh, North Carolina
NEIU Archives	Northeastern Illinois University Archives, Chicago, Illinois

NIAU Archives	University of Northern Iowa Special Collections and University Archives, Cedar Falls, Iowa
NMSU Archives	Hobson-Huntsinger University Archives, New Mexico State University, Las Cruces, New Mexico
NMU Archives	Northern Michigan University Archives, Marquette, Michigan
NOWU Archives	Northwestern University Archives, Evanston, Illinois
OC Archives	Occidental College Archives, Los Angeles, California
OSU Archives	Oregon State University Archives, Corvallis, Oregon
OTTU Archives	Ottawa University Archives and Collections, Ottawa, Kansas
PC Archives	Special and Archival Collections, Providence College, Providence, Rhode Island
PSU Archives	Pittsburg State University Archives, Pittsburg, Kansas
RPI Archives	Rensselaer Polytechnic Institute Archives and Special Collections, Troy, New York
ROSC Archives	Rosemont College Archives, Bryn Mawr, Pennsylvania
ROSU Archives	Roosevelt University Archives, Chicago, Illinois
RWU Archives	Roger Williams University Archives, Bristol, Rhode Island
SAPC Archives	St. Andrews Presbyterian College Archives, Laurinburg, North Carolina
SJU Archives	Saint John's University Archives, Collegeville, Minnesota
SKIC Archives	Skidmore College Archives, Saratoga Springs, New York
SIUC SC	Southern Illinois University Carbondale Special Collections Research Center, Carbondale, Illinois
SORU Archives	Southern Oregon University Archives, Ashland, Oregon
SPC Archives	Saint Peter's College Archives, Jersey City, New Jersey
SRU Archives	Slippery Rock University Archives, Slippery Rock, Pennsylvania
STAU Archives	The Special Collections and University Archives Department, St. Ambrose University, Davenport, Iowa
STCST Archives	St. Cloud State University Archives, St. Cloud, Minnesota
STCU Archives	St. Catherine University Archives, St. Paul, Minnesota
STOC Archives	St. Olaf College Shaw-Olson Center for College History, Northfield, Minnesota
SUNYB Archives	College Archives, The College at Brockport, State University of New York Archives, Brockport, New York
TCU Archives	Texas Christian University Archives and Historical Collection, Fort Worth, Texas
THIC Archives	Thiel College Archives, Greenville, Pennsylvania
TOGC Archives	Tougaloo College Archives, Tougaloo, Mississippi
TRAN Archives	Transylvania University Archives, Lexington, Kentucky
TRIC Archives	Trinity College Archives, Trinity, Connecticut
TRIU Archives	Trinity University Special Collections and Archives, San Antonio, Texas
TRSU Archives	Truman State University Archives, Kirksville, Missouri

TSTC Archives	H. Council Trenholm State Technical College Archives, Montgomery, Alabama
TUU Archives	Tulane University Archives, New Orleans, Louisiana
UA Archives	University of Alabama Archives, Tuscaloosa, Alabama
UAF Archives	University of Arkansas at Fayetteville Archives, Fayetteville, Arkansas
UAK Archives	Archival Services of University Libraries, The University of Akron, Akron, Ohio
UC Archives	Ursuline College Archives, Pepper Pike, Ohio
UCLA Archives	University of California, Los Angeles Archives, Los Angeles, California
UCSAN Archives	University of Santa Barbara Archives, Santa Barbara, California
UDAY Archives	University of Dayton Archives, Dayton, Ohio
UGA Archives	University of Georgia Archives, Athens, Georgia
UHOU Archives	University of Houston Archives, Houston, Texas
UIA Archives	The University of Iowa Archives, Iowa City, Iowa
UIC Archives	University of Illinois at Chicago Archives, Chicago, Illinois
UKS Archives	University of Kansas Archives, Lawrence, Kansas
UMAD Archives	University of Massachusetts Dartmouth Archives and Special Collections, North Dartmouth, Massachusetts
UMES Archives	University of Maryland Eastern Shore Archives, Princess Anne, Maryland
UMSTL Archives	University of Missouri–St. Louis University Archives, St. Louis, Missouri
UMT Archives	The University of Montana Archives and Special Collections, Missoula, Montana
UMU Archives	Robert Herman Carr Historical Room, University of Mount Union, Alliance, Ohio
UMW Archives	University of Mary Washington Archives, Fredericksburg, Virginia
UNAL SC	University of North Alabama Special Collections, Florence, Alabama
UNC Archives	The University of North Carolina at Chapel Hill Archives, Manuscripts Department, Chapel Hill, North Carolina
UNCC Archives	The University of North Carolina at Charlotte Archives, Charlotte, North Carolina
UND Archives	The University of North Dakota Archives, Grand Forks, North Dakota
UO Archives	University of Oregon Archives, Eugene, Oregon
UP Archives	University of the Pacific Archives, Stockton, California
USA Archives	University of South Alabama Archives, Mobile, Alabama
USF Archives	University of San Francisco Archives, San Francisco, California
UTC Archives	Utica College Archives, Utica, New York

UTNK Archives	University of Tennessee Archives, Knoxville, Tennessee
UTA Archives	University of Texas at Arlington Archives, Arlington, Texas
UTXA Archives	University of Texas at Austin Archives, Briscoe Center for American History, Austin, Texas
UUTAH Archives	University of Utah University Archives, Salt Lake City, Utah
UVA SP	Albert and Shirley Small Special Collections Library, University of Virginia, Charlottesville, Virginia
UWM Archives	University of Wisconsin at Milwaukee Archives Department, Milwaukee, Wisconsin
UWOSH Archives	University of Wisconsin at Oshkosh Archives, Oshkosh, Wisconsin
VC Archives	The Catherine Pelton Durrell '25 Archives and Special Collections Library, Vassar College, Poughkeepsie, New York
VTU Archives	Virginia Polytechnic Institute and State University Archives, Blacksburg, Virginia
VU Archives	Vanderbilt University Archives, Nashville, Tennessee
WARC Archives	Wartburg College Archives, Waverly, Iowa
WC Archives	Wellesley College Archives, Wellesley, Massachusetts
WCSU Archives	Western Connecticut State University Archives, Danbury, Connecticut
WEBU Archives	Webster University Archives, St. Louis, Missouri
WFU Archives	Wake Forest University, Winston-Salem, North Carolina
WIC Archives	Wilmington College Archives, Wilmington, Ohio
WILC Archives	Wilson College C. Elizabeth Boyd '33 Archives, Chambersburg, Pennsylvania
WPU Archives	Wilcox Library Archives, William Penn University, Oskaloosa, Iowa
WSSU Archives	Winston-Salem State University Archives, Winston-Salem, North Carolina
WU Archives	Washington University Archives, St. Louis, Missouri
XUO Archives	Xavier University Archives, Cincinnati, Ohio

Research Venues

CEMA	California Ethnic and Multicultural Archives, Department of Special Collections, University of California at Santa Barbara, Santa Barbara, California
CESKAA	The Center of Excellence for the Study of African Americans, Blazer Library, Kentucky State University, Frankfort, Kentucky
KHS	Special Collections and Archives, Kentucky Historical Society, Frankfort, Kentucky

LBJL   Lyndon Baines Johnson Library and Museum, Austin, Texas
PALL   Paley Library, Temple University, Philadelphia, Pennsylvania
SCHBG   Schomburg Center for Research in Black Culture, New York
        Public Library, New York, New York
SHC   Southern Historical Collection, The Wilson Library,
        The University of North Carolina at Chapel Hill, Chapel Hill,
        North Carolina
WTXC   The Dr. Ralph R. Chase West Texas Collection, Porter Henderson
        Library, Angelo State University, San Angelo, Texas

**Campus Periodicals (with abbreviations
of institutional archives)**

AH   *Alcorn Herald*, ASU Archives
AJR   *The A&J Register*, NATU Archives
ARR   *The Arrow*, CSUP Archives
AT   *Arkansas Traveler*, UAF Archives
ATN   *Afro-Times Newsletter*, MSSU Archives
BDH   *Brown Daily Herald*, BRWU Archives
BQ   *The Bristol Quill*, RWU Archives
BUTM   *Butler Magazine*, BUTU Archives
BW   *The Brown & White*, LEHIU SC
CC   *College Chips*, LUTC Archives
CE   *Campus Echo*, NCCU Archives
CHO   *Choragos*, MHC Archives
CP   *The College Profile*, HEC Archives
COE   *The Colby Echo*, COC Archives
COR   *College Reporter*, F&MC Archives
CR   *Collegian Reporter*, MORC Archives
CUR   *Currents*, MMC Archives
CRW   *Crimson-White*, UA Archives
CW   *Catherine Wheel*, STCU Archives
DB   *Daily Bruin*, UCLA Archives
DC   *Duke Chronicle*, DKU Archives
DCK   *Dickinsonian*, DICC Archives
DCN   *Defiance Crescent-News*, DEC Archives
DI   *The Daily Iowan*, UIA Archives
DN   *Daily Nexus*, UCSAN Archives
FLU   *Flush*, MITU Archives
GK   *Gannon Knight*, GAU Archives
GUI   *The Guilfordian*, GC Archives
HARD   *Harambee*, DKU Archives
HC   *The Harvard Crimson*, HARU Archives
HEIA   *Heidelberg Alumni*, HEIU Archives
HT   *Hornet Tribune*, ALSU Archives

KEY   *The Keystone*, KUP Archives
KT   *The Kentucky Thorobred*, KSU Archives
LA   *Lawrence Alumnus*, LAWU Archives
LAFA   *Lafayette Alumnus*, LAFC Archives
LUG   *The Langston University Gazette*, LGU Archives
MM   *The Manitou Messenger*, STOC Archives
MNL   *Middlebury News Letter*, MIDC Archives
MTL   *Michigan Tech Lode*, MITU Archives
NI   *Normal Index*, AAMU Archives
NIA   *Northern Iowan*, NIAU Archives
NS   *The Northwest Student*, IUN Archives
OGB   *Old Gold and Black*, WFU Archives
OTTC   *The Ottawa Campus*, OTTU Archives
PP   *Post Pioneer*, CWPLIU Archives
PSAC   *The Paper SAC*, STAU Archives
RA   *Ra* (Claremont Colleges Black Studies newspaper), CLAC Archives
RB   *The Red and Black*, UGA Archives
RP   *The Ram Page*, WTXC
RU   *Round Up*, NMSU Archives
SFF   *The Skiff*, TCU Archives
STA   *The Stag*, FARU Archives
STY   *The Stylus*, SUNYB Archives
TA   *The Arbiter*, BSU Archives
TAN   *Tangerine*, UTC Archives
TAR   *The Arrow*, CARC Archives
TB   *The Billboard*, WILC Archives
TBC   *The Black Collegian*, WU Archives
TC   *The Chronicle*, TOGC Archives
TCC   *The College Chronicle*, STCST Archives
TCE   *The Creightonian*, CU Archives
TCO   *The Cowl*, PC Archives
TCOL   *The Collegio*, PSU Archives
TCOR   *The Courier*, CLAU Archives
TDAR   *The Dartmouth*, DARC Archives
TDC   *The Daily Cougar*, UHOU Archives
TDEL   *The Delphian*, ADU Archives
TDP   *The DePauw*, DEPW Archives
TDS   *The Dakota Student*, UND Archives
TDT   *The Daily Texan*, UTXA Archives
TE   *The Eagle*, AU Archives
TECH   *The Technician*, NCSU Archives
TELB   *Tel-Buch* (yearbook), UAK Archives
TEM   *Tempo*, CSTU Archives
TF   *The Franklin*, FC Archives

TFA	*The Flor-Ala*, UNAL SC
TFOG	*The Foghorn*, USF Archives
THAT	*The Hatchet*, GWU SC
TIN	*The Index*, TRSU Archives
TL	*The Lance*, SAPC Archives
TLAF	*The Lafayette*, LAFC Archives
TMAR	*The Marcolian*, MAC Archives
TMIR	*The Mirror*, ACSD Archives
TMN	*The Miscellany News*, VC Archives
TN	*Technology News*, IIT Archives
TNA	*The News Argus*, WSSU Archives
TO	*The Occidental*, OC Archives
TOW	*Tower*, CATU Archives
TPAR	*The Parthenon*, MARSU Archives
TPC	*The Penn Chronicle*, WPU Archives
TQ	*The Quill*, UC Archives
TRA	*The Rambler*, TRAN Archives
TRAM	*The Rambler*, ROSC Archives
TREF	*The Reflector*, MSSU Archives
TRI	*Trinitonian*, TRIU Archives
TS	*The Signal*, UTXA Archives
TSL	*The Student Life* (Pomona College student newspaper), CLAC Archives
TT	*Trinity Tripod*, TRIC Archives
TTH	*The Thielensian*, THIC Archives
TTIG	*The Tiger*, CLEU Archives
TTO	*The Torch*, ROSU Archives
TV	*The Voice*, FASU Archives
VA	*Vanguard*, USA Archives
WAT	*Watani*, UMT Archives
WEB	*The Web*, WEBU Archives
WEL	*Wellesley* (magazine), WC Archives
WIT	*Witness*, WIC Archives
WT	*The Wartburg Trumpet*, WARC Archives
XUN	*Xavier University News*, XUO Archives

Community Periodicals

AA	*Afro-American*, Baltimore, Maryland, ProQuest Historical Newspapers (hereafter PHN)
AR	*The Alliance Review*, Alliance, Ohio
ADW	*Atlanta Daily World*, Atlanta, Georgia, PHN
BG	*Boston Globe*, Boston, Massachusetts, PHN
BSB	*Bay State Banner*, Boston, Massachusetts, ProQuest Ethnic

NewsWatch: A History (hereafter ENWH)

CD	*The Chicago Defender*, Chicago, Illinois, PHN
CH	*Clarion Herald*, New Orleans, Louisiana
CHE	*The Chronicle of Higher Education*, Washington, DC
CJ	*The Courier-Journal*, Louisville, Kentucky
CRP	*The Cedar Rapids Gazette*, Cedar Rapids, Iowa
CT	*Chicago Tribune*, Chicago, Illinois, PHN
EB	*Ebony*, Chicago, Illinois
FPM	*Fish Piss Magazine*, Montreal, Quebec
JG	*The Journal & Guide*, Norfolk, Virginia
LK	*Look*, Des Moines, Iowa
NBH	*The New Britain Herald*, New Britain, Connecticut
NE	*Newsweek*, New York, New York
NYAN	*New York Amsterdam News*, New York, New York, PHN
NYE	*New York Evangelist*, New York, New York, Pro-Quest American Periodical Series Online (hereafter PAPS)
NYOC	*New York Observer and Chronicle*, New York, New York, PAPS
NYT	*New York Times*, New York, New York, PHN
NYTM	*New York Times Magazine*, New York, New York, PHN
OP	*The Oakland Post*, Oakland, California, ENWH
PC	*Pittsburg Courier*, Pittsburg, Pennsylvania, PHN
PT	*Philadelphia Tribune*, Philadelphia, Pennsylvania, PHN
SFC	*San Francisco Chronicle*, San Francisco, California
SNS	*Springfield News-Sun*, Springfield, Ohio
SO	*The Sacramento Observer*, Sacramento, California, ENWH
SOBUN	*SOBU Newsletter*, Greensboro, North Carolina, SOBU Publications, box 2, folder: newsletters, ECSU Archives
SR	*Sun Reporter*, San Francisco, California, ENWH
ST	*The Seattle Times*, Seattle, Washington
TBS	*The Baltimore Sun*, Baltimore, Maryland, PHN
TB	*The Blade*, Toledo, Ohio
TC	*The Crisis*, New York, New York
TH	*The Herald*, Rock Hill, South Carolina
TL	*The Liberator*, Boston, Massachusetts, PAPS
TMG	*The Guardian*, London, England, PHN
TN	*The Nation*, New York, New York
TNR	*The New Republic*, Washington, DC
TP	*The Philanthropist*, Cincinnati, Ohio, PAPS
TSD	*Tri-State Defender*, Memphis, Tennessee, ENWH
TWP	*The Washington Post*, Washington, DC, PHN
WSJ	*The Wall Street Journal*, New York, New York, PHN
WT	*Watertown Times*, Watertown, Wisconsin

Notes

Introduction

1. "Troops Sent to U. of Wisconsin," *NYT*, February 13, 1969; Calvin B. T. Lee, *The Campus Scene, 1900–1970: Changing Styles in Undergraduate Life* (New York: McKay, 1970), pp. 147–148; Judith Lyons and Morgan Lyons, "Black Student Power," in *Academic Supermarkets: A Critical Case Study of a Multiversity* (San Francisco: Jossey-Bass, 1971), pp. 303–321; "Troops Use Tear Gas at U. of Wisconsin," *NYT*, February 14, 1969.

2. Rodney Stark, "Protest + Police = Riot," in *Black Power and Student Rebellion*, eds. James McEvoy and Abraham Miller, (Belmont, CA: Wadsworth, 1969), p. 170; "BSA Asks Black Studies," *TTO*, February 17, 1969, ROSU Archives; Joy Ann Williamson, *Black Power on Campus: The University of Illinois, 1965–75* (Urbana, IL: University of Illinois Press, 2003), pp. 94–97; Allan Kornberg and Joel Smith, "'It Ain't Over Yet': Activism in a Southern University," in *Black Power and Student Rebellion*, pp. 107–109.

3. Conrad M. Dyer, "Protest and the Politics of Open Admissions: The Impact of the Black and Puerto Rican Students' Community (of City College)," (PhD. diss., City University of New York, 1990), pp. 105–110; "Vandals Attack C.C.N.Y. Buildings," *NYT*, February 18, 1969; Joy Ann Williamson, *Radicalizing the Ebony Tower: Black Colleges and the Black Freedom Struggle in Mississippi* (New York: Teachers College Press, 2008), pp. 140–141; Daniel Harris and Joseph Honcharik, *Staff Study of Campus Riots and Disorders, October 1967–May 1969* (Washington, DC: U.S. Government Printing Office, 1969), p. 25.

4. I did not find any record of black campus activism at any of the institutions in Alaska.

5. Darlene Clark Hine, William Hine, and Stanley Harrold note that "some observers describe the period of activism between 1968 and 1975 as the 'second phase' of the black students' movement." See Darlene Clark Hine, William C. Hine, and Stanley Harrold, *The African-American Odyssey, Combined Volume* (Upper Saddle River, NJ: Prentice Hall, 2008), p. 625.

6. Ibram H. Rogers, "The Black Campus Movement: The Case for a New Historiography," *The Sixties: A Journal of History, Politics and Culture* 4 (December 2011), pp. 169–184; Larry Neal, "The Black Arts Movement," *The Drama Review: TDR*, 12 (Summer 1968), pp. 29–39; James H. Cone, *Risks of Faith: The Emergence of a Black Theology of Liberation, 1968–1998* (Boston, 1999); Kimberly Springer, *Living for the Revolution: Black Feminist Organizations, 1968–1980* (Durham, NC: Duke University Press, 2005), p. 8. In addition, quite a few scholars have already described this struggle as a movement. See William W. Sales Jr., *From Civil Rights to Black Liberation:*

Malcolm X and the Organization of Afro-American Unity (Boston: South End Press, 1994), p. 169; Manning Marable, *How Capitalism Underdeveloped Black America: Problems in Race, Political Economy, and Society* (Boston: South End Press, 1983), p. 218; William L. Van Deburg, *New Day in Babylon: The Black Power Movement and American Culture, 1965–1975* (Chicago: University of Chicago Press, 1992), p. 71. For the *NYT* citation, see "The Campus Revolutions: One is Black, One White," *NYT*, May 12, 1969. For the scholars who distinguished between the two racial movements, see Andrew Barlow, "The Student Movement of the 1960s and the Politics of Race," *Journal of Ethnic Studies* 19 (Fall 1991), p. 1; John Erlich and Susan Erlich, "Introduction," in *Student Power, Participation and Revolution*, eds. John Erlich and Susan Erlich (New York: Association Press, 1971), p. 12.

7. There were interrelated, age-old gender, class, and sexual aspects of the constitution of higher education, which the New Left movements probably changed as well; these changes will not be intimately covered in this study. For example, capitalist and patriarchal culture have also been presented and masked as normal.

8. There was a lot of black campus activism during the BCM at urban community colleges, activism that is not explored in this work. For black power marginalization, see Ibram Rogers, "The Marginalization of the Black Campus Movement," *Journal of Social History* 42 (Fall 2008), pp. 175–182. For examples of marginalization in studies on "student" activism, see David C. Nichols, *Perspectives on Campus Tensions: Papers Prepared for the Special Committee on Campus Tensions* (Washington, DC: American Council of Education, 1970); Gerald J. De Groot, *Student Protest: The Sixties and After* (Reading, MA: Addison Wesley Publishing, 1998); Philip G. Altbach, Robert S. Laufer, and Sheila McVey, ed., *Academic Supermarkets*; Lee, *The Campus Scene*; Elvin Abeles, *The Student and the University: A Background Book on the Campus Revolt* (New York: Parents' Magazine Press, 1969); Roger Rapoport and Laurence J. Kirshbaum, *Is the Library Burning?* (New York: Random House, 1969). For these campus studies, see Williamson, *Black Power on Campus*; Wayne Glasker, *Black Students in the Ivory Tower: African American Student Activism at the University of Pennsylvania, 1967–1990* (Amherst, MA: University of Massachusetts, 2002); Stefan M. Bradley, *Harlem vs. Columbia University: Black Student Power in the Late 1960s* (Urbana, IL: University of Illinois Press, 2009); Richard P. McCormick, *The Black Student Protest Movement at Rutgers* (New Brunswick, NJ: Rutgers University Press, 1990); Donald Alexander Downs, *Cornell '69: Liberalism and the Crisis of the American University* (Ithaca, NY: Cornell University Press, 1999); William H. Exum, *Paradoxes of Protest: Black Student Activism in a White University* (Philadelphia: Temple University Press, 1985; Dikran Karagueuzian, *Blow It Up!: The Black Student Revolt at San Francisco State and the Emergence of Dr. Hayakawa* (Boston: Gambit, 1971); Jack Bass and Jack Nelson, *The Orangeburg Massacre* (Macon, GA: Mercer, 1984); Tim Spofford, *Lynch Street: The May 1970 Slayings at Jackson State College* (Kent, OH: Kent State University Press, 1988). There are merely two books that include national examinations of black student activism in this period at HWCUs—a monograph and an anthology, both published during the movement. See Harry Edwards, *Black Students* (New York: Free Press, 1970); James McEvoy and Abraham Miller, eds., *Black Power and Student Rebellion*.

9. For a recent text on activism in the late 1960s at HBCUs, see Jeffrey Alan Turner, *Sitting In and Speaking Out: Student Movements in the American South, 1960–1970* (Athens, GA: University of Georgia Press, 2010). For a few of the many recent studies on black power women, see Bettye Collier-Thomas and V. P. Franklin, eds., *Sisters in the Struggle: African American Women in the Civil Rights—Black Power Movement*

(New York: New York University Press, 2001); Dayo F. Gore, Jeanne Theoharis, and Komozi Woodard, eds., *Want to Start a Revolution?: Radical Women in the Black Freedom Struggle* (New York: New York University Press, 2009); Rhonda Y. Williams, "Black Women and Black Power," *OAH Magazine of History*, 22 (July 2008), pp. 22–26; Rhonda Y. Williams, "'We're Tired of Being Treated Like Dogs': Poor Women and Power Politics in Black Baltimore," *The Black Scholar*, 31 (Fall 2001), pp. 31–34. For scholars who claimed that the movement began in 1967 or 1968, see Robert Allen, *Black Awakening in Capitalist America: An Analytical History* (Garden City, NY: Doubleday, 1969), pp. 101–102, 216–221; Fabio Rojas, "Social Movement Tactics, Organization Change and the Spread of African-American Studies," *Social Forces* 84 (2006), pp. 2147–2166; John H. Bunzel, "Black Studies at San Francisco State," *The Public Interest* 13 (Fall 1968), pp. 22–38; Lawrence Crouchett, "Early Black Studies Movements," *Journal of Black Studies* 2 (December 1971), pp. 189–200; William H. Exum, *Paradoxes of Protest: Black Student Activism in a White University* (Philadelphia: Temple University Press, 1985), p. 7; Edwards, *Black Students*, pp. 3, 62; Earl Anthony, *The Time of the Furnaces: A Case Study of Black Student Revolt* (New York, Dial Press, 1971), p. 11. For claims that the Orangeburg Massacre and King's death triggered the movement, see (respectively) Hine, Hine, and Harrold, *The African-American Odyssey*, p. 625; Martin Kilson, "The Black Student Militant," *Encounter* 37 (1971), pp. 80–85.

1   An "Island Within": Black Students and Black Higher Education Prior to 1965

1. George James, *Stolen Legacy: Greek Philosophy Is Stolen Egyptian Philosophy* (Trenton, NJ: Africa World Press, 1993); John Fleming, "Blacks in Higher Education to 1954: A Historical Overview," in *Black Students in Higher Education: Conditions and Experiences in the 1970s*, ed. Gail E. Thomas (Westport, CT: Greenwood Press, 1981), p. 11; Henry N. Drewry and Humphrey Doermann, *Stand and Prosper: Private Black Colleges and Their Students* (Princeton, NJ: Princeton University Press, 2001), p. 32.
2. Joanne Pope Melish, *Disowning Slavery: Gradual Emancipation and "Race" in New England, 1780–1860* (Ithaca, NY: Cornell University Press, 1998), pp. 39–41. Drewry and Doermann, *Stand and Prosper*, p. 32; Peter J. Knapp, *Trinity College in the Twentieth Century: A History* (Hartford, CT: Trustees of Trinity College, 2000), p. 337.
3. Frank Bowles and Frank A. DeCosta, *Between Two Worlds: A Profile of Negro Higher Education* (New York: McGraw-Hill, 1971), p. 13; Carter G. Woodson, *Education of the Negro Prior to 1861: A History of the Education of the Colored People of the United States from the Beginning of Slavery to the Civil War* (Washington, DC: Associated Publishers, 1919), pp. 257.
4. Woodson, *Education of the Negro*, pp. 256–260, 290 (first quote); Herbert Aptheker, *Nat Turner's Slave Rebellion* (Mineola, NY: Dover Publications, 2006), pp. 23–24; Emeline Burlingame-Cheney, *The Story of the Life and Work of Oren B. Cheney: Founder and First President of Bates College* (Boston: Morningstar, 1907), p. 32–33 (last quote); Bowles and DeCosta, *Between Two Worlds*, p. 23.
5. Woodson, *Education of the Negro*, pp. 265, 268–269.
6. Ibid., pp. 266–273. See also "Avery College Historical Marker," ExlporePAhistory.com, accessed July 31, 2011, http://explorepahistory.com/hmarker.php?markerId=1-A-37E.
7. Drewry and Doermann, *Stand and Prosper*, p. 33.
8. "Educating Colored Students," *NYOC*, November 15, 1845.

9. Robert Johnson Jr., "The African-American Legacy at Bowdoin" (unpublished manuscript, February 26, 1997), African American Society Records, box 1, folder 12, BOWU Archives; William H. Watkins, *The White Architects of Black Education: Ideology and Power in America, 1865–1954* (New York: Teachers College Press, 2001), pp. 18–29; Anthony R. Mayo, "Charles Lewis Reason," *Negro History Bulletin* 5 (June 1942), pp. 212–215; Stephanie Y. Evans, *Black Women in the Ivory Tower, 1850–1954: An Intellectual History* (Gainesville, FL: University Press of Florida, 2007), pp. 22–23.

10. Dorothy Sterling, *The Making of an Afro-American: Martin Robison Delany* (Garden City, NY: Doubleday, 1971), pp. 122–135.

11. Robert Samuel Fletcher, *A History of Oberlin College*, Vol. 2 (Oberlin, OH: Oberlin College, 1943), pp. 534–535; Ellen N. Lawson, "Sarah Woodson Early: Nineteenth Century Black Nationalist 'Sister,'" *Umoja: A Scholarly Journal of Black Studies* 5 (Summer 1981), pp. 15–26.

12. Christopher J. Lucas, *American Higher Education: A History, Second Edition* (New York: Palgrave Macmillan, 2006), p. 122; James D. Anderson, *The Education of Blacks in the South, 1860–1935* (Chapel Hill, NC: The University of North Carolina Press, 1988), p. 5 (AMA quote); W. E. B. Du Bois, *Black Reconstruction in America: An Essay Towards a History of the Part Which Black Folk Played in the Attempt to Reconstruct Democracy in America, 1860–1880* (New York: Atheneum, 1971), p. 123.

13. Lucas, *American Higher Education*, pp. 168–169.

14. Ibid., pp. 165, 168–169 (first and last quotes); Anderson, *The Education of Blacks in the South*, p. 34, 39.

15. Drewry and Doermann, *Stand and Prosper*, pp. 58–59; Anderson, *The Education of Blacks in the South*, p. 29–30 (quote).

16. "Maryville College," *NYE*, July 6, 1876; Elisabeth S. Peck, *Berea's First Century: 1855–1955* (Lexington, KY: University of Kentucky Press, 1955), pp. 40–43; Maurice W. Britts, *Blacks on White College Campuses* (Minneapolis, MN: Challenge, 1975), p. 3. When the University of Arkansas was established in 1871, it was theoretically open to all races. But even though the state superintendent of public instruction was black at the time, the attendance of blacks was discouraged until it was written into law two years later. See Robert A. Leflar, *The First 100 Years: Centennial History of the University of Arkansas* (Fayetteville, AK: University of Arkansas Foundation, 1972), pp. 273–274.

17. Booker T. Washington, *Up From Slavery: An Autobiography* (Garden City, NY: Doubleday, 1963), pp. 30–44; Mark S. Giles, "Special Focus: Dr. Anna Julia Cooper, 1858–1964: Teacher, Scholar, and Timeless Womanist," *The Journal of Negro Education* 75 (Fall 2006), pp. 623–625; Jeanne L. Noble, *The Negro Woman's College Education* (New York: Columbia University, Teachers College, 1956), pp. 22–24; Bowles and DeCosta, *Between Two Worlds*, p. 33.

18. W. E. B. Du Bois, *Dusk of Dawn: An Essay Toward An Autobiography of a Race Concept* (New York: Harcourt, Brace and Company, 1940), pp. 22–24, 32–33, 34–37.

19. "Closed Against Negro Students," *CT*, September 15, 1890 (Maryland quote); Ralph Waldo Lloyd, *Maryville College: A History of 150 Years, 1819–1969* (Maryville, TN: Maryville College Press, 1969), p. 200; Peck, *Berea's First Century*, pp. 51–53; Jacqueline Anne Goggin, *Carter G. Woodson: A Life in Black History* (Baton Rouge, LA: Louisiana State University Press, 1993), p. 13; "Notes," *TN*, May 10, 1888.

20. Joy Ann Williamson, *Radicalizing the Ebony Tower: Black Colleges and the Black Freedom Struggle in Mississippi* (New York: Teachers College Press, 2008). pp. 24–26 (Alcorn quote); "Negroes in a Normal School," *NYT*, September 16, 1894 (Council quote); Raymond Wolters, *The New Negro on Campus: Black College Rebellions of the 1920s* (Princeton, NJ: Princeton University Press, 1975), pp. 192–193.

21. W. E. B. Du Bois, "The Talented Tenth," in *Du Bois Writings*, ed. Nathan Huggins (New York: The Library of America, 1986), p. 842; Washington, *Up From Slavery*, p. 161. Also, for his activities concerning civil rights causes, see David H. Jackson, *Booker T. Washington and the Struggle Against White Supremacy: The Southern Educational Tours, 1908–1912* (New York: Palgrave Macmillan, 2008) and *A Chief Lieutenant of the Tuskegee Machine: Charles Banks of Mississippi* (Gainesville, FL: University Press of Florida, 2002).

22. Watkins, *The White Architects of Black Education*, pp. 18–20, 23.

23. Barbara Ransby, *Ella Baker and the Black Freedom Movement: A Radical Democratic Vision* (Chapel Hill, NC: University of North Carolina Press, 2003), pp. 60–61; "Why A Student 'Strike,'" *AA*, February 28, 1925; "Carnegie at Tuskegee," *TWP*, April 6, 1906; "Tuskegee Celebrates its Twenty-Fifth Year," *NYT*, April 5, 1906.

24. Allen B. Ballard, *The Education of Black Folk: The Afro-American Struggle for Knowledge in White America* (New York: Harper & Row, 1973), pp. 23–24.

25. Lucas, *American Higher Education*, p. 181; "Won't Study with Negroes," *NYT*, November 21, 1908; "Medical Students Stir Up Race Issue," *NYT*, January 15, 1911; "University of Michigan," *NYT*, December 15, 1912; "African Americans," in Encyclopedia Brunoniana, ed. Martha Mitchell (Providence, RI: Brown University Library, 1993), http://www.brown.edu/Administration/News_Bureau/Databases /Encyclopedia/search.php?serial=A0080, accessed November 3, 2011; "Textures: Perspectives on African-American History at Butler," *BM*, Fall 2001, BUTU Archives; John R. Anderson, "Impacts of Iowa State University: Its National and International Presence and Its Enduring Legacies," in *A Sesquicentennial History of Iowa State University: Tradition and Transformation*, eds. Dorothy Schwieder and Gretchen Van Houten (Ames, IA: Iowa State University, 2007), p. 310.

26. Pamela Riney-Kehrberg, "Foundations of the People's College: The Early Years of Iowa State," in *A Sesquicentennial History of Iowa State University*, pp. 17–18; Wolters, *The New Negro on Campus*, pp. 322–323; "Student Snowballed and Stoned, Knifes an Assailant," *PT*, February 21, 1914; "Disarmed Negro students," *TBS*, December 14, 1906.

27. Martin Bauml Duberman, *Paul Robeson* (New York: Ballantine, 1989), pp. 19–23.

28. Lawrence C. Ross Jr., *The Divine Nine: The History of African American Fraternities and Sororities* (New York: Kensington, 2000), pp. 5–7.

29. W. E. B. Du Bois, *The College-Bred Negro American* (Atlanta: Atlanta University Press, 1910).

30. Paul Giddings, *In Search of Sisterhood: Delta Sigma Theta and the Challenge of the Black Sorority Movement* (New York: William Morrow and Company, 1988), pp. 29–30, 43–44.

31. Ross, *The Divine Nine*, pp. 46–48, 102–103, 133–134, 266, 298; Giddings, *In Search of Sisterhood*, pp. 46–53; "Textures," BUTU Archives.

32. Giddings, *In Search of Sisterhood*, pp. 18–19, 21.

33. Fleming, "Blacks in Higher Education to 1954," p. 13; Wolters, *The New Negro on Campus*, p. 257; Williamson, *Radicalizing the Ebony Tower*, p. 17; Drewry and Doermann, *Stand and Prosper*, pp. 59–60.

34. Langston Hughes, *The Big Sea* (New York: Hill and Wang, 1963), pp. 306–310; Langston Hughes, "Cowards from the Colleges," *TC*, August 1934, pp. 226–228.

35. Frederick Rudolph, *The American College and University: A History* (New York: Vintage Books, 1962), pp. 329–354; George Ruble Woolfolk, *Prairie View: A Study in Public Conscience, 1878–1946* (New York: Pageant Press, 1962), pp. 187, 197; Yolanda L. Watson and Sheila T. Gregory, *Daring to Educate: The Legacy of the Early Spelman College Presidents* (Sterling, VA: Stylus, 2005), p. 92; Williamson, *Radicalizing the Ebony Tower*, p. 27; Drewry and Doermann, *Stand and Prosper*, p. 128.

36. Noble, *The Negro Woman's College Education*, pp. 28–30.
37. The information on the NACW is from Linda M. Perkins, "The National Association of College Women: Vanguard of Black Women's Leadership and Education, 1923–1954," *Journal of Education* 172 (September 1990), pp. 65–75.
38. Drewry and Doermann, *Stand and Prosper*, p. 75; Charles S. Johnson, *The Negro College Graduate* (Chapel Hill, NC: University of North Carolina Press, 1938), pp. 10, 13, 20; B. Baldwin Dansby, *A Brief History of Jackson College: A Typical Story of the Survival of Education Among Negroes in the South* (Jackson, MS: Jackson College, 1953), pp. 83–84 (quote).
39. Joe M. Richardson and Maxine D. Jones, *Education for Liberation: The American Missionary Association and African Americans, 1890 to the Civil Rights Movement* (Tuscaloosa, AL: University of Alabama Press, 2009), p. 136; Paul Cooke, "Desegregated of Higher Education the District of Columbia," *The Journal of Negro Education* 27 (Summer 1958), p. 344; Glasker, *Black Students in the Ivory Tower*, pp. 20–21; "Columbia Negro Student Gets Two 'Death' Letters," *TBS*, April 6, 1924; "Threats Reach Negro Student," *BG*, April 5, 1924; "Columbia Whites in Arms Against Colored Student," *PT*, April 5, 1924; Charles Hamilton, *Adam Clayton Powell, Jr., The Political Biography of an American Dilemma* (New York: Maxwell Macmillan International, 1991), pp. 47–51.
40. George M. Waller, *Butler University: A Sesquicentennial History* (Bloomington, IN: Indiana University Press, 2006), pp. 192–194; "Textures," BUTU Archives (quote).
41. "Negro Graduates Protest," *NYT*, January 13, 1923 (bulletin quote); Lani Guinier, *Lift Every Voice: Turning a Civil Rights Setback into a Strong New Vision of Social Justice* (New York: Simon & Schuster, 1998), pp. 58–61.
42. "Plan to Stop Segregation at Univ. of Michigan," *PC*, February 21, 1931; "Supreme Court Forces Ohio U. to Accept Negro Students," *PT*, February 9, 1933; "'Big Ten' Universities Are Full of Prejudice," *PC*, October 13, 1934; "Color Bar Is Up at Williams College Now," *AA*, October 5, 1935; "California," *CD*, September 26, 1936; "California News," *CD*, March 24, 1934; "California Students Lodge Protest," *PT*, March 14, 1935; "Bar Discrimination on U. of Cal. Campus," *PC*, March 16, 1935; "California State News," *CD*, December 5, 1936; "Metropolitan Oakland Newsettes," *CD*, September 14, 1940. "San Francisco, Cal.," *PC*, October 16, 1937; "San Francisco, Cal.," *PC*, October 16, 1937; John H. Johnson, "What the People Say," *CD*, October 30, 1937; "Attend Negro History Week Tea," *CD*, February 24, 1940; "Cast Will Be Entertained on U. of Chicago Campus," *CT*, January 29, 1945; "Howard U. Professor Thrills Big Audience at Univ. of Chicago," *CD*, February 6, 1937.
43. Florence Ridlon, *Black Physician's Struggle for Civil Rights: Edward C. Mazique, M.D.* (Albuquerque, NM: University of New Mexico Press, 2005), pp. 67–68; "Atlanta Aroused By a Murder Case," *NYT*, August 3, 1930; "Guilty of Killing Negro Student," *BG*, July 29, 1930; Leroy Davis, *A Clashing of the Soul: John Hope and the Dilemma of African American Leadership and Black Higher Education in the Early Twentieth Century* (Athens, GA: University of Georgia Press, 1998), p. 313.
44. Drewry and Doermann, *Stand and Prosper*, p. 58.
45. Ibid., pp. 74–77; Fleming, "Blacks in Higher Education to 1954," p. 14; Whiting, *Guardians of the Flame*, p. 19.
46. Drewry and Doermann, *Stand and Prosper*, p. 78; "End of Exploitation Asked By First Lady," *NYT*, October 8, 1943; Frederick D. Patterson, "Would It Not Be Wise For Some Negro Schools to Make Joint Appeal to Public For Funds?" *PC*, January 30, 1943; Richard L. Plaut, "Prospects for the Entrance and Scholastic Advancement of Negroes in Higher Educational Institutions," *Journal of Negro Education* 36 (Summer 1967), p. 230 (NSSFNS quote).

47. Williamson, *Black Power on Campus*, p. 10; "More Negro Students," *NYT*, April 18, 1945.

48. Albert N. Whiting, *Guardians of the Flame: Historical Black Colleges Yesterday, Today, and Tomorrow* (Washington, DC: American Association of State Colleges and Universities, 1991), p. 16.

49. Paul Drederic Lawrence, *College Primer for Negro Students* (Palo Alto, CA: Pepsi-Cola Scholarship Board, 1948); W. E. B. Du Bois, "The Talented Tenth: Memorial Address," *Boule Journal* 15 (October 1948), pp. 3–13.

50. Du Bois, "The Talented Tenth," p. 3–13; Martha Biondi, *To Stand and Fight: The Struggle for Civil Rights in Postwar New York City* (Cambridge, MA: Harvard University Press, 2003), pp. 98–99; Edward N. Saveth, "Fair Educational Practices Legislation," *Annals of the American Academy of Political and Social Science* 275 (May 1951), p. 41; "College Color Line Cracking in South," *NYT*, October 23, 1950; "Approximately 200 Colored Students in Dixie Colleges," *PT*, November 11, 1950; "In Two Decades: What Progress in Faculty Desegregation?" *CHE*, May 20, 1968; Tommy L. Bynum, "'Our Fight Is For Right': The NAACP Youth Councils and College Chapters' Crusade for Civil Rights, 1936–1965" (Ph.D. diss., Georgia State University, 2007), pp. 99–100.

51. Robert C. McMath Jr., Ronald H. Bayor, James E. Brittain, Lawrence Foster, August W. Giebelhaus, and Germaine M. Reed, *Engineering the New South: Georgia Tech, 1895–1995* (Athens, GA: University of Georgia Press, 1985), p. 281; Lucas, *American Higher Education*, p. 261.

52. Thomas D. Hamm, *Earlham College: A History, 1847–1997* (Bloomington, IN: Indiana University Press, 1997), p. 203; "Northwestern U. Dean Upholds Segregation of Negro Students," *CD*, March 8, 1947; "Racism and the University of Illinois," *CD*, September 22, 1945; "Klan Cross Is Burned on Harvard U. Campus," *AA*, March 1, 1952; "Rocks Thrown in Windows of LSU Negro Students," *ADW*, March 19, 1953; Donald Landon, *Daring to Excel: 1905–2005: The First 100 Years of Southwest Missouri State* (Marceline, MO: Walsworth, 2004), p. 236.

53. Richard Robbins, *Sidelines Activist: Charles S. Johnson and the Struggle for Civil Rights* (Jackson, MS: University Press of Mississippi, 1996), pp. 150–154.

54. Bowles and DeCosta, *Between Two Worlds*, p. 53; Arnold H. Taylor, *Travail and Triumph: Black Life and Culture in the South Since the Civil War* (Westport, CT: Greenwood, 1976), pp. 130–135; "The End of Uncle Tom Teachers," no date, circa early 1960s, General Files, ASU Archives.

55. McMath et al., *Engineering the New South*, p. 312; "Five Colleges, Universities This Summer Have for the First Time Admitted Negro Students," *CD*, July 14, 1962; "Chicago Appoints Negro Professor," *NYT*, April 14, 1963.

56. Charles Rogers to Harold Levy, April 26, 1965, Papers of Lyndon B. Johnson: Presidential Papers, White House Central Files, 1963–1969 (hereafter WHCF): Human Rights, box 50, folder: HU 2-5 Education – Schooling 11/22/63 – 9/6/65, LBJL.

57. Alford A. Young, *Revolt of the Privileged: The Coming Together of the Black Community at Wesleyan University, 1965–1976* (Middletown, CT: Wesleyan University, 1988), pp. 5–6; Richard McCormick, *The Black Student Protest Movement at Rutgers* (New Brunswick, NJ: Rutgers University Press, 1990) pp. 14; "More Negroes Accepted by Exclusive Colleges," *CD*, May 5, 1965; "Colleges Beckon Negro Students," *NYT*, May 15, 1966; "Strongest Minority Representations in Oxy History Due to Little-Publicized Committee," *TO*, September 24, 1965, OC Archives; "UCLA Drive Seeks More Negro Grads," *DB*, August 27, 1963, UCLA Archives.

58. For a few examples of exchange programs, see "Xavier Begins Exchange Program," *CH*, November 4, 1965; "Submersion in Negro Culture Reveals Need for More

Exchange Programs," *CW*, May 9, 1969, STCU Archives; "Fisk Exchange," *TDEL*, January 15, 1969, ADU Archives; "White on Black," *TSL*, November 4, 1969, CLAR Archives; "Southern Colleges Seek Top Negroes," *NYT*, January 29, 1967; "Thurgood Marshall Scholarship Opens," *PC*, March 28, 1964; "Firms, Roosevelt U. Launch Unique Scholarship Program," *CD*, August 11, 1964; "Chicago Youth Gets 4-Year College Grant," *CD*, July 14, 1965; "V.P.I. to Recruit Negroes," *NYT*, November 28, 1965; "Negroes Get Free College Admissions," *NYAN*, October 30, 1965; "250 Top Students Awarded 4-Year College Scholarships," *CD*, February 8, 1966; "NAACP Education Committee Awards College Scholarships to 38 Students," *BSB*, June 22, 1967; Antoinette Frederick, *Northeastern University: An Emerging Giant, 1959–1975* (Boston: Northeastern University, 1982), pp. 344–345; John Egerton, *State Universities and Black Americans: An Inquiry into Desegregation and Equity for Negroes in 100 Public Universities* (Atlanta: Southern Education Reporting Service, 1969), pp. 4, 6.

2   "God Speed the Breed": New Negro in the Long Black Student Movement

1. Jacquelyn Dowd Hall, "The Long Civil Rights Movement and the Political Uses of the Past," *Journal of American History* 91 (March 2005), p. 1235.
2. Peniel E. Joseph, "Introduction: Community Organizing, Grassroots Politics, and Neighborhood Rebels: Local Struggles for Black Power in America," in *Neighborhood Rebels: Black Power at the Local Level*, ed. Peniel E. Joseph (New York: Palgrave Macmillan, 2010), pp. 10–11.
3. John Newton Templeton, *The Claims of Liberia* (Athens, OH: Maurice Press, 1980), http://www.seorf.ohiou.edu/xx057/john_newton_templeton.htm, accessed November 3, 2011.
4. Ibid.
5. "Speech of Thomas Paul," *TL*, February 29, 1841.
6. Lucy Stanton, "A Plea for the Oppressed," in *Lift Every Voice: African American Oratory, 1787–1900*, eds. Philip S. Foner and Robert James Branham (Tuscaloosa, AL: University of Alabama Press, 1998), pp. 220–223.
7. Vincent Harding, *There Is a River: The Black Struggle for Freedom in America* (New York: Harcourt Brace & Company, 1981), pp. 210–213; Stephanie Y. Evans, *Black Women in the Ivory Tower: 1850–1954* (Gainesville, FL: University Press of Florida, 2007), p. 23.
8. Joy Ann Williamson, *Radicalizing the Ebony Tower: Black Colleges and the Black Freedom Struggle in Mississippi* (New York: Teachers College Press, 2008), pp. 24–25.
9. "No War of Races," *NYT*, March 3, 1887; "War in a University," *NYT*, March 2, 1887; Leroy Davis, *A Clashing of the Soul: John Hope and the Dilemma of African American Leadership and Black Higher Education in the Early Twentieth Century* (Athens, GA: University of Georgia Press, 1998), pp. 70–71.
10. James D. Anderson, The Education of Blacks in the South, 1860–1935 (Chapel Hill, NC: The University of North Carolina Press, 1988), 60–62.
11. Rackman Holt, *Mary McLeod Bethune: A Biography* (New York: Doubleday, 1964), pp. 33–37.
12. Grif Stockley, *Ruled By Race: Black/White Relations in Arkansas from Slavery to the Present* (Fayetteville, AR: University of Arkansas Press, 2009), pp. 135–136.
13. "Negro Students in Riot," *CT*, December 9, 1905; "Howard's President Resigns," *TBS*, December 28, 1905; "Howard's New President," *TWP*, May 8, 1906; "Trustees Remain Firm," *TWP*, January 27, 1906; "Negro Students Strike," *TBS*, January 25, 1906.

14. "Atlanta Massacre," *TMG*, September 26, 1906; Darlene Clark Hine, William C. Hine, and Stanley Harrold, *The African American Odyssey, Combined Volume* (Upper Saddle River, NJ: Prentice Hall, 2008), pp. 431–432; Rebecca Burns, *Rage in the Gateway City: The Story of the 1906 Atlanta Race Riot* (Athens, GA: University of Georgia Press, 2009), pp. 136, 161–162.

15. "Negro Students Rebel," *TBS*, October 22, 1911; "Expels Negro Students," *NYT*, October 23, 1911; "Color Line at Cornell," *TWP*, March 8, 1911 (tired and Clark quote); "Color Line at Cornell," *NYT*, March 13, 1911 (Martin quote); "Race Issue at Cornell," *NYT*, March 28, 1911; "Colored Co-Eds Explain," *NYT*, April 3, 1911 (Ray and Vassar statement); "No Race Line at Cornell," *TWP*, April 11, 1911.

16. Paul Giddings, *In Search of Sisterhood: Delta Sigma Theta and the Challenge of the Black Sorority Movement* (New York: William Morrow and Company, 1988), pp. 27–28, 43, 55–60.

17. "Negro Students Revolt," *BG*, January 4, 1914; "Students Go on Strike at Shaw University," *AA*, January 10, 1914; "Striking Students Return," *AA*, January 24, 1914; "700 Students at Howard Go on a Strike," *AA*, April 8, 1916; Raymond Wolters, *The New Negro on Campus: Black College Rebellions of the 1920s* (Princeton, NJ: Princeton University Press, 1975), p. 276.

18. James R. Grossman, "A Chance to Make Good: 1900–1929," in *To Make Our World Anew, Volume Two: A History of African Americans Since 1880*, eds. Robin D. G. Kelley and Earl Lewis (New York: Oxford University Press, 2000), pp. 118–120.

19. Herbert Aptheker, "The Negro College Student in the 1920s—Years of Preparation and Protest: An Introduction," *Science and Society* 33 (Spring 1969), p. 151.

20. Valerie Boyd, "Zora Neale Hurston: The Howard University Years," *The Journal of Blacks in Higher Education* 39 (Spring 2003), p. 107.

21. Carter G. Woodson, *A Negro in Our History* (Washington, DC: Associate Publishers, 1922); Benjamin Brawley, *A Social History of the American Negro* (New York: The Macmillan Company, 1921), p. 386; Alain LeRoy Locke, ed., *The New Negro* (New York: Albert and Charles Boni, 1925).

22. Alain Locke, "The New Negro," in *The New Negro*, p. 3 (Old Negro quote); Aptheker, *The Negro College Student*, p. 156 (McKay quote).

23. The following section, particularly the major protests at Wilberforce, Fisk, FAMU, Howard, Lincoln (MO), and Hampton, aside from the discussion on the American Federation of Negro Students, is from Wolters, *The New Negro on Campus*, boosted by citations. Lucas, *American Higher Education*, p. 210 (flappers quote); "Students Strike at Biddle University," *CD*, March 12, 1921.

24. Aptheker, "The Negro College Student"; Mary Church Terrell, *The New Student* 2 (February 24, 1923), p. 1.

25. W. E. B. Du Bois, "Harvard," *Crisis* 25 (March 1923), p. 199; "Negro Graduates Protest," *NYT*, January 13, 1923; "Harvard Overseers Ban Discrimination in Race or Religion," *NYT*, April 10, 1923.

26. "Storer College Boys Quit, Say Ku Klux Threatened," *AA*, November 17, 1922; Barbara Ransby, *Ella Baker and the Black Freedom Movement: A Radical Democratic Vision* (Chapel Hill, NC: The University of North Carolina Press, 2003), pp. 59–60; Lisa Frederiksen Bohannon, *Freedom Cannot Rest: Ella Baker and the Civil Rights Movement* (Greensboro, NC: Morgan Reynolds Publishing, 2005), pp. 29–33.

27. "Students Hold National Meet in Washington," *CD*, April 21, 1923; J. Alpheus Bulter, "The Negro Youth Awakening," *The New Student* 2 (April 21, 1923), p. 4.

28. "Initiate Mammoth Business Scheme," *PT*, December 1, 1923; "Youth Movement Begun By Lincoln Student Spreading Over the Entire Country," *PT*, March 15, 1924;

"'Ten Greatest Negroes American Has Produced,'" *PT*, March 29, 1924; "Annual Youth Movement Ends in Dixie City," *CD*, April 19, 1924, 9; "Federation Urges Youth to Cease Selling Labor," *CD*, June 7, 1924; "Youth Movement Debates Votes on 'Ten Greatest Negroes,'" *PC*, March 15, 1924; "Abbott is Names Among Big 10," *CD*, May 3, 1924; "President of Youth Movement Strikes Back at Tirade of Local Columnist," *PC*, December 27, 1924; "The Prominent Men to Address Youth Movement Conference," *PC*, August 8, 1925.

29. W. E. B. Du Bois, "Diuturni Silenti," in *The Education of Black People, Ten Critiques, 1906-1960*, ed. Herbert Aptheker (Amherst, MA: The University of Massachusetts Press, 1973), pp. 41–60.

30. W. E. B. Du Bois, "The Dilemma of the Negro," *The American Mercury* 3 (October 1924), pp. 183–184.

31. "Why A Student 'Strike,'" *AA*, February 28, 1925.

32. "New Strike Threatened at Howard," *CD*, August 1, 1925.

33. "Another Student Strike," *CD*, May 23, 1925; "School Disturbances," *PC*, May 23, 1925; "Dean Flees School as Students Stage Revolt," *CD*, November 7, 1925; "Students at Knoxville in Faculty Row," *CD*, December 12, 1925.

34. Oakley C. Johnson, "The Negro-Caucasian Club," *Negro History Bulletin* 33 (February 1970), pp. 35–41; Aptheker, "The Negro College Student," pp. 162–163, 165.

35. "Another Student Strike," *CD*, May 23, 1925; George Ruble Woolfolk, *Prairie View: A Study in Public Conscience* (New York: Pageant Press, 1962), pp. 207–208, 246.

36. "Another Student Strike," *CD*, May 23, 1925; Woolfolk, *Prairie View: A Study in Public Conscience*, pp. 207–208, 246; "College Students Strike," *PC*, November 6, 1926; Bohannon, *Freedom Cannot Rest*, p. 33; "St. Augustine Students Out On A Strike," *AA*, November 26, 1927; "St. Augustine Strike Ends," *AA*, December 3, 1927.

37. "Howard U. Football Squad on Strike," *CD*, October 8, 1927; "Howard Strike Unsettled," *PC*, October 15, 1927.

38. "Student Strikes," *PC*, October 29, 1927.

39. "Negroes Complain of Bias at N.Y.U.," *NYT*, December 31, 1927.

40. Wolters, *The New Negro on Campus*, pp. 319–320.

41. "Western University Student Strike Ends," *AA*, January 28, 1928; "Kittrell College Girls Accused Prexy," *AA*, February 25, 1928; Zella J. Black Patterson, *Langston University: A History* (Norman, OK: University of Oklahoma Press, 1979), pp. 131–140.

42. "8 Strikes Show Revolt Among Race Colleges," *AA*, January 26, 1929.

43. "Strike Looms After 'Coed' Is Expelled," *PT*, February 7, 1929 (womanhood quote); "Nine Youth Ousted From Langston U," *CD*, February 16, 1929; "The Week," *CD*, February 16, 1929 (unrest quote); "Students Seek Ousting of S.C. College Dean," *AA*, March 23, 1929; "Fifty N.C. College Students on Strike," *AA*, May 4, 1929; "Another North Carolina College Erupts," *AA*, May 11, 1929; "Students Win African Riotous Strike at Brick College," *AA*, May 18, 1929; Wolters, *The New Negro on Campus*, p. 277.

44. "God Help Shaw, Says Alumnus After Strike," *AA*, January 25, 1930; "Situation at Paine Caused Student Row," *CD*, April 19, 1930; "Columbia, S.C.," *PC*, April 26, 1930; "A. & T. College Students Return to Classrooms," *AA*, May 10, 1930.

45. Howard students did threaten a protest in 1931. See "Students Threatened a Strike Unless Dr. Johnson Was Retained," *AA*, April 18, 1931. For the citations of protests in 1932, see "Union Prof.," *AA*, January 23, 1932; "Knoxville, Tenn. College Strike Ended Friday," *AA*, January 30, 1932; "Union Prof.," *AA*, January 23, 1932; "Gammon Theologs Declined Prexy's Bid to 'Pray' During Strike," *AA*, March 12, 1932; "Langston Univ. Students in Upheaval," *AA*, May 7, 1932; "Storer President Fears Student Strike," *ADW*, June 11, 1932.

46. "Howard Students Stage One-Day-Class Strike," *PT*, May 11, 1933; "300 Students Strike Because of Food," *PC*, October 28, 1933; "They Chose Between Closing School and Having President Resign," *AA*, December 16, 1933; "Lincoln U. Head Says Strikes Has Ended," *AA*, December 30, 1933; Jervis Anderson, *Bayard Rustin: Troubles I've Seen: A Biography* (Berkeley, CA: University of California Press, 1997), p. 35; "Threat of Student Strike Stirs Wilberforce," *PC*, May 19, 1934; "Cossacks Rule Virginia Campus," *AA*, June 2, 1934; "Strike at Howard Law School Is Called Off," *AA*, December 22, 1934.

47. "Dismiss 1 Prof. 31 Students in Alcorn Strike," *CD*, December 21, 1935; "Howard University Co-Eds Strike Over Board Raise," *ADW*, January 20, 1936; "Students Picket for 'Hungry' H.U. Football Team," *AA*, November 21, 1936; "Students at Morgan Strike After Insult," *AA*, February 29, 1936; "4 Days of Riot End at A&T," *AA*, November 28, 1936; "St. Augustine, Shaw Hunger Strikes Ended," *AA*, November 28, 1936; "Langston University Students in Quiet Strike," *ADW*, December 7, 1936; "Student Strike at Prairie View Denied," *PC*, December 26, 1936; "Another Student Strike Flares, It's W. KY. This Time," *PC*, December 12, 1936.

3   "Strike While the Iron Is Hot": Civil Rights in the Long Black Student Movement

1. Jacquelyn Down Hall, "The Long Civil Rights Movement and the Political Use of the Past," *Journal of American History* 91 (August 1935), p. 1235.

2. Johnetta Richards, "Fundamentally Determined: James E. Jackson and Ester Cooper Jackson and the Southern Negro Youth Congress – 1937–1946," *American Communist History* 7 (2008), p. 192 (CIM quote); Maurice Gates, "Negro Students Challenge Social Forces," *TC*, August 1935; John Hope Franklin, *Mirror to America: The Autobiography of John Hope Franklin* (New York: Farrar, Straus and Giroux, 2005), pp. 52–55.

3. "Negro Students Rush Congress Restaurant in Vain Effort to Test Rule Barring Race," *NYT*, March 18, 1934; "Protest March of H. U. Students, Who Hope to 'Crash' Headlines, May Defeat DePriest Petition," *PC*, March 24, 1934.

4. For example, see Robert Cohen, *When the Old Left Was Young: Student Radicals and America's First Mass Student Movement, 1929–1941* (New York: Oxford University Press, 1997).

5. "'Too Pacific,' Youth Leader Says of Negro," *PT*, July 18, 1935; "'Town Meeting of Youth' Set for Feb. 7, 8, 9," *CD*, February 1, 1941.

6. Julie S. Doar, "National Council of Negro Youth," in *Organizing Black America: An Encyclopedia of African American Associations*, ed. Nina Mjagkij (New York: Taylor & Francis, 2001), p. 392; "Youth Urge Passage of Anti-Poll Tax Law," *ADW*, October 3, 1942 (Norman quote).

7. Robert Cohen, "Student Movements, 1930s," in *Encyclopedia of the American Left*, eds. Mari Jo Buhle, Paul Buhle, and Dan Georgakas (New York: Oxford University Press, 1998), pp. 799–802; "H. U. Students Join National Antiwar Strike," *AA*, May 2, 1936; John H. Johnson, "Along the Youth Front," *CD*, May 1, 1937.

8. Gates, "Negro Students Challenge Social Force," p. 251; "Ex-Richmonder, 5 Others to Appeal Red Convictions," *AA*, August 11, 1956; "Anti-Lynch Speaks," *AA*, March 23, 1940; "Boy Appointed to Wesleyan U. Staff," *CD*, October 15, 1938; "Students Fight Discrimination," *NYAN*, January 4, 1936; "Student Union Takes Rap at Restaurant Discrimination," *PC*, September 14, 1940; "Student Union OK's Antilynching Bill,"

AA, January 8, 1938; "Report on American Student Union," *CD*, January 22, 1938; "Is Elected Delegate to Students Conference," *PT*, December 23, 1937; "Student Union Hears a Plea for Tolerance," *CD*, January 14, 1939 (Davis quote); "4 Plan Appeal in Café Suit," *AA*, March 12, 1938; "Refuses to Serve Columbia Student," *NYAN*, April 11, 1936; "White Students Aid Boycott of Theaters," *AA*, January 29, 1938; "Anti-Lynch Speaks," *AA*, March 23, 1940; "Club Victory Spurs Move," *AA*, May 11, 1940; "'Red' Changes Give Campus Jitters," *NYT*, December 6, 1940; Cohen, "Student Movements, 1930s."

9. For works on CORE, see August Meier, *CORE: A Study in the Civil Rights Movement* (Urbana, IL: University of Illinois Press, 1973).

10. Hall, "The Long Civil Rights Movement," p. 1245.

11. "Youth Conference Marks Start of New Epoch in Race Equality Struggle," *PT*, February 18, 1937; Robin D. G. Kelley, *Hammer and Hoe: Alabama Communists During the Great Depression* (Chapel Hill, NC: The University of North Carolina Press, 1990), p. 200, 207, 212.

12. See Johnetta Gladys Richards, "The Southern Negro Youth Congress: A History, 1937–1949" (Ph.D. dissertation, University of Cincinnati, 1987); Johnetta Richards, "Southern Negro Youth Congress (1937–1949)," Blackpast.org, http://www.blackpast.org/?q=aah/southern-negro-youth-congress-1937-1949, accessed November 3, 2011; "Progress Seen in Activity of Youth Groups," *CD*, December 14, 1940; "Robeson Is Greeted with Enthusiasm at Tuskegee," *CD*, May 2, 1942; "New World Order Coming, Says Dr. Bethune," *ADW*, December 2, 1944; "Negro Youth Told Future Is in South," *NYT*, October 21, 1946 (Du Bois quote).

13. "Ask Dies to Investigate Ku Klux Klan," *CD*, November 11, 1939; Richards, "Fundamentally Determined," pp. 193–199, 201; "Youth Congress Launches Vote Crusade," *CD*, July 22, 1939; Kelley, *Hammer and Hoe*, p. 201–202, 212–219, Patricia Sullivan, "Five Decades of Activism," *The Journal of the Southern Regional Council* 12 (1990), pp. 5–6; Richards, "Fundamentally Determined," p. 202.

14. Unless otherwise cited, the following section on the NAACP youth councils and college chapters is from Thomas L. Bynum, "'We Must March Forward!': Juanita Jackson and the Origins of the NAACP Youth Movement," *Journal of African American History* 94 (Fall 2009), pp. 487–508 and "'Our Fight is For Right': The NAACP Youth Councils and College Chapters' Crusade for Civil Rights, 1936–1965" (Ph.D. diss., Georgia State University, 2007).

15. "Hampton Institute Students Form Chapter," *AA*, December 21, 1940; "LeMoyne N.A.A.C.P. Branch Sponsors Negro History Group," *PT*, February 6, 1941; "NAACP, with 160,000 Members Says 1942 Was Banner Year," *AA*, January 2, 1943; Pauli Murray, interview by Genna Rae McNeil, February 13, 1976, interview G-0044, transcript, Southern Oral History Program Collection (#4007), series G.1. Southern Women: Individual Biographies, SHC.

16. Arthur L. Johnson, *Race and Remembrance: A Memoir* (Detroit: Wayne University Press, 2008), pp. 22–25; Laura T. McCarty, *Coretta Scott King: A Biography* (Westport, CT: Greenwood Press, 2009), p. 12.

17. "Council on Minority Equality to Meet Thursday in Union," *TDP*, October 10, 1951; "Minority Equality Committee Visits Local Negro Church to Discuss Racial Problems," *TDP*, November 5, 1951, DEPW Archives; "Pa. Students Picket Barbers on Negro Bar," *WP*, December 11, 1948. For a few examples of the turmoil, see "Negroes Cautioned on Resistance Idea," *NYT*, November 23, 1946; "Boston Youth NAACP Suspended for Backing 'Red' Candidate," *ADW*, November 22, 1946. For a new take on the NAACP in these early years, see Patricia Sullivan, *Lift Every Voice: The NAACP and the Making of the Civil Rights Movement* (New York: The New Press, 2009).

18. There are many examples of this marginalization, starting to a certain extent with the books cited in this section.

19. "North Carolina Has Negro Student Row," *NYT*, April 2, 1933; Kenneth Robert Janken, *White: The Biography of Walter White, Mr. NAACP* (New York: The New Press, 2003), pp. 184–185; "Hocutt Loses Suit against College," *CD*, April 8, 1933.

20. "Negro Court Test Faces University," *NYT*, September 1, 1935; Alice Jackson to the Rector and Board of Visitors, U.Va., September 28, 1935, Papers of the Office of the President (RG 2/1/2.491), subseries II, box 18, folder: Negro Admissions and Scholarship Fund, UVA SC; J. Douglas Smith, *Managing White Supremacy: Race, Politics, and Citizenship in Jim Crow Virginia* (Chapel Hill, NC: The University of North Carolina Press, 2002), p. 248.

21. Rawn James Jr., *Root and Branch: Charles Hamilton Houston, Thurgood Marshall, and the Struggle to End Segregation* (New York: Bloomsbury, 2010), pp. 67–75.

22. Joy Ann Williamson, *Black Power on Campus: The University of Illinois, 1965–1975* (Champaign, IL: University of Illinois Press, 2003) p. 11; Christina Asquith, "For Missing Civil Rights Hero, a Degree at Last," *Diverse: Issues in Higher Education*, May 4, 2006, http://diverseeducation.com/article/5827/, accessed November 3, 2011.

23. "Negro Enrolls in University Law School," *AT*, February 3, 1948; "Students Voice Opinions on Admittance of Negro Students," *AT*, February 3, 1948, UAF Archives; Guerdon D. Nichols, "Breaking the Color Barrier at the University of Arkansas," *Arkansas Historical Quarterly* 27 (Spring 1968), pp. 3–21.

24. Williamson, *Black Power on Campus*, pp. 11–12; George Henderson, *Race and the University: A Memoir* (Norman, OK: University of Oklahoma Press, 2010), p. 75.

25. "City College Lists Course by M. Yergan," *NYAN*, September 25, 1937; "James Weldon Johnson, Max Yergan on Faculties of New York University and City College of New York," *ADW*, October 14, 1937; "Nine Wilberforce Student Strikers Expelled," *ADW*, May 4, 1938; "Turmoil Grips Campus as Students Strike," *ADW*, March 26, 1939; "Trustees to Probe Strike of Students at A. And T.," *ADW*, May 21, 1939; "Hampton Goes 'Radical'—Students Strike," *PC*, June 3, 1939.

26. "Jim Crow At N.Y.U. Fought," *CD*, March 22, 1941; "Walsh Joins Race Protest at Harvard," *BG*, April 15, 1941; "H.U. Women Strike; Dean Called Hitler," *AA*, May 31, 1941; "Tuskegee Students Tell 'Inside' Story of Strike," *NYAN*, January 25, 1941; "Tuskegee Students Strike Over Cafeteria Conditions," *ADW*, January 16, 1941; "Spelman Students Strike for Better Food, Socials," *ADW*, February 27, 1942; "Livingston Student Strike Upheld by Court Decision," *PT*, February 9, 1946; "Benedict Students Stage Strike," *ADW*, February 3, 1944; "Food Strike Ended at Benedict," *PT*, November 29, 1947; "More Food Strike Won by Alabama A. & M. Students," *PT*, November 4, 1947; "800 Alabama State College Students Strike Over Food," *AA*, March 13, 1948; "Clark Students Strike Over Food," *PC*, January 22, 1944; "Students Strike at J. C. Smith U.," *AA*, November 20, 1943; "No Action Against Morgan Strikers Yet," *AA*, November 27, 1943; "A. and T. College Strike Ended," *AA*, March 17, 1945; "Lincoln (Mo.) Students Go on Strike over Dismissal," *PT*, June 8, 1948; "51 Striking Co-eds Out at Fort Valley State College," *ADW*, April 19, 1949; "Students Strike at Kentucky State," *AA*, May 23, 1953; "Eggs Cause Bowie Strike," *AA*, November 22, 1941; "Striking Del. Students Defiantly Return to Class," *PT*, April 4, 1942; "St. Augustine Students Back in Class After 8-Day Strike," *PT*, May 1, 1943; "Students of Morris College on 'Strike,'" *ADW*, December 18, 1943; "New Instructor Charged with Fomenting Del. State Riot," *AA*, April 23, 1949; "Students, College Head Clash over Bans," *CD*, November 14, 1942; "One-Day Strike Ends at Va. Union; 1st in History," *AA*, April 8, 1944.

27. "Should College Students Have the Right to Strike," *AA*, February 12, 1944; "U. of C. Students Strike Hits Faculty Jim Crow," *CD*, June 23, 1945; Williamson, *Black Power on Campus*, pp. 17–18; Charles Evers and Andrew Szanton, *Have No Fear: The Charles Evers Story* (New York: John Wiley & Sons, 1997), pp. 55–64.

28. "Oust Three in Wiley U. Strike," *CD*, October 18, 1947; "Wiley Students Strike; Protest Social Curbs," *CD*, October 11, 1947; "J. C. Smith Professors Get 1-Year Contracts after Student Strike," *AA*, May 23, 1942; "Instructor Fired, Students Strike," *PC*, May 28, 1949; "Langston Students in Protest Strike," *ADW*, February 2, 1949.

29. "Students Resume Strike on Professors Charged with Bias," *CD*, April 30, 1949; Bynum, "'Our Fight Is for Right,'" pp. 96–97, 99–100.

30. "Decision a Challenge, Say 2 N.C. Students," *CD*, June 12, 1954.

31. "Student Strike Ends at Ala. State as Investigation Starts," *ADW*, October 23, 1954; Russell Freedman, *Freedom Walkers: The Story of the Montgomery Bus Boycott* (New York: Holiday House, 2006) pp. 33–34; Jo Ann Gibson Robinson, *The Montgomery Bus Boycott and the Women Who Started It* (Knoxville, TN: University of Tennessee Press, 1987), pp. 45–46.

32. E. Culpepper Clark, *The Schoolhouse Door: Segregation's Last Stand at the University of Alabama* (New York: Oxford University Press, 1995), p. xvii; Also, for white student reaction, see "College Editors Look at Alabama University," *XUN*, March 9, 1956, XUO Archives.

33. "New Dining Room and Kitchen to Be Constructed at Cheyney," *PT*, November 27, 1956; Jeffrey A. Turner, *Sitting In and Speaking Out: Student Movements in the American South: 1960–1970* (Athens, GA: University of Georgia Press, 2010), pp. 67–68.

34. Ana Maria Spagna, *Test Ride on the Sunnyland Bus: A Daughter's Civil Rights Journey* (Lincoln, NE: University of Nebraska Press, 2010), pp. 27–28; Gregory B. Padgett, "The Tallahassee Bus Boycott," in *Sunbelt Revolution: The Historical Progression of the Civil Rights Struggle in the Gulf South, 1866–2000*, ed. Samuel C. Hyde Jr. (Gainesville, FL: University Press of Florida, 2003), pp. 190–208.

35. Joy Ann Williamson, *Radicalizing the Ebony Tower: Black Colleges and the Black Freedom Struggle in Mississippi* (New York: Teachers College Press, 2008), pp. 39–40.

36. Williamson, *Radicalizing the Ebony Tower*, pp. 40–42.

37. "Impact of Alcorn Students' Strike," *CD*, March 12, 1957; "Allen Students Upset State!" *PC*, January 25, 1958.

38. Bynum, "'Our Fight Is for Right,'" p. 127.

39. John Lewis and Michael D'Orso, *Walking with the Wind: A Memoir of the Movement* (New York: Harcourt, Brace and Company, 1998), pp. 74–75.

40. "FAMU Students Get Action; Call Off Class Strike," *CD*, May 5, 1959; "FAMU Students Vow to Press Fight for Justice," *CD*, May 6, 1959; "Negro Students Go on Strike," *MG*, May 5, 1959; James Max Fendrich, *Ideal Citizens: The Legacy of the Civil Rights Movement* (Albany, NY: State University of New York Press, 1993), pp. 13–14.

41. Fendrich, *Ideal Citizens*, pp. 14–15.

42. Harvard Sitkoff, *The Struggle for Black Equality: 1954–1992* (New York: Hill and Wang, 1993), p. 59.

43. Lewis and D'Orso, *Walking with the Wind*, pp. 75–87.

44. Bynum, "'Our Fight Is for Right,'" pp. 136–137 (McNeill quote); Darlene Clark Hine, William C. Hine, and Stanley Harrold, *The African American Odyssey: Combined Volume, Fourth Edition* (Upper Saddle River, NJ: Pearson Education, 2008), pp. 584–585; Sitkoff, *The Struggle for Black Equality*, p. 63; Cleveland Sellers and Robert Terrell, *The River of No Return: The Autobiography of a Black Militant* (Jackson, MS: University of Mississippi Press, 1990), pp. 18–19 (rat quote).

45. Hine, Hine, and Harrold, *The African American Odyssey*, pp. 584–586; Sitkoff, *The Struggle for Black Equality*, pp. 64–69, 74–75.

46. Williamson, *Radicalizing the Ebony Tower*, pp. 44–45; Sellers and Terrell, *The River of No Return*, pp. 23–24; Sitkoff, *The Struggle for Black Equality*, p. 69; John A. Hardin, *Onward And Upward: A Centennial History of Kentucky State University 1886-1986* (Frankfort, KY: Kentucky State University, 1987), p. 50, CESKAA; "Trial Delayed in Suit of 13 against K.S.C.," *CJ*, April 30, 1963.

47. Hine, Hine, and Harrold, *The African American Odyssey*, p. 586; Sellers, *The River of No Return*, pp. 33–38; Sitkoff, *The Struggle for Black Equality*, p. 83.

48. Turner, *Sitting In and Speaking Out*, pp. 105–107.

49. Williamson, *Radicalizing the Ebony Tower*, pp. 53–54.

50. Sitkoff, *The Struggle for Black Equality*, pp. 103–106.

51. Turner, *Sitting In and Speaking Out*, pp. 107–110; Sitkoff, *The Struggle for Black Equality*, pp. 114–115; Frank Lambert, *The Battle of Ole Miss: Civil Rights v. States' Rights* (New York: Oxford University Press, 2010), pp. 116–138.

4   "March That Won't Turn Around": Formation and Development of the Black Campus Movement

1. "Militant Stand Taken by New All-Black Youth Group," *Young Socialist*, September 1963; Donna Jean Murch, *Living for the City: Migration, Education, and the Rise of the Black Panther Party in Oakland, California* (Chapel Hill, NC: The University of North Carolina Press, 2010), pp. 71, 73; H. Lawrence Ross to Malcolm X, February 8, 1962, box 4, folder 3; Audrey Johnson to Malcolm X, August 31, 1962, box 3, folder 17, Malcolm X Collection: Papers, 1948-1965, SCHBG; Muhammad Ahmad, *We Will Return in the Whirlwind: Black Radical Organizations, 1960-1975* (Chicago: Charles H. Kerr Publishing Company, 2007), pp. 95–99.

2. "A Few Beers with Herman Carter at the Cock n' Bull," *FPM*, 2000, http://www.fishpiss.com/archives/148, accessed November 11, 2011; "Interview with Herman Carter by Gabriel Tordjman," Dawson College Humanities/Philadelphia Department Newsletter, March 10, 2005, http://dc37.dawsoncollege.qc.ca/humanities/newsletter/Issue1/herman.htm, accessed November 11, 2011; Edward Leroy Whitfield, interview by Bridgette Burge, February 26, 2006, transcript, Heirs to a Fighting Tradition: Oral Histories of North Carolina Social Justice Activists, Heirs Project, Knightdale, North Carolina; Henry N. Drewry and Humphrey Doermann, *Stand and Prosper: Private Black Colleges and Their Students*, (Princeton, NJ: Princeton University Press, 2001) p. 32; Bridgette Sanders and Lois Stickell, "Black Student Activism at UNC Charlotte in the Late 1960s" (paper presented at the 90th annual convention of the Association for the Study of African American Life and History, Buffalo, New York, October 20–23, 2005), paper in author's possession, courtesy of UNCC Archives; Chester Grundy, interview by Betsy Brinson, June 23, 1999, interview 20 B 24, Civil Rights Movement in Kentucky Oral History Project, The Kentucky Oral History Commission, KHS, http://205.204.134.47/civil_rights_mvt/util.aspx?p=1&pid=14987, accessed November 11, 2011.

3. Ahmad, *We Will Return in the Whirlwind*, p. 105; Harvard Sitkoff, *The Struggle for Black Equality: 1954-1992*, (New York: Hill and Wang, 1993), pp. 130–132 (Conner quote).

4. "Afro-American Club," *HC*, May 10, 1963; "Past Officers Discuss History of Afro," *HC*, April 29, 1974; "College Negro Club Adopts Constitution," *HC*, April 29, 1963; "Negro Students' Challenge to Liberalism," *HC*, May 31, 1967, HARU Archives.

5. Thomas J. Sugrue, *Sweet Land of Liberty: The Forgotten Struggle for Civil Rights in the North* (New York: Random House, 2008), p. 302; Martin Luther King, "Letter from Birmingham City Jail," in *A Testament of Hope: The Essential Writings and Speeches of Martin Luther King Jr.*, ed. James M. Washington (San Francisco: Harper, 1986), p. 292; Sitkoff, *The Struggle for Black Equality*, pp. 145–146 (Kennedy quote); Jelani Favors, "Shelter in a Time of the Storm: Black Colleges and the Rise of Student Activism in Jackson, Mississippi" (PhD diss., The Ohio State University, 2006), pp. 215–216.

6. Sitkoff, *The Struggle for Black Equality*, pp. 144–145; Kareem Abdul-Jabbar and Peter Knobler, *Giant Steps* (New York: Bantam Books, 1983), pp. 60–61.

7. Ann Grundy, interview by Betsy Brinson, February 9, 1999, interview 20 B 7, transcript, Civil Rights Movement in Kentucky Oral History Project, The Kentucky Oral History Commission, KHS, http://205.204.134.47/civil_rights_mvt/util.aspx?p=1&pid=14973, accessed November 11, 2011.

8. William H. Orrick Jr., *SHUT IT DOWN! A College in Crisis, San Francisco State College October, 1968–April, 1969: A Report to the National Commission on the Causes and Prevention of Violence* (Washington, DC: US Government Printing Office, 1969), pp. 77–78; "Black Student Association," Office of Multicultural Affairs, The University of Memphis, accessed July 27, 2011, http://www.memphis.edu/multiculturalaffairs/organizations.htm; Ahmad, *We Will Return in the Whirlwind*, p. 104; Payson S. Wild to Faculty Member, May 8, 1968, General Files, folder: Black Student Protest—I, April–May 1968, NOWU Archives.

9. "Police in Jackson Break Up Protest," *NYT*, February 4, 1964; "College Students Shot Down by Miss. Police," *CD*, February 5, 1964; "Alcorn 1966: An Incident," Pamphlet of the Southern Student Organizing Commission, Nashville, Tennessee, Delos P. Culp Records, 1924–1974, box 124, folder 9, ETSU Archives; "Student Strike Threat at Norfolk State," *JG*, May 23, 1964; Jeffrey A. Turner, *Sitting In and Speaking Out: Student Movements in the American South: 1960–1970* (Athens, GA: University of Georgia Press, 2010), p. 181; Ahmad, *We Will Return in the Whirlwind*, pp. 115–118; Maxwell C. Stanford, "Revolutionary Action Movement (RAM): A Case Study of an Urban Revolutionary Movement in Western Capitalist Society" (M.A. Thesis, Atlanta University, 1986), p. 91.

10. Jabbar and Knobler, *Giant Steps*, pp. 71–76; Joseph Boskin, "The Revolt of the Urban Ghettos, 1964–1967," *Annals of the American Academy of Political and Social Science* 382 (March 1969), p. 7.

11. Darlene Clark Hine, William C. Hine, and Stanley Harrold, *The African-American Odyssey, Combined Volume* (Upper Saddle River, NJ: Prentice Hall, 2008), p. 594; Cleveland Sellers and Robert Terrell, *The River of No Return: The Autobiography of a Black Militant* (Jackson, MS: University of Mississippi Press, 1990), p. 94; Kay Mills, *This Little Light of Mine: The Life of Fannie Lou Hamer* (New York: Dutton, 1993), p. 132.

12. Sellers, *River of No Return*, p. 111.

13. Robin Gregory, "Howard University, 1967–1968: 'You Saw the Silhouette of Her Afro,'" in *Voices of Freedom: An Oral History of the Civil Rights Movement from the 1950s Through the 1980s*, Henry Hampton, Steve Fayer, and Sarah Flynn (New York: Bantam Books, 1990), pp. 427–429, 433–436.

14. Bettina Aptheker, *The Academic Rebellion in the United States* (Secacus, NJ: The Citadel Press, 1972), pp. 21–23, 156–158; Rogers A. Fischer, "Ghetto and Gown: The Birth of Black Studies," *Current History* 57 (November 1969), p. 291.

15. "Negro Students Fighting Apathy," *NYT*, December 20, 1964; "New College Magazine Aimed at Ending Negro Indifference," *NYT*, April 16, 1966.

16. The following section on Malcolm's ideological influence on black students is taken from Ibram H. Rogers, "'People All Over the World Are Supporting You': Malcolm X, Ideological Formations, and Black Student Activism, 1960–1972," *The Journal of African American History* 96 (Winter 2011), pp. 14–38; Malcolm X, "The Harvard Law School Forum of December 16, 1964," in *Malcolm X Speeches at Harvard*, ed. Archie Epps (New York: Paragon House, 1991), p. 161.

17. Stokely Carmichael and Ekwueme Michael Thelwell, *Ready for Revolution: The Life and Struggles of STOKELY CARMICHAEL (KWAME TOURE)* (New York: Scribner, 2003), pp. 253, 259–260; "1500 Hear Integration—Non-Segregation Debate," *TSD*, November 18, 1961; For the letter of thanks from the Howard student body, see Michael Winston to Malcolm X, November 7, 1961, box 3, folder 17, Malcolm X Collection: Papers, 1948–1965, SCHBG.

18. Martin Kilson, "Open Letter to a Negro Student at Harvard," *THC*, March 17, 1965, HARU Archives; "The Murder of Malcolm X," February 1967, Student Nonviolent Coordinating Committee Papers, 1959–1972, Microfilm Reel 22, No. 253, PALL; Photo to the right of "Purpose of Demands Told at AABL Meeting," *TDT*, March 6, 1969, UTXA Archives.

19. Vincent Harding, Robin D. G. Kelley, and Earl Lewis, "We Changed the World, 1945–1970," in *To Make the World Anew: A History of African Americans from 1880*, eds. Robin D. G. Kelley and Earl Lewis (New York: Oxford University Press, 2000), pp. 238–239.

20. For a firsthand account of "Bloody Sunday," see John Lewis and Michael D'Orso, *Walking with the Wind: A Memoir of the Movement* (New York: Harcourt, Brace and Company, 1998), pp. 335–362.

21. "Howard University Student Body Petition," March 9, 1965, WHCF: Human Rights, box 27, folder: GEN HU 2/ ST 1 3/9/65, LBJL; James Forman, *Sammy Younge, Jr.: The First Black College Student to Die in the Black Liberation Movement* (New York: Grove Press, 1968), pp. 79–80; Harding, Kelley, and Lewis, "We Changed the World," p. 239.

22. Biographical information on Gwen Patton is from the biography in the Gwendolyn M. Patton Papers, 1955–, TSTC Archives, http://www.trenholmtech.cc.al.us/index .php?id=235#c277, accessed November 11, 2011.

23. Robert J. Norrell, *Reaping the Whirlwind: The Civil Rights Movement in Tuskegee* (New York: Alfred A. Knopf, 1985), p. 173.

24. Forman, *Sammy Younge, Jr.*, p. 110.

25. Norrell, *Reaping the Whirlwind*, p. 173 (first quote); Gwen Patton, "The Student Movement in Introspective Retrospective (The National Association of Black Students, NABS—1969–1972)," in *Black Liberation Movement: Papers Presented at 6th National Council for Black Studies Conference 1982*, ed. Gerald A. McWorter (Urbana, IL: Afro-American Studies and Research Program, University of Illinois, 1982), p. 3 (second quote); Gwendolyn M. Patton, "Insurgent Memories," *Southern Exposure* 9 (Spring 1981), pp. 58–63.

26. Jimmy Garrett, "Watts Thoughts on a Rebellion," *Students for a Democratic Society Bulletin*, 1965, http://content.cdlib.org/view?docId=kt4w1003tt&brand=calisphere &doc.view=entire_text, accessed November 11, 2011.

27. "The Black Student Union at SFSU Started It All," *SFC*, February 1, 2010.

28. Scot Brown, *Fighting for US: Maulana Karenga, the US Organization, and Black Cultural Nationalism* (New York: New York University Press, 2003), pp. 38–39; William L. Van Deburg, *New Day in Babylon: The Black Power Movement and American Culture, 1965–1975* (Chicago: University of Chicago Press, 1992), p. 31; Earl Anthony, *The Time of the Furnaces: A Case Study of Black Student Revolt* (New York: Dial Press, 1971),

pp. 23–25 (Lewis quote); see Maulana Karenga, *The Quotable Karenga* (Los Angeles: US Organization, 1967).

29. "White People Are Deciding Blacks' Fate, Karenga Tells Experimental College," *DB*, October 18, 1967; "Column Directed to Black Students," *DB*, October 24, 1967, UCLA Archives; George Henderson, *Race and the University: A Memoir* (Norman, OK: University of Oklahoma Press, 2010), p. 81.

30. Forman, *Sammy Younge, Jr.*, pp. 185–196; Nancy Regina Hooten to President Lyndon B. Johnson, January 4, 1966, WHCF Name File: Sammy Younge Jr., LBJL.

31. Sellers and Terrell, *The River of No Return*, pp. 149–151. For a study of the movement in Lowndes County, see Hasan Kwame Jeffries, *Bloody Lowndes: Civil Rights and Black Power in Alabama's Black Belt* (New York: New York University Press, 2009).

32. Peniel E. Joseph, *Waiting 'Til the Midnight Hour: A Narrative History of Black Power in America* (New York: Henry Holt and Company, 2006), p. 141–142; Sellers, *River of No Return*, pp. 164–167; Stokely Carmichael and Charles Hamilton, *Black Power: The Politics of Liberation in America* (New York: Vintage Books, 1967), p. 44.

33. "Carmichael Urges Negro Unity: 'We're going to turn our ghettoes into communities of love for each other," *BSB*, August 27, 1966; Adrienne Manns, "Howard University, 1967–1968,'" pp. 429–431.

34. "Appearance of Stokely Carmichael at Morgan State College, Baltimore, Maryland," United States Department of Justice, Federal Bureau of Investigation, January 24, 1967, Papers of Lyndon B. Johnson: Presidential Papers, Office Files of Mildred Stegall, box 73B, folder: Student Nonviolent Coordinating Committee (Stokely Carmichael) Aug.–Dec. 1966, LBJL. See also Joel Rosenthal, "Southern Black Student Activism: Assimilation vs. Nationalism," *The Journal of Negro Education* 44 (Spring 1975), p. 124 (Howard speech). A transcript of the UC Berkeley speech can be found in Joanne Grant, ed., *Black Protest: History, Documents, and Analyses: 1619 to the Present* (New York: Faucet Publications, 1968), pp. 459–466; "How Did Stokely Carmichael Affect Us?" *TC*, April 1967, TOGC Archives (Tougaloo quote); "Appearance of Stokely Carmichael in Texas," United States Department of Justice, Federal Bureau of Investigation, April 21, 1967 (Houston quote); Turner, *Sitting in and Speaking Out*, p. 177 (Fisk quote); "The Times They Have A-changed," *ST*, January 22, 2002 (Seattle quote). For an inventory of FBI reports on some of his speeches during the spring of 1967, see the above folder at the LBJL.

35. Huey P. Newton and J. Herman Blake, *Revolutionary Suicide* (New York: Harcourt Brace Jovanovich, 1973), pp. 110–113.

36. Mike Floyd, interview by Arthur Murphy, *DCK*, March 7, 1969, DICC Archives (Dickinson quote); "Radicals on Campus," *ST*, November 5, 1968; "Duke University Afro-American Society Ten-Point Program: What We Want and Why We Want It," *HARD*, February 5, 1969, in Black History at Duke Reference Collection, box 1, folder 15, DKU Archives; "B.S.A. & S.Q.E to All Teachers, Administrators & Staff," April 28, 1969, Student Activities Collection, box: NB-STUD-V-BSP, folder: R.U.-N&B-News Releases-General-Black Studies Protest-1969 I, ROSU Archives; "Black Renew Demands, Rap Campus' 'Racism,'" *RB*, May 6, 1969, UGA Archives; "Organization Seeks Black Studies," *COR*, April 15, 1969, F&MC Archives (F&M quote); Franz Schulze, Rosemary Cowler, and Arthur Miller, *30 Miles North: A History of Lake Forest College, Its Town, and Its City of Chicago* (Chicago: Lake Forest College, 2000), p. 158; Jeffrey O. G. Ogbar, *Black Power: Radical Politics and African American Identity* (Baltimore: The John Hopkins University Press, 2004), p. 140.

37. "King in Plea for Rights, Peace," *TO*, April 14, 1967, OC Archives; Jerry Avon, *Up Against the Ivy Wall: A History of the Columbia Crisis* (New York: Atheneum, 1968),

p. 20; H. Rap Brown, *Die Nigger Die! A Political Autobiography* (Chicago: Lawrence Hill Books, 2002), p. 99.

38. "Mrs. King Speaks at Harvard," *BSB*, June 20, 1968; "Rep. Chisholm Is Cheered by Howard Grads," *CD*, June 9, 1969; "Negro Leaders and Opponents of War Play Major Role as Graduate Speakers," *NYT*, June 9, 1969; "Militant Jones Coddles Carthage," *TAR*, March 6, 1969 (Jones quote 2); "The Black Movement: A World of Black Change," *TAR*, March 6, 1969 (Trotter quote), CARC Archives.

39. "9 Hours in February: The Takeover," *DC*, February 23, 1999, DKU Archives; Williamson, *Radicalizing the Ebony Tower*, pp. 140–141 (White quote).

40. "Muhammad Ali at Fairleigh Dickinson," *NYAN*, April 20, 1968.

41. "Presidential Candidate Speaks on Pitt Campus," *TCOL*, September 27, 1968, PSU Archives.

42. "Barbour Prognosticates Bloodshed," *TT*, October 6, 1967, TRIC Archives; "Groppi: 'Black Is Beautiful; Black Power is Christian,'" *TCOR*, January 19, 1968, CLAU Archives; "Fr. Groppi Speaks at Tech on Protest and Racial Revolution," *Michigan Tech Lode*, January 25, 1968, MITU Archives; "Black Students at NCC Accused of Betrayal," *CD*, October 21, 1967.

43. "College Observes 'Black Week,'" *TV*, January 26, 1969, FASU Archives.

44. "Black Cats Working Here; Desperation Spurs Action," *TL*, February 27, 1969, SAPC Archives.

45. "Black America Does Exist," *TTH*, December 13, 1968, THIC Archives; "Black Cats Working Here; Desperation Spurs Action," *TL*, February 27, 1969, SAPC Archives; "Black Coalition Joins CU Blacks, Whites," *TCE*, April 26, 1968, CU Archives; Robert Johnson Jr., "The African-American Legacy at Bowdoin" (unpublished manuscript, February 26, 1997), African American Society Records, box 1, folder 12, BOWU Archives.

46. Richard P. McCormick, *The Black Student Protest Movement at Rutgers* (New Brunswick, NJ: Rutgers University Press, 1990) pp. 17–18; "The Basis of Our Ethos," *WEL*, Spring 2008, WC Archives.

47. "A Dream Defended: The African-American Institute Reaches Ahead as It Looks Back on Thirty Years," *N.U. Magazine Online*, May 1998, http://www.northeastern .edu/magazine/9805/9805page&images/aai.html, accessed November 11, 2011; "Youth Conference Manifesto," *DB*, November 21, 1967, UCLA Archives.

48. "Negro College Students Discuss Ghetto Needs," *NYT*, April 12, 1968; "Negro Students Plan Aid Project," *NYT*, April 13, 1968; "Princeton Talk Exhorts Negroes," *NYT*, April 11, 1968; James E. Cheek to Presidents of Predominantly Negro Colleges, April 16, 1968, George Owen Papers, box 4, folder 15, TOGC Archives.

49. "Negro Students Seek Relevance," *NYT*, November 18, 1968; "Howard Students Discuss Reforms," *NYT*, November 15, 1968; Jerrold Wimbish Roy, "Student Activism and the Historically Black University: Hampton Institute and Howard University, 1960–1972" (PhD. diss, Harvard University, 2000), pp. 125–129; "FSC Students Attend Black Conference," *TV*, February 26, 1969, FASU Archives.

50. David Bishop, "Civil Rights and Race Relations in Durham and in the State: The Shepard, Elder, Massie and Whiting Models," in *A History of N.C. Central University; A Town and Gown Analysis*, ed. George W. Reid (North Carolina: George W. Reid, 1985), p. 78, General Files, NCCU Archives.

51. Lynne Anderson to the editors of Harambee, no data, circa 1969, Black Student Alliance Records, 1969–2005, box 1, folder: Afro-American Society materials, 1969–1971, DUKU Archives.

52. John A. Centra, "Black Students at Predominantly White Colleges: A Research Description," *Sociology of Education* 43 (Summer 1970)," pp. 328–334; Patricia Gurin and Edgar Epps, *Black Consciousness, Identity, and Achievement: A Study of Students*

in Historically Black Colleges (New York: John Wiley & Sons, 1975), pp. 197–233; *The Report of the President's Commission on Campus Unrest* (New York: Arno Press, 1970), pp. 94–96; Allen B. Ballard, *The Education of Black Folk: The Afro-American Struggle for Knowledge of White America* (New York: Harper & Row, 1973), pp. 90–95; Harry Edwards, *Black Students* (New York: The Free Press, 1970), p. 92.

53. "28% of Students in Poll Protested," *NYT*, May 25, 1969; Gurin and Epps, *Black Consciousness, Identity, and Achievement*; John S. Jackson, "The Political Behavior and Socio-Economic Backgrounds of Black Students: The Antecedents of Protest," *Midwest Journal of Political Science* 15 (November 1971), pp. 661–686; Frank L. Ellsworth and Martha A. Burns, *Student Activism in American Higher Education* (Washington, DC: American College Personnel Association, 1970), p. 21.; "The Negro Wants to Belong," *NYT*, March 17, 1968; "The Student Scene: Angry Militants," *NYT*, November 20, 1967; Rodney T. Harnett, "Differences in Selected Attitudes and College Orientations Between Black Students Attending Traditionally Negro and Traditionally White Institutions," *Sociology of Education* 43 (Fall 1970), pp. 419–436; "The Negro at Integrated College: Now He's Proud of His Color," NYT, June 3, 1968.

54. For a few examples, see "Black Womanhood Conference," *STY*, March 28, 1969, SUNYB Archives; "Who Is She," *TBC*, February 19, 1971, Thomas H. Eliot Chancellor Papers, series 8, box 1, folder: Association of Black Collegians, 1969–1970, WU Archives.

55. "To Be Young, Black and Female: A Predicament," *CE*, May 10, 1971, NCCU Archives; "The Basis of Our Ethos," WC Archives.

5 "Shuddering in a Paroxysm of Black Power": A Narrative Overview of the Black Campus Movement

1. "A.B.C. List Goals, Objectives," *GK*, November 8, 1968, GAU Archives; "Blacks, Whites Air Views at Forum," *TL*, December 5, 1968, SAPC Archives; "Lawrence Blacks Live One Life Two Ways," *LA*, May-June 1969, LAWU Archives; "Afro-Americans Explain Grievances to University," *DI*, May 30, 1969, UIA Archives; "Night and Day," *FLU*, no date, circa late 1960s, MITU Archives.

2. "BCC Celebrates Its 30th Anniversary," *Polytechnic Online*, November 14, 2001, http://poly.rpi.edu/old/article_view.php3?view=1026&part=1, accessed November 4, 2011; "Blacks Cite Racist Campus Incidents," *CR*, February 12, 1970, MORC Archives; "14 Related Racial Incidents," *TPAR*, May 8, 1969, MARSU Archives; "Black Student's Car Set Ablaze," *TDS*, September 20, 1968; "Why Black Reference?" *TDS*, October 4, 1968, UND Archives; *OGB*, October 31, 1966; "First Fall Carnival Brings in $1300," *OGB*, October 31, 1966; *The Howler* 65 (1967), pp. 14–15, WFU Archives; "Pep Rally Draws 2000; Bonfire, Spirits High," *TECH*, September 27, 1966, NCSU Archives; "The Negro at Integrated College: Now He's Proud of His Color," *NYT*, June 3, 1968; "Negroes in Siege of Cornell Office," *NYT*, April 5, 1968; "Negroes, Resenting Satire Burn Copies of Magazine at Columbia," *NYT*, May 21, 1967; "Columbia Acting on Race Tension," *NYT*, May 28, 1967. For examples, see "Charges Fly at Meeting," *SNS*, February 26, 1970; Jackie Butler Blackwell, interviewed by Tamara Kennelly, April 29, 1995, transcript, Black Women at Virginia Tech History Project, http://spec.lib.vt.edu /archives/blackwomen/butlerhp.htm, accessed November 4, 2011, VTU Archives; "Discrimination Now Subtle, but Still Seen at Ole Miss," *DB*, March 28, 1968, UCLA Archives; "Apathy Leads to Iowa State Negro Unrest," *ISD*, May 3, 1968, ISU Archives; "Cornell Cautioned on Punishing Sit-ins," *New York Times*, May 2, 1968.

3. "Black Reflections," *TRI*, April 24, 1970, TRIU Archives; "The Negro at Integrated College: Now He's Proud of His Color," *NYT*, June 3, 1968 (Yale quotes).
4. "Reporter Discovers Unique Black Power at Tougaloo," *TREF*, March 19, 1968, MSSU Archives; Jeffrey A. Turner, *Sitting In and Speaking Out: Student Movements in the American South: 1960-1970* (Athens, GA: University of Georgia Press, 2010), pp. 189–190.
5. Turner, *Sitting in and Speaking Out*, pp. 178–179.
6. Jerrold Wimbish Roy, "Student Activism and the Historically Black University: Hampton Institute and Howard University, 1960-1972" (PhD. diss, Harvard University, 2000), pp. 60–67.
7. "KU Civil Rights Council Protests Discrimination," *TCOL*, March 12, 1965, PSU Archives; "Rules Announced for Campus Students," *TNA*, June 1, 1965, WSSU Archives; "Students' Revolts March 19 Shakes Campus," *CE*, March 31, 1965, NCCU Archives.
8. Lyndon Baines Johnson, "To Fulfill These Rights: Commencement Address at Howard University," in *Affirmative Action: Social Justice or Reverse Discrimination?*, eds. Francis J. Beckwith and Todd E. Jones (Amherst, New York: Prometheus Books, 1997), p. 57; Lawrence B. de Graaf, "Howard: The Evolution of a Black Student Revolt," in *PROTEST! Student Activism in America*, eds. Julian Foster and Durward Long (New York: William & Morrow & Company, 1970), pp. 323–324.
9. Gerald D. Saxon, *Transitions: A Centennial History of the University of Texas at Arlington, 1895-1995* (Arlington, 1995), p. 113; Turner, "Conscious and Conflict," pp. 269–271 (Carter quote); Robert J. Norrell, *Reaping the Whirlwind: The Civil Rights Movement in Tuskegee* (New York: Alfred A. Knopf, 1985), pp. 173, 178; "Diverse Campuses," *WSJ*, December 22, 1965.
10. William Barlow and Peter Shapiro, *An End to Silence: The San Francisco State College Student movement in the '60s* (New York: Pegasus, 1971), p. 87; "SOUL Seeks Action on Food Discrepancies," *AJR*, March 4, 1966, NATU Archives; "Evers Seeks Ouster of Boyd," *NYT*, April 6, 1966.
11. "Sit-in Is Staged at Marquette," *WT*, December 3, 1966, General Information File: Students United for Racial Equality, MARU Archives; "Senior Women of Jamerson Hall Demand Extension of Closing Hour," *TC*, December 1966, TOGC Archives; William H. Orrick Jr., *SHUT IT DOWN! A College in Crisis, San Francisco State College October, 1968-April, 1969: A Report to the National Commission on the Causes and Prevention of Violence* (Washington, DC: US Government Printing Office, 1969), pp. 114–115.
12. William H. Exum, *Paradoxes of Protest: Black Student Activism in a White University* (Philadelphia: Temple University Press, 1985), pp. 44–45; Alford A. Young, *Revolt of the Privileged: The Coming Together of the Black Community at Wesleyan University, 1965-1976* (Middletown, CT: Wesleyan University, 1988), pp. 21–22.
13. "What's New on Campus," *NYT*, February 26, 1967.
14. Barlow and Shapiro, *An End to Silence*, pp. 125–128.
15. "We, the Undersigned, Register Our Grievances," April 18, 1967, Records Group 11: Student Organizations, 11-8: Black Student's Association, 11- 8/1/2: Black Student's Association: Black Issues 1965-1969: Petitions and Committees, IWESU Archives; *The Black Student at Vanderbilt* (Nashville, TN: Office of Undergraduate Admissions, 1970), p. 23, VU Archives; Gretchen Cassel Eick, *Dissent in Wichita: The Civil Rights Movement in the Midwest, 1954-1972* (Urbana, IL: University of Illinois Press, 2001), pp. 121–123. For examples of traditional routes to courses, see "Students Get Black History at Northeastern," *BSB*, October 12, 1967; "Northeastern Students Ask for Black History," *BSB*, May 20, 1967.
16. "Behind the Student Black College Revolt," *EB*, August 1967.

17. "New Black Consciousness Takes Over College Campus," *CD*, December 4, 1967; "The Black Revolt Hits the White Campus," *LK*, October 31, 1967 (Dunbar quote); Joe Palermo, "Black Power on Campus; The Beginnings," *San Jose Studies* 14 (1988), pp. 34–37; "Negro Students Protest at Berea," *New York Times*, December 10, 1967; Barlow and Shapiro, *An End to Silence*, p. 119–120; Turner, "Conscious and Conflict," pp. 275–276; "Ohio School Reopens Despite Death Plot Report," *NYT*, November 28, 1967.

18. "Orangeburg Events Cause Outrage," *BSP*, February 29, 1968 (Brown quote); de Graaf, "Howard University, 1967–1968," pp. 439–440.

19. Antoinette Frederick, *Northeastern University: An Emerging Giant: 1959–1975* (Boston: Northeastern University, 1982), pp. 402–403; "300 See Black-White Confrontation," *TO*, 26 January 1968, 1; "Begin to Open: Decade of Desegregation," *University of Mary Washington Today* 29 (Winter 2005), pp. 17–18, UMW Archives; "CRAC Hits NMS on Discrimination Charges," *RU*, February 17, 1968; "SLC Hears, Approves BSU Goals," *DB*, February 19, 1968, UCLA Archives; Jaribu Hill, "Excerpts from a Life Standing at the Well," *The Black Scholar* 36 (Spring 2006), pp. 31–32.

20. James L. Palcic, "The History of the Black Student Union at Florida State University, 1968–1978" (PhD. diss, Florida State University, 1979), p. 78; *The Report of the President's Commission on Campus Unrest* (New York: Arno Press, 1970), p. 137; "Colleges' Negro-aid Activities Spurred by Dr. King's Death," *CHE*, April 22, 1968; "Peace Again Reigns at Tennessee State," *CD*, April 27, 1968; "Outbreak in Missouri," *NYT*, April 6, 1968; Robert H. Brisbane, *Black Activism: Racial Revolution in the United States 1954–1970* (Valley Forge, PA: Judson Press, 1974), pp. 230–231; Lawrence E. Eichel, "The Founding of the Afro-American Studies Department: The Crisis of 1969," in *Blacks at Harvard: A Documentary History of African-American Experience at Harvard and Radcliffe*, eds. Werner Sollors, Caldwell Titcomb, and Thomas A. Underwood (New York: New York University Press, 1993), pp. 230–231; "The Negro at Integrated College: Now He's Proud of His Color," *NYT*, June 3, 1968 (Vassar quote).

21. See Stefan Bradley, *Harlem vs. Columbia University: Black Student Power in the Late 1960s* (Urbana, IL: University of Illinois Press, 2009); Ibram H. Rogers, "The Black Campus Movement: An Afrocentric Narrative History of the Struggle to Diversify Higher Education, 1965–1972" (PhD. diss, Temple University, 2009), pp. 100–133.

22. "Colleges' Negro-aid Activities Spurred by Dr. King's Death," *CHE*, April 22, 1968.

23. "Tuskegee Students Lock In Trustees," *NYT*, April 8, 1968; "Black Students Win Many Demands After 38-Hour Bursar's Office Sit-in," *DN*, May 6, 1968, NOWU Archives.

24. "Columbia's Black Students Showed Maturity," *NYAN*, May 11, 1968; Daniel Bell, "Columbia and the New Left," in *Black Power and Student Rebellion: Conflict on the American University*, eds. James McEvoy and Abraham Miller (Belmont, CA: Wadsworth Publishing Company, 1969), pp. 52–55; Jack D. Douglas, *Youth in Turmoil: America's Changing Youth Cultures and Student Protest Movements* (Chevy Chase, MD: National Institute of Mental Health, 1970), p. 226 (restructure quote); "The End of a Siege—and an Era," *Newsweek*, May 13, 1968 (Hayden quote). For the most thorough study of the BCM at Columbia, see Bradley, *Harlem vs. Columbia*.

25. William R. Corson, *Promise or Peril: The Black College Student in America* (New York: W. W. Norton & Company, 1970), p. 65 (Howard militants citation); "BOSA-CUA Seeks Black Awareness," *TOW*, October 18, 1968, CATU Archives; "Black Group Causes Varied Feelings," *OGB*, November 26, 1968, WFU Archives; "The Negro at Integrated College: Now He's Proud of His Color," *NYT*, June 3, 1968 (Yale quote).

26. "Northeastern Teachers 'Afro,'" *BSB*, December 19, 1968; "Predict Many College Outbreaks This Fall," *CD*, August 20, 1968; War, Political Frustration, Race Issues Presage Deeper Student Unrest," *CHE*, July 22, 1968.

27. Joy Ann Williamson, *Black Power on Campus: The University of Illinois, 1965–1975* (Urbana, IL: University of Illinois, 2003), pp. 81–86; Jan Stradling, *More Than a Game: When Sport and History Collide* (Millers Point, NSW: Pier 9, 2009), p. 175.

28. For an example at Ottawa University, see "Black Concerns," OTTC, January 10, 1969, OTTU Archives. For the SF State protest, see Barlow and Shapiro, *An End to Silence* and Dikran Karagueuzian, *Blow It Up! The Black Student Revolt at San Francisco State College and the Emergence of Dr. Hayakawa* (Boston: Gambit, 1971).

29. "Black Thursday at Oshkosh," *TC*, November 1969; President Morse to Members of the Afro-American Society of Case Western Reserve University, December 13, 1968, Records of Afro-American Studies Program, box 1, folder 6, CWRU Archives; "Black Student Union Issues Demands," *TFOG*, November 8, 1968, USF Archives; "Their Crowning Glory," TDC, February 26, 2002, UHOU Archives; Robinson Block, "Afro-Americans for Black Liberation and the Fight for Civil Rights at the University of Houston," *Houston History* 8 (Fall 2010), p. 25.

30. "Violence Plagues S.F. State; Race Issues Flare Elsewhere," *CHE*, December 9, 1968 (Smith quote); "The Eleven Days at Brandeis—As Seen from the President's Chair," *NYT*, February 16, 1969; "Queens Students Ransack Office," *New York Times*, January 14, 1969; Daniel Harris and Joseph Honcharik, *Staff Study of Campus Riots and Disorders, October 1967–May 1969* (Washington, DC: US Government Printing Office, 1969), p. 21; "Racial Tensions Still Trouble Ohio Colleges," *CD*, January 21, 1969; "Militants Eliminated From Campus," *WEB*, February 14, 1969, WEBU Archives (Shaw citation); "Protest at Wittenberg University, Documentation," in *Themes and Events of Campus Unrest in Twenty-Two Colleges and University*, Helen S. Austin, Ann S. Bisconti, Michele Herman, and Richard Hofrichter (Washington, DC: Bureau of Social Science Research, 1969), pp. C-138–C-166; Rodney Stark, "Protest + Police = Riot," in *Black Power and Student Rebellion*, pp. 167–185; "Swarthmore College Prexy Dies Amid Dissension," *CD*, January 18, 1969; Scot Brown, *Fighting for Us: Maulana Karenga, the US Organization, and Black Cultural Nationalism* (New York: New York University Press, 2003);Two Negroes Slain at UCLA Meeting of Black Students," *NYT*, January 18, 1969.

31. "Reform Needed at Universities," *BW*, February 7, 1969, LEHIU SC; Claudrena N. Harold, "'Of the Wings of Atalanta': The Struggle for African American Studies at the University of Virginia, 1969–1995," *Journal of African American Studies*, online first, accessed July 28, 2011, doi: 10.1007/s12111-011-9172-3; "SGA Stages Sit-in," *AJR*, February 14, 1968, NATU Archives; "BATU Issues List of Demands," *FN*, February 11, 1969, UDAY Archives; "Protesters Draw Up Demands in Austin," *TDT*, February 16, 1969, UTXA Archives (Huston-Tillotson citation); "Purpose of Demands Told at AABL Meeting," *TDT*, March 6, 1969; "Protest at Mills College," *NYT*, March 22, 1969; Richard P. McCormick, *The Black Student Protest Movement at Rutgers* (New Brunswick, NJ: Rutgers University Press, 1990), pp. 39–64; Cathy Meeks, *I Want Somebody to Know My Name* (Nashville: Thomas Nelson Publishers, 1978), pp. 68–81; Winston A. Grady-Willis, *Challenging U.S. Apartheid: Atlanta and Black Struggles for Human Rights, 1960–1977* (Durham, NC: Duke University Press, 2006), pp. 144–168; "Students: The New 'Feel' on Campus," *WSJ*, March 20, 1969.

32. Donald Alexander Downs, *Cornell '69: Liberalism and the Crisis of the American University* (Ithaca, NY: Cornell University Press); Harvard Negroes Get Faculty Vote," *NYT*, April 23, 1969; Conrad M. Dyer, "Protest and the Politics of Open Admissions: The Impact of the Black and Puerto Rican Students' Community (of City College)," (PhD. diss, City University of New York, 1990), pp. 114–126; Roy, "Student Activism and the Historically Black University," pp. 69–85; Armed Students Takeover Voorhees

College Building," *CD*, April 29, 1969; "Student Protests Interrupt Spring Semester," *HT*, May 1969, ALSU Archives; "The Siege of Greensboro," *NE*, June 2, 1969.

33. "Student Secessionists," *NYT*, August 28, 1969; "Black Walk Out at NSA Convention," *SO*, August 28, 1969.

34. "The Negro Colleges: Victims of Progress," *NYT*, October 6, 1969.

35. "Unrest Is Found to Be Widespread among Faculty Members as well as Students; Many Groups Are Split," *CHE*, September 15, 1969.

36. For the trials at San Francisco State, for example, see DeVere Pentony, Robert Smith, and Richard Axen, *Unfinished Rebellions* (San Francisco: Jossey-Bass, 1971), pp. 172–176; "S.F. State Strike Trials—A Mixed Bag of Repression," *SR*, November 29, 1969. "Blacks Make Own School in Calif. Area," *CD*, March 20, 1971; "Malcolm X University to Open in Durham as Militants' School," *NYT*, October 28, 1969.

37. Clifford A. Bullock, "Fired by Conscience: The 'Black 14' Incident at the University of Wyoming and Black Protest in the Western Athletic Conference," *Annals of Wyoming: The Wyoming History Journal* 68 (1996), pp. 4–13; "ROTC Is Primary Issue in Unrest during October," *CHE*, November 3, 1969; "Students Interrupt Convocation Speech," *TPAR*, October 3, 1969, MARSU Archives; "S.G.A. Appropriates $1,000 to Blacks," *PSAC*, October 30, 1969, STAU Archives; George W. McDaniel, *A Great and Lasting Beginning, The First 125 Years of St. Ambrose University* (Helena, MT: Sweetgrass Books, 2006), p. 202; "Chronology of Events Friday November 21st," *STA*, December 10, 1969, FARU Archives; "35 Negro Girls Seize Part of a Building at Vassar and Sit In," *NYT*, October 31, 1969; "Fisk Students Want Black University," *CD*, December 15, 1969 (Fisk quote).

38. "Sympathy for Workers and Strikes Spur Students Protests," *CHE*, December 15, 1969; "Harvard Sit-in over Black Painters' Pay," *BSB*, November 27, 1969; "Building Campus Integration," *NYT*, November 8, 1969 (quote); "Black Leaders Speak at Boston College," *BSB*, December 11, 1969; Yohuru Williams, 'A Red, Black and Green Liberation Jumpsuit,'" in *The Black Power Movement: Rethinking the Civil Rights— Black Power Era*, ed. Peniel Joseph (New York: Routledge, 2006), pp. 181, 183–184, 190–191. On the Hampton/Clark murder, see Jeffrey Haas, *The Assassination of Fred Hampton: How the FBI and the Police Murdered a Black Panther* (Chicago: Lawrence Hill Books, 2010).

39. "About the Issue," "Some Words from Black Alumni," *LAFA*, Winter 1970, LAFC Archives.

40. Robert Johnson Jr., "The African-American Legacy at Bowdoin" (unpublished manuscript, February 26, 1997), African American Society Records, box 1, folder 12, BOWU Archives; "Black in the Chapel," *COE*, March 6, 1970, COC Archives; Tiffany McClain, "The Integration Experiment: Black Women at Mount Holyoke College, 1964–1974" (unpublished manuscript, May 1, 2001), pp. 1, 6–8, MHC Archives; Leon Glaster to President James K. Sours, March 12, 1970, James Sours Collection, box 4, folder: Black Student Union, SORU Archives; "Black Student Union Proposals," "The President's Response to the Black Student Union Proposals," *HEIA*, Spring 1970, HEIU Archives; "Black Students Leave: Demands Under Study by Mount Union Officials," *AR*, March 7, 1970; "CCC Has Sit-in, No Bomb," *BW*, March 17, 1970, LEHIU SC; "'It Couldn't Happen Here': Blacks Give Stratton 11 Demands," *KEY*, April 22, 1970, KUP Archives; Ralph W. Schlosser, *History of Elizabethtown College, 1899–1970* (Elizabethtown, PA: Elizabethtown College, 1971), pp. 319–321; "Black Students Suggest Positive Improvements," *TRAM*, April 1970, ROSC Archives; Luther J. Carter, "U. of Michigan: Black Activists Win a Change in Priorities," *Science* 168 (April 10, 1970), pp. 229–231; "Negroes Pleased With Talks at TU," *TB*, May 9,

1970; Palcic, "The History of the Black Student Union at Florida State University," pp. 110–118; "Black Want Own College, 5 Student Board Members," *TCE*, February 27, 1970, CU Archives; "Black Students Sit-in At Maucker Home," *NIA*, March 20, 1970, NIAU Archives; "Dallas Students Ousted by Police," *NYT*, February 13, 1970; "Mississippi Students Rebel at Itta Bena," *ADW*, February 27, 1970.

41. "Black Studies Out at San Fran College," *NYAN*, April 4, 1970; "More Trouble at S.F. State," *SR*, March 7, 1970; "Emergency Declared at College," *SO*, May 21, 1970; "Stanford Confab: Black Students Call for Unity," *SR*, May 9, 1970.

42. "A Week of Tragedy: Disorders Flare, 4 Students Die as U.S. Action in Cambodia Inflames Many Campuses," *CHE*, May 11, 1970; "Are College Protests Racist?" *PC*, May 23, 1970; "Will Blacks also Revolt?" *PC*, May 16, 1970; Seymour Martin Lipset, *Rebellion in the University* (Boston: Little and Brown, 1972), pp. 91–92.

43. Spofford, *Lynch Street*, pp. 29, 56–79; "F.B.I. Investigating the Killing of 2 Negroes in Jackson," *NYT*, May 16, 1970.

44. "Jackson State Shootings Stir New Wave of Unrest," *CHE*, May 25, 1970.

45. "Black Presidents Assail Nixon Policies," *CHE*, June 1, 1970; "Evers Blasts College Killings," *PC*, July 11, 1970; "Kent, Jackson and Augusta," *NYAN*, June 13, 1970 (McKissick quote); "Jackson State Travesty," *NYAN*, April 15, 1972; see *The Report of the President's Commission on Campus Unrest* (New York: Arno Press, 1970).

46. "Campuses Quiet but not Content," *NYT*, December 20, 1970.

47. "Jim Brown Meets Syracuse," *BSB*, September 10, 1970; "Syracuse U. Sets Query," *CD*, September 22, 1970; Jane Kehoe Hassett, *As Strong as the Granite: Vitality and Vision: Fontbonne at 75* (St. Louis: Fontbonne College, 2000), pp. 76–78; "We the Members of the Organization of Afro-American Students Demand," no date, circa October 1970, The Student Government Association Records, box 1, folder 34, WCSU Archives; John Craig Stewart, "The University of South Alabama: The First Thirteen Years," p. 446–448, John Craig Stewart Papers, box 1, file 9, USA Archives; "Riot Flares in Norfolk St. College," *New Pittsburg Courier*, November 21, 1970; "St. Mary's OK's Black Coach," *CD*, February 2, 1971; "Prairie View College Closed Down," *Chicago Daily Defender*, March 1, 1971; Janet Lynn Brewer, 'Keep the Lights Burning': Leadership in Church-Related Institutions" (PhD. diss, University of Kentucky, 2008), pp. 126–135; "Walkout Spurs Black Outcry," *SFF*, February 5, 1971, TCU Archives; "Black Action Association Presents 17 Demands," *ARR*, March 5, 1971; "A Time for Action," *TCO*, April 28, 1971, PC Archives; "Students at University of Ga. Give 3 Point Demands," *ADW*, May 9, 1971; "Florida U. Students Mod Home of President After Police Battle," *NYT*, April 16, 1971; "Florida U Head Disavows Racism," *NYT*, April 18, 1971; "Six Students Resume Classes on Probation," *ADW*, April 27, 1971; "Campus Protests Follow D.C. Activities; Many Involve Blacks," *CHE*, May 17, 1971.

48. For what happened to these voices, see Alphonso Pinkney, *Red, Black, and Green: Black Nationalism in the United States* (New York: Cambridge University Press, 1976), pp. 103–104, 116–117, 142–146. Ralph D. Gray, *IUPUI—The Making of an Urban University* (Bloomington, IN: Indiana University Press, 203); "Rebuttal To President's Speech," October 6, 1971, George A. Owens Papers, box 4, folder 16, TOGC Archives; "Special Committee to Study Human Relations," *WT*, October 22, 1971, WARC Archives; Stephanie Kadel Taras, *On Solid Rock: The Founding Vision of Florida Presbyterian/Eckerd College* (St. Petersburg, FL: Eckerd College, 2008), p. 180; "Classes Canceled at Wilberforce," *CHE*, October 26, 1971; "U of H Blacks Hold Building During Night," *NBH*, November 10, 1971; Warren L. D'Azevedo, "The Ethnic Minority Experience at the University of Nevada, 1874–1974," *Nevada Historical Society Quarterly* 41 (Winter 1998), pp. 225–292; "An Underground

Message: Help Liberate The Rambler," Inserted in the 1971–1972 volume of TRA, TRAN Archives.

49. "72 Sees Calmer Days on College Campuses," *CD*, June 3, 1972; "The Traditionally White Institutions: For Most, Still a Long Way to Go," *CHE*, May 20, 1972; "Higher Education and the Black American: Phase 2," *CHE*, May 30, 1972.

50. "BSU Demands Are Viewed by Dean Park," *TF*, October 5, 1972, FC Archives; "ASU Officials Hear Requests of Minorities," *RP*, December 8, 1972, WTXC; "Too Few Blacks on Faculty," *TFA*, October 23, 1972, UNAL SC; Tae Y. Nam, "A Manifesto of the Black Student Activists in a Southern Black College Under the Integration Order," *The Journal of Negro Education* 46 (Spring 1977), pp. 168–185.

51. Tim Thomas, "The Student Movement at Southern University," *Freedomways* 13 (Winter 1973), pp. 17–27; "Southern U.—Tragedy on a Toured Campus," *CHE*, November 27, 1972; "Black Student Unity in New Orleans," *SR*, November 18, 1972; "Disturbance at S.U. Continues," *CD*, November 16, 1972; "'Cops Fired into Crowd,'" *CD*, November 22, 1972; "Student Group Calls Shooting 'Premeditated...Murder,'" *CHE*, November 27, 1972; "Racial Commission Blames Governor, Sheriff for Southern U. Slayings," *PC*, December 2, 1972; "Police 'Possibly' Shot Pair, Admits Governor Edwards," *OP*, November 22, 1972; "Southern U.—Tragedy on a Toured Campus," *CHE*, November 27, 1972; "Panel Says One Blast Killed Two," *OP*, December 20, 1972.

52. "Students Protest Southern Killings," *SR*, November 25, 1972; "Black-College Heads Urged to Confer on Southern U.," *CHE*, November 27, 1972; "Rally Protests Southern U Deaths," *SR*, December 2, 1972.

53. "Black Unity," *LUG*, May 1972, LGU Archives; "Toward Black Unity at MSU," *AFT*, September 30, 1972 (quote one); "Open Letter to Black Students," *AFT*, November-December 1972 (quote two), Presidents Papers: President William L. Giles, accession A81-25, box 49, folder: Student Affairs—Black Students, MSSU Archives; "Harris Discusses Black Milieu," *BW*, December 8, 1972, LEHIU SC; J. K. Obatala, "Black Students: Where Did Their Revolution Go?" *TN*, October 2, 1972.

54. "Black Students Honored With Apathy Award," *TCOL*, January 19, 1973, PSU Archives.

6   "A Fly in Buttermilk": Black Campus Movement Organizations, Demands, Protests, and Support

1. "OASATAU: Black Men Lost," *TE*, March 1, 1968, AU Archives; "Orientation '69," Collection of the Black Students Union Orientation Handbook, 1969, box 1, folder 1, UTNK Archives.

2. See James Baldwin, *Nobody Knows My Name: More Notes of a Native Sun* (New York: Dial Press, 1961).

3. Lawrence B. de Graaf, "Howard: The Evolution of a Black Student Revolt," in *PROTEST! Student Activism in America*, eds. Julian Foster and Durward Long (New York: William & Morrow & Company, 1970), p. 331.

4. Nelson Johnson, interviewed by William Chafe, October 24, 1978, interview 4.23.654, transcript, William Henry Chafe Oral History Collection, 1933–1988 and undated, box 2, file: Johnson, Nelson, 1978, Oct. 24, DKU SC; "Hart Runs for President," *TNA*, March-April 1970, WSSU Archives.

5. "Black Student Union," *TNA*, October 1969, WSSU Archives.

6. Frank Morral and Arthur Gropen, "Memorandum on Negro-White Education at Carleton," December 1, 1967, Willis D. Weatherford Papers, box 40, folder 12, BERC

Archives; "Afro-American's Seeking More Campus Involvement," *CRW*, May 9, 1968, UA Archives.

7. "Black Action Affairs Council: A Historical Perspective," Monmouth College Oral Histories Collection, box 2, folder: History of Blacks in Monmouth II, MONC Archive; "Black Student Union Promotes Black Pride," *KT*, February 1972, KSU Archives.

8. "BSU," *TF*, November 20, 1970, FC Archives; "President Peters Breaks It Down," *Ra*, October 8, 1969, CLAC Archives; "Explains Philosophy of Afro-American Society," *NIA*, December 16, 1969, NIAU Archives; "OASATAU: Black Men Lost," AU Archives.

9. Gary S. Gaston, "Crisis of Affiliation: The Merger of Arkansas Agricultural and Mechanical College with the University of Arkansas" (PhD. diss., University of Arkansas at Little Rock, 1997), p. 97; "Negroes Create Group for Political Purposes," *COR*, May 5, 1967, F&MC Archives; "Black Student Union Forms at MC," *TMAR*, March 7, 1969, MAC Archives.

10. "Black Union Goal; Get Blacks Involved," *TAN*, November 13, 1970, UTC Archives; "Statement of Purpose of the Afro-American Society," *COR*, March 28, 1968, MORC Archives; "The New Black Generation," *PP*, November 22, 1968, CWPLIU Archives; "Black Power Talk in Action," *TCOR*, October 4, 1968, CLAU Archives; "Black American Does Exist," *TTH*, December 13, 1968, THIC Archives; "BASIB," *GUI*, November 8, 1968, GC Archives; "Constitution, Afro-American Society, Case Western Reserve University," no date, circa late 1960s, Records of Afro-American Society, box 1, folder 5, CWRU Archives.

11. "Objectives and Goals Listed by Black United Students," *TPAR*, March 7, 1969, MARSU Archives; Gwen Patton to Brothers and Sisters, September 1969, Student Organizations Records, 67/13 Black Student Union, box 1, folder 2, UKS Archives.

12. "Rallies Demand Action," *TO*, May 28, 1968, OC Archives; "It's Oliver, Shabino, Ylitalo and Jorgensen!" *MM*, April 19, 1968; "Panel Recommends Handbook, Course in Negro Politics," *MM*, May 3, 1968, STOC Archives; "Renee Jones Wins Top Office," *TQ*, April 2, 1969, UC Archives; "Big Man on Campus," *EB*, August 1971.

13. Clifford Hand to Jack, December 12, 1969, Miscellaneous Student Organizations A-L Series: Bodies Affiliated with University Collection, Sub-Series: Small Collections, box: 5.4.1.2.1, folder: Black Student Union, UP Archives; "The Black Demands," February 13, 1969, Allen Building Takeover Collection, 1969–2002, box 1, folder 3, DKU Archives; AABL Statement Presented to Dr. Hoffman, February 7, 1969, President's Office Records, 1927–1981, series 1, sub-series 17, box 44, folder 22, UHOU Archives; "Protest at Mills College," *NYT*, March 22, 1969.

14. "Black Students, SIE Deliver Demands to Administration," *RU*, May 2, 1969, NMSU Archives; Ronald G. Weber to the Parents of Union College Students, Alumni, and Other Friends of the College, 26 March 1970, Historical Collection, Envelope: Black Student Union, UMU Archives.

15. Ernest Stephens, "The Black University in America today: A Student Viewpoint," *Freedomways* 7 (Spring 1967), p. 131; de Graaf, "Howard University, 1967–1968," p. 326.

16. John Hope Franklin, *Mirror to America: An Autobiography of John Hope Franklin* (New York: Farrar, Straus and Giroux, 2005), pp. 247–248.

17. "Attention!!," no date, circa spring 1971, Vertical Files: Multiculturalism/Multicultural Affairs, 1954–1997, SKIC Archives; "Blacks Walkout Draws Response," *BDH*, December 6, 1968, BRWU Archives.

18. "The Following Demands Are Being Presented," September 29, 1969, Records Group 11: Student Organizations, 11-8: Black Student's Association, 11- 8/1/2: Black

Student's Association: Black Issues 1965–1969: Petitions and Committees, IWESU Archives; "Black Student Union Issues Demands," *TFOG*, November 8, 1968, USF Archives; "Statement of Demands," 1970, Office of the Dean of Students—Student Life Collection, box 12, folder: Integration – Racial, 1923–1965, GOC Archives; Claudrena N. Harold, "Of the Wings of Atalanta: The Struggle for African American Studies at the University of Virginia, 1969–1995," *Journal of African American Studies*, Online First, accessed November 21, 2011, doi: 10.1007/s12111-011-9172-3; "A Time for Action," *TCO*, April 28, 1971, PC Archives; "Concerned Black Students' Demands," *WIT*, April 23, 1971, WIC Archives; "The Black Demands," DKU Archives; Black Student Association to Paul Hardin, March 13, 1970, Administrative Records, Series—Office of the Dean (Dr. Harold Jacoby), box 3, folder: Black Studies, MILLC Archives; "Statement to Members of the Black Student Organization of The John Hopkins University," May 17, 1968, Records of the Office of the President, series 9, box 40, folder: Students Affairs—Black Students' Organization, 1968, JHU Archives; Dale W. Patton, "Memo on Meeting with Negro Students – May 28, 1968, June 4, 1968," Records of the President, 1965–1970, box 12 (6F.7b), folder 10, STCST Archives.

19. "Afro Center Establishes Cultural Identity," *TDP*, February 3, 1970, DEPW Archives; "Black Cultural Centers," *MNL*, Summer 1972, MIDC Archives; Eugene R. McPhee to Each Regent and President Guiles, November 27, 1968, "November 21, 1968 Incident" Records, 1968–1971, series 1, box 1, folder 7, UWOSH Archives.

20. "Text of Demands Presented by BSA," April 7, 1969, Records of Student Unrest, box 1, folder 7, CSU Archives; "Commentary: Black Studies—The Things We Need to Know," *CHO*, November 14, 1968, MHC Archives.

21. Black Students Association to Dean of Instruction, no date, circa February 1969, Student Activities Collection, NB-STUD-V-BSP, folder: R.U.-N&B—News Releases—General—Black Studies Protest—1969, I, ROSU Archives; "Demands and Recommendations from the Maryland State College Student Body," April 19, 1970, Student Government Association Records (RG #132), box 1, folder: 1970, UMES Archives; AABL Statement, UHOU Archives; "Reed College Bars Autonomous Center for Negro Studies," *NYT*, January 27, 1969; "Blacks Want Own College 5 Student Board Members," *TCE*, February 27, 1970, CU Archives; "Demands," no date, circa 1969, Vice President for Business and Finance Series (5B/3/356), box: Black United Students, folder: Injunction File, UAK Archives; "Negro Students Press Demands," *NYT*, February 8, 1969 (Stony Brook quote); "The May Demands: A Restatement of Intentions," *TMN*, November 7, 1969, VC Archives; Rollin S. Armour to Joe Adams, May 25, 1970, General Files: Integration, STU Archives; *The Bulletin of Beloit College*, March 1969, Willis D. Weatherford Papers, box 40, folder 12, BERC Archives; John Coffee, *A Century of Eloquence: The History of Emerson College, 1880–1980* (Boston: Alternative, 1982), p. 385.

22. Robert McCray to Daniel Walker, March 16, 1973, Chancellor's Central Files (RG # 3-1-2), series 3, box 51, folder 725, UIC Archives.

23. "In Recent Years Saint Peter's College," early February 1969, RG-15 Student Activities and Campus Life, 15.7 Black Action Committee, Accession 015—XX-0002, SPC Archives; "On Niggers and Honkies," *TDS*, February 21, 1969, UND Archives; "Stanford Fails to Win Approval of Militants With Pioneer Program," *WSF*, June 11, 1969; "Racism at Howard," *The Spear and Shield*, February 3, 1970, Student Movement Records, Liberal/Left Archival Studies Papers, MS2096 series 2, box 4, folder 7, GWU SC.

24. "Documents on Demands," *XUN*, November 19, 1969, XUO Archives; Black Student Demands at Providence College, March 16, 1971, General Files: Afro-American

Society of Providence College, PC Archives; Demands of Roosevelt Black Students Association, no date, circa May 1968, Student Activities Collection, NB-STUD-V-BSP, folder: R.U.-N&B—News Releases—General—Black Studies Protest—1969, I, ROSU Archives

25. "Concerned Black Students' Demands," WIC Archives; "Black Students Demands," February 20, 1969, Student Demonstrations, 1960–Present Collection, box 001, folder 3, EMU Archives; Demands of the Organization of Afro-American Students, no date, circa early 1970s, The Student Government Association Records, box 1, folder 34, WCSU Archives; "Demonstration at Coe in Support for Negro Demands," *CRP*, May 20, 1968; "What the B.S.A. Wants," no date, circa late 1960s, Student Life Collection, box 20, folder: Black Student Alliance, 1968-1977, RPI Archives.

26. The Black Student Union Demands to Administration, November 21, 1969, Black Student Union Scrapbook 1969–1991, University Records Collection – UR 38, box 1, folder 1, UMAD Archives; "ASU Officials Hear Requests of Minorities," *RP*, December 8, 1972, WTXC; Frank McClellan to McCloskey, May 7, 1969, Unprocessed Student Affairs Records, DQU Archives; "Text of the Statement Presented to President Umbeck, Dean Salter and Dean Harlan by Allied Blacks for Liberty and Equality on February 11, 1969," Organization Series: A.B.L.E., "10 Demands," 1969, KC Archives.

27. "Demands," UAK Archives; Edward D. Eddy to Members of the Faculty and Staff and the Students of Chatham College, March 3, 1970, Alphabetical Files: Black Student Union, CHU Archives; Warren L. D'Azevedo, "The Ethnic Minority Experience at the University of Nevada, 1874–1974," *Nevada Historical Society Quarterly* 41 (Winter 1998), pp. 225–292.

28. David Simons, "Perspectives: A Brief History of CBS's roots," Concerned Black Students of Grinnell College, http://www.grinnell.edu/student/groups/cbs/history /manifesto, accessed November 5, 2011; "Students Tell Demands," *DCN*, April 9, 1970, DEC Archives; "In Recent Years Saint Peter's College," SPC Archives; "Black Student Problems Given Top Priority," *BQ*, April 3, 1972, RWU Archives; Press Release on Black Students Demands, no date, circa 1971, Records of the Affirmative Action/ Equal Opportunity Office, box 5, folder 2, SRU Archives; "Black Students Present Demands," *TIN*, April 2, 1969, TRSU Archives.

29. John Craig Stewart, "The University of South Alabama: The First Thirteen Years," p. 446–448, John Craig Stewart Papers, box 1, file 9; USA Archives; AABL Statement, UHOU Archives; Memo from the Black Student Organization Regarding their Demands, May 6, 1968, Records of the President (R 3/13), box 1, folder 7, KAC Archives; "Text of Demands Presented by BSA," April 7, 1969, Records of Student Unrest, box 1, folder 7, CSU Archives.

30. President Morse to Members of The Afro-American Society of Case Western Reserve University, December 13, 1968, Records of the Afro-American Studies Program, box 1, folder 6, CWRU Archives; Urban Institute, "Student Unrest A Chronology, 1964–June 1969," Martin K. Gordon Collection, box 1, folder 6, GWU SC; Demands to President Jerome Sachs Northeastern Illinois State College, May 27, 1968, General Files: Student Life and Customs – Clubs and Organizations M3/46 to M3/51, folder: Student Life and Customs – Clubs and Organizations – Memos M3/51, re: Student Black Caucus Demonstration in History Department, NEIU Archives; "CCC Has Sit-in, No Bomb," *BW*, March 17, 1970, LEHIU SC; Black Student Demands at East Tennessee State University, no date, circa May 1972, D. P. Culp Papers, box 60, folder 5, ETSU Archives; John Egerton, *State Universities and Black Americans: An Inquiry into Desegregation and Equity for Negroes in 100 Public Universities* (Atlanta: Southern Education Reporting Service, 1969), p. 82.

31. Earl Anthony, *The Time of the Furnaces: A Case Study of Black Student Revolt* (New York: Dial Press, 1971), pp. 50–51.

32. "Racism Uproots Murphy," *PC*, March 30, 1968; "The Angry Black Athlete," *NE*, July 15, 1968; Harry Edwards, *Black Students* (New York: Free Press, 1970) pp. 144–155.

33. John Matthew Smith, "'Breaking the Plan': Integration and Black Protest in Michigan State University Football during the 1960s," *The Michigan Historical Review* 33 (Fall 2007), pp. 50–55.

34. Gayraud S. Wilmore, *Black Religion and Black Radicalism* (Garden City, NY: Doubleday, 1972), p. 281; "Black Militants' Demands Are Changing Churches," *NYT*, May 25, 1969; "Union Seminary Back to Normal," *NYT*, May 14, 1969; "Protest Delays Exams at Seminary," *CD*, May 13, 1969; "Social Welfare Accepts BSU Demands," *DB*, April 16, 1969, UCLA Archives; The Black Graduate Student Union to Milton Eisenhow, May 5, 1971, Records of the Office of the Presidents, series 13, box 4, folder: "Black Students," JHU Archives; Harry Alpert to R. D. Clark, May 15, 1972, Office of the President Records, Robert D. Clark (UA 16), box 68, folder: Black Graduate Student Council, UO Archives. Cone's major text was *Black Theology and Black Power* (New York: Seabury Press, 1969).

35. "Protest at Wittenberg University," pp. C-138–C-166; Winston A. Grady-Willis, *Challenging U.S. Apartheid: Atlanta and Black Struggles for Human Rights, 1960–1977* (Durham, NC: Duke University Press, 2006), pp. 146–148; Jeffrey Alan Turner, "Conscious and Conflict: Patterns in the History of Student Activism on Southern College Campuses, 1960–1970" (PhD. diss, Tulane University, 2000), pp. 356–363; Payson S. Wild to Faculty Member, May 8, 1968, General Files, folder: Black Student Protest—I, April-May 1968, NOWU Archives.

36. "A Position Concerning Black Survival, Part I," November 11, 1970, General Folders: Black Student Union Minority Issues, 1969–1970, SJU Archives.

37. "Strider," "Blacks," *COE*, March 6, 1970, COC Archives.

38. *Staff Study of Campus Riots and Disorders, October 1967–May 1969* (Washington, DC: US Government Printing Office, 1969) p. 16. Howard and City College protests are cited in previous chapter.

39. "When Black Students Take Over a Campus," *TNR*, April 13, 1968; Jerrold Wimbish Roy, "Student Activism and the Historically Black University: Hampton Institute and Howard University, 1960–1972" (PhD. diss, Harvard University, 2000) pp. 73–85.

40. Zira DeFries and Lilo Grothe, "'Les Jours De Mai' 1968—Barnard College," *Adolescence* 4 (Summer 1969), pp. 158–160; de Graaf, "Howard University, 1967–1968," p. 447.

41. "Negroes Stage Radcliffe Sit-in; Colleges Act on Their Demands," *NYT*, December 11, 1968.

42. "Blacks Walkout Draws Response," BRWU Archives.

43. "Presidents Speaks With Blacks About Student Relations Center," *TPAR*, October 2, 1969, MARSU Archives; "200 Students March Quietly to Rice Hall," *THAT*, April 30, 1968, GWU SC; Adam Gray, "African American Activism at Northern Michigan University: 1968–1970" (unpublished manuscript, no date), Student Papers, box 1, folder 30, NMU Archives; Steven C. Phillips, *Justice and Hope: Past Reflections and Future Visions of the Stanford Black Student Union, 1967–1989* (Stanford, CA: Stanford Black Student Union, 1990), pp. 15–18.

44. Alford A. Young, *Revolt of the Privileged: The Coming Together of the Black Community at Wesleyan University, 1965–1976* (Middletown, CT: Center for Afro-American Studies, Wesleyan University, 1988) pp. 33–34; Alexander W. Astin, Helen S. Astin, Alan E. Bayer, and Ann S. Bisconti, *The Power of Protest: A National Study of Student and Faculty Disruptions with Implications for the Future* (San Francisco: Jossey-Bass,

1975), pp. 98–105; Franklin, *Mirror to America*, pp. 247–248; "Fisk Students Want Black University," *CD*, December 15, 1969.

45. *Staff Study of Campus Riots and Disorders*, p. 34; "Armed Troopers Patrol Lane College," *CD*, March 25, 1969; "Fear More Violence at Lane College," *CD*, March 24, 1969; "Rebellion, Fires Hit Quinn Campus," *CD*, July 30, 1970; "Negro Student Is Charged in Bluefield College Bombing," *NYT*, November 25, 1968; Roy, "Student Activism and the Historically Black University," p. 85–90; "Prairie View College Closed Down," *CD*, March 1, 1971; "Queens Students Ransack Office," *NYT*, January 14, 1969.

46. Fabio Rojas, *From Black Power to Black Studies: How a Radical Social Movement Became an Academic Discipline* (Baltimore: The John Hopkins University Press, 2007), p. 55; "The Eleven Days at Brandeis—As Seen from the President's chair," *NYT*, February 16, 1969; Ione D. Vargus, *Revival of Ideology: The Afro-American Society Movement* (San Francisco: R & E Research Associates, 1977), pp. 118–119; Richard P. McCormick, *The Black Student Protest Movement at Rutgers* (New Brunswick, NJ: Rutgers University Press, 1990) pp. 3–4, 50–60; "Negroes at Rutgers Main Campus Stage Protest," *NYT*, February 26, 1969. See also Ernesto "Che" Guevara, *Guerilla Warfare* (New York: Ocean Press, 2006); Robert Taber, *The War of the Flea: Guerrilla Warfare Theory and Practice* (London: Paladin, 1970).

47. Richard E. Peterson, *The Scope of Organized Student Protest in 1967–1968* (Princeton, NJ: Institutional Research Program for Higher Education, Educational Testing Service, 1968), pp. 11, 13; Alan Bayer and Alexander Astin, "Violence and Disruption on the U.S. Campus, 1968–1969," *Educational Record* 50 (Fall 1969), pp. 337–350; *Student Protests, 1969* (Chicago: Urban Research Corporation, 1969); "Student Strikes: 1968–1969," *Black Scholar* 1 (January-February 1970), pp. 65–75; Alexander Astin, "New Evidence on Campus Unrest, 1969–70," *Educational Record* 52 (Winter 1971), pp. 41–46; Dale Gaddy, *The Scope of Organized Student Protest in Junior Colleges* (Washington, DC: American Association of Junior Colleges, 1970); "Demonstrations Occur at Rate of One a Day in 1970; Major Protests Hit Michigan, Washington U," *CHE*, April 6, 1970.

48. "Brooklyn College Resumes Class after Arrest of 42," *NYT*, May 22, 1968; "Police Break Up Sit-in in Brooklyn College at College Office," *NYT*, May 21, 1968; "Sit-in a Fraud Dean Declares," *NYT*, May 21, 1968.

49. "Minority Students Present Ultimatum to Regents," *TMIR*, November 14, 1969, ACSD Archives; See Jeffrey O. G. Ogbar, "Rainbow Radicalism: The Rise of the Radical Ethnic Nationalism," in *The Black Power Movement: Rethinking the Civil Rights— Black Power Era*, ed. Peniel E. Joseph (New York: Routledge, 2006), pp. 193–228.

50. Statement by Forty Faculty Members Who Actively Supported the Association of Black Collegians, April 14, 1968, Box: Colgate—Vietnam Era, COLU Archives; "Alumni Request Ghetto Recruitment," *TMAR*, May 10, 1968, MAC Archives.

51. "Negro Students Continue Their Protest at Brandeis," *NYT*, January 16, 1969; "Black Students Alive and Well at Malcolm X U.," *BSB*, January 16, 1969; Tuskegee—Students Take Care of Business!!, George Owens Papers, box 4, folder 15, TOGC Archives; Attached FBI Bulletin on University of Hawaii, December 11, 1968, Papers of Lyndon B. Johnson: Presidential Papers, Office Files of Mildred Stegall, box 73B, folder: Students for a Democratic Society [1968], LBJL; Loretta Johnson to President Harrison, February 22, 1969; Willie J. Wiley to Sir, February 26, 1969; Sammy Roberts to Mr. Harrison, no date, circa February 1969; Mary Dixon to President Harrison, February 24, 1969; Afro-American Student Union to President Harrison, February 27, 1969; David L. Uhuru to Mr. Harrison, March 3, 1969, Franklin Harrison Papers, box 4, folder 8, UTA Archives.

7   "Black Jim Crow Studies": Opposition and Repression

1. This opening narrative about the Cornell protest comes from Donald Alexander Downs, *Cornell '69: Liberalism and the Crisis of the American University* (Ithaca, NY: Cornell University Press, 1999) and William H. Friedland and Harry Edwards, "Confrontation at Cornell," *Trans-action* 6 (June 1969), pp. 29–36, 76.
2. "Cornell Faculty Votes Down Pact Ending Take-over," *NYT*, April 22, 1969; "Peaceful Sit-in at Cornell Ends New Seizure Threat," *NYT*, April 23, 1969; Friedland and Edwards, "Confrontation at Cornell," p. 34; "Cornell Faculty Reverses Itself on Negroes," *NYT*, April 24, 1969.
3. "What People Are Saying about Campus Disorders: A Sampler," *CHE*, May 5, 1969; "Backlash Grows in Congress as Campus Protests Intensify," *CHE*, May 5, 1969; "Negro Professor Quits Cornell, Charges Leniency Hurts Blacks," *NYM*, June 2, 1969; "Response to Armed Negroes Divides Cornell Community," *CHE*, May 5, 1969; "Cornell Blacks," *CD*, April 29, 1969.
4. "Mississippi Police Rout 1,000 Negroes with Gas and Clubs," *NYT*, April 6, 1966.
5. "Rioting Nashville Negroes Fire on Cars, Stone Police," *NYT*, April 10, 1967; *The Report of the President's Commission on Campus Unrest* (New York: Arno Press, 1970), pp. 414–416; Joy Ann Williamson, *Radicalizing the Ebony Tower: Black Colleges and the Black Freedom Struggle in Mississippi* (New York: Teachers College Press, 2008), p. 137; "University in Ohio Closes Doors to Avert a Renewal of Violence," *NYT*, November 15, 1967; "Central State College Closes over Campus Black Power," *NYAN*, November 25, 1967; "Texas Cops Beat Students," *BSB*, May 27, 1967; "Bricks without Straw," *TH*, August 31, 2007; "Texas Indicts 5 in Police Killing," *NYT*, June 3, 1967; "Shot Kills Texas Policeman in Riot at a Negro College," *NYT*, May 18, 1967; "Texas Student Charged with Murder," *BSB*, August 3, 1967; "NAACP Protests: Reinstate Students," *NYAN*, November 11, 1967.
6. "ACLU Statement on Demonstrations," *CHE*, May 17, 1967; "Unrest Campus Style," *PC*, June 10, 1967; "One Method Versus Another," *NYAN*, May 13, 1967.
7. "Afro-American Society Pushes for Administrative Approval in Council," *CR*, March 21, 1968, Unprocessed Files of Tim Orwig, MORC Archives; "Action Gets Heavy During Senate Passage of Black Student Union Constitution," *TA*, February 26, 1971, BSU Archives; "'Segregation,'" "Acknowledgement," *TT*, May 2, 1967, TRIC Archives; Downs, *Cornell '69*, p. 62; Wayne Glasker, *Black Students in the Ivory Tower: African American Student Activism at the University of Pennsylvania, 1967–1990* (Amherst, MA: University of Massachusetts, 2002), p. 31.
8. Clarence L. Mohr and Joseph E. Gordon, *TULANE: The Emergence of a Modern University, 1945–1980* (Baton Rouge, LA: Louisiana State University Press, 2001), pp. 357–358.
9. "We Are Afro-Americans," *TEM*, February 21, 1968; "Rebuttal: Being Black a State of Mind," *TEM*, February 28, 1968, CSTU Archives; "Student Speaks Out against Wilson's Negro Non-Acceptance," *TB*, November 10, 1967; "An Open Letter to Madelyn," *TB*, November 17, 1967, WILC Archives; Jeffrey Alan Turner, *Sitting In and Speaking Out: Student Movements in the American South, 1960–1970* (Athens, GA: University of Georgia Press, 2010), p. 190.
10. Jeffrey Alan Turner, "Conscious and Conflict: Patterns in the History of Student Activism on Southern College Campuses, 1960–1970" (PhD. diss, Tulane University, 2000), p. 276; "National Guardsmen Sent to 3 Troubled Campuses," *CHE*, June 16, 1969; Cleveland Sellers and Robert Terrell, *The River of No Return: The Autobiography of a Black Militant* (Jackson, MS: University of Mississippi Press, 1990), pp. 210–212, 218.

11. "Overuse of Force on Negroes Found," *NYT*, February 25, 1968; "My View," *PC*, March 16, 1968; "Police Slayings of 3 Students Arouse South," *CHE*, March 11, 1968; "6 Hurt in Clashes at Negro College," *NYT*, February 22, 1968; Williamson, *Radicalizing the Ebony Tower*, pp. 154–155; "South Carolina Verdict," *CD*, June 12, 1969; "Carolina Patrolmen Cleared of Liability in Orangeburg Suit," *NYT*, November 14, 1970.

12. "Negro Students Seize Colgate Fraternity House," *NYT*, April 8, 1968; "Colgate Students Fraternity Bias," *NYT*, April 10, 1968; "Colgate Bans 2 Biased Frats after Shooting," *PC*, April 27, 1968; "Two Bias Incidents Hit Students after 'Black Week,'" *CD*, May 10, 1969; "OSU Indictments Likened to Lynching," *CD*, April 2, 1969; Durward Long, "Black Protest," in *PROTEST! Student Activism in America*, eds. Julian Foster and Durward Long (New York: William Morrow and Company, 1970), p. 473; "Patrolmen Guard Ohio State Campus," *NYT*, May 1, 1968; "34 at Ohio State Gain Settlement," *NYT*, July 29, 1969.

13. "My View," *PC*, August 10, 1968; "Surveillance on Campus: Some Administrators Are Shocked, Others Cooperate," *CHE*, May 3, 1971 (first quote); "FBI Approved Hiring Student Informers, Sen. Weicker Says," *CHE*, June 18, 1973 (second quote); Interdepartmental correspondence to Robert E. Smith, September 30, 1968, Chancellor James Bugg's Papers, box 1, folder 29, UMSTL Archives; "Chicano and Black Student Demands and Rationale," no date, circa 1969, Campus Unrest Collection, box 2, folder: Ethnic Minorities; African American students, 1968–1971 and undated, CSUFRES Archives. Also see "How the FBI Tried to Subvert Campus Rebellion," *CHE*, September 15, 1975; "FBI is Reported Active on Campuses since 1968," *CHE*, April 12, 1971; "FBI, under Hoover, Sought to Discredit Texas U., Antioch," *CHE*, December 1, 1975; "F.B.I. Planned to Neutralize Key Activists," *CHE*, December 17, 1973; Kenneth O'Reilly, *Racial Matters: The FBI's Secret File on Black America, 1960–1972* (New York: Free Press, 1989).

14. "Incidents Urge Respect of Blacks," *CC*, March 14, 1969, LUTC Archives; "Rights for the Whites, Inc." to University of Utah, October 28, 1971; "A Loyal Tennessee Fan" to President, October 29, 1971, Student Affairs Office Records, 1970–1977, Box 4, Folder 14, UUTAH Archives.

15. "Silent Majority" to "NIGGERS," no date, circa late 1960s, Center for African American Studies, Administrative Subject Files, 1969–, box 16, folder (Black Faculty/ Staff of So. Calif 1968–1969), UCLA Archives; Block, "Afro-Americans for Black Liberation," p. 26; "Blacks Take Credit for DeKalb Rioting," *CD*, March 24, 1969; "Riot Hits NIU Campus," *CD*, March 24, 1969.

16. John Craig Stewart, "The University of South Alabama The First Thirteen Years," p. 449, John Craig Stewart Papers, box 1, file 9; "Whiteurs Discusses Shooting," *VA*, March 12, 1971, USA Archives; "Events of Yesterday," no date, circa late 1960s, Jose Joel Garcia Collection CEMA 73, series 3, box 1, folder 18, CEMA.

17. Rusty L. Monhollon, *This is America?: The Sixties in Lawrence, Kansas* (New York: Palgrave Macmillan, 2002), pp. 100–106; Beryl Ann New, "A Fire in the Sky: Student Activism in Topeka, Kansas and Lawrence, Kansas High School in 1969 and 1970" (Masters Ed., Washburn University, 2002), pp. 52–54; Judith Jackson Fossett, *Race Consciousness: African-American Studies For the New Century* (New York: New York University Press, 1997), pp. 248 (Garrett and BSU quotes); Bryce Nelson, "Kansas: Police-Student Violence Imperils University," *Science* 169 (August 7, 1970), pp. 567–569.

18. "Black Thursday at Oshkosh," *TC*, November 1969; "100 Negro Students Seized in Wisconsin Protest," *NYT*, November 22, 1968; "Black Students Ransack Oshkosh Prexy's Office," *PC*, November 30, 1968; "200 Students Storm Wisconsin Regents to

Press Demands," *NYT*, December 7, 1968; "Negro Student Is Charged in Bluefield College Bombing," *NYT*, November 25, 1968.

19. Anonymous to Thomas H. Eliot, December 11, 1968 (first quote); C. L. Husbands to Thomas H. Eliot, December 16, 1968 (second quote); Ex-Student to Thomas H. Eliot, December 12, 1968 (third quote), series 11, box 1, folder: Student Demonstrations WU, Correspondence A–K, 1968–1969, WU Archives.

20. This narrative is from Dikran Karagueuzian, *Blow It Up!: The Black Student Revolt at San Francisco State and the Emergence of Dr. Hayakawa* (Boston: Gambit, 1971), pp. 168–169; William Barlow and Peter Shapiro, *An End to Silence: The San Francisco State College Student Movement in the '60s* (New York: Pegasus, 1971), pp. 236–264; "Police Repel Students at College in San Francisco," *NYT*, December 4, 1968.

21. "Incident in Minneapolis," *NYT*, January 15, 1969; "Students End Siege on U. of Minnesota Campus," *NYT*, January 16, 1969; Calvin B. T. Lee, *The Campus Scene, 1900–1970: Changing Styles in Undergraduate Life* (New York: McKay, 1970), pp. 147–148 (bath quote); "Black Culture at SSC," *TS*, March 31, 1970, CSUSTAN Archives; "Marquette Head Criticized, Kenosha News, May 22, 1968, Office of Student Affairs Records, series 3, box 3, folder: Institutional Racism Protest Newspaper Clippings, May 21–26, 1969, MARU Archives; "UCSB Black Studies Dept. Built From 1968 Black Student Union Protest," *DN*, February 12, 2001, UC SAN Archives; "Coast Negroes Seize University Center," *NYT*, October 14, 1968; Richard D. Strahan to Hugh C. Smith, March 11, 1969, 1969 Demonstrations Collection, DSU Archives.

22. Barlow and Shapiro, *An End to Silence*, pp. 299–301; Karagueuzian, *Blow It Up*, pp. 183–184; "House Committee Opens Hearings on Impact of Student Protests," *CHE*, February 10, 1969; "Negro Students Push Demands; Reaction Grows," *CHE*, January 27, 1969; "CORE's Chief Assails Wilkins Stand," *NYT*, January 22, 1969; "NAACP Opposes Student Control of Black Studies," *SR*, February 1, 1969.

23. "The Case for Separatism: 'Black Perspective'"; "The Case Against Separatism: 'Black Jim Crow,'" *NE*, February 10, 1969.

24. Allan Kornberg and Joel Smith, "'It Ain't Over Yet': Activism in a Southern University," in *Black Power and Student Rebellion*, pp. 107–109; Alan Kornberg and Mary L. Brehm, "Ideology, Institutional Identification, and Campus Activism," *Social Forces* 49 (March 1971), pp. 445–446; Stark, "Protest + Police = Riot," in *Black Power and Student Rebellion*, pp. 186–190.

25. "Silbert Attacks Afro Demands As 'Unrealistic, Vague, Racist,'" *TDT*, February 28, 1969, UTXA Archives; "United We Welsh," no date, circa early 1969, Student Demonstrations, 1960–Present Collection, box 001, folder 3, EMU Archives; Bill Kost, "Minority Groups," *TPC*, December 6, 1968, WPU Archives; Eugene G. Williams to the Editors, November 22, 1968, "November 21, 1968 Incident" Records, 1968–1971, series 1, box 1, folder 7, UWOSH Archives; "Campus Backlash: Students Protest Protests," *NYT*, February 26, 1969; "'Black Studies Furora Fad,' says Brinley," *OP*, February 27, 1969 (Huntley quote); "Separate Is Not Equal," *NYAN*, February 22, 1969 (Rustin quote); "Reactions to Disorders Gains in Intensity," *CHE*, March 10, 1969; "Tough Responses to Dissent Seen Stifling Reforms," *CHE*, March 10, 1969; "Governors Reject Hard Line on Colleges," *CHE*, March 10, 1969; "Poll Shows Adult Public Favors Hard Line as Campus Protests Continue to Spread," *CHE*, March 29, 1969.

26. "A.C.E. Special Report: Text of the Memorandum from the Office for Civil Rights, Dated March, 1969," Willis D. Weatherford Papers, box 40, folder 12, BERC Archives;

"Black Students Blamed in New Jim Crow," *CD*, March 1, 1969; "Dozen Colleges Warned on Excluding Whites," *CHE*, March 10, 1969; "Is Crow-Jim Democratic," *CD*, March 8, 1969 (first quote); "Clark Scores Separatism at Antioch," *New York Times*, May 23, 1969 (second quote)

27. Turner, "Conscious and Conflict," pp. 311–314; "Fly 'Black Flag' at Southern," *CD*, April 16, 1969; "Cops Nab 109 MSU Students," *CD*, April 30, 1969; "Armed Students Takeover Voorhees College Building," *CD*, April 29, 1969; "Voorhees College Students on Trial for Rioting," *SR*, July 25, 1970; "Negro Students Reach Accord with Pratt Institute President," *NYT*, May 11, 1969; "20 Arrested at Howard as Campus Siege Ends," *NYT*, May 10, 1969; "365 Held in Alabama," *NYT*, May 6, 1969.

28. Dyer, "Protest and the Politics," pp. 127–129; "Rash of Vandalism at QC Brings 500 Cops," *NYAN*, May 10, 1969; "2 More Campuses of City U. Closed after Disorders," *NYT*, May 3, 1969.

29. "Negro Students Criticized by Rustin," *NYT*, April 28, 1969; "Negro Students Reply to Critics," *NYT*, May 17, 1969; "Allen Comments on Protests," *NYT*, June 1, 1969.

30. "U. of Louisville Expels 9," *NYT*, May 3, 1969; "Student Revolutionaries Condemned by President," *CD*, April 30, 1969.

31. "The Siege of Greensboro," *NE*, June 2, 1969; "Greensboro Calm as Guard Leaves," *NYT*, May 25, 1969.

32. "Thurgood Marshall Denounces Militants," *SR*, May 17, 1969; "Negro Leaders and Opponents of War Play Major Role as Graduate Speakers," *NYT*, June 9, 1969; "Negro Extremists Scored at Parley," *NYT*, July 3, 1969 (Kilson quote one); "Professor Scores Black Separatism," *NYT*, September 7, 1969 (Kilson quote two); "The Case against Black Studies," *PC*, August 2, 1969 (Lewis quote).

33. "Black Problem Unsolved," *BW*, September 23, 1969, LEHIU SC (Mills quote); Glen R. Driscoll to Robert, June 11, 1970, Papers of the Chancellors, Glen Driscoll (1969–1972), box 4, folder 205, UMSTL Archives.

34. "Initiators Withdraw Referendum Petition," *CR*, February 26, 1970, MORC Archives; "Why Put a Color on the Center," *TCC*, November 22, 1968, STCST Archives; "Olaf Black Population Alienates Most Whites," *MM*, November 17, 1969; "Olaf Black Say Union Open to All," *MM*, November 25, 1969, STOC Archives

35. "House Action on Disorders Appears Near," *CHE*, June 16, 1969; "Campus Disorder Brings Demands for States to Act," *NYT*, May 4, 1969; Janet Harris, *Students in Revolt* (New York: McGraw-Hill Book Company, 1970), p. 165–167; "Campus Gun Ban Is Voted in Albany," *NYT*, May 1, 1969; "Assembly Votes Campus Gun Ban," *NYT*, April 29, 1969; "Many State Legislatures Act against Campus Disrupters," *CHE*, June 16, 1969; "Disorders Puzzle Legislators," *CHE*, August 11, 1969; "Police Seeking to Avoid Clashes with Students," *CHE*, July 14, 1969; "Confrontations Alter Role of Campus Officers," *CHE*, July 14, 1969.

36. "Stern Anti-Disruption Warnings Greet Returning Students, but so Do Conciliatory Moves Giving Them More Say," *CHE*, September 29, 1969 (Ohio quote); "Colleges Strengthen Security and Rules; Students Warned on Disruptions," *CHE*, September 28, 1970.

37. "68 Colleges Cut Off Funds to Disrupters," *CHE*, October 20, 1969; DeVere Pentony, Robert Smith, and Richard Axen, *Unfinished Rebellions* (San Francisco: Jossey-Bass, 1971), pp. 172–176; "S.F. State Strike Trials—A Mixed Bag of Repression," *SR*, November 29, 1969; "2 at Minnesota U. Guilty in Protest," *NYT*, November 8, 1969; "Students Trial Is Seen as Vital," *NYT*, September 21, 1969; "Valley State Students Face New Troubles," *SR*, December 13, 1969; "NAACP Defends College Students," *TC*, November 1969; "2 Decisions Set Precedents in Curbing Campus Disorders," *CHE*, December 8, 1969;

"Campus Militants Given 1–25 Years," *NYT*, February 1, 1970; "Judicial Lynching of Calif. Students," *CD*, February 21, 1970; Earl Anthony, *The Time of the Furnaces: A Case Study of Black Student Revolt* (New York: The Dial Press, 1971) pp. 87–100.

38. Clifford A. Bullock, "Fired by Conscience: The 'Black 14' Incident at the University of Wyoming and Black Protest in the Western Athletic Conference," *Annals of Wyoming: The Wyoming History Journal* 68 (1996), pp. 4–13; "Wyoming U Still Tense," *CD*, October 25, 1969; "Black Athletes Having Their Day in Court," *CD*, November 11, 1969; "Court Disclaims Black-14s Petition," *CD*, October 19, 1971.

39. "Rule of Law at Harvard," *NYT*, December 13, 1969; "Negroes Skip Harvard Classes," *NYT*, December 17, 1969; "Students Suspended: Blacks Press Harvard for Jobs," *BSB*, December 18, 1969; "Dean at Harvard Charges 40 Students in Take-over," *NYT*, December 20, 1969; "Harvard Acts against Blacks," *CD*, January 3, 1970; "Harvard Hearings Boycott," *NYT*, January 10, 1970; "Black Students Judge Harvard," *BSB*, January 22, 1970.

40. Williamson, *Radicalizing the Ebony Tower*, pp. 140–141; "Mississippi Students Rebel at Itta Bena," *ADW*, February 27, 1970; "894 Students Are Arrested at a Mississippi College," *CHE*, March 2, 1970; "Dallas Students Ousted by Police," *NYT*, February 13, 1970; Turner, "Conscious and Conflict," pp. 294–296; James Forman, *Sammy Younge, Jr.: The First Black College Student to Die in the Black Liberation Movement* (New York: Grove Press, 1968), pp. 262–282.

41. "OBC Protest Dean's Letter," *TTH*, March 6, 1970, THIC Archives; "Brandeis Quiet Despite Student Sit-in," *NYT*, January 15, 1969.

42. "Campus Protests Follow D.C. Activities; Many Involve Blacks," *CHE*, May 17, 1971; Jerrold Wimbish Roy, "Student Activism and the Historically Black University: Hampton Institute and Howard University, 1960–1972" (PhD. diss, Harvard University, 2000), pp. 90–93.

43. "A Settlement—And Why We Signed It," *Black Fire*, May 3, 1969, Author's Personal Collection, Supplied by Bernard Stringer.

8   "Black Students Refuse to Pass the Buck": The Racial Reconstitution of Higher Education

1. "Black Scholarship," *NYT*, January 23, 1969; "Harvard Report Calls for Degree in Negro Studies," *NYT*, January 22, 1969; Henry Rosovsky, "Black Studies at Harvard: Personal Reflections Concerning Recent Events," *The American Scholar* 38 (Autumn 1969), pp. 562–572; Roger Rosenblatt, *Coming Apart: A Memoir of the Harvard Wards of 1969* (Boston: Little, Brown and Company, 1997), p. 141; "Among the Harvard Faculty, an Intense Feeling of Uncertainty," *NYT*, April 24, 1969; "Harvard Negroes Get Faculty Voice," *NYT*, April 23, 1969; Lawrence E. Eichel, Kenneth W. Jost, Robert D. Luskin, and Richard M. Neustadt, *The Harvard Strike* (Boston: Hougton Mifflin Company, 1970), pp. 268–269, 284–286.

2. "Boycotting Students at Howard Threaten an Injunction," *NYT*, May 13, 1969; "Nkrumah for Howard U.," *CD*, June 3, 1969; "20 Arrested at Howard as Campus Siege Ends," *NYT*, May 10, 1969; "Howard Prexy Maps Plans for 'Black Education,'" *CD*, September 24, 1969; Jerrold Wimbish Roy, "Student Activism and the Historically Black University: Hampton Institute and Howard University, 1960–1972" (PhD. diss, Harvard University, 2000), pp. 138–147.

3. "Colleges Step Up Changes in Bid to Avert Disruption," *NYT*, May 11, 1969 (Roose quote); "'Education Authority Crisis' Discussed by Ford Fund," *CHE*, March 10,

1969 (Ward quote); "Black Collegians," *WSJ*, July 28, 1969; W. Todd Furniss, "Racial Minorities and Curriculum Change," *Educational Record* 50 (Fall 1969), p. 360–370; "Vast Changes on Campuses Seen in 70s," *CHE*, December 8, 1969; "More Negroes, Women Joining Trustee Ranks," *CHE*, April 6, 1970.

4. "C. E. Daye Delivers 'State of Campus,'" *CE*, February 28, 1966, NCCU Archives.

5. Joy Ann Williamson, *Radicalizing the Ebony Tower: Black Colleges and the Black Freedom Struggle in Mississippi* (New York: Teachers College Press, 2008). p. 39.

6. "Disruptive Tactics May Not Be Used Again," *AJR*, March 7, 1969, NATU Archives; "Demands and Recommendations from the Maryland State College Student Body," UMES Archives.

7. "Temporary Accord Ends Bowie Demonstration," *THAT*, April 2, 1968, GWU SC; "Alcorn 1966: An Incident," ETSU Archives; George Henderson, *Race and the University: A Memoir* (Norman, OK: University of Oklahoma Press, 2010), p. 26.

8. *Special Financial Needs of Traditional Negro Colleges: A Task Force Report* (Atlanta: Southern Regional Education Board, 1969).

9. "46 Black College Heads Appeal for U.S. Funds," *CD*, May 29, 1971.

10. Vivian W. Henderson, "Blacks and Change in Higher Education," *Daedalus* 104 (Fall 1974), p. 74; "A Professor's Point of View," *NI*, June 1969; "Board of Trustees Gets First Black Chairman," *AJR*, November 7, 1969, NATU Archives.

11. Robert W. Morse to Raymond A. Henry, December 1, 1969, Records of the Afro-American Society, box 1, folder 4, CWRU Archives.

12. Ronald Walters and Robert Smith, "The Black Education Strategy in the 1970s," *The Journal of Negro Education* 48 (Spring 1979), pp. 158, 165–166; "Black Youths' Share of Enrollment Grows," *CHE*, December 15, 1975; 12% of College Frosh in '74 Were Blacks," *CD*, December 10, 1975; "Enrollment of Black Freshmen Slowed This Year, Study Indicates," *CHE*, February 11, 1974; "Black Enrollment Rising Again," *CHE*, March 17, 1975; See Susan T. Hill, *Participation of Black Students in Higher Education: A Statistical Profile from 1970–71 to 1980–81* (Washington, DC: National Center for Education Statistics, 1983).

13. Alexander W. Astin, Helen S. Astin, Alan E. Bayer, and Ann S. Bisconti, *The Power of Protest: A National Study of Student and Faculty Disruptions with Implications for the Future* (San Francisco: Jossey-Bass, 1975), pp. 148–149; See Reuben R. McDaniel Jr. and James W. McKee, *An Evaluation of Higher Education's Response to Black Students* (Bloomington, IN: Student Association of Higher Education, 1971).

14. Ama Mazama, ed., *The Afrocentric Paradigm* (Trenton, NJ: Africa World Press), pp. 4–5.

15. AABL Statement Presented to Dr. Hoffman, UHOU Archives; "Educational Reform Discussion Target," *RU*, October 9, 1970, NMSU Archives; "Racism at Howard," GWU SC; Roy, "Student Activism and the Historically Black University," pp. 69–73 (Masingale quote); "BSU News Release," *RB*, April 8, 1969, UGA Archives; Students for a Black University, "Week of Reckoning, Toward a Black University" Pamphlet, no date, circa late 1969, FU SC; Paul E. Wisdom and Kenneth A. Shaw, "Black Challenge to Higher Education," *Educational Record* 50 (Fall 1969), pp. 352–353.

16. "No More Inferior Education," *TNA*, March 1969; "Black Student Union," *TNA*, October 1969, WSSU Archives; Jeffrey A. Turner, *Sitting In and Speaking Out: Student Movements in the American South: 1960–1970* (Athens, GA: University of Georgia Press, 2010), pp. 165, 180 (Morehouse and graduate dean quotes).

17. "Student Strikes: 1968–69," *The Black Scholar* 1 (January-February 1970), p. 65.

18. Genna Rae McNeil to the Faculty and Administration of Kalamazoo College, May 19, 1969, Records of the President (R 3/13), box 1, folder 8, KAC Archives.

19. Astin, Astin, Bayer, and Bisconti, *The Power of Protest*, pp. 148–149; McDaniel Jr. and McKee, *An Evaluation of Higher Education's Response to Black Students*; "Education Find Black Studies Are Changing Higher Education," *NYT*, June 4, 1972; "Black Studies on the Rise," *CD*, March 12, 1974; "The State of Black Studies," *CHE*, December 8, 1975; Nick Aaron Ford, *Black Studies: Threat or Challenge* (Port Washington, NY: Kennikat Press, 1973).

20. "Anguish over Relevance Strains Three Social Sciences, Psychologists: One Session Taken Over, Five Dissident Groups Seek Changes," *CHE*, September 15, 1969; "*Disciplines Experiencing Rifts Between Old Guard and Proponents of Change*," *CHE*, September 15, 1969; "Many Geographers Urge Focus on Urban Problems," *CHE*, September 15, 1969.

21. "Two Types of Instructors in Negro Colleges—Daye," *CE*, May 18, 1966; "Prairie View A&M Re-Opens," *SOBU Newsletter*, March 20, 1971, ECSU Archives.

22. "'The New Alcorn,'" *AH*, October 1969, ASU Archives.

23. "Demands Made by Black Caucus," *NS*, May 2, 1969, IUN Archives; "Proposal for Establishing a Black Studies Program," no date, circa late 1960s, Chancellor James Bugg's Papers, 1940–1978, box 1, folder 29, UMSTL Archives; "Education or Indoctrination," *AFT*, October 31, 1972, Presidents Papers: President William L. Giles, accession A81-25, box 49, folder: Student Affairs—Black Students, MSSU Archives; "Statement of the Black Student Alliance," no date, circa 1968, Student Protest Files of the Vice President for Student Affairs, 1965–1971, box 1050H, folder 11, MSU Archives; Gregory, "'Howard University, 1967–1968,'" p. 428; Barbara Garrison, Statement of the Alliance of Black Students, February 13, 1969, Communication & Media Relations Records (AR 134), box 11, folder 35, UWM Archives.

24. Gilbert L. Lycan, *Stetson University: The First 100 Years* (DeLand, FL: Stetson University Press, 1983), pp. 462–463; "Proposal for Establishing a Black Studies Program," no date, circa late 1960s, Chancellor James Bugg's Papers, 1940–1978, box 1, folder 29, UMSTL Archives.

25. "Black Students Speak Out," *TELB*, 1970, UAK Archives; Black Students Association to Dean of Instruction, "A Minority Report," no date, early 1969, Student Activities Collection, box: NB-STUD-V-BSP, folder: R.U.-N&B-News Releases-General-Black Studies Protest-1969 I, ROSU Archives; The Black Students Alliance of the University of Chicago to Lyndon B. Johnson, March 1, 1968, WHCF Name File: Black, S, LBJL; "Blackwell Calls for End To 'Whitewashing' of Blacks," *XUN*, March 11, 1970, XUO Archives; Gwen Patton to Brothers and Sisters, UKS Archives.

26. "Black Student Union Demands," May 1, 1968, Vertical Files: Black Student Union, 1968–1975, CLAC Archives.

27. "Campus Dis-unity," *Harambee*, February 14, 1969, TOGC Archives.

28. Gregory D. Stanford to John P. Raynor, S.J., November 23, 1967, Office of Student Affairs Records, series 3, box 3, folder: Institutional Racism Protest – Students United for Racial Equality (SURE) Correspondence, 1967–1968, MARU Archives. Two examples of the AP story's publication are "Marquette May Never Be Same," *The Rhinelander Daily News*, May 24, 1968; "Crisis Over, but Marquette May Never Be Same," *Beloit Daily News*, May 24, 1968, All-University Faculty Committee Records, series 3, box 2, folder: Association for Interracial Justice—Students United for Racial Equality (SURE) General Correspondence n.d., MARU Archives.

29. "Tough Responses to Dissent Seen Stifling Reforms," *CHE*, March 10, 1969 (Birenbaum quote); "Gould Foresees Hope and Accomplishment Arising from Today's Agony of Nation's Universities," *CHE*, October 6, 1969 (Gould quote); Harold L. Enarson, "Higher Education and Community Services," in *The Campus and the Racial Crisis*, eds. David C. Nichols and Olive Mills (Washington, DC: American

Council of Education, 1970), p. 241; Robert H. Finch, "Challenge and Response in the American Educational Environment," in *The Campus and the Racial Crisis*, p. 302.

30. "The Negro Colleges: Victims of Progress," *NYT*, October 6, 1969 (Pitts quote); "Black Colleges Offer Negro Youths Road Out of the Ghetto," *CT*, May 24, 1970 (Gates quote).

31. "Black Colleges Starved of Funds," *BG*, December 28, 1969; Henderson, "Blacks and Change in Higher Education," p. 74; "Dowdy Says Leaders Needed," *AJR*, October 3, 1969.

Epilogue: Backlash and Forward Lashes
of the Black Campus Movement

1. Peter Louis Goldman, *The Death and Life of Malcolm X* (Urbana, IL: University of Illinois Press, 1979), p. 16.

2. "The SAT's Growing Gaps," *Inside Higher Ed*, August 27, 2008, http://www .insidehighered.com/news/2008/08/27/sat, accessed November 7, 2011.

3. I am defining egalitarian exclusion as exclusion utilizing principles of equality, while inclusive exclusion is slightly different—the mutual inclusion and exclusion of African Americans. Amy S. Blodgett, "The Fight for Racial Equality at Dickinson College During the Sixties," pp. 5–6 (unpublished manuscript, May 5, 1982), DICC Archives.

4. "Black Monday," *TNA*, November 1971, WSSU Archives; Student Organization for Black Unity, "Save Black Schools: What Is the Future of Black Higher Education in North Carolina, A Report on the Crisis in Black Higher Education in North Carolina," April 1971, SOBU Publications, box 2, folder: reports, ECSU Archive; "July Merger Threatens AM&N," *SOBUN*, March 20, 1971.

5. "A.C.E. Special Report," BERC Archives; Reply by Chancellor J. Carlyle Sitterson to Demands Presented by Black Student Movement, January 24, 1969; New University Conference at Chapel Hill, Statement on Chancellor Sittersen's reply to Black Student Movement's demands, February 1, 1969, Office of the Chancellor of North Carolina Chapel Hill: Joseph Carlyle Sitterson Records, 1966–1972 (#40022), box 1, folder: Black Student Movement: Statements, 1968–1969, UNC Archives; Jeffrey Alan Turner, "Conscious and Conflict: Patterns in the History of Activism on Southern College Campuses, 1960–1970" (PhD. diss, Tulane University, 2000), pp. 345–354; "35 Negroes March in Student Protest at North Carolina," *NYT*, February 22, 1969.

6. "Black Protests Air Problems," *CD*, May 25, 1974; Roderick Kieth Linzie, "Analysis of the Anti-Racist Student Movement at the University of Michigan—Ann Arbor" (PhD. diss, University of Michigan, 1993); "Campus Cops End Student Takeover," *CD*, May 6, 1975; "25 Protesters Arrested at Santa Barbara," *CHE*, May 12, 1975; "Student Protest, 1975: Stress on Economic Issues," *CHE*, June 9, 1975.

7. "The Bakke Decision: Attack on Your Civil Rights!" no date, circa 1978, Student Activities Collection, box: NB-STUD-V-BSP, folder: R.U.-N&B-News Releases-General-Black Studies Protest-1969 I, ROSU Archives; "Demonstration on Bakke Suit," *TWP*, April 16, 1978; "30,000 Join March Against Bakke," *NYAN*, April 22, 1978.

8. Mary Frances Berry, "Atlanta and Affirmative Action, 1973–1980,'" in *Voices of Freedom: An Oral History of the Civil Rights Movement from the 1950s Through the 1980s*, Henry Hampton, Steve Fayer, and Sarah Flynn (New York: Bantam Books, 1990), pp. 644–645.

9. Hampton University Dress Code, accessed August 10, 2011, http://www.hamptonu.edu/student_life/dresscode.cfm.

10. I choose not to define "real diversity," because it differs at every college in America, depending on its location, whether it is private or public, its mission, its local, regional, and national drawing power, and so forth. I think the communities of each institution can define real diversity.

11. *Status and Trends in the Education of Racial and Ethnic Minorities*, National Center for Education Statistics Publication # 2010015, July 2010, http://nces.ed.gov/pubsearch/pubsinfo.asp?pubid=2010015,accessedNovember7,2011;USCensusBureau, "Estimates of the Resident Population by Race and Hispanic Origin for the United States and States: July 1, 2008 (SC-EST2008-04)," published May 14, 2009, http://www.census.gov/popest/states/asrh/SC-EST2008-04.html, accessed November 7, 2011; Nathan E. Bell, *Graduate Enrollment and Degrees: 1999 to 2009* (Washington, DC: Council of Graduate Schools, 2010), p. 41, http://www.cgsnet.org/portals/0/pdf/R_ED2009.pdf, accessed November 7, 2011; "More Blacks, Latinos in Jail Than College Dorms," *MSNBC*, last modified September 27, 2007, http://www.msnbc.msn.com/id/21001543/ns/us_news-life/t/more-blacks-latinos-jail-college-dorms/, accessed November 7, 2011; "U.S. Women and Minority Scientist Discourage from Pursuing STEM Careers, National Survey Shows," Bayer Corporation, March 22, 2010, http://www.bayerus.com/News%5CNewsDetail.aspx?ID=862593F0-F489-B4D0-283DB12C656EA899, accessed November 14, 2011; Noliwe Rooks, *White Money/Black Power: The History of African American Studies and the Crisis of Race in Higher Education* (Boston: Beacon Press, 2006); Michelle Alexander, *The New Jim Crow: Mass Incarceration in the Age of Colorblindness* (New York: The New Press, 2010); "Classrooms or Prison Cells?," *The Daily Beast*, June 28, 2010, http://www.thedailybeast.com/newsweek/2010/06/28/classrooms-or-prison-cells.html, accessed November 7, 2011.

12. "African Americans in Higher Education: Now for the Good News," *The Journal of Blacks in Higher Education*, accessed on August 10, 2011, http://www.jbhe.com/news_views/48_blacks_highereducation.html; "Ranking the Nation's Leading Universities and Liberal Arts Colleges on Their Numbers of Black Faculty," *The Journal of Blacks in Higher Education*, accessed on August 10, 2011, http://www.jbhe.com/news_views/65_blackfaculty.html; "Faculty Diversity: Too Little for Too Long," Harvard Magazine, March-April 2002, http://harvardmagazine.com/2002/03/faculty-diversity.html, accessed November 7, 2011; "Doctoral Degree Awards to African Americans Reach Another All-Time High," *The Journal of Blacks in Higher Education*, accessed August 10, 2011, http://www.jbhe.com/news_views/50_black_doctoraldegrees.html.

13. Rooks, *White Money/Black Power*, p. 78 (Bundy quote); Robert Allen, "Politics of the Attack on Black Studies," *Black Scholar* 6 (September 1974), pp. 2, 5.

14. Robert McCray to Daniel Walker, March 16, 1973, Chancellor's Central Files (RG # 3-1-2), series 3, box 51, folder 725, UIC Archives.

15. Rojas, *From Black Power to Black Studies*, p. 21.

16. Nathan Hare, "Appendix 4: A Conceptual Proposal for a Department of Black Studies," in William H. Orrick, *Shut It Down! A College in Crisis San Francisco State College October, 1968–April 1969* (Washington, DC: US Government Printing Office, 1969), pp. 160–161.

Index

A. Phillip Randolph Institute, 138
AAAS, *See* African and Afro-American
   Association
AABL, *See* Afro-Americans for Black
   Liberation
AAO, *See* Afro-American Organization
AAS, *See* Afro-American Society
Abbott, Robert S., 39
ABC, *See* Association of Black Collegians
Abernathy, Ralph, 100
abolition, 9, 11–12, 30, 42
accommodating separatists, 10–13, 17, 25,
   28, 39, 45
ACE, *See* American Council on Education
ACLU, *See* American Civil Liberties
   Union
ACS, *See* American Colonization Society
Adams, Osceola, 34
Adams, Ruth, 87
affirmative action, 92, 161–4
AFNS, *See* American Federation of Negro
   Students
African and Afro-American Association
   (AAAS), 145–6
African Methodist Episcopal Church
   (AMEC), 11, 13, 15, 32, 57
Africana Studies, 6, 90, 152, 168–9
Afro-American (Baltimore), 41, 58
Afro-American Congress, 131
Afro-American Organization
   (AAO), 80, 162
Afro-American Society (AAS), 68, 80–1, 83,
   110, 122, 127–9, 131, 145–6, 150, 169
Afro-American Student Movement, 71
Afro-American Student Organization, 157
Afro-American Studies Institute, 138
Afro-Americans for Black Liberation, 152

Afros, 1–2, 117, 169
Ahmad, Muhammad, 68
Alabama A&M University, 16, 58, 150
Alabama State University, 58–9, 64,
   98, 138
Alcindor, "Lew," 70–1, 77
Alcorn State University, 16, 26, 32, 45–6,
   58, 61, 71, 92, 108, 130, 133, 149, 155
Alexander, Jim, 96
Alexander, Michelle, 167
Ali, Muhammad, 81, 116, 131
All-Southern Negro Youth Congresses, 52
Allen, Robert, 168
Allen, Jr., James E., 139
Allen University, 57, 61
Alliance of Black Students, 156
Allied Blacks for Liberty and Equality, 116
AMA, *See* American Missionary
   Association
AMEC, *See* African Methodist Episcopal
   Church
American Association of State
   Colleges, 154
American Baptist Theological, 61
American Civil Liberties Union
   (ACLU), 131
American Colonization Society
   (ACS), 10–12
American Council on Education (ACE),
   147, 158
American Federation of Negro Students
   (AFNS), 38–9
The American Mercury, 40
American Missionary Association
   (AMA), 13
American Political Science
   Association, 154

American Psychological Association, 154
American Sociology Association, 154
American Student Union (ASU), 50–3, 65
American University of, 109–10
American Youth Congress, 50
Amherst College (MA), 56
Amistad Society, 70
Anderson, James D., 14, 32
Anderson, Lynne, 85
Angelo State University, 104, 116
antebellum era, 10, 13, 29–30
Antioch College, 54
Armah, George, 69
Armstrong, S. C., 13–14, 32
Asante, Molefi Kete, 169
Asian students, 2, 124, 130, 161, 168
Association of American
    Geographers, 155
Association of Black Collegians (ABC), 89,
    109, 133–4, 156
Association of Black Psychologists, 154
Association of Black Psychology
    Students, 154
ASU, See American Student Union
Atlanta Exposition (1895), 17
Atlanta Race Riot (1906), 33
Atlanta University, 15–16, 18, 33, 38, 52
Atlanta University Center, 90
Attica Prison massacre (NY), 104
Atwood, R. B., 58, 64
Augustana College (IL), 84, 124
Autherine Lucy episode (1956), 25, 60,
    64, 69
The Autobiography of Malcolm X, 93, 121

Baker, Ella, 18, 43, 62, 64
Baker, Sam, 43
Bakke, Allan, 164
Baldwin, James, 73, 82, 93, 107
Ballard, Allen, 18
Banks, W. R., 42
Banneker, Benjamin, 9
Barber-Scotia College (NC), 32
Barnes, Jr., Ervin, 155
Barnhill, M. V., 55
Barry, Marion, 62
The Battle of Algiers (1966) (film), 123
BCCs, See Black Cultural Centers
Beckwith, Byron De La, 69
Beloit College (WI), 115, 122

Benedict College (SC), 45
Berea College (KY), 15–16, 42, 70, 94
Berry, Mary Frances, 164
Bethune, Mary McLeod, 32, 50, 52
Birenbaum, William M., 158
The Birth of a Nation (1915) (film), 34
Black Arts Movement, 3
black campus activists, 3
Black Campus Movement (BCM)
    before 1965, 9–28
    demands of, 111–20
    formation of, 67–87
    future of, 161–9
    and higher education, 145–59
    and the long black student movement,
        See long black student movement
    narrative overview of, 89–106
    opposition to, 127–43
    organizing, 107–11
    and protests, 120–5
Black Capitalism Movement, 110, 117, 159
Black Cultural Centers (BCCs), 81
Black Feminist Movement, 3, 86
Black 14 affair, 142
black lines, 167–8
black nationalism, 36, 68, 70, 72, 86, 131
Black Panther Party, 74, 79–80, 96–7, 100,
    127, 158
Black Power Movement (BPM), 3, 29, 67,
    76, 82, 87, 89–106, 112, 133, 159
The Black Scholar, 153
Black Student(s) Alliance (BSA), 1, 114,
    116, 133, 137, 156–7, 168–9
Black Student(s) Unions (BSUs), 3, 22–3,
    68, 70, 77, 79–80, 82–3, 85–6, 92–7,
    107–11, 113–25, 131–7, 140–3, 148,
    152, 156–8, 162, 164, 169
black student movement
    narrative overview of, 89–106
    opposition to, 127–43
    organizing, 107–11
    and protests, 120–5
    black student newspapers, 84–5
Black Student Psychology Association, 118
Black Studies, 1, 3, 80–2, 93–9, 101, 104,
    110, 113–15, 119–20, 124–5, 129, 133,
    137–8, 140, 145–7, 153–4, 156–8, 163,
    168–9
black suasion, 67, 70, 109–11
Black Theology Movement, 3, 118

Black United Students (BUS), 156–7
"Black University" concept, 3, 94, 108, 112, 146, 162
Blackwell, Ken, 157
Blair, Jr., Ezell, 62–3
Blake, Elias, 154
Bloody Sunday (March 7, 1965), 73, 75, 86, 91, 112
Bloody Tuesday (December 3, 1968), 136
Bluefield State (WV), 43, 97, 122, 131
Boise State University (ID), 131
Bond, Horace Mann, 23
Bond, Julian, 81, 133
Boston, LeRoy, 142
Boston College, 100
Bowdoin College (ME), 122
Bowie State University of (MD), 58, 148
Bowser, Ben, 110
Boyd, J. D., 61, 92, 155
BPM, *See* Black Power Movement
Bracey, Jr., John, 70
Bradley, Stefan, 95
Bradley University (IL), 133
Brandeis University (MA), 123, 125, 143
Brandler, Mark, 142
Branson, Herman, 150
Brawley, Benjamin, 36
Brick Junior College (NC), 45
Brimmer, Andrew F., 149
Brooklyn College, 124
Brooklyn League of Afro-American Collegians, 124
Brown, Benjamin, 130
Brown, Elaine, 80
Brown, H. Rap, 79–80, 94
Brown, Jim, 81
Brown, Jr., Ewart, 108
Brown, Roland, 101
Brown v. Board of Education of Topeka (1954), 4, 25, 59, 147
Brown University, 18–19, 32, 97, 113
BSA, *See* Black Student(s) Alliance
BSUs, *See* Black Student(s) Unions
Bumpers, Dale, 163
Bunche, Ralph, 22
Bundy, McGeorge, 168
Butler, Reggie, 90
Butler University of, 18–19, 22

C. W. Post Campus (Long Island University), 110
California State University, Dominquez Hills, 109
California State University, Fresno, 85, 101, 109, 113, 123, 134
California State University, Long Beach, 134
California State University, Northridge, 77, 141
California State University, Stanislaus, 136
campus activism, 3, 5–6, 39, 41, 46, 49, 57–9, 64, 70–4, 79–80, 91, 95–6, 104, 110, 120, 130, 133, 141–3, 162, 166, 181n4, 182n8
Canton, Calvin, 115
Capital Press Club, 150
Carleton College (MN), 109
Carlos, John, 97
Carlson, Bill, 142
Carmichael, Stokely, 2, 40, 64, 74, 78–9, 81, 83
Carnegie, Andrew, 18
Carnegie Corporation, 17
Carney, Phillita, 134
Carter, Alprentice ("Bunchy"), 97
Carter, Herman, 68, 92
Carter, Jimmy, 164
Carthage College (WI), 81
Carver, George Washington, 18, 39
Case Western Reserve University, 97, 110, 117, 150–1
Catholic University, 22, 96
Cedar Crest College (PA), 101, 117
Central State University (OH), 68, 94–5, 108, 130
Chaney, James, 71
Chatham University (PA), 116
Chatman, Archie, 142
Chavis, Ben, 9, 68
Chavis, John, 9
Cheek, Cordie, 50
Cheek, James E., 83, 103, 146
Cheyney University (PA), 11, 60, 139
Chicago Defender, 23, 39–41, 45, 61, 94, 129, 138, 142, 146
Chicago State University, 131–2
Chicano/a students, 2, 124, 130
Chisholm, Shirley, 81
Choat, Wray, 44

Christian, Dwight, 109
The Chronicle of Higher Education, 97, 104, 154
City College of New York, 2, 42, 57–8, 80, 98, 120–1, 138–9
Civil Rights Act (1964), 4, 27, 72, 138, 147, 161, 163
Civil Rights Movement (CRM), 7, 26–7, 44, 47, 49, 53, 59, 65, 67–8, 71–3, 79, 87
"civil rights unionism," 51–2
Claflin College (SC), 60
Claremont Colleges, 109, 157
Clark, E. Culpepper, 60
Clark, Hilton, 72
Clark, James B., 33
Clark, Jim, 74–5
Clark, Kenneth B., 72, 138
Clark, Madelyn, 132
Clark, Mark, 100
Clark, Ramsey, 132
Clark University (Atlanta), 33–4, 58, 90, 150, 159
Clarke University (IA), 110
Cleaver, Eldridge, 80, 96, 157
Cleveland State, 158
Coe College (Iowa), 116
COINTELPRO, *See* Counter-Intelligence Program
Colby College (ME), 119
Cold War, 53
Colgate University of, 22, 42, 124–5, 133, 158
College of William & Mary, 19
colonization, 10–11, 13–14, 30, 42, 61
Colorado State University of, 117
Columbia University of, 5, 11, 22, 27, 51, 54, 59, 72, 80–1, 83, 90, 92, 96, 109, 121, 139
communism, 26, 49–53, 55, 58–9, 61
Cone, James, 118
Confederacy, 74–5, 89, 92
Congress of African People, 158
Congress of Racial Equality (CORE), 51, 57, 62, 64–5, 68, 77, 81, 87, 100, 103, 137, 158
Cooper, Anna Julia, 152
Cooper, Ester, 52
Cooper, Julia Haywood, 15
Copeland, John, 31

CORE, *See* Congress of Racial Equality
Cornell University, 5, 19, 33–4, 38, 54, 59, 68, 90, 98, 120, 127–31, 138, 145–6
Cornwell, Don, 111
Coulter, Richard C., 13
Councill, W. H., 16
"counter center," 168–9
Counter-Intelligence Program (COINTELPRO), 133
Creighton University (NE), 115
CRM, *See* Civil Rights Movement
CUBE, *See* Cultural Union for Black Expression
Cullen, Countee, 35
Cultural Union for Black Expression (CUBE), 141
curricular relevance, 152
Currier, Theodore, 122

Dancer, Eddie Lee, 142
Dartmouth College, 12, 30, 45, 79, 116
Davis, Allison, 25
Davis, Angela, 81
Davis, Bill, 51
Davis, John P., 45
Day Law (1904), 16
Daye, Charles E., 148, 155
De La Beckwhit, Byron, 69
De Priest, Oscar, 50
De Saille Tucker, Thomas, 16
Deep South, 2, 25–7, 52, 56, 62, 64
Defiance College (OH), 116
Delany, Martin, 12
Delaware State University, 58
Delta Sigma Theta, 34
Delta State University of (MS), 136
Delta Upsilon International Fraternity (DU), 127–8, 133
Democratic National Convention (1964), 71, 73
Denmark, Leon, 139
Dennett, Tyler, 22
Department of Health, Education, and Welfare (HEW), 81, 138, 158, 163
DePauw University (IN), 54
desegregation, 25–7, 55, 57, 61–4, 69, 87, 112–13, 140, 150
Dickinson College (PA), 80, 162
Dillard University, 23
Diop, Cheik Anta, 152

diversity, 6, 87, 95, 99, 101, 116, 119, 147, 151, 161–2, 164, 166–9, 220n10
Dixon, Aaron, 79
Dixon, James P., 138
Dobbins, Preston, 163
Douglass, Frederick, 39, 111
Dowdell, Rick ("Tiger"), 134–5
Driscoll, Glen R., 140
DU, *See* Delta Upsilon International Fraternity
Du Bois, W. E. B., 13, 16–17, 20, 25–6, 28, 33, 37–41, 52, 82, 152
Du Bois, Yolanda, 40
Duke University, 1, 55, 59, 80–1, 85, 111, 114, 137
Dunbar, Ernest, 94
Dunbar, Paul Laurence, 39
Duncan, Charles, 139
Duquesne University (PA), 116
Durkee, J. Stanley, 41
Dymek, Eugene, 127

Earlham College (Indiana), 26
East St. Louis riot (1917), 34
East Tennessee State, 117
Eastern Michigan, 116
Easton, David, 154
Eaton, Lloyd, 142
Educational Opportunity Programs (EOPs), 85
Educational Record, 152
Edwards, Edwin, 105
Edwards, Harry, 85, 117–18
egalitarian elitism, 10–11, 162
Egypt, 9
Eiffinger, Dean John R., 42
Elam, Jack, 139
Eliot, Charles William, 18
Eliot, Thomas H., 135
Elizabeth City State University (NC), 58
Elizabethtown College (PA), 101
Emerson College (Boston), 115
Enarson, Harold L., 158
Equal Protection Clause (14th Amendment), 56, 164
Ethos, 83, 87
Eurocentrism, 3, 5, 79, 114, 151–2, 156
Eusan, Lynn, 97

Evans, Eric, 129
Evers, Charles, 58, 61, 69, 92, 103
Evers, Medgar, 69

Fairfield University (CT), 100
Fairley, Carrier, 164
Fanon, Franz, 82, 93
Farmer, Fran, 145
Fauset, Jessie, 35
Favors, Jelani, 69
Fayetteville State University (NC), 82, 84
Federal Bureau of Investigation (FBI), 98, 133–4
Federal Reserve Board, 140
Fellowship of Reconciliation (FOR), 51, 61–2
Finch, Robert, 158
First Annual Convention of the People of Color, 11
Fischer, Roger A., 72
Fisk University, 16, 18–19, 23, 26, 39–41, 50, 52, 71, 79, 93, 100, 108, 113, 122, 152
Florida A&M University, 16, 39, 43, 60, 62, 95
Florida State University, 62, 101
Floyd, Mike, 80, 162
Ford, Nick Aaron, 154
Ford Foundation, 27, 147
Fordham University (NY), 97
Forman, James, 76
Fort Valley State University (GA), 58, 125
Foster, Walker ("Moose"), 107
Fourteenth Amendment, 56, 161, 164
Franklin, Aretha, 121
Franklin, John Hope, 50, 81, 122
Franklin & Marshall College (PA), 80, 110
Franklin College (IN), 109
fraternities, 19–20, 22, 38, 90, 125, 127, 133
Frazier, E. Franklin, 36, 73–4
Free Angela (Davis) campaign, 104
Free Huey Day, 80
Freedom's Journal, 9
Freeman, Elmer, 83
Fritz, Jolee, 59
Fugitive Slave Act, 30
Fuller, Howard, 82, 99–100

Gaines v. Canada, 56–7
Gallagher, Buell, 2

Gandhi, Mohandas, 62
Gannon University (PA), 33, 46, 89
Garrett, Jimmy, 77, 93, 109, 164
Garrett, William, 134
Garrison, William Lloyd, 30
Garvey, Marcus, 29, 35, 38, 112
Gates, Betty, 159
George Washington University
    (DC), 18, 122
Georgia Tech University, 19, 26–7, 64
Ghana, 146
G. I. Bill (Servicemen's Readjustment Act),
    24, 54
Giddings, Paula, 19–20, 121
"golden age of black educational
    opportunity" (1965–1973), 151
Goodman, Andrew, 71
Goodman, Robert, 153
Gordon, John, 33
Goucher College (Baltimore), 113
Gould, Samuel B., 158
Grambling State University (LA), 90, 94,
    106, 108, 117, 132
Granger, Augustus, 18
Great Depression, 24, 45
Great Migration, 20, 34–6
Greek language, 12, 14–15, 23
Greek system, 19–20, 22, 26, 38, 82, 90–1,
    113, 125, 127, 133–4
Greensboro Four, 63–4
Gregg, Howard, 46
Gregg, James, 43–4
Gregory, Dick, 81
Gregory, Robin, 72, 156
Grimes, Willie, 139
Grinnell College (IA), 116
Grundy, Ann Beard, 70
Grundy, Chester, 68, 70
Guerilla Warfare (Guevara), 123
Guevara, Ernesto ("Che"), 82, 123
Guilford College (NC), 110
Guinier, Ewart, 22, 147

Hall, Jacquelyn Dowd, 29, 51–2
Hall, Mildred Marshall, 22
Hamer, Fannie Lou, 71, 81
Hamilton, Charles, 78, 83
Hammond, Samuel, 132
Hammond, Smith, 132
Hampton, Fred, 80, 100

Hampton University (VA), 13–15, 18, 21,
    32, 43–4, 53, 57, 78, 80, 91, 98, 100,
    121–2, 143, 152, 166, 189n23
Hansberry, William Leo, 23
Hare, Nathan, 124, 136–7, 169
Harlem Youth Action Project, 71
Harris, Nathan, 106
Hart, Earl, 153
Harvard University, 12, 16, 18, 22, 26–7,
    37, 42, 45–6, 57, 69, 74, 79, 81, 95, 98,
    100, 117, 140, 142, 145–7, 164
"The Hate that Hate Produced"
    (documentary) (1959), 73
Hayakawa, S. I., 101, 135–6
Hedgeman, Ethel, 19
Henderson, Clarence, 63
Henderson, Vivian W., 150, 159
Henry, Raymond A., 150
Herndon, Angelo, 52
Herring, Stan, 89
HEW, See Department of Health,
    Education, and Welfare
Hitler, Adolf, 53, 57–8, 129
Hocutt, Thomas, 55
Hodges, Guinnevere, 149
Holland, Jerome, 91
Holmes, Hamilton, 64
Hood, James, 69
Hoover, J. Edgar, 133
Hope, John, 18, 32
House Special Education
    Subcommittee, 137
House Un-American Activities
    Committee (HUAC), 26
Houston, Charles Hamilton, 55–6
Howard, Bertie, 81
Howard, Jeff, 95
Howard, William Schley, 23
Howard University, 13–14, 18–21, 23,
    32–6, 38–43, 45–6, 50–4, 57, 64,
    71–5, 78–9, 81–3, 92, 94–6, 98, 103,
    108, 112, 115, 120–1, 124, 138, 146–7,
    152, 156, 164
HUAC, See House Un-American
    Activities Committee
Hudson, Roy, 143
Hughes, Donald, 91
Hughes, Langston, 20–1, 35
Humphreys, Richard, 11
Hunt, Ida Gibbs, 15

Hunt, Silas, 56
Hunter, Charlayne, 64
Hunter College (NY), 79
Huntley, Chet, 137
Hurston, Zora Neale, 35, 63, 152
Husbands, C. L., 135
Huston-Tillotson University (TX), 22, 98

"If We Must Die" (poem) (McKay), 34
Illinois Wesleyan, 93, 109, 113
Indiana University, 19, 117, 169
Indiana Northwest University, 156
Innis, Roy, 100, 137
Institute of Nonviolent Resistance to
     Segregation (Spelman College)
     (1959), 62
"integration," 168–9
invisibility, 22

Jabbar, Kareem Abdul, 70–1, 77
Jackson, Alice C., 55
Jackson, Fanny M., 13
Jackson, James, 52–3
Jackson, Jesse, 165
Jackson State University, 5, 21, 64, 71, 84,
     95, 101–3, 106, 130, 132, 135, 143
   massacres (1970), 5, 101–3, 132
Jacobs, C. D., 46
Jakes, Wilhelmina, 60
Jeannes Foundation, 17
Jena 6 affair (Louisiana) (2007), 165
Jet magazine, 59
Jim Crow, 25, 39, 49–50, 54–7, 60,
     137–8, 167
John Birch Society, 136
John Brown's raid (1859), 31, 46
Johnson, Andrew, 51
Johnson, Arthur, 54
Johnson, Charles, 26
Johnson, James Weldon, 39
Johnson, John H., 23
Johnson, Lyndon B., 92, 132, 157
Johnson, Mordecai, 41, 54
Johnson, Nelson, 108
Johnson C. Smith University (NC), 36,
     43, 58
Johnson Publishing Company, 23
Jones, Angela, 109
Jones, Edward A., 9–10, 50
Jones, LeRoi, 81

Jones, Renee, 111
Jones, Thomas Elsa, 41
Joseph, Peniel, 29
Joseph Jr., Wilhelm, 2
Jourdain Jr., Edwin B., 37
Journey of Reconciliation (CORE) (1947),
     51, 64
Julius Rosenwald Fund, 25

Kafka, Franz, 77
Kalamazoo College (MI), 117, 153
Karenga, Maulana (Ron), 77–8, 83, 97
Kelley, Robin D. G., 52
Kennedy, John F., 65, 69–70
Kennedy, Keith, 127
Kent State, 101, 103, 122, 135
Kentucky State University, 16, 58,
     64, 108–9
Kilson, Martin, 140
King, Clennon, 25, 61
King, Coretta Scott, 54
King, Jr., Martin Luther, 6, 54, 60–1, 64,
     73–6, 80, 83, 90, 94–5, 97, 103, 112–
     14, 117, 122–3, 133, 148, 157
   assassination (1968), 6, 73, 83, 94–5, 97,
     103, 112–14, 117, 122–3, 133, 148
King, Sr., Martin Luther, 98
Kittrell College (NC), 44
Knox College (IL), 116
Knoxville College (TN), 42, 46, 58
Ku Klux Klan (KKK), 22, 53, 60, 64,
     102–3, 130
Kutztown University (PA), 101

ladder altruism, 4–5, 17, 20, 25, 45, 61, 87,
     90–1, 147, 153, 156–8, 161–2, 165
Laing, Daniel, 12
Lake Forest College (IL), 80
Lane College (TN), 122
Langston University (OK), 44–6,
     57–8, 106
Latin, 12–14, 23, 132
Latino Studies programs, 124
Latino/a students, 2, 124, 130, 161
Lawrence University (WI), 89, 134
Lawson, James, 62
LBSM, *See Long* Black Student Movement
Lee, J. R. E., 39
Lehigh University (PA), 106
Lehman College (NY), 122

LeMoyne-Owen College (TN), 13, 32, 53, 120–1
Lewis, Arthur, 140
Lewis, John, 61–2, 64
Lewis, Robert A., 77, 142
LGBTs, 161
Liberal Arts College (LAC), 9, 15, 20, 83, 101, 132, 134, 147
Lincoln, Abraham, 69
Lincoln Institute (KY), 42
Lincoln University (MO), 43, 46, 56, 58, 93–5
Lincoln University (PA), 11–12, 20, 38, 150
Lindley, Ernest, 44
Lindsay, Clyde, 146
Littrell, Wayne O., 141
Livingston College (NC), 58
Locke, Alain, 36, 38, 152
Locke, Gene, 134
Logan, Rayford, 46
Long Black Student Movement (LBSM) (1919 to 1972), 3–4, 7, 28, 29–47, 49–65, 67, 71, 73, 90, 122, 131, 139, 143, 147–8, 165, 169
　and civil rights, 49–65
　and the new negro, 29–47
Long Civil Rights Movement, 29
Long Island University (NY), 54, 110
Lorch, Lee, 26
Lord, Nathan, 12
Louisiana State University, 26, 125
Lucy, Autherine, 25, 60, 64, 69
Luther College (IA), 134
lynching, 11, 18, 30, 40, 50–3, 59, 133, 142

Macalester College (MN), 164
Mahorney, Amelia, 18
Malcolm X, 1, 65, 67–9, 73–4, 78–80, 82, 93, 96, 98–100, 106, 111, 116–17, 121, 157, 161
Malcolm X College (IL), 80
"Malcolm X Liberation School," 1–2
Malcolm X Liberation University (MXLU) (NC), 82, 99–100
Malcolm X Speaks, 73
Malone, Vivian, 69
Manley, Albert E., 132
Manns, Adrienne, 79
Marietta College (OH), 110, 125
Marquette, 93, 136, 158

Marshall, Thurgood, 55, 140
Marshall University (WV), 100, 111, 122
Martin, Gertrude, 33
Maryville College, 16
Masingale, Sharon, 152
Massachusetts Anti-Slavery Society, 30
Massachusetts Institute of Technology (MIT), 27
Matthews, Calvin, 148–9
Mayfield, Curtis, 1
Mays, Benjamin E., 133
Mazama, Ama, 152
McAllister, Don, 136
McCain, Franklin, 62–3
McCarthyism, 26, 53, 59
McCray, Robert, 168
McCullough, Vincent, 108
McEwan, Ernest, 61
McKay, Claude, 34
McKenzie, Fayette, 39–41
McKissick, Sr., Floyd, 57
McLaurin, George, 57
McLaurin v. Oklahoma State Regents, 57
McLeod, Mary Jane Bethune, 32
McNeil, Genna Rae, 153
McNeill, Joseph McNeill, 62–3
Meharry Medical, 38
Memphis State, 138
Meredith, James, 65
Merritt College (CA), 74, 79
Metamorphosis (Kafka), 77
Michigan State University, 85, 109, 118, 156
Michigan Tech University, 89
Michot, Louis, 105
Middleton, Delano, 132
Miles College (AL), 159
Miller, Loren, 44
The Millionaire, 46
Mills, Robert H., 140
Mills College (CA), 98, 109, 111
Millsaps College (MS), 114
Miner, Myrtilla, 11
Mississippi Freedom Democratic Party (MFDP), 71–2
Mississippi Freedom Summer (1964), 71–2
Mississippi State University, 106, 156
Mississippi Valley State University, 60–1
Missouri ex. rel. Gaines v. Canada, 56
Missouri State University, 26

Mobley, Mamie Till, 59
Moore, Fred, 60
Mootry, Primus J., 131–2
moralized contraption, 4–5, 14, 17, 19,
    21, 36, 39, 41, 45–7, 87, 90–1, 147–8,
    161–2, 165
Morehouse College, 23, 32, 34, 38, 52, 54,
    98, 104, 153, 159
Morgan State University (MD), 46, 52,
    58, 79
Morningside College (IA), 110, 131, 140
Morris Brown College (GA), 15
Morris College (SC), 58
Morse, Robert W., 150
Mount Holyoke College (MA), 101, 114
Muhammad, Elijah, 73
Mulholland, Joseph P., 122
Munn, Clarence ("Biggie"), 118
Murch, Donna, 68
Murphy, Calvin, 117–18
Murphy, Hardy, 152
Murray, Donald, 56
Murray, Pauli, 57
Murray State University (KY), 104

NAACP, *See* National Association for the
    Advancement of Colored People
Nabrit, James, 146
NABS, *See* National Association of Black
    Students
NACW, *See* National Association of
    College Women
Nash, Diane, 62
Nation of Islam (NOI), 73–4
National Association for the
    Advancement of Colored People
    (NAACP), 24–5, 33, 35, 37, 39, 44, 46,
    49, 52–7, 59–65, 67–9, 92, 96, 99–100,
    131, 137, 139–40, 142
National Association of Black Students
    (NABS), 98, 111, 157
National Association of College Women
    (NACW), 21
National Black Feminist Organization,
    86, 158
National Conference of Negro Youth
    (1937), 50
National Council of Methodist Youth, 53
National Football League (NFL), 117
National Guardsmen, 1, 69, 101, 132, 139

National Negro Congress (NNC), 52
National Organization of Women (NOW),
    54, 57
National Scholarship Service and Fund for
    Negro Students, 24
*National Survey of the Higher Education of
    Negroes,* 24
National Urban League, 65
National Youth Administration, 50
Native American students, 2, 124, 130,
    161, 168
Nazi party, 51, 131
NCC, *See* Negro-Caucasian Club
Negro History Week (1926), 20
"Negro Student Clubs," 23
Negro Students Association (NSA), 70
"Negro University," 3, 146
Negro-Caucasian Club (NCC), 42
Netterville, G. Leon, 104–5
New England Anti-slavery Society, 11
New England Consulate of the Republic of
    New Africa, 142
"new humanism," 147
"The New Jim Crow," 167
New Mexico State University, 85, 94,
    112, 152
New Negro, the term, 35–6
The New Negro (anthology), 36
New Negro Campus Movement (NNCM),
    3, 20, 29–30, 35–7, 40–4, 46–7, 49–50,
    65, 87
New Negro Movement, 29–30,
    35–6, 87
The New Student, 45
New York University (NYU), 5, 27, 37, 44,
    57, 68, 93
Newton, Huey P., 79, 157
Nixon, Richard, 101, 103, 137, 139, 150
Nkrumah, Kwame, 146
NNC, *See* National Negro Congress
NNCM, *See* New Negro Campus
    Movement
NOI, *See* Nation of Islam
Norfolk State University (VA), 71, 104, 143
normalized mask of whiteness, 4–5, 14, 17,
    20, 36, 42, 82, 87, 114, 147, 151–5, 161
Norris, Frances J., 13
North Carolina A&T State University (NC
    A&T), 33, 46, 57–8, 62, 92, 98, 108,
    139, 143, 148, 150, 153, 159

North Carolina Central University (NC Central), 55, 58–9, 85–6, 92, 148
Northeastern Illinois State University, 117
Northeastern University (MA), 83, 94, 96
Northern Michigan University, 122
Northwestern University, 26, 38, 70, 95, 119
Notre Dame University, 27
NOW, *See* National Organization of Women
Noyes Academy (Canaan, New Hampshire), 11, 30
NSA, *See* Negro Students Association
Nunn, Louis B., 139

Oakwood University (AL), 21
OASATAU, *See* Organization of African and Afro-American Students at American University
Oberlin College (OH), 12–13, 15, 18, 30–1, 36–8, 52, 83, 104
Oberlin Ladies Literary Society, 30
Occidental College, 27, 80, 94, 111
Ogbar, Jeffrey, 80
Ogletree, Kathryn, 95
Ohio State University, 22, 103, 113, 133, 141
Ohio University, 30, 141
"Old Negro," 36
Olds, Merton R., 135
Oliver, Lee, 111
Olympics (1968), 70, 97
Orangeburg Massacre (South Carolina State University) (February 8, 1968), 5, 6, 94, 103, 132–3, 135, 157
Organization of African and Afro-American Students at American University (OASATAU), 107
Osborne, J. G., 42
Otis, Jesse R., 61

Paine College (GA), 46, 108, 125
Pan-Africanism, 10, 12, 35, 82, 104, 111, 138, 169
Parent, Ronald R., 101
Parks, L. O., 33
Parks, Rosa, 59
paternalism, 2–4, 6–7, 10–14, 17, 22–3, 27–8, 32–3, 37, 39, 42, 45–6, 73, 76, 87, 90, 112, 120, 148, 162, 165–6

and conservatism, 10–14, 17, 28, 39, 73
and liberalism, 11–14, 22, 28, 33, 45–6, 73
Patterson, Carrie, 60
Patterson, Frederick D., 24
Patterson, John, 64
Patterson, Mary Jane, 12–13, 15
Patton, Gwen, 75–6, 78, 91–2, 98, 111, 157
Paul, Michele, 71
Paul, Thomas, 30
Paul Quinn College (TX), 122
Payne, Daniel A., 11
Peabody Education Fund, 17
Peacock, J. L., 45–6
Peck, David John, 12
Penn State University, 54
Pepperdine University (CA), 98, 143
Peters, Franklin, 109
Phenix, George P., 44
Phillips, Ulrich B., 42
Pike, Orlando, 124
Pitts, Lucius, 159
Pittsburg State University (KS), 81, 106
Pittsburgh Courier, 44, 46
Powell, Jr., Adam Clayton, 22, 81
Prairie View A&M University (TX), 21, 42, 46, 104, 122, 155
Pratt Institute (NY), 138
Princeton University, 9, 27, 79, 83–4, 117
prisons, 141–2, 167
Project CURE, 159
Providence College (RI), 104, 113, 115
Psychologists for a Democratic Society, 154
Psychologists for Social Action, 154
Puerto Rican students, 2, 123–4, 139
Puryear, Bebbet, 14
Pusey, Nathan, 146

Queens College (NY), 97, 122, 139

Radcliff College, 121
RAM, *See* Reform Action Movement
Ramapo College (NJ), 86
Randall, Leanear, 106
Randolph, A. Phillip, 61
Ray, Pauline, 33–4
Raynor, John P., 158
Reagan, Ronald, 165
Reason, Charles L., 12

Reconstruction, 13–15, 17, 29, 31–2, 56, 58, 153

"Red Summer" (1919), 34

Reed College (WA), 115

Reform Action Movement (RAM), 68, 71, 158

Rensselaer Polytechnic Institute (NY), 116

Reserve Officers' Training Corps (ROTC), 41, 90, 112, 146, 148

Revels, Hiram, 32

"reverse discrimination," 119, 140, 161–4

revolting black nationalism, 12

Rice, Harry Nicholas ("Nick"), 135

Richardson, Clement, 43

Richmond, David, 62

Riley, Billy, 131

Riley, Chuck, 131–2

Rising Tide of Color (Stodard), 42

Robeson, Paul, 19, 52

Robinson, Ethel, 19

Robinson, James H., 53

Robinson, Jo Ann, 59–60

Rockefeller, Sr., John D., 17

Rockefeller Foundation, 27

Roger Williams University, 32, 116

Rogers, J. A., 152

Rojas, Fabio, 168

Roosevelt, Franklin D., 50, 53

Roosevelt University (IL), 1, 27, 70, 80, 109, 114–15, 156, 164

Rosemont College (PA), 101

Rosenwald Fund, 17

Rush, Benjamin, 12

Rush, Betty, 71

Russian Revolution (1917), 35

Russwurm, John, 9–10

Rustin, Bayard, 46, 62, 73, 137–40

Rutgers University, 5, 19, 27, 83, 98, 123, 164

SAAS, *See* Society of African and Afro-American Students

St. Ambrose University (IA), 100

St. Andrews Presbyterian University (NC), 83, 89

Saint Augustine's College (NC), 15, 21, 43, 46, 58

St. Cloud State University (MN), 114, 140

St. Olaf College (MN), 111, 140

Saint Paul's College (VA), 21

Saint Peter's College (NJ), 115–16

Sayers, Gayle, 91

Scarborough, William, 36

Schurman, Jacob G., 34

Schwerner, Michael, 71

science, technology, engineering, and mathematics (STEM), 167

SCLC, *See* Southern Christian Leadership Conference

Scott, Bob, 162–3

Scott, W. H., 32

Scottsboro Boys, 52, 55

SDS, *See* Students for a Democratic Society

Seale, Bobby, 74, 79

Search for Education, Elevation, and Knowledge (SEEK), 122–3

SEEK, *See* Search for Education, Elevation, and Knowledge

segregation/segregationists, 4, 7, 13, 16, 19, 22–3, 25, 27–8, 31, 33, 39, 50–5, 57, 59, 61–5, 68, 70–1, 74–5, 82, 91, 112–13, 131–2, 140, 155, 162, 169

Sellers, Cleveland, 71–2

Selma to Montgomery marches (1965), 74–6, 79, 91

SF State, 1, 5, 23, 70, 74, 77, 81, 83, 85, 92–4, 97, 101, 108–9, 115, 120, 122, 124–5, 135–6, 141, 143, 164, 169

SGAs, *See* Student Government Associations

Shabazz, Betty, 81, 100

Shaw, Kenneth A., 152

Shaw University (NC), 18–19, 34, 36–7, 43, 46, 64, 83, 97, 163

Shellcroft, John, 111

Shepard, James, 55

Shields, Perry, 32

Shull, A. Franklin, 42

Simmons College, 41–2

Sinclair, Roxanne E., 143

Sipuel, Ada Lois Fisher, 56–7

Sipuel v. Board of Regents, 56–7

sit-ins, 42, 49, 62–3, 77, 83, 91, 121–2, 125, 131, 135

Sitterson, J. Carlyle, 163

Sixteenth Street Baptist Church bombing (1963), 70

Skidmore College (NY), 113

Slater, John F., 16–17

Slater Fund, 17

slavery, 4, 9–13, 15, 18, 23, 30–2, 40, 42, 52, 61, 65, 69, 92–4, 101, 143, 152–3, 162

Slippery Rock University (PA), 116

Slowe, Lucy, 21

Smith, Barbara, 114

Smith, Courtney, 97

Smith, Henry, 132

Smith, Johnson C., 58

Smith, Lenoir Beatrice, 42

Smith, Robert, 135

Smith, Tommie, 97

Smith, William, 63

SNCC, See Student Non-Violent Coordinating Committee

Snowden, Isaac, 12

SNYC, See Southern Negro Youth Congress

SOBU, See Students Organized for Black Unity

Society of African and Afro-American Students (SAAS), 72, 131

sororities, 19–20, 26, 38, 134

Southern Association of Colleges and Secondary Schools, 24

South Carolina State University (SC State), 5, 60, 93–4, 132, 143, 157

Southern Christian Leadership Conference (SCLC), 64–5, 68–9, 74, 100

Southern Negro Youth Congress (SNYC), 52

Southern Oregon University, 101

Southern Regional Education Board, 149

Southern Student Organizing Committee, 149

Southern University (LA), 15, 68, 104–6, 132, 138, 143, 159

Sowell, Thomas, 129

Sowle, Claude R., 141

Spelman, 15, 21, 52, 58, 62, 99, 132

Spencer, Howard, 90

Stamp, Neal, 127

standardization of exclusion, 4–5, 12, 15, 18, 36, 47, 57, 59, 87, 90–1, 93, 147–9, 151, 161

Stanford, 27, 83–4, 101, 115, 122

Stanford, Jr., Max, 68

Stanton, Lucy, 12, 30–1

Starr, Steve, 129

"The State of Black Studies" (1975), 154

Staten Island Community College, 158

STEM, See science, technology, engineering, and mathematics

Stephens, Ernest, 112

Stephens, Patricia, 62

Stephens, Priscilla, 62

Stetson University (FL), 113, 115, 156

Stewart, Benny, 109, 143

Stewart, John S., 150

Stewart, Maria, 9

Stifler, William, 32

Stillman College (AL), 21

Stith, David W., 59

Stodard, Lothrop, 42

Storer College, 46

Stowe, Lucy, 45

Streator, George, 40

Strider, Robert E. L., 119–20

Student Government Associations (SGAs), 3, 39, 60–1, 76, 80, 83, 86, 93, 95–6, 107–8, 111, 113, 117, 119–21, 125, 143, 148, 155, 158, 163, 169

Student Non-Violent Coordinating Committee (SNCC), 61–2, 64–5, 67–8, 71–80, 87, 93–4, 118, 158

Students for a Democratic Society (SDS), 124, 127–9

Students Organized for Black Unity (SOBU), 108, 111, 152, 163

Students United for Racial Equality, 158

The Stylus, 35

SUNY Stony Brook, 115, 158

Swarthmore College, 97

Sweatt v. Painter, 57

Taber, Robert, 123

Taft, William H., 18

Talladega College (AL), 18, 33, 159

Tanner, Henry O., 39

Temple University, 51, 141, 169

Templeton, John Newton, 30

Tennessee State, 95

Terrell, Beulah, 37

Terrell, Mary Church, 15, 37

Texas Southern University, 83, 93, 130

Thiel College (PA), 83, 110, 143

Third World Liberation Fronts, 124

Thirkield, Wilbur, 33

TIAL, *See* Tuskegee Institute Advancement League
Till, Emmett, 59
Tougaloo College, 20, 79, 84–5, 90, 93, 104, 108, 125, 157
Trimble, Frank Levi, 32
Trinity College (CT), 9, 82, 131
Trinity University (TX), 90
Trotter, Joe, 81
Truman, Harry, 54
Truman State University (formerly Northeastern Missouri State University), 116
"TSU Five," 131
Tufts University (MA), 100
Tulane University (LA), 131
Turner, Benner C., 60
Turner, James, 95
Turner, Nat, 9, 112
Tuskegee (AL), 14–15, 17–18, 21, 24, 36, 38–9, 52, 58, 75–6, 78, 91–2, 95, 98, 112, 125, 143, 157
Tuskegee Institute Advancement League (TIAL), 75–6
Twilight, Alexander, 9–10

UNCF, *See* United Negro College Fund
Union Theological Seminary (NY), 118
United Negro College Fund (UNCF), 24, 26
United Press International, 154
University of Akron, 115–16, 156–7
University of Alabama, 25, 27, 60, 69, 109, 164
University of Arkansas, 56, 104, 110, 163
University of California, Berkeley (UC Berkeley), 1, 22–3, 72, 79, 96–7, 124, 137, 140
University of California, Davis (UC Davis), 109, 164
University of California, Los Angeles (UCLA), 27, 77–8, 85, 94, 97, 100, 118
University of California Regents v. Bakke, 164
University of California, Riverside (UC Riverside), 109
University of California, Santa Barbara (UC Santa Barbara), 109, 134, 136, 164

University of Chicago, 23, 25, 27, 38, 51, 58, 154, 157
University of Dayton, 98
University of District of Columbia, 11
University of Florida, 104
University of Georgia, 25, 27, 64, 80, 85, 104, 152
University of Hawaii, 125
University of Houston, 79, 97, 111, 114, 117, 134, 152
University of Illinois, 1, 5, 26, 51, 58, 96–7, 109, 168
University of Indiana, 56
University of Iowa, 22, 89
University of Kansas, 18, 44, 91, 134–5, 143
University of Kentucky, 68, 70
University of Louisville, 139
University of Mary Washington (VA), 94
University of Maryland, 16, 56, 85, 112, 114
University of Maryland-Eastern Shore, 112, 114, 148
University of Massachusetts Amherst (UMASS-Amherst), 97
University of Massachusetts Dartmouth (UMASS-Dartmouth), 116
University of Memphis, 70
University of Michigan, 18, 22, 42, 79, 101
University of Minnesota, 84, 136, 141
University of Mississippi, 25–7, 65, 142, 149
University of Missouri-St. Louis, 84, 134, 140, 156
University of Montana, 85
University of Mount Union (OH), 101, 112
University of Nevada, 104, 116
University of New Mexico, 59
University of Niagara, 117–18
University of North Carolina at Chapel Hill (UNC Chapel Hill), 55
University of North Carolina at Charlotte (UNC Charlotte), 9, 68
University of North Dakota, 84, 89–90, 115
University of Northern Iowa, 109
University of Oklahoma, 56–7, 78, 84, 149
University of Oregon, 118
University of Pacific (CA), 111

University of Pennsylvania (UPENN), 5, 18, 22, 53, 131, 169
University of San Francisco, 97, 113
University of South Alabama, 104, 117, 134
University of South Carolina, 25, 61, 111
University of Southern California (USC), 109
University of Tennessee, 107
University of Texas, 26
University of Texas at Arlington, 92, 125
University of Texas at Austin, 57, 74, 98, 117, 125, 137
University of Texas at El Paso (UTEP), 84
University of Utah, 134
University of Virginia (UVA), 50, 55–6, 98, 113
University of Wisconsin-Madison (UW Madison), 1, 59, 136
University of Wisconsin-Milwaukee (UW Milwaukee), 156, 169
University of Wisconsin-Oshkosh (UW Oshkosh), 97, 114, 135, 137
University of Wyoming, 142
Up From Slavery (Washington), 93
Ursuline College (OH), 111
US Army, 141
US Civil War, 11, 13, 25, 31, 46
US Declaration of Independence, 111
US Organization, 77, 85, 97, 158
US Senate, 32
US Supreme Court, 25, 56–7, 59, 164
Utica College, 110

Vanderbilt University of, 62, 93
Varnado, Jerry, 109, 136
Vassar, Rosa, 33–4
Vassar College (NY), 95, 100, 115
Vietnam War, 78, 80, 101, 139
Virginia Union University, 38, 46, 49–53, 55, 58, 112
Virginia University of Lynchburg, 46
The Voice of the Twentieth Century, 32
Von Bismarck, Otto, 16
Voorhees College (SC), 21, 64, 98, 138
Voter Education Project, 65, 159
Voting Rights Act (1965), 74

Waddell, Charles M., 105
Waddy, Marianna, 92, 109

Wake Forest University, 96
Walker, Harry, 111
Walker, Madam C. J., 39
Wallace, George, 69
Wallace, Michelle, 86
The War of the Flea (Taber), 123
Ward, F. Champion, 147
Wartburg College (IA), 104
Washington, Booker T., 15, 17–18, 33–4, 38, 43, 82, 93
Washington, George, 31
Washington, Walter, 155
Washington University (MO), 135
Watkins, Irma, 157
Watkins, William H., 17
Watts Rebellion (1965), 76–7, 92
"We're a Winner" (song) (Mayfield), 1
Wellesley College, 83, 87
Wells-Barnett, Ida B., 34
Wells, Frederick W., 22
Wells, I. J. K., 38
Wesleyan University (CT), 27, 122
West Africa, 9
West Kentucky Community & Technical College (KY), 46
West Virginia State University, 38
West Virginia University, 19
Western Athletic Conference (WAC), 142
Western Connecticut State University, 116
Western University (KS), 13, 44
Wheatley, Phillis, 9
White, J. H., 81
White, Madree, 34
White, Walter, 55–6
white nationalism, 22, 81, 114
"white" philanthropy, 20
White Student Movement, 124
White Studies, 5, 93, 114
white suasion, 67
Whiteness Studies, 168
Whitfield, Edward, 68, 128–9
Whiting, Albert, 85
Whitted, Gerry, 86
Wichita State, 93
Widener University (PA), 134
Wilberforce University (OH), 11, 13, 36, 46, 57, 97, 104, 189n23
Wiley College, 58
Wilkins, Roy, 61, 96, 99, 100, 131, 137
William Penn University (IA), 137

Williams, Robert F., 67–8
Williams, Yohuru, 100
Williams College (MA), 22
Williamson, Joy Ann, 148
Wilmington College (OH), 113, 116
Wilson, Woodrow, 35
Wilson College, 132
Winston-Salem State University (NC), 63, 91–2, 108, 153
Wisdom, Paul E., 152
Witherspoon, John, 9
Wittenberg University (OH), 119
Women's Consortium of Psychologists for Social Action, 154
Woodson, Carter G., 10, 16, 20, 36
Woodson, Sarah Jane, 13
World War I, 3, 17–18, 20–2, 29, 35, 46, 72
World War II, 24, 27, 51, 53–4, 58

The Wretched of the Earth (Fanon), 93
Wright, Jr., Nathan, 51
Wright, Richard, 15, 93
Wynn, E. R., 139

Xavier University, 115, 157

YAF, See Young Americans for Freedom
Yale, 27, 38, 83, 90, 96, 168
Yergan, Max, 57
Young, Colonel Charles, 39
Young, Nathan B., 43
Young, Thomas W., 44
Young Americans for Freedom, 136
Young Republicans, 136
Younge, Jr., Sammy, 78, 92
Youth Organization for Black Unity, 111